SOMETIMES ALWAYS TRUE

Undogmatic Pluralism in Politics, Metaphysics, and Epistemology

Jeremy Barris

Fordham University Press
New York   2015

Copyright © 2015 Fordham University Press

All rights reserved. No part of this publication may be reproduced, stored in a retrieval system, or transmitted in any form or by any means—electronic, mechanical, photocopy, recording, or any other—except for brief quotations in printed reviews, without the prior permission of the publisher.

Fordham University Press has no responsibility for the persistence or accuracy of URLs for external or third-party Internet websites referred to in this publication and does not guarantee that any content on such websites is, or will remain, accurate or appropriate.

Fordham University Press also publishes its books in a variety of electronic formats. Some content that appears in print may not be available in electronic books.

Library of Congress Cataloging-in-Publication Data

Barris, Jeremy.
    Sometimes always true : undogmatic pluralism in politics, metaphysics, and epistemology / Jeremy Barris. — First edition.
        pages cm
    Includes bibliographical references and index.
    ISBN 978-0-8232-6214-4 (cloth : alk. paper)
  1. Pluralism. I. Title.
  BD394.B26 2014
  110—dc23

                                        2014008830

Printed in the United States of America

17 16 15 5 4 3 2 1

First edition

Contents

Preface		vii
Acknowledgments		ix
	Introduction: Sometimes Always True	1
1.	Comparing Different Cultural or Theoretical Frameworks: Davidson, Rorty, and the Nature of Truth	32
2.	An Internal Connection between Logic and Rhetoric, between Frameworks, and a Legitimate Foundation for Knowledge	54
3.	Pluralism, Legitimate Self-Contradiction, and a Proposed Solution to Some Shared Fundamental Problems of Political and Mainstream Epistemology	78
4.	The Logic of Genuine Political Pluralism and Oscar Wilde's Artificiality of Wit and Style	102
5.	Foucault's Pluralism and the Possibility of Truth and of Ideology Critique	129
6.	How to Be Properly Unnatural: The Metaphysics of Heterosexual Normativity and the Importance of the Concepts of Essence and Nature for Pluralism	150
7.	The Necessary Inconclusiveness of Heideggerian Interpretation of Metaphysics and the Undecided Nature of Essential or Logical Connection	179

8.	The Formal Structure of Metaphysics and *The Importance of Being Earnest*	202
9.	The Logical Structure of Dreams and Their Relation to Reality	231
	Coda: Overviews	259
	References	281
	Index	293

Preface

The problem with philosophy, and with the aspects of our experience of which it is an expression, is not that, in contrast to the natural sciences, it gives no definitively established answers. On the contrary, the problem is that it gives too many definitive answers, answers that often conflict with and even contradict each other and yet are nonetheless definitive.

Many insights of philosophy clearly have their finger on something right. It may not be clear exactly how we can express this something without being misleading in some important way or ways, or what the limits of applicability of this something are, but it is often clear that there is something there that needs to be taken into account.

In fact, with respect to this uncertainty of expression, philosophy is exactly like the natural sciences, whose forms of expression always go beyond the experimental results and theoretical proofs—in fact, are always partly metaphorical—in ways whose precise character and misleading effects on theory the most experienced practitioners cannot specify.[1] But it is clear that well-confirmed scientific results nonetheless definitely have their finger on something, and that with careful specifications we can and should rely on them.

---

[1] See, for example, Bruno Latour and Steve Woolgar, *Laboratory Life: The Social Construction of Scientific Facts* (London: Sage, 1979), who argue, for instance, that scientific work centrally involves "the art of interpreting confused texts (texts comprising slides, diagrams, other paper, and curves) and of writing persuasive accounts. . . . Exegesis and hermeneutics are the tools around which the idea of scientific production has historically been forged" (257, 261, n. 24).

The contradictory clashes between definitive philosophical insights do not mean that one invalidates another and that we cannot decide which is the valid one, so that philosophy again offers no definitive answers. They each have something definitively right. As a result, what their clashes mean is that the world is a contradictory place. We might say that while there are ultimate and definitive ways in which the world makes sense, the world is too big to make sense in only one consistent kind of way, for only one consistent kind of sense to define its character. By way of analogy, infinity can have infinitely large parts, and even if each way of making sense is infinitely (or unlimitedly) and so exclusively valid, an infinite world of sense can accommodate multiple unbounded and so mutually exclusive ways of making sense. Sometimes, for example, we face loss or despair in which consolation is truly inconceivable, and yet it is also true that we and our world come to shift into consolation, and then that same inconsolable grief or despair is itself in turn truly no longer conceivable.

Our task is not to decide between the definitive answers but to find ways of understanding and working with their simultaneous and yet wholly mutually exclusive truth.

This is one perspective toward which this collection of essays works.

Acknowledgments

I am deeply thankful for and to Steve de Wijze, Roy Blumenthal, Jim Mills, Greg Galford, Jeff Ruff, and Paul Turner, for being a home to me.

I am also very grateful to Kathy Chezik, Irene Klaver, and Andrea Walter for many years of loving support.

I thank Irene Klaver, Paul Livingston, and the Press's anonymous reader for their encouragement and advice about this book. Because of Irene Klaver's and Paul Livingston's suggestions in particular, it is much more the book I would like it to be. I also thank Peter Manchester for his acutely thoughtful encouragement and friendship over the years.

I am grateful to the late Helen Tartar, editorial director at Fordham University Press, for giving my distinctly counterintuitive work a chance. And I thank the editorial and production staff at the Press for their careful, very helpful work on the book.

Apart from the Introduction and the Coda, the chapters of this book are modified versions of essays that were previously published in various journals. I am grateful to the publishers of the journals for permission to republish these essays here.

Chapter 1 was originally published as "The Problem of Comparing Different Cultural or Theoretical Frameworks: Davidson, Rorty, and the Nature of Truth," *Method and Theory in the Study of Religion* 18, no. 2 (2006): 124–43, published by Brill.

Chapter 2 was originally published as "An Internal Connection between Logic and Rhetoric, and a Legitimate Foundation for Knowledge," *Philosophy and Rhetoric* 40, no. 4 (2007): 353–71. Copyright © 2007 The

Pennsylvania State University Press. This article is used by permission of The Pennsylvania State University Press.

Chapter 3 was originally published as "Epistemology and the Civil Union of Sense and Self-Contradiction: A Coordinated Solution to the Shared Problems of Political and Mainstream Epistemology," *Pli* 19 (2008): 78–99.

Chapter 4 was originally published as "Oscar Wilde's Artificiality and the Logic of Genuine Pluralism," *Contemporary Justice Review* 8, no. 2 (2005): 193–209, reprinted by permission of the publisher, Taylor & Francis Ltd., http://www.tandf.co.uk/journals.

Chapter 5 was originally published as "That Foucault Justifies Truth and Ideology Critique," *Quarterly Journal of Ideology* 20, nos. 3–4 (1997): 61–98.

Chapter 6 was originally published as "How to Be Properly Unnatural: Nature, Essences, and the Metaphysics of Heterosexual Normativity," *Review Journal of Political Philosophy* 7, no. 1 (2009): 75–94.

Chapter 7 was originally published as "On Reading and Re-Reading the History of Metaphysics: The Necessary Inconclusiveness of Heideggerian Interpretation," *Existentia* 16, nos. 3–4 (2006): 243–54.

Chapter 8 was originally published as "The Formal Structure of Metaphysics and *The Importance of Being Earnest*," *Metaphilosophy* 39, nos. 4–5 (2008): 546–70, published by John Wiley and Sons. © 2008 The Author. Journal Compilation © 2008 Metaphilosophy LLC and Blackwell Publishing Ltd.

Chapter 9 was originally published as "The Logical Structure of Dreams and Their Relation to Reality," *Dreaming* 20, no. 1 (2010): 1–18. Copyright © 2010 by the American Psychological Association. Reproduced and adapted with permission. The use of this information does not imply endorsement by the publisher.

Sources for the epigraphs on page xiii are as follows:

José Ortega y Gasset, *What Is Knowledge?*, ed. and trans. Jorge García-Gómez (Albany: State University of New York Press, 2002), 190, translator's insertions.

Bertrand Russell, "The Philosophy of Logical Atomism," in *Logic and Knowledge: Essays 1901–1950*, ed. Robert Charles Marsh (London: George Allen & Unwin, 1956), 193.

Takuan Sōhō, *The Unfettered Mind: Writings of the Zen Master to the Sword Master*, trans. William Scott Wilson (New York: Kodansha International, 1986), 23–24, my insertions. "*Abiding place* means the place where the mind stops" (19); "not stopping the mind is called *immovable*" (21). For some brief elaboration on this kind of contradiction in the context of Zen, see the Introduction, note 19.

There are certain ridiculous things that have to be said, and philosophers exist for that purpose.... Don't you think that it is an easy task to discharge. It demands a courage of a sort that great warriors and the cruelest of revolutionaries have usually lacked. Both [groups] have usually [consisted of] rather vain people who got cold feet when, simply, it was a question of becoming ridiculous. Hence, it would be advisable for humanity to take advantage of the philosopher's special brand of heroism.
—*Ortega y Gasset*

The point of philosophy is to start with something so simple as not to seem worth stating, and to end with something so paradoxical that no one will believe it.
—*Bertrand Russell*

When one practices discipline and moves from the beginner's territory to immovable wisdom [in which the mind does not stop], he makes a return and falls back to the level of the beginning, the abiding place [where the mind stops].... The ignorance and afflictions of the beginning, abiding place and the immovable wisdom that comes later become one.
—*Takuan Sōhō*

Introduction

Sometimes Always True

The essays in this book explore three themes that are really different expressions of the same set of fundamental concerns. First, the essays identify and try to resolve a particular contemporary problem connected with pluralism. Second, they develop an approach to the "big questions" of philosophy, in the context of understanding this kind of questioning to be (as they argue) an essential dimension of human life. By the "big questions" I mean questions like "What is reality?," "What is it to be a good person?," and "How is knowledge possible?" While the essays explore this approach to fundamental questions in its own right, they also try to show that the contemporary problem is itself rooted in and an offshoot of the big philosophical questions. Third, the essays discuss the concrete, intimate texture of our experience of existence and of the meaning and value of our conduct. This intimate experience of existence and value, as the essays show, is really the other side of the same coin as the concerns of the apparently more impersonal "big question" philosophy, together with those of the contemporary problem that is its offshoot.

Some elements of this aspect of our experience directly comprise both the intimate and the impersonal sides of this coin. Among these, for example, are our moral and political values and the connected, appropriate self-approval or shame we feel in living or not living up to the standards those values embody. In our deeply pluralist contemporary context, successfully living out our moral and political values presents a particularly difficult problem. These essays suggest that the roots themselves of this and related difficulties also offer a morally livable and even, in some respects, morally happy resolution.

1. The Contemporary Problem

The contemporary problem with which these essays are concerned is that we need, and do not yet have, a genuine, undogmatic pluralist standpoint in political theory, epistemology, and metaphysics. The essays identify and address a more general and a more specific form of this problem. I shall first describe the more general form of the problem and outline the kind of solution the essays variously propose before moving on to the more specific form.

A widespread aim of Western intellectual life for the last few decades, in both postmodern and more traditional approaches, has been to find an adequately pluralist mode of thought, one that respects fundamental difference of outlook, meaning, and values. This aim has been strongly visible in social and political thought, for example in the contexts of multiculturalism, gender politics, queer theory, postcolonialism, political liberalism, communitarian political theory, and some versions of neo-Marxism. It has also shaped a great deal of the work in hermeneutics, epistemology, and metaphysics, partly in light of the political pluralist concerns and partly as a consequence of these subdisciplines' own recent history of being confronted with the importance of deep differences between frameworks of meaning.

In all these contexts, this pluralist aim suffers from a contradiction: that making room for truly fundamental difference means making room for outlooks that exclude this pluralist aim itself. This is perhaps most easily seen in the case of political theory. Pluralist political positions are very much in the minority, so that respect for other standpoints very often means respecting positions that deny the legitimacy of these pluralist positions themselves.[1]

---

[1] In the context of discussing toleration, John Horton argues that "the very idea of tolerating everything is incoherent. Tolerating something must imply intolerance towards its negation"; John Horton, "Three (Apparent) Paradoxes of Toleration," *Synthesis Philosophica* 17 (1994): 16. As a result, this idea does not need to be pursued, and the paradox is only apparent. This argument presupposes, however, that the incoherence can be avoided. At the very least, it does not take into account the possibility of different general frameworks that are in a position to make a meaningful case for what the tolerating standpoint excludes, a case that cannot be immediately dismissed without arbitrariness, and so *necessitate* the incoherence for that tolerating standpoint. In this context, Horton seems to identify a problem and mistake it for a solution.

This is really only one expression of a more general problem. In fact, this more general problem is a concern not only for standpoints committed to pluralism but, as I argue in the next section, for all standpoints concerned with truth, and in a way that necessitates their engaging very deeply with the same concerns that motivate pluralism. This is the problem that it is arguably possible for standpoints to differ so fundamentally that the meanings that are central to one framework do not exist for and are excluded by the meanings of another. In other words, their worlds are literally inconceivable and meaningless to one another.[2] As a result, for one of these frameworks of sense to engage with another's meanings, even to justify its own against them, requires that it work with a system of meanings from which its own are altogether excluded. The result is the same kind of contradiction as the one involved in openness to non-openness: to engage with the other framework is to deny the meaningfulness of one's own engagement with it. We can already see that this is a concern for nonpluralist frameworks too, insofar as they are committed to responsible thought, since they also need to justify themselves over against other frameworks.

More immediately, since these frameworks understand the sense and therefore the truth of the same things in incompatible ways, and yet the legitimacy of one cannot be established over the legitimacy of another, the possibility of this kind of deep divergence between frameworks creates a

[2] This is a familiar idea in philosophy of science, political philosophy, and in treatments of disagreements between whole philosophical systems. In philosophy of science, see, for example, Paul Feyerabend, *Against Method,* 3rd ed. (London: Verso, 1993), especially chapter 16; Thomas S. Kuhn, *The Structure of Scientific Revolutions,* 2nd ed. (Chicago: University of Chicago Press, 1970); Ludwig Wittgenstein, *Remarks on Frazer's Golden Bough,* trans. A. C. Miles (Atlantic Highlands, NJ: Humanities Press, 1979). In political philosophy, see, for example, Jean-François Lyotard, *The Differend: Phrases in Dispute,* trans. Georges Van Den Abbeele (Minneapolis: University of Minnesota Press, 1988); Alasdair C. MacIntyre, *Whose Justice? Which Rationality?* (Notre Dame, IN: University of Notre Dame Press, 1988); Charles Taylor, *Philosophical Papers, Volume 2: Philosophy and the Human Sciences* (Cambridge: Cambridge University Press, 1985), especially chapters 3–5. With respect to philosophical systems, see, for example, Robin George Collingwood, *An Essay on Metaphysics* (Oxford: Clarendon Press, 1940); Everett W. Hall, *Philosophical Systems: A Categorial Analysis* (Chicago: University of Chicago Press, 1960); Henry W. Johnstone, Jr., *Validity and Rhetoric in Philosophical Argument: An Outlook in Transition* (University Park, PA: Dialogue Press of Man and World, 1978), e.g., 114.

problem for establishing truth. (It is true that if the different frameworks give different meanings to the same things, they are really different things, so that there is no conflict between the truths about them. But I argue that there is an important sense in which they are nonetheless also still the same things.)[3] Further, because in this situation incompatible statements are arguably true of the same thing, truth has to be said to allow what it excludes, and this contradiction creates a problem even for a coherent understanding of the nature of truth.

I discuss this more general problem in its own right throughout these essays. But I focus on the directly pluralist form of it here because it makes the problem more sharply clear, and also allows us to see more easily why the essentials of the same problem exist for frameworks of sense generally as for pluralist standpoints. I discuss this connection with sense frameworks in general in more detail in the next section, where I explore the theme of big question philosophy and the way in which the contemporary pluralist problem is rooted in its concerns.

This problem, both in its directly pluralist form and in its more general form, is increasingly recognized by postmodern theorists and their successors. Judith Butler, for example, notes that particular groups often have "notions of universality" that are intrinsic to their character, are part of what make their viewpoints what they are. As a result, a commitment to recognition of different particular viewpoints sometimes itself requires us to respect ideas of universal truth. What is more, different particular groups may have notions of universality of this kind that differ from and conflict with those of other groups, so that we are even required to respect conflicting versions of universal truth.[4] Again, the anthropologist Bruce Kapferer argues that the attempt to adopt a perspective from which all cultural views are simply equivalently valid in fact "flattens out" differences "in a homogenising, globalising sweep. This contradicts the significance of the postmodern notion of multiple modernities . . . involving distinct . . . ori-

---

[3] On this issue, see the quotation by Alasdair MacIntyre in section 4 of Chapter 1, and the discussions in section 6 of Chapter 3 and in the first sections of Chapters 8 and 9.

[4] Judith Butler, "Competing Universalities," in *Contingency, Hegemony, Universality: Contemporary Dialogues on the Left*, ed. Judith Butler and Slavoj Žižek (London: Verso, 2000), 166–67.

entations to reality."⁵ Alain Badiou comments, analogously, on the rejection of "grand narratives" in postmodern theory, "The announcement of the 'End of the Grand Narratives' is as immodest as the Grand Narrative itself, the certainty of the 'end of metaphysics' proceeds within the metaphysical element of certainty."⁶ Or, as David Simpson laconically asks in this connection, "What, we might wonder, is the grand narrative behind the compulsive appeal of little stories?"⁷ In queer theory, a number of writers have pointed out that its commitment to open-ended inclusiveness requires it to accept the legitimacy of fixedly exclusive personal identities. Ann Cvetkovich, for instance, argues against the assumption that "the queer . . . is the undoing of the identity politics signified by the category lesbian, or that lesbian culture is hostile to queer formations."⁸ As Biddy Martin writes, "Postmodernism, for its rhetorical attention to otherness and difference, enacts its own form of othering, of anything that looks too stable, too fixed, too certain."⁹

While these various theorists recognize the problem of this kind of self-contradiction, however, there are few who offer a way of resolving or negotiating it, and I argue that those few really do not succeed in doing so but instead reduplicate the problem in different ways.

The essays in this collection aim to show, in a variety of the contexts I have mentioned, that this contradiction exists, that it is inescapable, and that a possible solution is to recognize it, accept it, and work with it. In other words, if we are to be properly or genuinely pluralist, we need a logic that makes sense of, and a conception of how to work with, a specific kind of contradiction, one that occurs in the negotiation of fundamental difference of outlook and of the corresponding sense of things. (Since the sense provided by these different outlooks is the sense of the world they are outlooks

---

⁵ Bruce Kapferer, ed., *Beyond Rationalism: Rethinking Magic, Witchcraft and Sorcery* (New York: Berghahn Books, 2003), 18–19.

⁶ Alain Badiou, *Manifesto for Philosophy*, ed. and trans. Norman Madarasz (Albany: State University of New York Press, 1999), 30–31.

⁷ David Simpson, *The Academic Postmodern and the Rule of Literature: A Report on Half-Knowledge* (Chicago: University of Chicago Press, 1995), 29.

⁸ Ann Cvetkovich, *An Archive of Feelings: Trauma, Sexuality, and Lesbian Public Cultures* (Durham, NC: Duke University Press, 2003), 11.

⁹ Biddy Martin, *Femininity Played Straight: The Significance of Being Lesbian* (New York: Routledge, 1996), 15.

on, the logic—and with it the type of contradiction—that these essays discuss does not just describe the ways in which our thinking makes sense but the ways in which reality itself makes sense and works. I return to this point in the section on the meaning of "logic," below.)

Despite the obvious objections to admitting the sense or workability of any kind of contradiction, there is a growing literature on the possible legitimacy of contradictions, which I discuss below. There is also a powerfully argued and very influential objection to the understanding of pluralism I begin with here that insists that the "very idea" of frameworks of sense as a whole (described from the "outside," as it were), and with it the idea of this kind of thoroughgoing conflict between them, has no meaning. As a result, both the pluralist aim as I have described it and the problem of contradiction it faces turn out to be illusory. Donald Davidson and Richard Rorty are perhaps the best-known representatives of this line of thought.[10] The first essay is devoted to responding to that line of thought, and several of the others add to that response.

In addition to showing the necessity, sense, and workability of this kind of logic, these essays attempt to sketch its character in broad outline, and to indicate and begin to draw on some of the resources we have with which to articulate and work with it. These resources exist, for example, in the fields of philosophy of language and meaning, rhetoric, literary and dramatic art, and some kinds of humorous sensibility.

I have given an extended account of the nature, sense, and justification of this logic in its own right elsewhere.[11] In the following essays I mostly give only a general outline of its character and viability in each context, in order to focus on its relevance to the various issues and, in turn, on the light these different contexts cast on its sense and role. In Chapter 8, on metaphysics and Oscar Wilde's *The Importance of Being Earnest*, I explore its

---

[10] See, for example, Donald Davidson, "On the Very Idea of a Conceptual Scheme," in *Inquiries into Truth and Interpretation* (Oxford: Oxford University Press, 1984); Richard Rorty, *Objectivity, Relativism, and Truth: Philosophical Papers, Volume 1* (New York: Cambridge University Press, 1991).

[11] Jeremy Barris, "The Convergent Conceptions of Being in Mainstream Analytic and Postmodern Continental Philosophy," *Metaphilosophy* 43, no. 5 (2012): 592–618; *The Crane's Walk: Plato, Pluralism, and the Inconstancy of Truth* (New York: Fordham University Press, 2009); *Paradox and the Possibility of Knowledge: The Example of Psychoanalysis* (Selinsgrove, PA: Susquehanna University Press, 2003).

nature and justification in detail, and I map out its functioning in the negotiation of fundamental difference of standpoint.

For the purposes of these essays, there is an especially important consequence of this paradox of eliminating the legitimacy of one's own standpoint in carrying out its principle of respect for deeply different others. This consequence is that the elimination itself is canceled, since the legitimacy of the standpoint that requires and exercises it is eliminated. (In fact, as I shall argue, the standpoint itself is altogether eliminated as having any meaning at all.) The essays argue that, as a result, the legitimacy of one's own standpoint is restored, or uneliminated. But this occurs as a consequence of a process of *reasoning,* and in particular a process that in one phase has eliminated the standpoint's legitimacy and so has moved completely outside it, and then on that basis restored it. In other words, these essays argue, the legitimacy of the standpoint is now *established* or justified, and through a process that goes beyond it and so does not circularly presuppose it. A similar logic applies to the justification of other, conflicting standpoints, each understood similarly from its own point of view.

Paradoxically, then, a properly carried through respect for deeply different standpoints is not an obstacle to establishing the truth of a single standpoint but instead provides the conditions for doing so. This truth and its context of meanings must now, however, be understood as in some contexts in coordination with meanings and truth that it excludes. In addition to arguing for this idea, these essays try to give an account of its sense and some of its implications.

What is more, as the essays argue, within the context of each position the truths established in this way are universal and absolute. I have already mentioned Judith Butler as arguing for the legitimacy of competing notions of universal truth. Nelson Goodman notes that "one might say that there is only one world but this holds for each of the many worlds. . . . The equivocation is stark—yet perhaps negotiable."[12] Similarly, Thomas Kuhn, who so influentially made the case for the importance of "incommensurable

---

[12] Nelson Goodman, "Notes on the Well-Made World," *Partisan Review* 51 (1984): 278. See also, for example, Bernard Williams, *Ethics and the Limits of Philosophy* (Cambridge, MA: Harvard University Press, 1985), 159: "Even if there is no way in which divergent ethical beliefs can be brought to converge by independent inquiry or rational argument, this fact will not imply relativism. Each outlook may still be

paradigms" (or mutually exclusive global frameworks) in the history of science, argues in his later work that "within the world of each practice, true laws must be universal, but some of the laws governing one of these worlds cannot even be stated in the conceptual vocabulary deployed in, and partially constitutive of, another. . . . The point is not that laws true in one world may be false in another but that they may be ineffable, unavailable for conceptual or observational scrutiny."[13] In a different tradition, Karl Jaspers argues for a related "contradiction and paradox" of conflicting absolute truths. He notes that when our thinking is at its deepest, our existence comes "before its final limits: that there are many truths in the sense of existential absolutes."[14]

(These thinkers do not, however, take into account the consequence for which I argue here, namely, that their own statements about this issue themselves become meaningless or "ineffable" in the context of legitimate "worlds" that are not theirs—and as a result their statements in fact become incoherent in the course of their referring to those worlds. This in turn, though, is not the end of the issue. As I noted above, and as the following essays argue further, taking this self-cancellation of meanings into account also allows us to see that it in turn undoes itself and restores the relevant meanings, so that neither the statements nor their incoherence is the final word.)

The kind of deep difference of standpoint at issue here means that each position excludes the fundamental relevant principles and therefore the relevant meanings of the others. Consequently, once each standpoint is restored from its self-elimination and its legitimacy established, it again excludes the meanings of all the other fundamentally conflicting standpoints. But this result is part of what has now been justified: it is now established that the meanings of the other standpoints are legitimately excluded. It follows that there are no longer any legitimate meaningful conflicts

---

making claims it intends to apply to the whole world, not just to that part of it which is its 'own' world."

[13] Thomas S. Kuhn, *The Road Since Structure: Philosophical Essays, 1970–1993, with an Autobiographical Interview*, ed. James Conant and John Haugeland (Chicago: University of Chicago Press, 2000), 249.

[14] Karl Jaspers, *Reason and Existenz: Five Lectures*, trans. William Earle (Milwaukee, WI: Marquette University Press, 1997), 112, 100.

with the relevant fundamental principles of the standpoint, since any meanings that might allow this are rightly excluded. For this and other reasons that the essays explore, a genuinely undogmatic pluralism therefore produces a diversity of absolutely justified positions. In this context, the established truth claims of each of these are what I call "sometimes always true." The essays argue, then, for a way of conceiving and working with multiple conflicting absolute truths, rather than for a relativist pluralism—although it follows from the argument that this standpoint too has its place.[15]

The second, more specific form of the problem of contemporary thought that these essays address concerns a central aim of specifically postmodern thought, an aim that is related to and interacts with the more generally pluralist commitment discussed above. This is the aim of establishing a mode of thought that does justice to concepts and terms that have been systematically but questionably subordinated to their binary opposites (for example, male and female, natural and artificial, literal and figurative, logical and rhetorical). Postmodern work often tries to achieve this goal by attempting to undo the notion of binary opposition in general and to replace it with the notion of difference rather than mutually exclusive opposition. This more general approach to the postmodern aim faces a contradiction related to the pluralist one: its own principle requires it to make room for the difference between difference and opposition themselves, and to grant legitimacy to opposition in its full difference from difference. The more particularly conceived postmodern aim of undoing the subordination of one opposed concept by another also faces a form of this contradiction: it cannot universally and in a permanently unquestionable way subordinate subordination itself to the relation of equal legitimacy—not without reinstating another subordination of this kind in that very act.

These essays argue, in the course of presenting the more generally pluralist theme, that "sometimes always truth" applies here too. Sometimes a term is meaningful and relevant only when conceived as one side of an opposition; in other contexts that same term is legitimately conceived only in nonoppositional relations to the systems of terms within which it belongs.

---

[15] Goodman proposes "a policy common in daily life and impressively endorsed by modern science: namely, judicious vacillation. . . . We are monists, pluralists, or nihilists . . . as befits the context" ("Notes," 278).

For example, one such opposition or difference the essays explore is that of "sense" and "nonsense." Several of the essays argue that sometimes sense is simply sense, cleanly and stably separated from nonsense, but sometimes that same sense is inherently or internally connected with nonsense and so is partly and inescapably constituted by it. Similar arguments are made about, among other terms, "construction" and "essence," "artificiality" and "nature," "essential issue" and "inessential issue," "superficiality" and "depth," and "logic" and "rhetoric."

As the essays argue, almost all of the existing literature in all of the fields I mentioned at the start of this section either suffers from the unacknowledged and unassimilated contradiction outlined above or, where it acknowledges the contradiction, does not successfully offer a way of resolving or negotiating it. One of the chapters argues that Michel Foucault's work is an exception, but it seems routinely not to be read in this way. (I believe that Jacques Derrida's version of deconstruction is demonstrably also an exception, but the literature that draws on Derrida seems universally not to allow, or only very inconsistently to allow, his own position to cancel itself, and so to establish limits to its applicability. Derrideans, then, are not an exception, even though I would argue that Derrida's own work—with occasional slippages natural for an innovator finding his way—is.)

It should already be clear that the issues I have discussed in connection with contemporary pluralism are often also issues for what I have called big question philosophy. I suggested at the start of this Introduction that the contemporary pluralist problem is itself rooted in and an offshoot of the big philosophical questions. I now turn to discussing its relevance to big question philosophy.

2. Big Question Philosophy

I mentioned at the start that these essays also develop an approach to the big questions of philosophy. Although they explore this approach in its own right, they also show that the contemporary pluralist problem is rooted in those fundamental questions. As a result, the exploration of one is also directly or indirectly the exploration of the other. This connection of deep pluralism with the fundamental philosophical questions began to emerge in the previous section with the discussion of the implications of deep pluralism for knowledge and for the ultimate nature of truth. By the big questions, again, I mean questions like "What is knowledge and how is it possible?," "What is the nature of being?," "What is the meaning of life?" In asking these questions, we try to get a vantage point on the whole of things, in some sense to stand outside everything and treat it all as a whole that can be wondered about.[16] Similarly, when general frameworks are contrasted in thinking about pluralism, we also try to get this kind of vantage point outside or beyond the whole. Doing so is not the aim of thinking about pluralist issues and only comes about incidentally in thinking about them, but it is nonetheless a necessary part of their context. As a result, the deep pluralist concerns of contemporary thought turn out to engage the fundamental and central dimensions of big question philosophy.

The big questions of philosophy share not only the same kind of vantage point with deep pluralist thinking but also the problem of the same kind of self-contradiction. I have mentioned the objections that the "very idea" of a vantage point on the whole makes no sense. One of these objections is that the idea is self-contradictory: our activity of "stepping outside" can only be part of the whole, so that to "step outside" the whole also means to remain within the whole. This is the same kind of contradiction as that of thinking in terms of two all-embracing and yet mutually exclusive standpoints at the same time. Each of these standpoints is outside the other, but since they are each all-embracing, each can only be inside the other.

Philosophy at its most fundamental, then, is self-undermining in the same way that genuine pluralism is. In trying to grasp the sense of the whole of reality or, equivalently, the whole of sense, it steps outside sense and consequently eliminates its own meaning.[17] (Expressing this in a way

---

[16] I argue for the need and legitimacy of this kind of grasp of the whole in several of the essays. See, for example, the references to Thomas Nagel's and Jacques Derrida's defenses of this idea in Chapter 9, note 5, and the accompanying text.

[17] Giorgio Agamben's exploration of the legal "state of exception" is one prominent contemporary recognition that this is the case, and that it is the inescapable and legitimate structure of deep thought and sense. (As will become clear below, I would argue instead that it is sometimes always inescapably and legitimately that structure.) As he explains, "On the one hand, the juridical void at issue in the state of exception seems absolutely unthinkable for the law; on the other hand, this unthinkable thing nevertheless has a decisive strategic relevance for the juridical order," and he points out that "the strategy of the exception . . . is the counterpart to the onto-theo-logical

that is more clearly a parallel with the pluralist case: in being open to the sense of reality as a whole, philosophy steps outside that sense and so eliminates even the meaning of its own openness.)

For example, if we think of everything as being essentially matter, then our thinking of it and our statements about it are matter too, and consequently do not mean or say anything: they are just brute, unintelligent material. Or, alternatively, in this view matter is able to signify, with the result that matter has the qualities of thought and intelligence that its meaning is supposed to exclude. Saying that all reality is matter is then the same as saying that reality includes immaterial thought and meaning. Similarly, if we think of everything as essentially spiritual (or ideal), we eliminate anything that might contrast with "spiritual" and give it the meaning for which we selected it. What we ordinarily think of as material is now included in the new meaning of "spiritual," which has simply come to mean "everything, whatever it may be." Again, if we think of all of life as meaningless, the idea that it is meaningless is itself meaningless too, and makes no difference for us to take into account. The same kind of self-cancellation happens to "all truth is relative." On the other hand, "all truth is absolute" loses the contrasts on which its meaning depends, in the same way as "all reality is spiritual."

Since big question philosophy and deep pluralism share this same problem, however, they also share the solution to that problem these essays propose. Just as these essays argue that we can successfully think in terms of two global and completely mutually exclusive standpoints at the same time, they argue that we can successfully think in the mutually exclusive terms of being wholly within a standpoint and yet wholly outside it at the same time.

This means, however, that, as in the case of pluralism, any philosophy must ultimately take as an inherent part of its meaning and procedure that, in one phase of its procedure and with occasionally lasting consequences, it also renders its own standpoint and statements meaningless. This is true whether the philosophy proceeds with a consistent commit-

---

strategy aimed at capturing pure being in the meshes of the *logos*. That is to say, everything happens as if both law and *logos* needed an anomic (or alogical) zone of suspension in order to ground their reference to the world of life." Giorgio Agamben, *State of Exception*, trans. Kevin Attell (Chicago: University of Chicago Press, 2005), 51, 59–60.

ment to sense and consequence, or whether it proceeds by accepting and working with contradiction, or even whether it insists on the necessity of moving beyond sense and meaning. Each of these either endorses an idea of how sense in general works, and to do so has to occupy a vantage point in some way outside sense itself, or else it already explicitly occupies that position in some way outside sense. This in turn means that it eliminates its own sense, and therefore eliminates the legitimacy of its idea of how sense (or non-sense) works.

We can see this necessity directly in the specific formulations of these various understandings of sense. An idea of sense as inconsistent must allow the legitimacy of inconsistency with its own sense: that is, it must endorse inconsistency with inconsistency itself or, in other words, consistency. And an idea of sense as consistent must think through the inconsistencies it finds with consistency to their inconsistency, and not instead explain them away so that it entirely eliminates what it was explaining. That is, it must endorse inconsistency as a part of the sense of some areas of reality.[18]

In general, the sense of philosophy—or, in other words, of the attempted articulation of fundamental sense—is constituted by the partly outside-of-sense contexts in which it operates. Consequently, whatever principle a philosophy is committed to (including a principle of "sometimes always" paradox), its own sense as philosophy makes unqualified room for what that same sense excludes, whether that is logical paradox or simple, unequivocal truth, or even a "sometimes always" coordination of both.

As I noted in the pluralism discussion, this self-cancellation of sense also cancels its own meaning, and so wholly restores the various relevant original forms of sense. But this self-cancellation is nonetheless also a cancellation of that sense. The sense of philosophy must therefore still be understood now as in some contexts in coordination with kinds of sense it excludes.[19] In addition, as I have argued and will argue further in these

---

[18] As Davidson argues, part of the "underlying paradox of irrationality, from which no theory can entirely escape, is this: if we explain it too well, we turn it into a concealed form of rationality"; Donald Davidson, "Paradoxes of Irrationality," in *Philosophical Essays on Freud*, ed. Richard Wollheim and James Hopkins (New York: Cambridge University Press, 1982), 303.

[19] I believe the relevant logic here has strong affinities with the logical tetrad of Taoism and Zen Buddhism, one formulation of which is "it is this, and that, and both, and neither." For example, in commenting on a Zen story in which a teacher

essays, the legitimacy of this philosophical or fundamental sense is only established through this self-canceling process. As a result, to the extent that our philosophy does not recognize its own necessary participation in this paradoxical process, it fails to see itself and the status of its own claims adequately.

I try to show this in detail in the essays with respect to particular philosophers, various areas of philosophy, and the various types of philosophical procedure I mentioned above. I discuss Davidson, Rorty, Foucault, and Martin Heidegger, for example, and I do so partly with respect to their own explicit understandings of truth, both in general and in the context of various issues, but partly also with respect to what their thinking illustrates about widely accepted principles of philosophical sense and procedure. Davidson and Rorty are committed to a thoroughgoing consistency of sense, while Heidegger ultimately proceeds through a form of systematically contradictory thought that has since been widely taken up in postmodern philosophy.[20] I argue, however, that Davidson, Rorty, and Heidegger all do not recognize the problem I discuss of the entire self-cancellation of their own meanings, or consequently the principles of

---

responds to a particular question about Buddha-nature or ultimate reality with the answer "no" or "nothing" (mu), the Zen master Mumon writes that the meaning of this answer "is not nothingness, the opposite of existence. . . . If you say yes or no, you lose your own Buddha-nature"; Mumon, *The Gateless Gate*, trans. Nyogen Senzaki and Paul Reps, in *Zen Flesh, Zen Bones*, ed. Paul Reps (Harmondsworth: Penguin Books, 1957), 95–96. Similarly, Shunryu Suzuki explains that the Buddhist goal of egolessness "does not mean to give up your own individual practice. . . . As long as you believe, 'My practice is egoless,' that means you stick to ego, because you stick to giving up ego-centered practice. . . . True egolessness . . . is not just egolessness. It also includes ego practice, but at the same time it is the practice of egolessness that is beyond ego or egolessness"; Shunryu Suzuki, *Not Always So: Practicing the True Spirit of Zen*, ed. Edward Espe Brown (New York: Harper, 2002), 86. More generally, "To develop . . . clear . . . judgment, it is important to give up, or be ready to give up everything, including your understanding of the teaching and your knowledge of Buddhism. . . . When you are trying to give up everything, you haven't given up everything yet" (117). On the comparison of the kind of logic I discuss here with the Zen tradition, see Jeremy Barris and Jeffrey C. C. Ruff, "Thoughts on Wisdom and Its Relation to Critical Thinking, Multiculturalism, and Global Awareness," *Analytic Teaching and Philosophical Praxis* 31, no. 1 (2011): 5–20.

[20] In fact, Heidegger thinks systematic consistency through to the point where it emerges as systematic contradiction.

sense and thought that follow from it, and that the adequacy of their thinking suffers as a result. While Davidson and Rorty endorse consistency and Heidegger endorses ultimate contradiction, then, they are all fundamentally committed to an unself-canceling consistency of their principles, whether a consistency of consistency or a consistency of inconsistency. I call this, among other things, a "simply continuously consistent" logic, in contrast to the "sometimes always continuously consistent" logic for which I argue.

I try to show that Foucault, on the other hand, does recognize and successfully negotiate the paradox I discuss and its consequences, although I think that he does not give an account of the logical (or, in Heidegger's language, essential) possibility of this kind of negotiation. I also discuss Oscar Wilde at length in two chapters, where I argue that he exemplifies this "sometimes always" logic in very illuminating ways. I am not sure that his work has the genuine weight of philosophy, but I think it may be something that in equally important ways, some themselves philosophical, is better than philosophy.[21]

Finally, to return in the light of this discussion to the relation between the pluralist problem I discussed in the first section and the concerns of big question philosophy: there are dimensions of deep pluralism that coincide with the big questions of philosophy. As a result, the pluralist contrast of global frameworks, of interpretations of being in general, also offers one way of framing those questions. These essays partly explore what insights into those deep questions this framing may yield, as well as the reverse.

---

[21] I have also discussed this logic and its consequences at length in relation to Plato in *The Crane's Walk*, to Derrida in *Paradox*, esp. 78–85, to Wittgenstein in "Convergent Conceptions," and to Lacan in *Paradox*. I argue that each of these thinkers articulates and works with this kind of logic. The different ways they do so are themselves very illuminating. In "Convergent Conceptions," I also explore ways in which Heidegger's thinking can be understood as true to this logic (although, as I argue in Chapter 7 of this book, that is not how his work ultimately carries it through). In Chapter 7 here, I sketch the difference between "sometimes always" logic and Hegel's; I discuss this in a little more detail in *The Crane's Walk*, as well as the difference between "sometimes always" logic and Schelling's, which in important ways is closer to it than Hegel's. On Hegel, see *The Crane's Walk*, 279, n. 20; 286–88, n. 2; 295, n. 23; 310, n. 19; on Schelling, see *The Crane's Walk*, 314, n. 53.

3. Our Experience of Existence and Value

Coming to the third theme the essays explore, I suggested that the global or "world" framing that the big questions of philosophy involve is another side of the same coin as, or is continuous with, the texture of our concrete, deeply personal experience of existence and of the meaning and value of our conduct. By our experience of existence and of the meaning of our conduct I mean, for example, our concerns with finding meaning in the events of our lives and in our lives as a whole, with our sense of identity and of our place in the world, with the deeply affecting confusions and clarities about the sense of things we encounter in growing and as we come across very different outlooks, with basic human decency and indecency in acknowledging or failing to acknowledge what is essential to others (and, for that matter, what is essential to ourselves), and with our and others' capacity for unshadowed enjoyment in the face of the profound uncertainties and evils of life. As the essays try to show, the apparently abstract and impersonal logic of the interaction of frameworks and of concepts connects directly with all of these. I noted above that the sense the frameworks offer is the sense of the world they are frameworks of. As a result, the logic of their interaction informs both the details of the sense of the world we react to and that part of it that is our experience itself, its own substance and texture.

In other words, the essays argue, for example, that experiences whose sense is given by mutually exclusive concepts or conceptual structures can also make room for each other and even constitute the bases for each other, while nonetheless remaining wholly mutually exclusive. For instance, unmitigated conflict between gender concepts, commitments, and experiences can coexist with and even be the basis of their mutual affirmation and support; strength and surrender, or power and vulnerability, can be the same thing, or the means to each other; failure to grasp and inability to know how to proceed can be the core and vehicle of clarity, expertise, and empowerment; and innocent trust and delight in the world can coexist with and mutually enable a full awareness of the overwhelming evils of the world and the unremitting need to work to remedy those that are ours to affect.

The reasons for this at this more specific level of particular concepts or conceptual structures are parallel to those I gave for the relations between incomparable global frameworks. Because these conceptual structures are mutually exclusive, they have no meaning in each other's terms, and so have no relevance to each other. (It is also true, as Wittgenstein, among others, shows, that concepts function only in connection and cooperation with a large variety of very different concepts. I am arguing this too, but I am arguing in addition that these kinds of concepts are also mutually exclusive in the ways I discuss here, so that their connection is in fact one between incomparable concepts. Consequently, it needs the kind of explanation I try to offer here.) In contexts where the contrast of these conceptual areas with other conceptual structures becomes relevant, however, a reflection on their own sense as one kind among others becomes meaningful, and they are then in the state I have described as being partly outside what for each of them respectively is all of sense. In that context, as I have argued, their own sense makes room for what it excludes. As a result, they are then also mutually meaningful and relevant. Since, however, it is by reflecting on their own exclusive sense that these structures of sense cancel themselves to result in this mutual meaningfulness, it is their mutual exclusiveness itself that produces their mutual relevance. Consequently, their mutual relevance does not in any way qualify their mutual exclusiveness but instead depends on it. They are unqualifiedly both mutually meaningless and mutually meaningful.

These essays try to give an account of the sense and importance of this kind of contradictory coordination of incompatible conceptual areas in the context of our concrete experience, as well as in the context of global frameworks.

Once each essay has sorted out the logic of the issues it deals with, the bearing of this logic on our existential experience and on our practice—how we conduct ourselves and how we negotiate problems—can emerge. In other words, the essays generally focus first on the large, apparently impersonal issues and move from there to the more intimately existential ones.

As I mentioned at the start of the Introduction, some of the elements of our experience, such as our moral and political values, directly comprise both the intimate and the impersonal sides of our experience at once. One moral and political issue in particular to which the "sometimes always true" theme is relevant is that we are so profoundly dependent on our social environment that we cannot but participate in its moral and political

18 *Introduction: Sometimes Always True*

structures, deeply flawed as these are. As a result, we are all inevitably complicit in our societies' moral and political evils. Because of this complicity, it seems that we can have no clear sense of decency or moral innocence, of a shame-free or prideworthy life. This problem is especially acute in our contemporary deeply pluralist societies, which explicitly make room for living out incompatible values. The essays present a framework in which we can absolutely acknowledge this inescapable complicity, and yet at the same time and in the same respects recognize room for living out an unequivocal truth to our moral and political values, and so for living in a morally clean and innocent way. This issue is most directly addressed by Chapter 6, in the context, rather nicely, of queer theory, and by the Coda.

4. The Meaning of "Logic"

I have mentioned logic a great deal, and the discussion so far will help me make clear what I mean by it. I do not take logic to be only or even primarily the rules of inference or of the derivation of truth (although it is the ultimate basis of these). Instead, as I have already suggested in the course of the discussion, I take it to be something like the fundamental anatomy of the sense of things. As the anatomy or blueprint of the sense of things in general, it is also the anatomy of the nature of reality, or, in other words, of what metaphysics explores. One traditional version of this conception is Kant's idea of "transcendental logic"; another is Wittgenstein's idea of "grammar."[22] In turn, ultimate reality and therefore logic are not only objects of our scrutiny, although they are that too; they are as importantly the structure of the stuff of which we, as well as our scrutiny itself, are made.[23] Metaphysics and logic are consequently

---

[22] Bertrand Russell also insists, for example, that when "the laws of logic" are regarded as "laws of thought . . . the true dignity of reason is very greatly lowered," since logic is a matter of "the very heart and immutable essence of all things actual and possible," and not "something more or less human and subject to our limitations"; Bertrand Russell, "The Study of Mathematics," in *Mysticism and Logic and Other Essays* (London: Unwin Books, 1963), 55.

[23] It follows that philosophy or deep thought is an activity of our substance or being, and not only (although it is also) a making and exploration of statements and

not only the most abstract of things but also the closest and most personal and intimate of things.

Against this conception of logic, it is a commonplace in contemporary philosophy that logical relations characterize only collections of statements or propositions, and not the world of events and things. I do not believe that this very widespread view of the field of application of logic is tenable. It is by now also a commonplace in a host of philosophical traditions that facts and events are "theory-laden," that what we *mean* by our references to things and events presupposes a grammar of the usage of the terms we are using to refer to them. In other words, anything we can mean by things and events, including what we can mean by their objectivity or their independence of us and of our language, is exactly a matter of grammatical meaning. Consequently, things and events are not ultimately separable from the relations of the propositions in which we articulate them, and so from the logic that characterizes those propositional relations.

For the last century and a half or so, logicians have achieved great success in approaching and handling the problems of logic by treating logic exclusively as rules for deriving the truth of statements from the truth of other statements. I imagine that the current view that this is what logic necessarily is results from confusing a feature of a prevalent and now habitual method of approaching and handling the subject with features of the subject itself. In this method's becoming an institutional habit, the awareness that it has presuppositions and a history that shaped it has been lost. But successful as it has been for the particular purposes that have struck its proponents as central, it is only a method of handling the problems of the subject, and not definitive of the subject itself. It is also only one possible method even for those purposes.

---

their connections, independent of our particularity. I explore how it is at once both activity or enactment of being and straightforward, stable descriptive statement (in the way of the coordination of sometimes always true alternatives whose logic I discuss in this book) briefly in Chapter 9, section 3, and at length in *The Crane's Walk*, esp. part 1, idea 2, but also throughout. Chapter 7 of the present book, which deals with a fundamental limitation of Heidegger's conception of truth as enactment of being, offers a detailed account of a closely related version of this coordination of conflicting alternatives in the course of pursuing its own focus.

5. The Possibility of Legitimate Logical Contradiction

With respect to the issue of contradiction, there is a growing literature on the admissibility of contradictions in the contexts of both formal and informal logic. In formal logic, the traditional view is that contradiction is logically unacceptable, since any statement at all can be validly derived from a contradiction,[24] so that if we accept a contradiction we are no longer saying anything, rather than anything else. But this is no longer uncontroversially understood to be the case.[25]

A recent discussion by Paul Livingston, for example, offers a very illuminating detailed account in this context of the paradoxes of self-reference demonstrated by Russell, Gödel, and Tarski. These logicians variously and famously demonstrate a fundamental conflict between the completeness of a logical or semantic whole and its logical consistency. This conflict has been taken to show in particular that we cannot refer to or grasp a framework of meaning or sense as a whole because the attempt to do so leads to logical contradiction. This is, of course, the same kind of logical conflict that I discuss as the paradox of reflecting on or grasping the sense of a framework as a whole. Livingston draws on an argument by Graham Priest to show that the demonstrations of these conflicts do not in fact prove "the incompleteness of any language [or framework], but rather face us with a choice, *between* incompleteness and inconsistency."[26] These paradoxes can only be taken to prove incompleteness if it is *presupposed* that inconsistency is unacceptable. Further, as Livingston also argues in some detail, "the attempt to *prohibit* self-reference . . . is . . . quite at odds with the actual commitments of ordinary speech and discourse," so that the at-

---

[24] For this principle, see, for example, Susan Haack, *Philosophy of Logics* (New York: Cambridge University Press, 1978), 22, 202.

[25] On the formal admissibility of contradictions see, for example, Graham Priest, *An Introduction to Non-Classical Logic* (Cambridge: Cambridge University Press, 2001). On the formally admissible existence of *true* contradictions, see, for example, Manuel Bremer, *An Introduction to Paraconsistent Logics* (Frankfurt: Peter Lang, 2005), 16, 19ff.; Priest, *Introduction*, e.g., pp. 67ff., 151. For useful discussion on both sides of this debate, see Graham Priest, J. C. Beall, and Bradley Armour-Garb, eds., *The Law of Non-Contradiction: New Philosophical Essays* (Oxford: Oxford University Press, 2004).

[26] Paul M. Livingston, *The Politics of Logic: Badiou, Wittgenstein, and the Consequences of Formalism* (New York: Routledge, 2012), 33, my insertion.

tempts to avoid it are "quite implausible."²⁷ We do, for example, talk about our own language as a whole, or make statements about truth in general that themselves claim to be true, in ways that are not easily shown to be without meaning or aptness. Consequently, there is very good reason, even in the context of formal considerations, to think that we should accept the legitimacy of logical inconsistency at least with respect to considering frameworks of meaning or sense as a whole.

It is important, however, that, as I commented in the previous section, despite how formal logic has at times been seen, it is not a representation of the essence of valid inference and so is not the final arbiter of questions about sense and its violations. On the contrary, it is only one limited model on whose basis to frame these questions. As Henry Johnstone argues, for example, since different frameworks of sense introduce conflicts of meaning, "cases of inconsistency subject to verification by every rational being can occur only in formal systems, in which the axioms and rules of inference are unambiguously stated and it is irrelevant to consider the meanings of the symbols. But clearly the assertion of a philosophical thesis is not like this, for the meanings of the symbols in terms of which the assertion is made are clearly essential to the enterprise of making the assertion."²⁸ Further, logical systems are themselves developed and justified on the basis of philosophical considerations, which are therefore more ultimate arbiters than they are. As Johnstone notes, "the very notion of inconsistency is itself subject to philosophical interpretation."²⁹ Philosophical thought occurs at a level before formal systems and their principles acquire their force, and their meaning and force themselves depend on that prior thought. Consequently, even where formal systems of logic do forbid contradiction, they meaningfully do so only within their own systems.³⁰ Whether contradiction is inadmissible in either a formal or an informal context, then, is not settled in advance of argument on the issue.

---

²⁷ Ibid., 30–31.
²⁸ Johnstone, *Validity and Rhetoric*, 45.
²⁹ Ibid., 45.
³⁰ For a defense and exploration of legitimate contradiction in the context of concrete, nonformalized philosophical issues, see, for example, Graham Priest, *Beyond the Limits of Thought* (Oxford: Oxford University Press, 2002).

To see this more plainly, one might ask on what principle, legitimated by what, can contradictions never conceivably contribute to logical sense? Would this be the principle of noncontradiction, magically validating itself? If, on the other hand, one says the principle is self-evident, one is relying on a psychological and therefore empirical fact—the fact of what people happen to find obvious—as somehow able to support a principle that recognizes no variable, empirical circumstances as affecting its validity.[31] But if the principle of contradiction does not validate itself and is not self-evident, then its own legitimacy cannot be taken as going without saying, and it is clearly not logically inadmissible to consider ways of thinking that do not respect it.

Given the status and difficulties of this debate, it is certainly legitimate at least to explore the possibility that contradictions may be part of logical sense. In these essays, therefore, I shall do so.

In addition to these general considerations, several of the essays develop their own detailed, contextualized accounts of the sense and viability of the kind of contradiction I am proposing here. In fact, then, given the unresolved nature of the debate, the essays may be taken as not simply depending on what the conclusions of the debate may turn out to be but as contributing to the debate and adding to the considerations on which its conclusions depend. And on the debate's positive side, with respect to the formal arguments for the possibility of true contradictions ("dialetheias") that some logicians offer, these essays provide a variety of concrete contexts in which that formal result has application and its meaning and consequences can be explored and elaborated.

Something worth noting here that I do not make a theme in its own right, although I work with it in Chapters 4 and 8, is that there do exist traditions of organized accounts of reality that are meaningful and yet include central inconsistencies without regarding them as requiring to be resolved. What is more, they also do so without always or even generally respecting inconsistency as legitimate. In other words, they are inconsistent, but also inconsistent with respect to the legitimacy of inconsistency. In this way, they have a kinship with the kind of "sometimes always" logic for which I argue. These traditions include, for example, myths in a wide variety of cultures and ancient Western biographical traditions. Both of-

---

[31] See, for example, Haack, *Philosophy of Logics*, 235–36.

ten offer a variety of very different alternative versions of each story, without a concern to reconcile or decide between them, and within each of these versions also often narrate or argue with explicit reference to the need for consistency. In the contemporary world, these traditions include storytelling in the sense, for example, of recounting on different occasions something that happened to one or retelling a part of one's family history, and joke telling. All these kinds of accounts are meaningful and convey possible truths despite their contradictions. I would argue that they are meaningful as accounts of reality not only despite those inconsistencies but also partly because of them. This book implicitly offers that argument. Chapters 4 and 8, on Wilde, do so explicitly with respect to certain kinds of story and a certain kind of humor.

6. Recurring Discussions in the Essays

Before turning to a brief description of each of the chapters, I should say a word about some discussions that recur across the essays. For example, I discuss objections to talking about global frameworks or the world as a whole from the outside (particularly Davidson's and Rorty's objections) in a number of the essays, and there is therefore some partial repetition of some of the themes of this discussion. I have left these repetitions in place because each essay recasts this discussion in keeping with its own focus. As a result, each essay addresses a different aspect of the issue, while the resources of its own focus also allow it to offer a different response to the overall problem.

Some other discussions partially reappear in several essays for the same reasons: the mutual meaninglessness of globally different frameworks, the problem of regarding the statements of thoroughly incompatible frameworks as referring to the same things and therefore as expressing genuinely conflicting interpretations, and discussion of some of the central problems of epistemology.

7. The Chapters

In Chapter 1, "Comparing Different Cultural or Theoretical Frameworks: Davidson, Rorty, and the Nature of Truth," I argue that, in comparing very different cultural, theoretical, or methodological standpoints, the nature of truth itself becomes a problem. If the standpoints have different conceptions of truth, a comparative approach that respects both involves the contradiction of resulting conflicting legitimate claims to truth. But if we reject this contradiction, we eliminate the possibility that standpoints can have legitimately different conceptions of truth. And with that we reject the sense of a genuine comparison in this respect, and replace it with a reading of one framework that either arbitrarily assimilates it to the conception of truth of the other or equally arbitrarily assimilates both to the conception of truth of the standpoint surveying the two.

Donald Davidson and Richard Rorty have mounted especially powerful arguments against the very sense of this kind of contradiction between frameworks, and so against the sense of this kind of pluralist comparison. Through a detailed discussion of their work, this chapter argues that the contradictory conception of truth is the right one, in part because, as their own work helps to show, the contradiction has the self-canceling character that I have outlined in this Introduction and as a result resolves itself. The chapter also argues that because the contradiction is self-canceling in this way, it is manageable. Consequently, a properly comparative approach is both possible and necessary, even where the interpretation of the nature of truth itself is part of the conflict between the frameworks. In particular, this chapter argues that this conception makes room for ideas of truth as both absolute and relative, and also (contradictorily but with due respect for many of the cultural and theoretical frameworks available for comparison) makes room for noncontradictory conceptions of truth.

Chapter 2, "An Internal Connection between Logic and Rhetoric between Frameworks, and a Legitimate Foundation for Knowledge," takes up some of the discussion of Chapter 1 more fully in the context of problems of knowledge rather than those of the nature of truth. That is, it focuses more fully on epistemology rather than on the metaphysics of truth. It is a common argument that theories that try to justify themselves fully are ultimately viciously circular (or infinitely regressive, though the chapter argues that they are so in a way that is here equivalent to circularity). The chapter argues that while this is true, the circularity in this context has a rhetorical dimension that offers a solution to this problem. Since the circle needs a contrast to be identified at all, closing the circle of justification means referring to another theoretical position. This is a reference to an audience—a matter of rhetoric. The contrasting position, however, is by definition outside the circle, that is, its meanings are irrelevant to the meanings constituted by the circle. Consequently, closing the circle establishes the meaninglessness of the contrasting position for the circular position. And this, by eliminating the contrast, establishes the meaninglessness of the circle itself, and therefore of the requirement to justify it. But the absence of this requirement has now been *established,* and with reference to meanings and truths outside the relevant position, or noncircularly. The theory is therefore now noncircularly justified.

Since this process involves the ultimate conditions of meaning and consequence, it is properly logical, and not only rhetorical. But because it is a specifically rhetorical process that is at the same time properly logical, the logical and rhetorical dimensions are internally connected, formally integral to each other. In other words, each standpoint is internally (logically) connected to standpoints that are nonetheless external (rhetorically and not logically relevant) to it.

The chapter argues further, again, that the type of contradictory self-elimination involved here is logically viable.

A pluralism of deeply different standpoints, then, is not an obstacle to establishing the truth of a single standpoint but can be drawn on to help do so.

Later in the book, I take up the discussion of the nature and status of internal (or essential) and external relations in their own right, in their fundamental connection with logic and with metaphysics and in particular with metaphysical pluralism. I discuss them most fully in Chapter 7. Chapter 2 also offers some broader context to those later discussions.

Chapter 3, "Pluralism, Legitimate Self-Contradiction, and a Solution to Some Shared Fundamental Problems of Political and Mainstream Epistemology," returns to a focus on the mutual meaninglessness and yet essential connection of globally different frameworks, and develops the relevance of this paradoxical connection for both political and mainstream, unpoliticized epistemology. The chapter discusses political epistemology primarily through the example of feminist epistemology. It argues, first, that the unresolved debates in the field of political epistemology show that it is still widely troubled by problems that it shares with the mainstream versions. Second, political epistemologists have typically engaged in debates within epistemology, and have not taken up the debates that have emerged between mainstream epistemologists and antiepistemologists. The chapter argues that a possible solution to the problems of both kinds of epistemology lies in coordinating the incommensurable insights of mainstream epistemology, explicitly politicized epistemology, and antiepistemology. Also inherent in this coordination are the means of coordinating and negotiating between epistemically incommensurable standpoints generally. This solution is necessarily self-contradictory. But it is conceivable given a specific reunderstanding of sense itself, a possibility of which the "sometimes always" logic I have outlined offers an account, and for which some postmodern and some specifically feminist work has opened the way.

In Chapter 4, "The Logic of Genuine Political Pluralism and Oscar Wilde's Artificiality of Wit and Style," I argue that the artificiality of Oscar Wilde's wit and style exemplifies both the logic and method of genuine, undogmatic political pluralism, and that it does so in a deeply consistent and illuminating way. (His work is also pluralist in more wide-ranging ways, but in this chapter I focus on its political side. I focus on his metaphysical pluralism, for example, in Chapter 8.) I argue that the most widely known current approaches to political pluralism, by contrast, suffer from the unacknowledged and unmanaged contradiction I discussed above in the section on the problem of contemporary pluralism. I try to show that Wilde's artificiality of style and wit presents the serious and unartificial possibility of things' being essentially otherwise than they are understood to be in any given standpoint. His aesthetic impact in fact consists in a fresh opening of essential—or constitutive or ontological—spaces or standpoints. But raising the possibility of thoroughly new meanings, entirely unrelated to all the familiar meanings we have access to in considering that possibility, is nonsensical. I argue that it is so in a way that is thoroughly self-canceling. As a result, it both opens the possibility of new essential spaces and is *also* a validation of familiar essential spaces *exactly as they are*. This validation, then, involves the self-canceling recognition of essentially different and therefore mutually exclusive "spaces."

The self-canceling principle at work is that constitutive difference between standpoints involves the meaninglessness of the organizing categories of each position to the others. A position that aims to understand and communicate with incompatible positions must therefore recognize the genuine meaninglessness of its own claims to them, and vice versa. In this way, paradoxically, mutually exclusive positions can be related without obscuring their mutual exclusivity. Wilde's nonsensically self-canceling aesthetic, as expressed in both his fictional and critical works, is a medium for exactly this kind of paradoxical coordination.

Chapter 5, "Foucault's Pluralism and the Possibility of Truth and of Ideology Critique," addresses the widely held view that Michel Foucault's pluralism of equally legitimate truth frameworks or "regimes of truth" ultimately abolishes the idea of truth and hence of truth-distorting ideology. As a result, it also abolishes the sense of ideology critique, that is, of identifying and questioning ideology. In other words, it removes any meaning from the notion of criticizing and so of justifiably rejecting or endorsing the systems of ideas under which we live our lives. But this chapter argues that Foucault's pluralism instead provides an unusually rigorous theoretical and ethical-political foundation for the notions of both truth and ideology critique.

Foucault works at two levels: within particular frameworks, and quasi-transcendentally outside all particular frameworks. Truth criteria are given only within particular frameworks. As a result, it is true that for discussion purely at the metalevel outside particular frameworks, questions of truth versus ideology are necessarily meaningless, but at the level of discussion within frameworks various traditional ideas of both truth and ideology are in fully legitimate force. Metalevel statements, however, are also not entirely without relation to the standards of truth. The criteria for the adequacy of metalevel statements are given indirectly by their successfully allowing the truths of the frameworks they coordinate to emerge in their own terms. Thought at the metalevel, then, is both not fully constrained by the truth of particular frameworks and also still related to it. As a result, metalevel thought allows unbiased—not precommitted to a decision between what is truth and what is ideology for any given framework—practical and theoretical negotiation between different truth commitments. In other words, it is not that Foucault's pluralism eliminates truth: the standards of truth play a role at both levels, and their limited, indirect relevance at the metalevel allows truth to be considered and established precisely without in that process prejudging it and so defeating their own role as standards of truth.

The chapter argues that while Foucault himself does not fully account for the logical possibility of coordinating the two levels, the self-canceling logic developed in this book does offer that kind of account.

In Chapter 6, "How to be Properly Unnatural: The Metaphysics of Heterosexual Normativity and the Importance of the Concepts of Essence and Nature for Pluralism," I develop an approach to what has become known as heterosexual normativity, the attitude and social norm that heterosexuality can be taken for granted as naturally the right way to be. This attitude presupposes the concept of "nature," or equivalents to it, and with this has excluded various sexualities as "unnatural." Sexuality and gender theorists have therefore largely rejected the concept of "nature" and with it the related concept of "essence," except when understood as constructed by social and historical processes. I argue that, for reasons involving both the sense of these concepts at the metaphysical level and, connected with that, their liberatory political significance, we desperately need to reclaim *construction-free* natures or essences, *and* that we need to think of them as ultimately constructed, *and* that these views are irreconcilably contradictory. I then propose a viable, because self-canceling, contradictory or "unnatural" logic, along the lines of the "sometimes always" logic sketched above, that allows us to reclaim the independent value of these conflicting ideas. I briefly discuss the relevance of this logic to the concept of nature in environmental thought in connection with the work of Bruno Latour. Finally, I explore some of the implications of this logic for our practice, experience, and relation to others whose ways of making sense are not our own.

Chapter 7, "The Necessary Inconclusiveness of Heideggerian Interpretation of Metaphysics and the Undecided Nature of Essential or Logical Connection," argues that there is a central problem with Martin Heidegger's widely influential understanding of the interpretation of metaphysical standpoints, a problem that much of contemporary continental philosophy consequently shares. As I explain below, it is also a problem that in a more general form most contemporary philosophy of all traditions shares. Heidegger frequently asserts *decisive* or definitive understandings of the history of metaphysics, a kind of assertion that contemporary continental work often echoes both explicitly and in tone. (It is true that he is often decisive about the necessity for a kind of permanent openness or *non*decisiveness of understanding, in the light of the central importance that our finitude has in his thinking; but this, as I have noted in connection with pluralism, is a more complicated version of the same fundamental attitude.) His understanding of interpretation, however, undermines the possibility of this kind of decisive understanding of metaphysical positions and their history, that precludes all readings that conflict deeply with it.

This is not to say that no decisiveness is possible in this context, only that it is not possible on the basis of Heidegger's interpretive framework. In fact, in criticizing Heidegger's tone of decisiveness, the chapter partly tries to make room for genuine kinds of decisiveness or definitiveness that his version excludes.

Although Heidegger asserts decisive understandings of metaphysical systems, he also understands the interpretation of metaphysical thought as necessarily involving a kind of "violence," a kind of distortion. It is not initially obvious that this is a problem: in the context of Heidegger's thinking, a dimension of something like distortion is integral to the nature or working of truth. As a result, violence, far from simply clashing with truth, is part of and necessary to its expression and pursuit. But this chapter argues that this kind of violence does in fact involve the ineliminable possibility of a simple clash with the truth of interpretation, in the classical sense that it distorts this truth. As a result, within the Heideggerian mode of interpreting the history of philosophy, there can be no decisive understanding of the history of metaphysics, precluding all readings that conflict deeply with it, but at best only meaningful, well founded, but inconclusive understandings.

The chapter also argues that this problem has its source in a particular, and questionable, understanding of the coherence of concepts or of the logic or essential nature of connection between the different items, elements, and dimensions of the world. This is the kind of logic I described above as a "simply continuously consistent" logic (which in Heidegger, as the chapter discusses, and in much of postmodern thought often turns out to produce continuously consistent paradox or logical "strife"), in contrast with the "sometimes always continuously consistent"—or "unnatural"—logic for which I argue in this book.

The profoundly thoroughgoing form in which Heidegger thinks this simply continuously consistent logic through has itself also been widely influential in contemporary continental philosophy. It is central, for example, to the work of philosophers of various understandings of immanence, such as Gilles Deleuze, Jean-Luc Nancy, and (I think equivocally, because more deeply thought) Giorgio Agamben. But this same logic in different ways also informs most of contemporary philosophy of all traditions. The discussion of the thoroughly developed form it takes in Heidegger should therefore also cast light on some features of the wide variety of other contemporary standpoints that draw on it, including the ways in which they take for granted the legitimacy of definitively asserting or relying on their fundamentals.

In Chapter 8, "The Formal Structure of Metaphysics and *The Importance of Being Earnest*," I argue that a central and perhaps the most fundamental type of metaphysical thought has a deeply pluralist formal structure, and I try to show that this structure is mapped out in Oscar Wilde's *The Importance of Being Earnest*. One frequent aim of metaphysics is to understand the world as a whole. We cannot gain such a global vantage point without separating ourselves from all the particular meanings things have for us within the world. But we start within the world, and so can only proceed on the basis of those particular meanings. Consequently we can only separate ourselves from them if they work to cancel themselves in favor of the global understanding. When the separate range of meanings is established, however, it and the meanings of all the particulars of the world it aims to understand no longer have any connection with each other. Metaphysics therefore succeeds by establishing and canceling its relevant meaning, all at once. I argue that precisely this self-canceling moment or process of thought constitutes a grasp of the world as a whole. Because it is self-canceling, it also makes room for different understandings of reality as a whole, and it allows them to recognize and enter into dialogue with each other. I argue, again, that this also makes room for truth to be both essentially absolute and essentially relative. I try to show that the climactic moments of *The Importance of Being Earnest* are structured as a map of this insight- and dialogue-granting process of the self-cancellation of a global range of meanings. That is, they express the formal structure of metaphysical thought in its fundamentally pluralist character. As the discussion proceeds, I also explore the character of this structure of thought in detail and try to justify its legitimacy.

Chapter 9, "The Logical Structure of Dreams and Their Relation to Reality," argues that the contradictions and non sequiturs often found in dreams (or, equivalently, dream narratives) are not always logical errors but express and work with a type of logic that characterizes the deepest dimensions of our waking reality. These are the dimensions in which we deal with ourselves as a whole, our lives as a whole, or the sense of reality as a whole. We do so, for example, when we encounter outlooks deeply different from our own, or in situations of deep personal transformation. The chapter argues that the logic of these situations is validly one of contradiction and non sequitur, that dreams sometimes express and work with these kinds of situation, and that these kinds of dreams therefore validly involve the same kind of logic. These kinds of dreams consequently also express insight into the sense that our lives or that existence as a whole has for us in the light of deeply contrasting possibilities for our general sense of things. In achieving that insight, they actively orient, situate, or resituate us in our relation to our lives or existence as a whole. In this respect they are in themselves a practice of metaphysics, and specifically of a pluralist metaphysics.

In the Coda, I discuss what it is or means to have an overview or general sense of the kind of situation where there are simultaneously relevant but wholly mutually exclusive frameworks of sense. I explore this not only as an issue of intellectual grasp but also with respect to what it requires of us and offers us to recognize and live with these kinds of self-cancelingly self-contradictory coordinations.

1. *Comparing Different Cultural or Theoretical Frameworks*

Davidson, Rorty, and the Nature of Truth

In comparing and considering dialogue between very different standpoints, whether cultural, subcultural, individual, or theoretical, the nature of truth itself becomes a problem. If, for example, we see the standpoints as genuinely but legitimately different with respect to the truth, we have the problem of conceiving how conflicting views can both be true. If they can, then within one of the standpoints, what the other takes as truth is equally legitimately taken as false, as the opposite of truth. In that case, are we dealing with *truth* at all anymore? Further, in comparing them, we occupy a more general framework that includes all the relevant views. That is, that framework consists in taking *both* (or more) conflicting views into account simultaneously, so that in our single comparison-making standpoint we are regarding one and the same thing as simultaneously both true and false.

If, on the other hand, we reject this contradiction within truth, we have to assume that standpoints cannot be legitimately different with respect to the truth. This view has been very powerfully argued by, for example, Donald Davidson. But this seems to eliminate the sense of a comparative perspective altogether, at least when it comes to conceptions of truth. Our view of the nature of truth in general, then, of whether truth can legitimately be construed in conflicting ways and so involve contradictions, or whether truth is ultimately universal, determines how we understand the nature of differences between standpoints, and so whether a properly comparative approach is ultimately appropriate or, instead, distorts the realities of intercultural and interperspectival understanding.

Richard Rorty has very subtly argued a third view of truth, largely on the basis of Davidson's work. This view is that there is no need for or point in talking about truth at all. Consequently there are no *logical* obstacles to comparison between conflicting standpoints: there is no worthwhile conception of truth at all, and so no conflict of conceptions of truth to trouble us. Comparison can then proceed as far as we have the energy and practical conditions for it. On the other hand, it is also a consequence of this view that there is no ultimate justification, no ultimate foundation, for anything. As a result, this view excludes in advance the possible legitimacy of all the many standpoints that do find the concepts of truth and ultimate foundations meaningful. This view too, then, seems troubling for the possibility of a genuinely comparative approach.

In contrast with these views, I want to show that it is in fact both possible and necessary to have a properly pluralist conception of standpoints, one that therefore allows and requires a properly comparative approach. That is, I want to defend a conception in which standpoints can have conflicting conceptions of truth without also, because these conceptions contradict each other, ultimately eliminating their sense altogether. In fact, I want to show that the contradictions involved in the ways in which truth is relative, and *only* those contradictions, *justify* the idea that there are ways in which the *same* truth *excludes* contradiction, that is, ways in which it is universal or absolute.

I shall argue, then, that truth is contradictory, but in ways that give rise to noncontradictory sense and knowledge.[1] More specifically, I shall argue that we sometimes can and must think of truth as both absolute and relative in the same respects, and also sometimes as just universally the one, sometimes as just universally the other. I approach this argument through a discussion of Davidson's and Rorty's work. I try to show how their own, cogent arguments lead, though entirely despite themselves, to the pluralist, proper comparison-requiring conclusions for which I argue. More precisely, I try to show that their arguments are productively self-canceling (that is, that they undermine their own sense), both in ways that they themselves insist on, and in a further way that leads to a properly comparative view.

Since absolute truth involves given or natural essences of things, and relative truth involves the construction of truths by the perspectives through which they are known, this discussion also applies to the ideas of truth as

---

[1] On the possibility of legitimate logical contradiction, see the Introduction, section 5.

given essences (essentialism) and as historical construction (constructionism).[2] Variations of these ideas of the nature of truth, and consequently of the fundamental nature of reality whose truth it is, are central in and perhaps foundational to the history of philosophy, and they are often also taken up in contemporary liberatory political and subcultural theory. I discuss essentialism and constructionism in their own right in Chapter 6 on heterosexual normativity, and the logic of essences or natures in the context of metaphysics most directly both there and in Chapter 7, on Heidegger.

1. Ethnocentrism and Antirelativism

Rorty argues that we cannot be anything but ethnocentric. That is, we can only take as true what appears true to "us." As he puts it, we "have to start from where we are"; we cannot escape from our historical circumstances.[3] He argues, however, that this claim does not mean that truth is relative. In fact, he argues that it means the reverse. To say that ethnocentrism implies that truth is relative is to say that there are positions other than ours to whose truths we can compare our own, so that our truths are relative to theirs. But, as Rorty points out, we cannot meaningfully talk *at all* about positions so radically other than ours that their most basic ideas about truth conflict with ours. Anything we say *about* such positions is inescapably bound to the basic ideas of truth in our own position. That is, we cannot meaningfully compare our truths with fully incompatible ones because the comparison itself is already limited to our ideas of truth. The idea that our truths are relative consequently does not make any sense from the start (25–26, 38, 215–16).

It also follows from this line of thought that we cannot meaningfully talk about a world of *objects* independent of our culture's beliefs, to which our beliefs could be relative. *Any* reference we make to objects is already

---

[2] See, for example, Judith Butler, *Gender Trouble: Feminism and the Subversion of Identity* (New York: Routledge, 1990); Diana Fuss, *Essentially Speaking: Feminism, Nature and Difference* (New York: Routledge, 1989); Eve Kosofsky Sedgwick, *The Epistemology of the Closet* (Berkeley: University of California Press, 1990).

[3] Richard Rorty, *Objectivity, Relativism, and Truth: Philosophical Papers, Volume 1* (New York: Cambridge University Press, 1991), 29, 50. Unless otherwise noted, further references to and citations of Rorty in this chapter are from this book.

made in the form of a belief (12, 50–51). That is, anything we can say about such objects, *including that they are independent of our beliefs, which is itself a belief*, is inescapably bound to the meanings and ideas available to us with which to speak or think. Even our sensory impressions only have meanings and roles for us in the context of our culturally given meanings, language, and beliefs. This side of the issue of relative truth will help clarify various aspects of Rorty's and Davidson's discussions of cross-cultural truth, and I occasionally draw on it.

Ethnocentrism, however, does not mean that we cannot test our beliefs. We can test them against each other, and against what we understand in the beliefs of other communities (41). What we ultimately settle on as the best understanding in and between such communities or cultures is true, since truth only has meaning as what we, who can only work with our culture's meanings, can stably understand (50). Rorty therefore sees legitimate science, for example, "as solidarity" and open-mindedness (38ff.).

Rorty relies heavily on Davidson in arguing the antirelativistic side of these points. Davidson argues against the relativistic idea defended by, for example, Thomas Kuhn and W. V. O. Quine, that it is possible for a culture or position to be so different from ours that we could not translate the meanings of its language into ours.[4] If this idea is justified, we cannot avoid the conclusion that truth is relative. The ideas of a position or culture like this would be "incommensurable" with ours: that is, it would have such different ideas about everything that there would be no common standard of meaning or sensemaking with which to compare its meanings with ours. As a result, there would be no way even to begin to compare its ideas with ours so as to decide which is right.

Against this view, Davidson argues that if a language were so fundamentally different from our own, we would not even be able to regard it or meaningfully talk about it as a language at all.[5] (Davidson notes that

---

[4] See, for example, Thomas S. Kuhn, *The Structure of Scientific Revolutions*, 2nd ed. (Chicago: University of Chicago Press, 1970); Willard Van Orman Quine, "Ontological Relativity," in *Ontological Relativity and Other Essays* (New York: Columbia University Press, 1969), 26–68.

[5] Donald Davidson, *Inquiries into Truth and Interpretation* (Oxford: Oxford University Press, 1984), 185–86. Unless otherwise noted, all further references to and citations of Davidson in this chapter are from this book.

"putting matters this way is unsatisfactory," and goes on to "improve" the "credibility of the position" (186). I address his subsequent arguments below in discussing translatability.) Consequently the idea of such a radically different language is literally meaningless (232). This is the same kind of argument Rorty offers in connection with cultures or positions radically other than "ours."

If, on the other hand, Davidson argues, we *are* able to regard a different language as a language—and this capacity is presupposed and so conceded by the very idea of a different *language*—then it has basic commonalities with our own meanings and we are then also able to translate it into our language. This would remove the basis for thinking that its and our truths are incomparable with each other and so inescapably relative to different standards. And we *are* in fact able to regard any different language as a language, for two related reasons that are also arguments supporting his claim that "languages" incommensurable with our own are rightly not regarded as languages at all.

First, Davidson argues, in order to make sense of the idea of a language at all, we have to assume that most of what the speakers of the language say is true (27, 137, 196). Davidson calls this assumption the principle of charity. If this assumption about languages were not true, no one could come to understand *any* language (200). If someone were trying to learn a language while the people around her or him were making mainly false statements, the words and sentences that person learned would not serve the communicative and practical functions that they do serve in a working language. To put this more accurately, the person would not be able to learn the meanings of the words and sentences at all, since they can only be learned in the course of serving those communicative and practical functions. Since languages are all learned, the assumption that most of what the speakers of the language say is true is involved in the very idea of a language. And in all cases this refers to how *we* understand truth, since it is *our* assumption. Consequently, if we are genuinely talking about languages, very different or not, the *same* connection with and standards for truth are *already* established with respect to all languages, in common.

Davidson expresses this by saying that the concept of truth is "primitive." As he states,

I shall call such theories *absolute* to distinguish them from theories that (also) relativize truth to an interpretation, a model, a possible world, or a domain. In a theory of the sort I am describing, the truth predicate is not defined, but must be considered a primitive expression. (216)

That is, the term "truth" is not analyzed into anything more basic. It does not require analysis to understand it beyond its immediate, unanalyzed meanings, because it itself is the basis of analysis and understanding (216–18).[6]

Since language is learned in the course of its communicative and practical functions, and since, in fact, its meanings partly *consist* in just those functions (one necessary test that someone understands what is said, for example, is that she or he reacts in certain ways and performs certain activities), Davidson points out that we can learn the meanings of a language by observing which statements people make in which specific circumstances (162). And because it is already part of the concept of a language that most of what its speakers say is true, we can establish the truth of what the speakers are talking about in the same way.

The second, related reason Davidson gives for our ability to translate any language into ours is that any disagreement we might have about truth, or about anything else, presupposes a background of innumerable agreements (153, 192). If we can say that we differ from another position in *any* respect, then we have already conceded that we share agreements with the other position about, for example, some of the characteristics of the issue or object we are disagreeing about. If we did not share such agreements, we could not begin to disagree, since we could not even refer to what it is we disagree about. Disagreeing languages, then, share innumerable agreements, and so have an extensive common basis for translating each other into their own terms.

---

[6] See, similarly, Donald Davidson, "A Coherence Theory of Truth and Knowledge," *Truth and Interpretation: Perspectives on the Philosophy of Donald Davidson*, ed. Ernest LePore (Cambridge, MA: Basil Blackwell, 1986), 308–9: "Truth is beautifully transparent compared to belief... and I take it as primitive.... The truth of an utterance depends on just two things: what the words as spoken mean, and how the world is arranged. There is no further relativism to a conceptual scheme, a way of viewing things, a perspective."

Davidson, then, argues for "a theory of absolute truth" (221; and see also 216, quoted above). And as he also insists, "we do not relinquish the notion of objective truth—quite the contrary.... We ... re-establish unmediated touch with the familiar objects whose antics make our sentences and opinions true or false" (198). He argues for this kind of absolute objectivity via a theory of "radical interpretation," based on the arguments discussed above for the possibility of "radical translation."

Rorty works out some of the social and scientific consequences of just this idea that we cannot meaningfully question our basic beliefs, although he rejects the terminology of truth, absolute or otherwise. He rejects this terminology because if, as he argues, there is no comparison between our beliefs and the world independent of our (culture's) beliefs, the idea of truth can contribute nothing to how we assess our beliefs beyond the relations of those beliefs among themselves. Consequently, "There is a human activity called 'justifying beliefs' ... but this activity does not have a goal called Truth." And if "one takes the principal use of the adjective 'true' to be endorsement [like a term of praise] rather than description, one can drop the notion that there are propositions out there that have a property called truth."[7] But as Rorty also explains, "Davidson has helped us realize that *the very absoluteness of truth is a good reason for thinking 'true' indefinable and for thinking that no theory of the nature of truth is possible.*"[8] Consequently, while Rorty insists that "On my interpretation ... Davidson joins the pragmatist in saying that 'true' has no explanatory use" (136),[9] he can also note, in a related discussion of Bernard Williams, that the "pragmatist wants to ... aim at what Williams thinks of as 'absolute' truth, while denying that this latter notion can be explicated in terms of the notion of 'how things really are'" (59).

It is important that, for the same reasons that Rorty rejects the terminology of "truth," both Rorty and Davidson also often tend to avoid the

---

[7] Richard Rorty, *Truth and Progress: Philosophical Papers, Volume 3* (New York: Cambridge University Press, 1998), 163, my insertion.

[8] Ibid., 3, Rorty's emphasis.

[9] And see Richard Rorty, *Contingency, Irony, and Solidarity* (New York: Cambridge University Press, 1989), 67, where Rorty argues that we need to be "content to call 'true' (or 'right' or 'just') whatever the outcome of undistorted communication happens to be, whatever view wins in a free and open encounter."

terminology of "meaning." If, as they argue, there is no world simply independent of the meanings given to us in language, words can only be explained in terms of other words and the activities associated with them. The idea of meanings, then, contributes nothing to explaining how words work: there is nothing outside other words and their associated activities for an "entity" like a "meaning" to reflect. But, as in the case of truth, the issue for Davidson and Rorty is really *what one takes to be the use* of the term "meaning," what one understands by it. If one understands meaning, for example, as nothing but the relations among words and their associated activities, then it no longer refers to something ultimately independent of language. And in that case it serves a perfectly satisfactory purpose in naming those relations between the elements of language. As a result Davidson is often content to use the language of "meanings," as well as that of "truth."

In the following discussion I largely use the language of meanings, to be taken, when I am discussing their arguments, in a Davidsonian and Rortian sense. As I occasionally indicate, the arguments work equally with the substitution of Davidson's and Rorty's preferred terminology. I also often use equivalents of the terms "useful" and "useless" as shorthand for the vocabulary that Rorty in particular uses in place of talking about "truth" and "meaning": for example, "useless for our purposes," "profitless," "pointless," "getting in the way of our preferred ways of talking."

2. The Explicit Self-Cancellation of Davidson's and Rorty's Standpoints

In this section I discuss a self-canceling step that Davidson and Rorty both explicitly take. This is a step in which they show how their arguments (productively) undermine their own sense. In the next section I try to show that their work requires them to take a further self-canceling step that they do not take, a step in which the first self-cancellation (also) cancels *itself*, undermines *its* own sense.

If it is meaningless—not wrong, but literally meaningless—to talk about our beliefs being relative given the contrasting beliefs of other cultures or communities, then it follows that it is *also* meaningless to talk about our beliefs *not* being relative in that way. It is meaningless to say that something meaningless is or is not true. Or, in language that Rorty might prefer, it does not contribute anything to say that a useless piece of language should be used in one way rather than another. The arguments Rorty and Davidson give are *radical* or foundational: they show that *any* talk or thought about beliefs that are sufficiently different to involve the relativity of truth is (literally and completely) meaningless, or profitless and pointless.

Davidson and Rorty, in different ways, both insist on this point. Davidson argues, for example, that "if we cannot intelligibly say that schemes [frameworks to which our beliefs might be relative] are different, neither can we intelligibly say that they are one" (198, my insertion). And even further (here with respect to the related denial of a *world* or objects independent of language), "we have erased the boundary between knowing a language and knowing our way around in the world generally. . . . I conclude that there is no such thing as a language, not if a language is anything like what many philosophers and linguists have supposed. . . . We must give up the idea of a clearly defined shared structure which language-users acquire and then apply to cases."[10] And Rorty writes, for example (here again with respect to the denial of a language-independent world),

> We are tempted to say that there were no objects before language shaped the raw material. . . . But as soon as we say anything like this we find ourselves ourselves accused (plausibly) of making the false causal claim that the invention of "dinosaur" caused dinosaurs to come into existence. . . . Davidson, however, has shown us how to make our point without saying anything susceptible to that misinterpretation. He suggests that we stop trying to say *anything* general about the relation between language and reality. . . . We should just refuse to discuss such topics as "the nature of reference."[11]

They both argue, then, that if it is literally meaningless or pointless to talk or think about fundamentally different belief systems (or a world independent of belief systems) *at all*, then it is just as meaningless or pointless to talk about them in trying to show that one cannot talk about them as it is in trying to show that one can.

As Davidson and Rorty imply in these quotations, we cannot avoid this paradox of language by distinguishing between the language we discuss (the object language: for example, "fundamentally different belief systems")

---

[10] Donald Davidson, "A Nice Derangement of Epitaphs," in LePore, *Truth and Interpretation*, 445–46.

[11] Rorty, *Truth and Progress*, 90, Rorty's emphasis.

and the language in which we discuss that language (the metalanguage: for instance, "phrases like 'fundamentally different belief-systems' are unhelpful"). It is true, for example, that one can specify or mention a meaningless sequence of sounds or letters ("inka dinka doo") and say that it is meaningless ("'inka dinka doo' is meaningless") without also making that metastatement meaningless. But, first, this kind of example really concedes the point: it states that this sequence of marks is not a piece of language at all, does not do anything other than being a set of sounds or marks, at any level of language. It does not itself specify anything. Any argument, then, at any level, that uses "inka dinka doo" to specify what we can or cannot say is only going through the motions of saying something, of using a piece of language. And similarly with "fundamentally different belief systems" and "language ultimately separate from objects." Davidson and Rorty are not discussing pieces of language but strings of marks that fall outside the constraints of meaningful or functioning language in general. And, of course, a metalanguage, like any language, is also subject to those constraints. Consequently, they cannot reject what those strings of marks refer to, since those strings do not refer to anything.

Second, Davidson and Rorty are not simply specifying or mentioning a meaningless or functionless sequence of marks but *establishing, justifying the claim that* a proposed piece of language is really just meaningless or functionless marks. And this justification must itself explore what the proposed piece of language purports to specify, its proposed meanings or functions, in order to show that it is meaningless or profitless. That is, it must make statements about what is specified by what it will show does not specify anything. In other words, the justification must itself repeat what it will show is the failure of this proposed piece of language to specify, contribute, or mean. Consequently, if it succeeds, it will show that what it itself has stated is largely meaningless or without useful function. Again, then, it is just as meaningless or pointless to talk about these issues in trying to show that one cannot talk about them as it is in trying to show that one can.

In fact, Davidson elaborates his theory of translation in a way that avoids relying on meanings, precisely to avoid this kind of self-referential paradox (71ff., 148–49). But the arguments he makes to justify this avoidance, being meaningful, have to rely on something that functions like meanings, and so functions in the ways I have described. Or, even if one successfully avoids the vocabulary of "meanings," his arguments have to function within the constraints they specify for language as a whole, with the result that these constraints still refer to the arguments that specify them. That is, his arguments are still paradoxically self-referential.

Even where the scope of this paradox extends beyond where Davidson and Rorty themselves insist on it, I am not trying to present it as simply an objection to their views. As I have mentioned, my aim is in fact to show that the paradox both resolves itself and offers solutions to the problem of truth in the context of genuine comparison between conflicting standpoints. But it does nonetheless have consequences for Davidson's conclusions and Rorty's, and I explore those in the next section.

3. Self-Cancellation of the Self-Cancellation

By demonstrating that discussion of the possibility of incommensurable beliefs is meaningless or pointless, Rorty and Davidson succeed in showing that the "possibilities" themselves are unintelligible or noncontributing. But now I want to try to show that, because they are dealing with the constraints for meaning or useful language *in general*—because there is no metalanguage immune to the range of their arguments—this meaninglessness or profitlessness of the discussion, including as it does their own contributions to it, *also* works to *invalidate* this conclusion. That is, I want to show that they have not *simply* shown that talk about fundamentally different belief systems is meaningless or noncontributing, and so that truth is not relative. As Hilary Putnam expresses a similar point, "if we agree that it is *unintelligible* to say, 'We sometimes succeed in comparing our language and thought with reality as it is in itself,' then we should realize that it is also unintelligible to say 'It is *impossible* to stand outside and compare our thought and the world.' . . . In this case to say that it is impossible to do '*p*' . . . involves a '*p*' which is unintelligible."[12] Rather, their arguments have produced a "liar's paradox" (on the model of the statement "I am lying"): if their arguments succeed in making their point, they have no meaning and so fail to make their point, and if they fail to

---

[12] Hilary Putnam, *Words and Life,* ed. James Conant (Cambridge, MA: Harvard University Press, 1994), 299.

make their point, they have the meaning that succeeds in making their point.

Let me emphasize this does not mean that their conclusion is false or unprofitable. On the contrary, it is exactly if their argument *succeeds*, if their conclusion is *true* or profitable, that they respectively fail and are false or unprofitable, and vice versa. This is a paradox that makes the meanings or functions of its own terms *undecidable*. It is precisely its truth or useful functioning that makes it false or useless, and precisely its falsehood that makes it true, and this means that the meanings of "true" and "false" incorporate *what they are defined by excluding*. These meanings or functions, then, turn out to be incompatible with themselves. It is not clear what those meanings or functions are any more, and they cannot be clarified, because these meanings or functions are not clear *as a result of their clarity*.

To put this in a less general context: there are further self-referential consequences of, for example, Davidson's comment that "if we cannot intelligibly say that schemes [frameworks to which our beliefs might be relative] are different, neither can we intelligibly say that they are one" (198, my insertion). One way of expressing the point of this comment is that, if there is no intelligible idea of different schemes, then there is no contrast that might make sense of the idea of a specific, single scheme. Similarly, given no contrast between language and the world it refers to, Davidson can conclude, as I quoted above, that "there is no such thing as a language" (at least as ultimately distinguishable from the world in general). It follows that, if, similarly, we eliminate the intelligibility or coherence of talk about, for example, both the alternatives of "fundamentally different belief systems" and "no fundamentally different belief systems," then we have *also* eliminated the contrast that might give sense to what we are referring to in arguing and stating that we *cannot talk about those alternatives*.

Another way of expressing the point of Davidson' comment is that, since an unintelligible idea does not specify anything, asserting *or* denying anything about what it specifies is equally unintelligible. It follows that, if both the alternatives that schemes are different and that they are the same are unintelligible, and so do not specify anything, then saying *anything* about what this combination of alternatives specifies is equally unintelligible. That is, it is unintelligible to say that what this combination of alternatives refers to is unintelligible. Now, again, appeal to a metalanguage does not help us avoid this result. As I noted in discussing the appeal to a metalanguage in the last section, Davidson's and Rorty's arguments are not simply *mentioning* an evidently meaningless or profitless string of marks here but trying to *establish that* a proposed piece of language is just a meaningless or profitless string of marks. That is, their arguments involve exploring *what this proposed piece of language purports to specify*, in order to show that those purported specifications are empty or noncontributing. Their arguments therefore repeat what they show is meaningless or profitless, and so are themselves meaningless or profitless. *Any* statements, then, about what *this* unintelligible idea specifies, *including statements that it is unintelligible*, are equally unintelligible.

In the language I have been using here, the self-cancellation of their arguments also cancels *itself*.

As I have argued, because this is a genuine paradox, it does not *simply* negate their argumentative strategy. Instead, it does so by virtue of the *success* of that strategy. As a result, it introduces an entirely different kind of problem. That it is *possible* to develop this kind of paradox means that the very ideas of "successful argument" and "failed argument" in this context already contain in themselves what they exclude. It shows that a successful argument can fail precisely in being successful, and vice versa. But what it means to be a successful argument is, precisely, that it does not fail. Consequently we cannot simply proceed, when this kind of paradox occurs, on the basis of the familiar meanings of the phrases "successful argument" and "failed argument." We need to reunderstand the meanings of these ideas before we can know what to say about this kind of paradox. That is, we are not in a position to say, for example, that arguments involving this paradox have failed. In this context the idea of "failing" no longer has the meaning that we are familiar with. If we say that the arguments have failed in this context, we literally do not know what we have said.

Now, while this paradox renders its own meanings meaningless, I have been arguing that it also renders its own results meaningless in the same act. Consequently, it restores its meanings in the very act of canceling them. In other words, it is both a self-cancellation of these meanings and a self-cancellation of that self-cancellation itself. In the language of undecidability, it is an indecision of meaning that is so fundamental that it is even undecidable as to whether it is undecidable. This paradox, then, maintains mutually exclusive, incompatible positions in one thought. I shall try to show, on this basis, that Davidson's and Rorty's arguments rigorously justify *both* their own position(s) on truth *and* the relativistic position they oppose.

4. Absolute Justification of Both Relativism and the Unintelligibility of Relativism

I have discussed Davidson's argument that we could not consider a language radically incommensurable with our own to be a language at all. If it were really incommensurable with our own, it would not do any of the things done by anything that we *could*, given our own language, consider a language. There is a tempting objection that this argument is circular. Now, in fact, presented at this level of the discussion, the objection is incorrect, but presented at a more comprehensive level it is, I suggest, *also* right, in keeping with the paradox we are exploring here. The importance of this discussion here is that Davidson's response to this objection is typical of his arguments that truth is absolute. Consequently, showing how his argument both is and is not circular will help me to show why relativism and the unintelligibility of relativism are both absolutely justified (and also relative).

The objection, then, is that the argument is circular. Davidson's argument seems to go: what *we* mean by "language" is the only meaning we can consider, because what *we* mean by "language" is the only meaning we can consider. But stated at this level the objection misses Davidson's point. Given the radical nature of his point about meaninglessness, the circle cannot even begin to occur. As soon as we use the word "language" in the context of incommensurability with our own meanings, we are, by definition, not saying or thinking anything that has meaning. There is no circularity, because the circle of argument cannot even get under way.

But the objection is only this simply incorrect if it stays at this level. To show why this is so, I need to make a fairly lengthy digression, though one that is helpful in its own right.

As I have argued, Davidson's argument itself is meaningless, whether as a circle or not. Consequently it justifies our considering the issue from the beginning again as though he had said nothing—which, on his own arguments, is in fact exactly what he has said.

Davidson, as I have discussed, makes the point that we could not learn an incommensurable "language" if we could not regard what its speakers say as true. And, if it is thoroughly incommensurable with our own language, so that its notions of what "truth" means have no connection with ours, we would not be able to regard what its speakers say as true. We would not, then, be able to learn the language, and any arguments about its incommensurability could not get under way. But this argument is another version of the self-canceling arguments I have discussed, and so, like them, renders itself and its conclusions meaningless.

And, what is more, it seems clear that we have all learned at least one language, our own, before having *any* language with *any* notion of what "truth" means, or, for that matter, any of the "vast common ground" of "shared belief" for which Davidson argues (200). There seems to be no difficulty, then, in accepting that we could learn another language, including its incomparable notions of the meaning of "true."[13] "Untranslatability," as Rorty puts it, "does not entail unlearnability" (48). The resulting situation would be one in which we can speak two or more incommensurable languages, and think in two or more incommensurable ways.

A natural objection here is that if the languages are in fact comprehensively different to the point of being incommensurable, then their statements cannot refer to the same things, and therefore cannot conflict with respect to the truth they express. They are simply statements about different things. As Alasdair MacIntyre argues, however, "each community, using its own criteria of *sameness* and *difference*, recognizes that it is one and the same subject matter about which they are advancing their claim; incommensurability and incompatibility are not incompatible."[14] I return to this issue

---

[13] Alasdair MacIntyre also argues that we can learn a second, incomparable language, with its own, different standards for truth, just as we learned the first one. Alasdair C. MacIntyre, *Whose Justice? Which Rationality?* (Notre Dame, IN: University of Notre Dame Press, 1988), e.g., 374: "Just as a child does not learn its first language by matching sentences with sentences, since it initially possesses no set of sentences of its own, so an adult who has in this way become a child again does not either." He makes this point specifically in response to Davidson's view, among others, that if "two rival points of view are successful in understanding one another, it must be the case that they share standards of rational evaluation," so that "translatability . . . entails commensurability" (371).

[14] Alasdair C. MacIntyre, "Relativism, Power, and Philosophy," in *Relativism: Interpretation and Confrontation,* ed. Michael Krausz (Notre Dame, IN: University of Notre Dame Press, 1989), 190.

in more detail in section 6 of Chapter 3 and in the first sections of Chapters 8 and 9.

But these considerations in no way affect Davidson's and Rorty's point that we could not *compare* the truths of the two or more languages or standpoints or communities at all. That is, truth is still not relative. But it is not *simply* absolute either. We have something like incompatible absolute truths, so that, as in the case of "true" and "false" discussed above, the meaning of "absolute," and with it the meaning of "relative," need to be reunderstood.

This situation only occurs when the meanings of both or more positions or communities are being considered at once. It is only that act of simultaneous consideration that links them. The meanings of each literally have no meaning for the others; only the simultaneous thought of both sets of meanings can connect them, and then only in a purely external way, with no logical or meaningful connection between them. But when each position is considered *simply* on its own, the other sets of "meanings" have no meaning in *any* relevant context and cannot meaningfully be thought or talked about.

(Actually, this last paragraph is not quite accurate. We cannot rule out in advance the possibility that incommensurable positions can meaningfully mention each other in some way because the arguments that successfully rule out that possibility, again, reduce *themselves* to meaninglessness. And this justifies us, as I have argued, in considering the issue from the beginning again.)

It is partly because this contradictory situation of conflicting absolutes is limited to certain kinds of context that it is manageable, and partly because, as I explore further below, it is self-canceling.

If, as this logic of self-cancellation suggests, then, a position can in some contexts make a space for the meaningful simultaneous consideration or mention of another incommensurable one at all (or, equivalently, if incommensurable positions can be spoken about at all: the position that talks about them would have to be incommensurable with at least one of them, since if it were commensurable with one, it would be incommensurable with the other), let me suggest that when two or more such positions are being considered together with respect to the truth of their claims, we have two or more circular *justifications*. For, first, if we can talk about incommensurable positions or languages, we can talk intelligibly about *entire* positions (or frameworks or conceptual schemes) in contrast with others, and so about their justification relative to each other. Now, since the two or more languages are nonetheless still meaningless to each other, each will ultimately justify itself exclusively on the basis of its own meanings. And it is just those meanings that are ultimately what is in dispute, so that each will really be justifying its own meanings on the basis of its own meanings. That is, each will justify itself as a whole circularly.

But, second, at the point at which the circle closes, when the position has justified its own meanings, the incommensurably-meaning other position(s), since its (their) meanings are excluded by the meanings that are now closed off, is (are) definitively established as meaningless. And at that point the circle itself also ceases to have existed meaningfully, since some of the connections in the circle consist in mentions of the meanings of the other position(s) against which the position and so its circle has identified itself, and upon the closing of the circle these meanings no longer exist in the relevant position. In one respect, then, the positions justify themselves circularly to each other, and in another respect there is neither a circle nor a meaningful need for this justification.

But, third, these two respects are the same: it is *only the closing* of the circle that makes the circle and the need for justification that produces it meaningless. The need for justification is first meaningful and is then given the *answer* that it is meaningless. In other words, the need for justification is *met*, or at least legitimately deflected. We are back to the paradox of successful argument that fails by being successful, here specifically in connection with circularity. If it is a circle, it is not, and vice versa. That is, this circle is self-canceling. Again, then, what "circular" and "noncircular" mean in this kind of context are not their familiar meanings, and we need to establish what their meanings are before we can conclude anything from their applicability here.

In short, then: at the point at which the circle closes, it loses meaning as a circle. But because there is then no circle and so no circularity in the argument, but the standpoint has nonetheless been able to consider itself *as a whole* in reaching that point at which the circle closes, the standpoint can in fact *fully justify* itself, that is, justify itself *absolutely*, at that point. This kind of circularity *itself* allows a noncircular kind of justification of positions, and of positions that conflict with them, (each) as a whole.

It follows that we *can* talk about incommensurably different positions each as a whole. As a result, we can distinguish between talk "inside" the position and talk "outside" it. As we have seen, inside a position, its standards for truth are absolute, since no contrasting standards can be meaningful. But from outside that position its standards for truth are relative to those of other positions. And each of these perspectives is literally meaningless in the context of the other. It follows that each position is sometimes simply absolute and sometimes simply relative.

I need to make one more point to try to show why the objection that Davidson's argument in particular is circular is ultimately right (as well as still being mistaken). As I have argued, again, the paradox in the meaninglessness of Davidson's argument justifies us in considering the issue from the beginning again. That is, it justifies our starting *on the basis of* considering two or more incommensurable positions simultaneously. And in fact if we do start on that basis, we develop a way of thinking about languages and positions that *can only* take both into account, or (how to speak accurately is becoming precisely the issue here, where incommensurable meanings are simultaneously relevant) take both into two incommensurable but simultaneous accounts, since that is the basis of this way of thinking. The reason we can *only* take both positions into account is as follows. Since we start with both, that is, since both are part of what we familiarly understand in speaking our language, we can speak meaningfully about both. But, as Davidson shows, this language and the "not even a single standpoint" language he is familiar with cannot consider each other to be languages at all. If we start on this alternative basis, then, we can only talk meaningfully in terms of the possibility of incommensurable positions. In this context, Davidson's arguments are not part of what we can consider a meaningful language at all. Like the initial objection of circularity against his position, they cannot even begin to get under way.

On the other hand, the justification of this other way of thinking relies on the same kind of appeal to the meaninglessness of alternative standpoints that Davidson's arguments do, and so also results in the same paradoxical meaninglessness that they do. Consequently, it too justifies our beginning again, for example with Davidson's basic assumption of considering only one "language" or "position" at a time. And here, as Davidson has shown, the counterarguments in turn cannot begin to get a purchase.

What we have, again, then, is two positions (here, positions on the possible relations of positions) that can only justify and/or explain themselves circularly to each other. Since the justification and/or explanation of either to the other ends in meaninglessness, there is no reason in advance to begin with Davidson's basic assumption rather than the basic assumption of two incommensurable positions or languages considered simultaneously[15] (although the position that begins on the basis of simultaneously considered incommensurable positions perhaps has more to recommend it, given that Davidson's arguments about the unlearnability of incommensurable languages do not hold up). Davidson's choice of his own position on the grounds of the meaninglessness of the other, then, amounts to a choice of his own position on the grounds of having chosen his own position. It is in this way, I suggest, that his argument is circular, once the initial *non*circularity of his argument has been taken into account.

Rorty, having abandoned the vocabulary of truth as expressing more than the justification of our beliefs by other beliefs, as well as the vocabulary of frameworks or positions-as-a-whole, is happy to acknowledge this kind of ultimate circularity: "the pragmatist cannot justify . . . without circularity, but then neither can the realist" (28–29). Again, "a circular justification of our practices, a justification which makes one feature of our culture look good by citing still another, or comparing our culture invidiously with others by reference to our own standards, is the only sort of justification we are going to get."[16] In fact, Rorty takes this inescapable circularity, our being necessarily limited to our own standpoint, as one of the justifications for abandoning the connection between justification or knowledge, on the one hand, and truth, on the other. As he argues, accepting that there is no truth outside our language and habits means that questions like "'How can we justify our knowledge claims without falling

---

[15] Hilary Putnam concludes a different line of argument by noting that "if one recognizes that the radical interpreter himself may have more than one 'home' conceptual scheme, and that 'translation practice' may be governed by more than one set of constraints, then one sees that conceptual relativity does not disappear when we inquire into the 'meanings' of the various conceptual alternatives: it simply reproduces itself at a meta-linguistic level!"; Hilary Putnam, *Realism with a Human Face*, ed. James Conant (Cambridge, MA: Harvard University Press, 1990), 104. And Peter Winch notes, against a position similar to Davidson's, that this kind of argument "does not in fact show that our *own* standards of rationality occupy a peculiarly central position." For "a formally similar argument could be advanced in *any* language containing concepts playing a similar role in that language to those of 'intelligibility' and 'rationality' in ours"; Peter Winch, "Understanding a Primitive Society," *American Philosophical Quarterly* 1, no. 4 (1964): 318.

[16] Rorty, *Contingency*, 57.

into infinite regress, or circularity, or relativism?'" will no longer "seem urgent."[17]

But circularity is not the end of the story. The objection of circularity is still *also* mistaken. As I have argued, this objection, like the arguments appealing to meaninglessness, is self-canceling. And if this is so, there is no reason to find Rorty's arguments *simply* persuasive. Not because they are circular, which he is content to insist on himself, but because their claim that circularity is all there is, is (not only right but also) *simply mistaken*. In that case, the "profitability" of a view, and its relation to "our standards," are no longer a necessarily ultimate consideration, since it is in fact possible that we can establish the truth of a view by balancing our senses of profitability and our standards with wholly different ones.

5. *The Truth of the Knower, and Negotiation between Truths*

What we necessarily have, then, at certain points of thinking through the nature and bases of truth, is a self-incompatible and self-canceling negotiation of incompatible positions, each circularly justified and/or explained against or to each other. Because this negotiation is between incommensurable positions, the meanings on which it is based, and so the negotiation itself, are, as I have argued, undecidable. I suggest that the negotiation is ultimately resolved partly by the knower's making honest or existential decisions between the positions. That is, she resolves the negotiation partly by establishing the truth of her own being in that particular context: what she finds herself honestly (as the truth of herself) committed to.

As I argued in the Introduction, logic, and therefore logical consequence, belong to the structure of reality itself and not only to statements about it. Let me note here that a fact of our being, such as one of our commitments, is not just a brute entity, meaningless in itself and so incapable simply on its own of offering a contribution to truth beyond the fact of itself. First, our being consists partly in a meaningful awareness, so that it is in itself in some sense inherently connected with what it reflects on. Second, constituted as our being is by the framework in which sense, including the

---

[17] Richard Rorty, "Transcendental Arguments, Self-Reference, and Pragmatism," in *Transcendental Arguments and Science: Essays in Epistemology*, ed. P. Bieri, R.-P. Horstmann, and L. Krüger (Dordrecht: D. Reidel, 1979), 100.

sense of our selves, is given to us, it is partly conceptual, consists partly but essentially in meanings, which in turn are constituted as the meanings they are partly by their relations to systems of other, connected and contrasting meanings. That is, our being is conceptually or logically connected with, among other meanings, the contrasting and also in many ways connected meanings of its contexts.

Again, that the decision turns partly on the truth of our own being does not mean that this is *simply* subjective relativism. One's own truth, and the truth of one's circumstances, are parts of reality in general (or as such) and hence of truth beyond the truth specifically of ourselves. In particular, this kind of subjective decision in particular contexts, that brings in the contribution of the truth of our own being as an element of the relevant circumstances, is part of the *establishing or justifying* of positions, and so of their ideas of truth themselves. It is therefore *prior* to the successful establishment of positions and ideas of truth, including the ideas that truth is relative or absolute. That is, one's existential decisions cannot be simply described as subjective and relative because those decisions partly *establish* what those terms *mean* and how they are to be assessed.

As Rorty puts what I think is a related point, "Nobody is being any more arbitrary than anybody else. But that is to say that nobody is being arbitrary at all. Everybody is just insisting that the beliefs and desires they hold most dear should come first in the order of discussion. That is not arbitrariness, but sincerity" (195).

6. Conclusion

As Davidson and Rorty make clear, it is in fact a real difficulty to find a way of talking about such incommensurable contexts in relation to each other that would *allow* talk like that of relativity, whether subjective or any other, and so would allow any sense to the idea of comparison between them. And this is part of what I have been trying to do by exploring the character of certain kinds of talking and thinking that are established as literally meaningless. These moments of meaninglessness and contradiction are the bridges that allow, and by canceling themselves make sense of, comparison between very different standpoints.

They are also what allow noncircular establishment of the truth of *singular* standpoints, considered without reference to others. And singular, non-comparison-permitting standpoints are, of course, relevant to the concerns of a comparative framework. A genuinely comparative framework must make room for the possible legitimacy of standpoints that rule out the relevance of reference to other standpoints, that is, that reject the sense of comparison between deeply different standpoints itself.

2. *An Internal Connection between Logic and Rhetoric, between Frameworks, and a Legitimate Foundation for Knowledge*

In this chapter I take up again the discussion of fundamental justification begun in Chapter 1 (section 4), but here in the context of problems of knowledge, rather than mainly those of the nature of truth. In other words, this chapter returns to some of the same issues but focuses more fully on epistemology rather than on what we might think of as the metaphysics of truth. This focus allows me to give a fuller account of the point, sense, and legitimacy of this kind of justification than I gave in the context of the previous chapter.

I argue here that there is an internal connection between logic and the rhetoric that occurs between different frameworks of sense, that in contexts involving different frameworks this connection affects the natures of logic and rhetoric, and that this transformation of their natures helps to provide a legitimate foundation for knowledge. By a "legitimate" foundation for knowledge, I mean a foundation that is not circular, not infinitely regressive, and not otherwise arbitrary.[1]

Later in the book, I discuss the nature and status of two fundamental kinds of relation in connection with logic and with metaphysical pluralism: essential or internal relations and happenstance or external relations. I argue there, as I argue here with respect to logic and rhetoric between

---

[1] The traditional objection of Western skepticism to the possibility of genuine knowledge is that attempted foundations of knowledge must end up being either circular, or infinitely regressive, or simply arbitrary. Michael Williams calls this "Agrippa's trilemma," after "the ancient sceptic [of about the second century CE] who appears first to have given it formal expression"; Michael Williams, *Unnatural Doubts: Epistemological Realism and the Basis of Scepticism* (Princeton, NJ: Princeton University Press, 1996), 60, my insertion.

frameworks, that there is an internal connection between these kinds of relation themselves that affects their respective natures, and that this transformation helps to provide a legitimate foundation for (in that case) metaphysics. Since logic works centrally with essential or internal relations between its elements, and rhetoric works centrally with happenstance or external relations between them, the present chapter also provides a broader, more clearly concrete context for those later discussions of these relations. I discuss internal and external relations in their own right most fully in Chapter 7.[2]

It has often been argued that a theory that tries to justify itself fully is either viciously circular or produces an infinite regress of justifications. Thinking that tries to establish ultimate foundations for itself seems in the end to base itself on nothing but its own insistence that it is right.[3] As a result, it offers no real knowledge. As Robert Almeder notes, for example, there is a strong appeal of arguments like "there is no non-question-begging way to answer questions such as 'Are you justified in believing your definition of justification?'"[4]

---

[2] I discuss the intimately connected topic of essence or nature in its own right most fully in Chapter 6.

[3] Plato, for example, has Socrates argue in the *Theaetetus* that, if knowledge involves justification (giving a *logos* for, or a rational account of, one's true opinion), then this justification must be based on simple elements for which no account is given, otherwise there would be an infinite regress of justifying one's justifications. But these simples would then not be known, since knowledge involves justification. And since all justification would depend on these unknown simples, if we still wanted to maintain that we had knowledge, we would be left with saying that we were justified without any further grounds. That is, we would be justified on our own say-so; we would be justified because we were justified. Plato, *Theaetetus*, trans. Robin H. Waterfield (Harmondsworth: Penguin Books, 1987), 200ff.

Aristotle, analogously, argues that demonstration, which alone gives knowledge, proceeds from universals, but that the "primary universals" themselves are known by means of induction. But induction proceeds from sensible particulars, "nor," he insists, "can one *know* [a thing] through sensation." In the end, then, knowledge is circular—universals are justified because they are justified, not on any further ground. Aristotle, *Aristotle's Posterior Analytics,* trans. Hippocrates G. Apostle (Grinnell, IA: Peripatetic Press, 1981), 81a41–81b10, 87b29–36, 100b5–7, translator's insertions and emphases.

[4] Robert Almeder, "On Naturalizing Epistemology," in *Foundations of Philosophy of Science,* ed. James H. Fetzer (New York: Paragon House, 1993), 470.

Since this is true of thinking that tries to justify itself most fully or rigorously, one reaction to this kind of argument is to think that we cannot regard *any* level of thinking as giving us knowledge. Another reaction has been to abandon the idea of epistemological foundations altogether, regarding foundations as unnecessary to knowledge. The argument goes that since such foundations have always been an illusion, we have in fact always gotten along perfectly well without them. And by recognizing the illusion, we no longer mislead ourselves or waste time and effort in pursuing it.[5]

I argue, however, that there is a genuinely epistemological solution to the problem of circular or infinitely regressive foundations, as opposed to simply eliminating the problem on the grounds that it rests on an illusion of what is conceivable and necessary. In fact, as will become clear, this solution *also endorses and incorporates* the reasons for dismissing the problem of foundations. It should therefore have something to recommend it to antifoundationalists as well.

Ultimate circularity and infinite regress express equivalent problems with respect to providing foundations of knowledge. In the case of circularity, the same claim is repeated in place of contributing something new that might therefore offer support for it. In the case of infinite regress, the same *form of justification* is repeated in place of contributing something new that might therefore justify that form of justification. The Almeder quotation above illustrates this equivalence. In the argument that follows, the same considerations therefore apply to both, and for the sake of convenience I discuss the problem only with respect to vicious circularity.

I want to approach the problem of circularity by combining it with another, possibly equally serious difficulty. On the basis of this combination, I shall argue that rigorous thought *is* in fact viciously circular, but that this circularity has peculiar *rhetorical* properties that allow it to offer genuine knowledge. In other words, I shall argue that it is possible to establish truth not only despite, but *because* of, the problem of ultimate cir-

---

[5] See, for example, Donna J. Haraway, "Situated Knowledges: The Science Question in Feminism and the Privilege of Partial Perspective," in *Simians, Cyborgs, and Women: The Reinvention of Nature* (New York: Routledge, 1991), 191; F. C. S. Schiller, *Formal Logic: A Scientific and Social Problem* (London: Macmillan, 1912).

cularity. This claim clearly involves a contradiction. In the later sections of this chapter I argue that this kind of contradiction is logically admissible.[6] I also argue that, although it is a contradiction, it does not work just as much against as for the success of the solution. In addition, it is this contradiction that allows the proposed solution to combine, as I noted, both foundationalist and antifoundationalist thinking. At a certain point, this contradiction produces an undecidability of meanings, and in the penultimate section I respond to some problems that potentially result from that undecidability. I end with some thoughts on the relevance of this paradoxical foundation of knowledge to our experience and conduct in everyday life.

1. Overview: The Usefully Contradictory Connection of Logic and Rhetoric

The second difficulty is this. As Henry Johnstone has argued, a philosophical position is necessarily contradictory. On the one hand, as a logical condition of its existence, it must recognize positions opposed to it.

> [The] philosopher's position . . . does not arise in a vacuum. It . . . arises in the attempt to combat an alien view. . . . If I cannot conceive any alternative to my view, then my view, like a logical tautology, conveys no information. . . . If my view is to be true in a nontrivial way, then at least one alternative to it must be conceivable.[7]

But, on the other hand, it is logically impossible for a philosophical position even to conceive positions opposed to it. Because a philosophical position is or involves a conception of reality in general, "each position claims possession of the only universe of discourse in which comparison can be made at all."[8] Again, for the same reason "a philosophical position always is, or implies, a decision as to what is to count as facts or evidence,"[9] so that for "a philosopher—say, Smith— . . . nothing his antagonist submits as

---

[6] See the Introduction, section 5, for a discussion of the general possibility of legitimate logical contradiction.
[7] Henry W. Johnstone, Jr., *Validity and Rhetoric in Philosophical Argument: An Outlook in Transition* (University Park, PA: Dialogue Press of Man and World, 1978), 117.
[8] Ibid., 48.
[9] Ibid., 55.

evidence can possibly be evidence for anything except Smith's own view."[10]

Johnstone does not see this contradiction as an alarming sign of error. He understands contradiction as altogether forbidden only for formal deductive systems. In contrast, philosophy occurs at a point before such systems acquire their force, because it is precisely philosophy's mandate to argue about such systems.[11] He resolves the contradiction, however, or at least shows how it is livable, through the role of the self, which exists as the tension involved in standing both inside and outside one's position at the same time and in the same respect.[12]

In this sense, he maintains, philosophical argument is always ad hominem.[13] Its only means of engaging legitimately with its opposition is by taking up the argument in its opposition's terms, because that opposition cannot unproblematically conceive the terms of other, conflicting positions. Philosophical argument, then, always includes and depends on the argument's persuasiveness to a particular audience: persuasiveness not in virtue of the logic or evidential weight of the argument considered on its own, but partly in virtue of the audience's pre-existing commitment to certain ways of conceiving both the relevant issues and what can count as evidence or support. That is, philosophical argument always includes and depends on a specifically *rhetorical* dimension.

This kind of appeal to an audience's preexisting commitments is central to the tradition of rhetoric. Chaim Perelman and L. Olbrechts-Tyteca, for example, see it as essential to the functioning of argument.[14] They understand this as a matter of the "universal audience" rather than particular audiences, but this is of course an ideal, and one always and variously conceived on the basis of locally experienced particular audiences.[15] By contrast, as any introductory textbook on logic insists, appeal to a particular audience is traditionally sharply excluded from logic, since it relies or turns on the

[10] Ibid., 114.
[11] Ibid., 45.
[12] Ibid., 60–61, 120ff.
[13] Ibid., 45.
[14] Chaim Perelman and L. Olbrechts-Tyteca, *The New Rhetoric: A Treatise on Argumentation*, trans. John Wilkinson and Purcell Weaver (Notre Dame, IN: University of Notre Dame Press, 1969), 17ff.
[15] Ibid., 33.

audience's commitments uncritically, that is, in such a way that the truth or falsity of these commitments makes no difference to the value of their contribution to the conclusion. These commitments function successfully in the argument as long as they simply help to cause psychological conviction, and their truth value does not enter into the issue at all.

This sharp contrast between logic and rhetoric connects directly with Johnstone's discussion. The contradiction Johnstone defends is that a philosophical position must take other philosophical positions into account, but cannot conceive any other such positions. In other words, a philosophical position ultimately relies both on an appeal to a particular audience and also entirely on reasoning that is not concerned with a particular audience, with particular commitments, at all (no other audience is conceivable, so one is simply addressing everyone possible). One way of formulating this contradiction is that a philosophical position depends on both purely consequential and evidential reasoning *and* the kind of uncritical appeal to an audience's unreflective commitments that this consequential reasoning excludes. That is, it depends both on logic and on the kind of rhetoric that logic specifically excludes.

But, Johnstone argues, a philosophical position depends on these things as a *logical condition of its existence*. This means, in our alternative formulation of the contradiction he defends, that the rhetorical dimension that logic excludes is a *logical* condition of a philosophical position's existence. To the extent, then, that a philosophical position consists in logical thought, this rhetorical dimension is *a logical condition of the logical thought that excludes it*. It is this implication of the contradiction Johnstone defends that I explore in this essay.

Such metaphilosophical considerations, which for Johnstone stem from explorations like those of Everett Hall of the relations of rival philosophical systems, have also been taken up in the context of work like Thomas Kuhn's on incommensurable scientific paradigms, and W. V. O. Quine's on translation between conflicting cultural frameworks.[16] Donald David-

---

[16] Everett W. Hall, *Philosophical Systems: A Categorial Analysis* (Chicago: University of Chicago Press, 1960); Thomas Kuhn, *The Structure of Scientific Revolutions,* ed. 2 (Chicago: University of Chicago Press, 1970); Willard Van Orman Quine, "Ontological Relativity," in *Ontological Relativity and Other Essays* (New York: Columbia University Press, 1969).

son and Richard Rorty, for example, whose work I discussed in Chapter 1, resolve the contradiction, in different but intersecting ways, by falling simply on the side that fundamentally opposed philosophical or cultural positions are simply inconceivable—or, in Rorty's case, entirely unprofitable to conceive.[17] Others, like Barbara Herrnstein Smith, have gone in the opposite direction, insisting that there is no position that can establish truth in any final way against the claims of other, deeply differing positions, so that truth is simply relative.[18]

I argue in this chapter that Johnstone is right to pose the contradiction as he does. But I want to show that the contradiction does not need to be resolved or mitigated in *any* way. On the contrary, I want to show that when it is combined with the otherwise troublesome fact of foundational circularity, it provides the means of solving both that problem and the problems of conceiving conflicting frameworks and truths that it itself is thought to express. (Again, I shall defend the legitimacy of this contradiction and its aptness for these purposes.)

Specifically, I try to show that this combination of difficulties solves the problem of foundational circularity by allowing us to conceive how we can combine the pure self-consistency of logic with the audience directedness of rhetoric. This combination in turn allows us to conceive how we can establish nonrelative truth (but truth that is therefore based entirely on itself, and so circular) while we also, contradictorily, simultaneously have *more than one, conflicting* nonrelative truth (so that each of them can be *non*circularly established, with reference to meanings and truths outside itself). This contradiction would, in other words, allow us to see how a framework can justify itself with reference to other frameworks while *also* legitimately taking all of them to be entirely irrelevant to itself.[19] In this way the combination escapes both circularity and relativism.

---

[17] See, for instance, Donald Davidson, "On the Very Idea of a Conceptual Scheme," in *Inquiries into Truth and Interpretation* (Oxford: Oxford University Press, 1984); Richard Rorty, "Pragmatism, Davidson, and Truth," in *Objectivity, Relativism, and Truth* (New York: Cambridge University Press, 1991).

[18] Barbara Herrnstein Smith, *Belief and Resistance: Dynamics of Contemporary Intellectual Controversy* (Cambridge, MA: Harvard University Press, 1997).

[19] I want to add, then, to Johnstone's reevaluation of the status of ad hominem argument as a legitimate and in fact essential dimension of philosophical argument an analogous reevaluation of the status of contradiction and of vicious circularity. And

For the same reasons, this combination of difficulties solves the problem of conceiving conflicting frameworks and truths. On the one hand, it makes room for the full force of the antifoundationalist and relativist arguments that there are always further meaningful questions about justification to be asked. And on the other hand, it also grants full force to the recognition that contrasting global frameworks, which questions about ultimate justification presuppose, are simply meaningless to each other, or, in Rorty-like terms, that they are "very unhandy languages" for each other. That is, in allowing us to conceive more than one conflicting but *nonrelative* framework and truth, it solves the problem of how to make sense of a genuine pluralism of truth in which each of the conflicting views of truth is not just undermined by also being false for each of the other views that it acknowledges to be legitimate, but is (also) *simply* a truth, without further question or qualification.

In fact, as my argument develops, I shall be able to suggest how the reference outside the framework's circle also allows us to conceive specifically how a theoretical framework can refer to and be grounded by not only other frameworks but also the *world* outside it. In other words, I shall argue that foundational circularity specifically allows a theory's correspondence with the world to be established, foundationally and (paradoxically) noncircularly.

As I have mentioned, the reference of frameworks to each other here is a rhetorical dimension of this combination of difficulties. It involves attempts to address a particular type of audience, to relate the terms of one point of view to those of another. The other side of the combination, the restriction to a single set of terms, is a purely logical dimension, involving only concerns of consistency and validity. But the combination involves both as part of one and the same contradictory structure and process.

This proposal, that rhetoric and logic combine integrally to form a foundation for knowledge, should not be confused with projects to *invert* the customary relation of logic to rhetoric, so that rhetoric is understood to be more fundamental to knowledge and inquiry than logic is. Walter Weimer, for example, argues that logical inference, and with it justification

---

since these foundational forms of circularity and contradiction involve a relation between truths that are also entirely irrelevant to each other, their legitimacy also involves the occasional legitimacy of non sequitur.

itself, are only secondary concerns for science as it is practiced and, in fact, as it is practicable. While he agrees that attempts to find foundational justifications have failed, he sees the solution in abandoning that kind of attempt, which, like Rorty and Smith, he argues is both unnecessary and misguided: "Justificationism is a self-stultifying metatheory—successful application of its tenets guarantees that even its most brilliant practitioners will succeed only in exhibiting the impossibility of success in their self-appointed tasks."[20] What is necessary and helpful to account for our concepts and acceptance of theories is a "psycho-sociological" explanation and "an understanding of rhetoric and the manner in which science is a rhetorical transaction."[21] For example,

> *the argumentative mode of discourse requires injunction rather than description.* Communication in science is primarily a matter of *commands*: correct description will not be attained unless an injunction is obeyed. Both scientific articles and research training given to novices *enjoin* their audiences to behave in a certain way . . . that will enable the researcher to have the appropriate experience: "Do this, and you will experience the world correctly!"[22]

The solution I am proposing, however, is that logical inference and justification, properly thought through, ultimately *already* involve a rhetorical dimension as, as it were, parts of themselves when they are functioning *as logic and justification*. And this rhetorical dimension *of logic* allows a successful foundational justification.

What is more, I am therefore proposing that at a deep level of analysis logical inference itself produces one type of contradiction, in a way analogous to a liar's paradox. Consequently reasoning *itself*, or truth-oriented sensemaking itself, involves, at this deep level, an element of nonsense. I am not arguing, in Weimer's terms, for "irrationalism" rather than rationalism,[23]

---

[20] Walter B. Weimer, *Notes on the Methodology of Scientific Research* (Hillsdale, NJ: Lawrence Erlbaum Associates, 1979), x.

[21] Ibid., 75.

[22] Walter B. Weimer, "Science as a Rhetorical Transaction: Toward a Nonjustificational Conception of Rhetoric," *Philosophy and Rhetoric* 10, no. 1 (1977): 12.

[23] For example, Weimer, *Notes*, 44.

but I am arguing that rationality itself contains an element of irrationality. And since this irrational element belongs to rationality itself, it is not an obstacle to rationality's fulfilling its rational aims. In fact, my proposal is precisely that it is what *allows* rationality to do so.

The field of epistemology is deeply divided as to whether we need logically and otherwise justified foundations for knowledge. I discuss the arguments that we do need a foundation of knowledge in logically consequential justification in Chapter 3.[24] (As I mentioned at the start of this chapter, I am really trying to show that we need to include both sides of this debate.) For the moment I am arguing only that this kind of foundation is possible. I note briefly, however, that although, as Weimer argues, logical inconsistency is not necessarily a problem for science when this kind of inconsistency occurs between different local contexts of inquiry, or with as yet unknown contexts,[25] we nonetheless clearly still need logical consistency *within any single* local context. Even given his argument, then, logical consistency remains a very basic requirement for science.

Returning now to my own proposal: the relation between the different contexts in which these metaphilosophical issues have been taken up that I mentioned above also indicates an intimate connection between logic and rhetoric in this context of foundations. Johnstone's focus is rhetorical, in that he is concerned with the "strife of systems," the fact of always-possible argumentation about philosophical positions and the implications of that fact for the worth and point of philosophy. Davidson and, in a sense, Rorty have instead a logical focus, in that they are concerned with the formal conditions of meaning and consequence. And each focus understandably claims to deal with the conditions of the other. A position on the conditions of meaning and consequence depends on an argument, but an argument equally depends on the conditions of meaning and consequence.

Part of my own aim is to show that both are right, and that rhetoric and logic *are* at the deepest levels conditions of each other. That is, at the level of philosophical foundations, rhetorical considerations *are* logical considerations, and vice versa. At the metaphilosophical level, then, or, equivalently,

---

[24] See also Jeremy Barris, "The Foundation in Truth of Rhetoric and Formal Logic," *Philosophy and Rhetoric* 29, no. 4 (1996): 314–28.

[25] For example, Weimer, "Science," 15–18.

at the metaconceptual level of discussions about such basic concepts as truth itself, reality itself, identity as such, and so on, rhetoric and logic are simply different dimensions of the same type of thinking. And the epistemological solutions I suggest here are rhetorical in a way that is logically relevant to—conceptually or internally related to—their logical dimensions, and vice versa.

In the two sections that follow I discuss the problem of foundational circularity, and the solution gained by combining this problem with that of the contradictory reference of all-embracing frameworks beyond themselves. In a brief fourth section, I discuss the correspondence of thinking with the world. In the fifth section I try to show that the contradiction involved in this proposed solution is viable and that, despite being a contradiction, it does not work as much against as for the success of this solution. The solution also involves a moment or phase of undecidability of meanings, and in the sixth section I discuss why that is not a problem either.

2. The Problem of Foundational Circularity

For the purposes of this discussion, I shall divide theoretical thinking into systematic thought and what I shall call episodic thought. Either way, if we are to have foundations for knowledge, we are faced with the problem of ultimate circularity.

A systematic theory tries to give mutually consistent reasons for the truth of everything it says. If it is *fully* systematic, this includes its starting point(s), and among these its own commitment to give reasons systematically for everything it says. Since it is committed to justifying *everything* that has any relevance to it, it leaves nothing outside itself on which its justifications can draw. It can therefore only justify itself on the basis of its own commitments or principles. It is necessarily circular.

One way in which this unhelpful circularity is clearly visible is in that more than one coherent set of assertions is conceivable, and if coherence is one's criterion of knowledge, there is no way to decide between them. As Quine, for example, points out, one need only adjust other parts of the "web of belief" to cohere with a new assertion, and the new assertion is then equally justified with old, incompatible ones: "Any statement can be held true come what may, if we make drastic enough adjustments elsewhere in the system."²⁶

Episodic thought, in contrast, does not justify its starting points. It just assumes them, and goes on from there. It is an episode among an indefinite number of possible unrelated episodes rather than a system with, as it were, a single self-coherent "plot" or connected narrative. Much of modern science is conducted as episodic thought. There is, however, a *foundational* form of episodic thought, which justifies its commitment to starting with unjustified assumptions. Almeder notes, for example, the argument that "the general sceptic . . . is in the logically contradictory position of asserting as . . . logically privileged or justified the position that no beliefs are justified." This, as he points out, "would serve as a fine *reductio ad absurdum* of the need to justify one's definition of justification."²⁷ Like foundational systematic thought, and for analogous reasons, however, foundational episodic thought can only justify itself, in the end, on the basis of its own commitments or principles. Like systematic thought, then, it is ultimately circular.

Davidson expresses the unhelpfulness of relying in this way on particular starting points that do not need further justification (as, for example, correspondence theories of truth aim to do) in the form of a dilemma. If, for the connecting link between our beliefs and the world, we rely on "something self-certifying," such as our subjective observation experiences, "it is so private as to lack connection with the sentences of the public language which alone are capable of expressing scientific, or even objective, claims. But if we start with sentences or beliefs already belonging to the public language (or what can be expressed in it), we find no intelligible way to base it on something self-certifying."²⁸

---

[26] Willard Van Orman Quine, "Two Dogmas of Empiricism," in *From a Logical Point of View: Nine Logico-Philosophical Essays* (Cambridge, MA: Harvard University Press, 1961), 43.

[27] Almeder, "On Naturalizing Epistemology," 470.

[28] Donald Davidson, "Empirical Content," in *Truth and Interpretation: Perspectives on the Philosophy of Donald Davidson*, ed. Ernest LePore (Cambridge, MA: Blackwell, 1986), 327.

It is true that before the ultimate point when the circle becomes apparent, circularity need not be vicious. The closing of the circle can be postponed by a progress through a variety of explanatory terms. Fruitful work is performed in the course of completing this circle. In fact, ultimate circularity is sometimes taken as the mark of full, adequate justification of a theory, since, if the steps that led to it are sound, it means that the theory has taken everything in the world into account in a way that works. The beginning and end of the theory are in harmony with themselves and everything else. Hegel, for example, famously defends this view.

But, in the end, reliance on circularity as a nonvicious justification itself depends on another vicious circle. If circularity is claimed to be the ultimate measure of successful explanation, this needs to be justified in turn. But here there is nothing else on which to base a justification. Everything else is already based on *it*, because it is the ultimate measure of explanation. A justification by nonvicious circularity therefore lands up in the new vicious circle of justifying circularity by itself.

But here we can helpfully introduce the second difficulty I mentioned, the self-contradictory reference of all-embracing standpoints to standpoints beyond themselves.

3. The Rhetorical Dimension of Foundational Circularity

In this section I take up again the type of foundational justification I discussed in Chapter 1 (section 4), but here in the context of the more specifically epistemological problems I have outlined and the rhetorical dimension of their logic. This allows me to account more fully for the sense and legitimacy of this kind of justification than I did in the context of that earlier discussion of the nature of truth.

A standpoint that is circular because it has justified everything that has any meaning for it leaves nothing meaningful outside itself on which its justifications can draw. It is therefore exactly the kind of all-embracing position Johnstone discusses. And in the light of Johnstone's argument, two things are clear in this connection. First, we *need* to be able to conceive such positions. This means that we cannot avoid the problem of foundational circularity, and we also cannot avoid the problem of the kind of contradiction that Johnstone notes. As I am about to try to show in the context of the second point here, however, we do not in fact need to avoid them, since the two problems together produce their own solution.

Second, which *is* the contradiction Johnstone notes, the only way such a fully circular or all-embracing position can exist as a particular, specifiable framework at all is by also contrasting itself with some other theory or framework outside its circle. In fact, without that contrast it cannot speak about itself even to name itself.[29] The moment it says, "this framework is now fully justified," it has differentiated itself as a whole from another framework. For that matter, the moment it *tries* to justify itself, it presupposes some other standpoint as the contrast with itself that gives meaning to the idea of "itself." It may see that other standpoint as wrong, or insufficiently rigorous (as in consisting in "mere opinion," or being "not up to scientific standards"), but it does presuppose its existence.

A foundational standpoint, then, depends on the *rhetorical* reference to another standpoint, a particular audience, to complete its own circle. And yet the completion of that circle means there is now nothing relevant to its justification outside itself. But to *state* that independence of anything outside itself, even to think it, again requires that it name itself in contrast to some alternative thinking that falls, if only by virtue of being mistaken, outside the circle of itself. This is all the more true if the completion of the circle is complex and so more than a naming. The very existence of foundational circularity presupposes a line of thought that is other than the lines of thought justified by the circle. The closing of the circle, then, is also the establishment of the existence of an independent and contrasting standpoint outside the circle. It is the establishment of an audience that is

---

[29] As I have mentioned, there is the diametrically opposed view that, for example, Davidson and Rorty argue, namely, that the "very idea" of a contrasting position is simply meaningless or irrelevant, so that the whole issue as I have framed it simply does not arise (including the specification of even a *single* global framework). As will become increasingly clear, I agree that such fully contrasting positions are meaningless or entirely irrelevant, but Davidson and Rorty conclude that they need not be taken into account at all, whereas I conclude that everything depends on taking them into account. My claim is that the character of the meaninglessness in question is such as to make meaningless—to cancel—*the claim of meaninglessness too*. Davidson and Rorty rely on this claim of meaninglessness without analyzing it further, as I argue needs to be done.

neither simply the circular standpoint itself nor, based on common ground, universal.

The closing of the circle, however, is a metaphor for an entire theory's final step of rigorous self-justification, the step of justifying the theory's own commitment to, for example, ultimately circular reasoning. But that circle only *needs* to be closed given the claims of another thought, a particular audience relying on its own, different commitments. For if no criticism can be meaningfully raised, no answer can be meaningfully required. And meaningful criticism of the circle itself, of the final step of rigorous self-justification, can only come from outside the circle. Criticism of the circle itself cannot come from within it, since it can only be identified as a circle from the outside, with reference to what contrasts with it as a whole circle. While the closing of the circle needs a contrasting standpoint, then, the other side of that coin is that the circle only needs to be closed, the standpoint only needs this full justification, if there is a contrasting standpoint. The *problem* of its closing or full justification only meaningfully exists in the first place if there is a contrasting standpoint.

But, as Johnstone argues, the other standpoint also literally has no meaning for the foundational standpoint, and so is irrelevant to its justification. And given that the problem of closing the circle, of full justification, exists only because of the other standpoint, this irrelevance of the other position means that the foundational standpoint is now fully justified. (I shall try to show the viability of the contradiction involved here.) On the one hand, the foundational standpoint can close its circle because the other position exists and so allows meaning to that circle. On the other hand, it does not also put itself in question by establishing the other position because the closing of its circle means that the other position then does not exist for it and so is irrelevant to it.[30] In other words, once the circle has been closed in the light of the other position's existence, the other position is then unable to raise meaningful questions, and consequently it is literally mean-

---

[30] Rorty in "Pragmatism" argues that, because the "other standpoint" is irrelevant, truth then stands in no need of justification: there is no relevant contrasting view to give a point to justification. My point, as I discuss more fully below, is that the irrelevance of the other standpoint is *established* only by the circle's closing, so that the other standpoint *must also be taken into account*, that is, must also be recognized as relevant, precisely so that its irrelevance can be established.

ingless to require a justification. As I have argued, that requirement can only come from outside the now complete circle, and this cannot happen.

The circle is then justified in not taking the final step of justifying itself. It is closed—finally justified—in not closing itself. And because this closure occurs with reference to another standpoint, it is not circular. It is only given another standpoint, relying on its own, different commitments, that the circle can even *exist* so as to be *required* finally to justify its commitment to circularity. That is, it is only given another standpoint that it both *can* be closed and *needs* to be closed. Consequently, given the other standpoint, its closure is possible, and, given that the other standpoint is also irrelevant, it is also justified. And because the circle is closed, which means that it leaves nothing relevant outside, it is *absolutely, foundationally*, justified. The standpoint, then, is foundationally and noncircularly justified as not needing justification—or, alternatively expressed, it is closed by not having to be closed.

In short, circularity allows full but noncircular justification of itself by rhetorical reference to the other standpoint(s), particular audiences relying on their own, different commitments, that it both excludes and presupposes.

And although this justification is a contradictory procedure that consequently cancels itself, that cancellation itself establishes that any justificatory procedure, including itself, is unnecessary. That is, this procedure is a justification because it *establishes* that it is contradictory and self-canceling, and in doing so *establishes* that it is redundant.[31]

---

[31] At this point it should be possible to see that this line of thought is, as I believe, an alternative expression of Wittgenstein's kind of approach to these issues. As he explains in the *Tractatus*, for example, "My propositions serve as elucidations in the following way: anyone who understands me eventually recognizes them as nonsensical, when he has used them—as steps—to climb up beyond them"; Ludwig Wittgenstein, *Tractatus Logico-Philosophicus*, trans. D. F. Pears and B. F. McGuinness (London: Routledge & Kegan Paul, 1961), 74, prop. 6.54. And in his later work there is the procedure of "dissolving" problems by exploring and so displaying their literal meaninglessness. So, for example, "My aim is: to teach you to pass from a piece of disguised nonsense to something that is patent nonsense"; Ludwig Wittgenstein, *Philosophical Investigations*, 2nd ed., trans. G. E. M. Anscombe (Oxford: Blackwell, 1958), no. 464. See also 51e, esp. no. 133. One way of conceiving my project here is as an attempt to articulate the kind of insight that Wittgenstein offers in a way that allows us to see that it can tell us some fundamental things about epistemological concerns as traditionally conceived (and not, say, as "dissolved" by philosophical therapy).

I note that this justification works only because the circularity really is vicious, based on nothing but itself. This is what, on the one hand, allows the circle to be completely and therefore foundationally closed. And, on the other hand, it is also what allows the other position both to be relevant to justifying the standpoint, so that the standpoint is in fact noncircularly justified with reference to what is outside its circle, and also to be wholly irrelevant to the standpoint, so that the circle of justification is not in the end reliant on something outside the standpoint, and therefore is not complete after all and so is not a vicious circle.

There is a crucial point that I should emphasize here. The problem of circularity cannot be avoided by saying that the circle simply need not be closed on the grounds that the other standpoint or position is irrelevant. First, the irrelevance of the other position is established only when the step of closing the circle is taken. Before that point of closure the other position cannot be said to be completely irrelevant to the first standpoint, since the boundaries of that standpoint are not definitively established. That the circle is not closed means that further justification of the standpoint as a whole is still required (or, more precisely, that further justification is required to establish the standpoint as a definite or complete whole), and this means that statements about the whole standpoint are not yet properly justified. One such statement is the assertion that another position is irrelevant in every respect, is irrelevant to this whole system of thought. Only when the circle is closed is it definitively clear that the other position is entirely irrelevant.

Second, until the circle has closed, there *is* no "standpoint as a whole" to *be* justified on the grounds that one can disregard the other position as irrelevant. The "standpoint as a whole" is just another way of talking about the complete circle. Before the circle is complete, then, there are only particular issues in particular contexts, and these can always call for further justification. In short, the circle must be closed both to allow the irrelevance of the existence of the other position and to establish it.

I maintained in my introduction to this chapter that this solution to the problem of foundational circularity also solves the problem of conceiving conflicting frameworks and truths. Clearly, when one standpoint is contrasted with another as a whole, the other standpoint is also set off as a whole. It is, after all, wholly excluded from the first standpoint. And this means that everything I have argued about the first standpoint also applies to the second. In other words, entirely conflicting standpoints actually can and do *justify* each other, rather than only putting each other in question.

The line of thought I am proposing, then, allows us to conceive a variety of conflicting views as each *simply and without qualification true*, and not only despite the conflict but also because of it.

4. Correspondence with the World

Another way of stating the paradox that ultimate justification involves is that the closing of the theory's circle cancels itself. It can only be closed on the (rhetorical) basis of reference to another theory, and as soon as it is closed the other theory becomes meaningless, since it is outside the completed "circle" of the first theory's meanings. And at that point, there is no meaning to the phrase, "the theory as a whole" (or "the circle"), since there is no contrast ("another theory") for it. Further, because this point of closure is the point at which a theory ultimately justifies itself, it is the point on which the whole theory depends. Consequently, the self-cancellation of its meaning is in fact the cancellation of the meaning of the entire theory. It follows that foundationally justified theories succeed by being constitutively—root and branch—self-canceling.

As a result, the integral interplay of consequential logic and rhetorical reference to an audience in foundational circularity also offers a solution to the problem of establishing a theory's correspondence with the world. I suggest that it is the means by which thinking can get itself out of its own way, by reducing itself to emptiness, so that the objects it is about are no longer "theory laden." The logico-rhetorical act of rigorously completing the vicious foundational circle is then the final step by which thought establishes its relation to the objects and actions that it is about, by getting even its enabling assumptions or framework and its process of justification themselves out of its way. What is left is the thoughtful action or understood thing.

5. The Viability and Aptness of the Contradiction

This proposed solution clearly rests on a contradiction. The existence of one standpoint as a whole is both relevant and irrelevant, at the same time and in the same respect, to another standpoint, an audience (as I have noted, obviously also contrasted as a whole). On the one hand, the mere existence of one position as a separate whole allows another to exist meaningfully as a whole, so that it can finally be justified. On the other hand, that completeness of the justified position *also* means that it cannot be contrasted with the other position, so that it does *not* exist meaningfully as a whole, and therefore does not have to be finally justified (justified as a whole). And this happens as one and the same event. It is a *whole* theory that does not exist as a whole, so that the theory is justified *as a whole*.

As I noted in the Introduction, the traditional view in formal logic is that contradiction is logically unacceptable, since any statement at all can be validly derived from a contradiction,[32] so that if we accept a contradiction we are no longer saying anything, rather than anything else. By contrast, however, this particular kind of contradiction really only occurs in a very limited context, and is self-canceling. As a result, it does not really violate the purposes that the law of contradiction expresses.

Once the circle has been closed and one has moved on to thinking *within* the standpoint's "circle" again, the paradoxes are irrelevant. The closing of the circle involves the loss of its own meaning as a circle. It has become universal or particular-audience-less, that is, without an "outside" to contrast with an "inside." Consequently the paradoxes arising from its closing no longer have meaning, until one returns to that last step of justification again. Our assumptions have been justified (or we have justified not justifying our assumptions), and we can think linearly on the basis of them. It is no longer true to say that one moves circularly after one has moved on from the closing of the circle. The circle only truly exists at the point of its closure. The metaphor has no meaning outside that context. What does it mean to say that "one thinks in a circular curve" without being able to refer to a possible terminus at which the circle emerges? The circle only emerges *as* a circle if it can be conceived as meeting up with itself, as complete. And in this case that completion is also the cancellation of the circle into meaninglessness.[33]

---

[32] For this principle, see, for example, Susan Haack, *Philosophy of Logics* (Cambridge: Cambridge University Press, 1978), 22, 202.

[33] It is worth noting that the fact that a metaphor, like "the circle," can be meaningfully used at one point of an analysis but has literally no meaning at all at another is another indication that rigorous theory cancels itself.

All the contradictions, then, exist before their resolution; but after the resolution, they no longer have meaning. At that point, it literally stops being meaningful even to say that they *have* existed. In fact, they occur *only* at the point of ultimate justification of theory, and at that point they are also immediately self-canceling. Outside that point they have *already* disappeared, in a way that amounts to their having never existed. As a result, they also do not lead to any further logical contradiction.

At that ultimate point, on the other hand, they have been reached by following the law of contradiction. Further, since they *are* the process of justification of any rigorous theory, including theories justifying rationality itself, they precede, as Johnstone notes, the establishment of the law of contradiction itself. That is, they do not violate the law, since it is not yet established at their level, and they themselves establish it for all other levels.

It might also be objected that the presence of the contradiction, since it is a contradiction, means that the justification fails as much as it succeeds. It is true that the contrasting position is, for example, relevant to the foundational standpoint exactly insofar as it is irrelevant, so that its irrelevance cannot simply "win out" over its relevance in a neatly accommodating sequence. But that is not how this idea of justification works. A crucial part of this idea is that the contradiction *cancels its meanings*, as contradictions do, and that as a result both it and the motivations of meaningful justification that produce it are *entirely replaced* by an all-embracing range of meanings (actually, by at least two all-embracing ranges of meanings). As I have argued, *within* the context of an all-embracing standpoint, the contradictory contrast between such standpoints does not meaningfully exist, and so the very idea of the standpoint as a whole, and with it the issue of its justification as a whole, have no meaning. And it is this idea and this issue that produce the contradiction. When the contradiction cancels itself, then, it is entirely replaced by a context in which even the motivation for formulating the contradiction has no meaning. And this means that the whole contradiction, *including both the relevance and the irrelevance* of the contrasting position, is no longer relevant even as a conceivable issue to the foundational standpoint. The whole issue vanishes altogether. It is *this* irrelevance, the irrelevance of *the whole contradiction of justificatory relevance and irrelevance*, that replaces and so eliminates the meaningfulness of both sides of the contradiction. It is not, in contrast, one side of the contradiction that replaces and eliminates the other. Both sides are simultaneously in force

74 *Logic, Rhetoric, and Knowledge*

as long as the contradiction meaningfully exists, and both sides lose their relevance when the whole contradiction loses its relevance.

A final comment: the point at which the circle is complete is the point at which we are justifying the position as a whole. Accordingly, to say that we have moved on from dealing with the whole circle is to say that we are no longer dealing with the final, foundational step of justification. The linear and nonparadoxical thinking that follows the closing of the circle, then, is less than fully or foundationally justified thinking. But it is now fully *justified* in being less than fully justified.

6. *The Problem of the Undecidability of Meanings*

The moment at which the circle closes involves an undecidability of meanings. It establishes mutually exclusive circles of meanings, but it is also a point of contact between them. Consequently it is a single point at which two or more conflicting circles of meanings of the "same" things are simultaneously in effect. And there can be no sense to the idea of a decision between them. Since each of these sets of meanings covers *everything*—this is what the completion of the circle means—they also cover the meanings involved in making decisions. As a result, a decision would be subject to exactly the same equivocity of meanings it is supposed to resolve.

Here the kind of issue that Jacques Derrida centrally explores might be raised. What if the two circles cannot be distinguished in the first place because their "own" meanings are *already* undecidable?[34] That is, a circle can *never* be fully or finally identified as a circle, not even "ultimately." It cannot reach the point of closing the circle because there *is* no fully decidable, consistent line of any kind to follow. Self-justification cannot get under way to start with because this "self" is, from the start, not the kind of thing that can be completely or definitively specified. Similarly, the distinctions between "particular speaker" and "particular audience" and between "particular interests" and "universal considerations," and so between purely logical and specifically rhetorical considerations, also cannot successfully be made. As a result one can never disentangle the conflicting

---

[34] See, for example, Jacques Derrida, "Différance," in *Margins of Philosophy*, trans. Alan Bass (Chicago: University of Chicago Press, 1982).

commitments of the different standpoints or, in fact, even clearly identify "which" belong to "whom."

But the meanings that make up this objection, as Derrida himself insists, are on its own grounds *also* undecidable. As a result, it is undecidable *whether* the "own meanings" of a position are undecidable. This frees us to explore the possibility that they are not undecidable. The meaning of the undecidability of meanings itself must be allowed to be undecidable.

It might be said, next, that this deconstructive objection applies equally to the argument that the meaning of undecidability must be allowed to be undecidable. This argument too is undecidable, since *its* rigorous meanings are undecidable. Consequently we have *not* succeeded in freeing the possibility of decidable meanings, which can be separated into their own circles of justification. But the same reply also applies here. We have, at worst, an infinite regress of the same objection with the same reply. If so, the point at which the undecidability is established is never reached, any more than the point at which decidability is established. This is enough, however, to establish the *possibility* of fully separate circles of meaning, or, in other words, to establish their conceivability. And that is enough to allow the kind of solution I have proposed. For once such circles of meaning are conceivable, there is no obstacle in principle to conceiving a situation in their terms, and exploring the results.

In fact, this infinite regress establishes an ultimate, complete, and decidable separation between the standpoint *that it can be established* that undecidability is inescapable and the standpoint *that it can be established* that decidability is possible. As a result, the "universal undecidability can be justified" standpoint can be circularly contrasted with the "sometimes-decidability can be justified" standpoint, and each can then be fully justified in the way I have proposed.

7. Relevance to the Experience and Conduct of Everyday Life

We can see the practical reasonableness of the contradictory idea that there can be different all-embracing but also justified circles of meanings in everyday life, in conflicts of views with fundamentally different priorities. One familiar example is the persistent miscommunication and mutual incomprehension that happen across the generation gap. First, here, two people can argue until they are blue in the face, but they will still only be able to understand and live in accordance with what they can find meaningful for themselves. And that will not be what the other person finds meaningful or a priority unless, as only sometimes happens, they go through a fundamental change on the spot. The audience here is *practically* meaningless. Second, however, in these everyday cases we can also see that this incorrigible separateness of meanings does not make truth simply relative. The truth *of* each person or "audience" as she or he is, limits and warts and also *possible falsehoods* and all, is still part of the truth of the situation inhabited by both parties, something that both need to work with in its own terms, for both practical and theoretical purposes. Everyday life, then, supports this idea of all-embracing yet conflicting, mutually irrelevant yet mutually justifying circles.

And conversely, one can begin to see here how this idea of separate all-embracing but also possibly justified circles of meanings might help to identify and account for some otherwise elusive textures of everyday experience. These include, for example, a sense of the kind of fairness based on accepting fundamental disagreements that are also about the nature of fairness itself in that situation; or a particular type of deep frustration resulting from one or more disputing parties' being unable to recognize that they are systematically mishearing another in terms of meanings that are not the other's, but that are nonetheless legitimately their own; or a kind of humaneness or sympathy practiced across deep differences in intelligible priorities and in how things can be held to make sense.

A final point: since I claim that circularity is both a problem for knowledge and required by it, one consequence of my argument is that knowledge is ultimately paradoxical. The argument suggests that knowledge is a problem for itself, and that being a problem for itself is what makes it truly knowledge. If I am right, this paradox extends to the attitude a knowing person has to have. This is the attitude of genuine open-mindedness. In order to have knowledge, one has to be open to the legitimacy of standpoints in which one's own ideas of things, including one's ideas of how knowledge and sense work, are literally meaningless. One has to be open to the possibility that one might need to learn how to make sense in new ways, and that as a result one might come to understand even the questions themselves, and therefore also what answers can look like, very differently.

And, on the other hand, as even the conventional view of open-mindedness implies, it must combine both openness to fresh ideas and a definite commitment to established ideas. Without this definite commitment it is not an open-mindedness involving *knowledge* (or, really, involving mindedness). Further, this openness and commitment are dependent on each other. One is *open* to *establishing* new ideas and becoming *committed* to them: otherwise one is not really open at all. And one is legitimately *committed* to established ideas because one *has been open* to their conflicting alternatives: otherwise those ideas have not been justified and have no claim to establishment and commitment.

3. *Pluralism, Legitimate Self-Contradiction, and a Proposed Solution to Some Shared Fundamental Problems of Political and Mainstream Epistemology*

> I have nothing
> Of woman in me: now from head to foot
> I am marble-constant: now the fleeting moon
> No planet is of mine.
> —*Antony and Cleopatra*[1]

In this chapter I return to a focus on the mutual meaninglessness and yet essential connection of globally different frameworks, and develop the relevance of this paradoxical connection for the political dimensions of epistemology. I also draw on this new context to expand the earlier discussion of mainstream or unpoliticized epistemology. I discuss political epistemology primarily through the example of feminist epistemology.

As I shall argue, the field of political epistemology is characterized by unresolved debates that show that it is still widely troubled by problems that it shares with mainstream epistemology. Another feature of this field of thought, one that I want to show is relevant to the first, is that political epistemologists have typically engaged in debates within epistemology, rather than in the debates between epistemologists and antiepistemologists. I argue in this chapter that a possible solution for both kinds of epistemology lies in coordinating, without reconciling, the incommensurable insights of mainstream epistemology, explicitly politicized epistemology, and antiepistemology. Also inherent in this coordination are the means of coordinating and negotiating between epistemically incommensurable

---

[1] William Shakespeare, *Antony and Cleopatra*, ed. Maynard Mack (Harmondsworth: Penguin Books, 1970), V, ii, 238–41.

standpoints generally. This solution is necessarily self-contradictory. But I argue that it is conceivable given a specific reunderstanding of sense itself, a possibility for which some postmodern and some specifically feminist work has opened the way.

1. Two Kinds of Debate in Mainstream Epistemology

It is useful in this context to distinguish two types of debate in contemporary mainstream epistemology. The first is between different types of epistemology, and the second is between epistemologists and those who reject epistemology itself altogether. I shall argue that a viable politically explicit epistemology needs to take the contradictory insights and results of both into account. As I mentioned, I shall focus particularly on feminist epistemology.

Examples of the first type of debate include debates between epistemologies based on coherence and correspondence theories of truth, or between different characterizations of knowledge as a sociological phenomenon and as the context-independent product of objective tests, or between different notions of the nature and role of objectivity. Feminist epistemology and philosophy of science have generally taken positions in this type of debate, attempting to identify and correct, or make use of or expand, gender characteristics of the various positions. This remains true even when feminists draw, as they often do, on work that is also drawn on in the second type of debate. For example, in the introduction to the fairly representative collection *Feminist Epistemologies,* many of whose contributors make use of work central to antiepistemology, Linda Alcoff and Elizabeth Potter write, "The authors included in this text are concerned with many of the problems that have vexed traditional epistemology, among them the nature of knowledge itself, epistemic agency, justification, objectivity. . . . But their essays . . . treat these issues in new ways."[2] These new ways do challenge the possibility of "a general account of knowledge," but still offer particular accounts of knowledge that attend to "the social context and status of knowers."[3] Similarly, the contributors to the

---

[2] Linda Alcoff and Elizabeth Potter, eds., *Feminist Epistemologies* (New York: Routledge, 1993), 1–2.
[3] Ibid., 1.

collection *Feminism and Science* are concerned with using, modifying the focus of, and adding to existing epistemologies and science.[4]

As I shall try to show, however, mainstream epistemology suffers from intractably unresolved conflicts even before feminist critique arrives on the scene. Feminist attempts to transform the political dimensions of mainstream theories leave these conflicts intact, and are consequently still caught in the same epistemological dilemmas.[5] In particular, I sketch some of the ways in which both mainstream epistemology and the feminist critique of it is characterized by unresolved conflicts about whether or not we need epistemological foundations, and whether or not we can find them if we do need them.

I should clarify that the second and third sections below, in which I discuss the conflicts within mainstream and feminist epistemologies, are not an attempt to argue that these epistemologies have failed, or, more particularly, that we need or do not need a foundation for knowledge. The same is true of the fourth section on antiepistemology. My aim instead is to rehearse some of the existing and ongoing debate and reservations in both mainstream and feminist epistemology in order to show the extent to which these fields are, understandably, conflicted and troubled by these questions. That is, in these sections my thesis is not that the various critiques of the various epistemologies are right but that it remains understandably unresolved among various influential versions and critiques of epistemology whether or not, for example, we need foundations and whether or not we can succeed in establishing them if we do need them.

The framework I propose in the later part of the chapter endorses *both* sides of *each* of these irresolutions, and it is by doing so that, I believe, it offers a solution.

---

[4] Nancy Tuana, ed., *Feminism and Science* (Bloomington: Indiana University Press, 1989). See, for example, in this collection Sandra Harding, "Is There a Feminist Method?," 29–30.

[5] I do not wish to claim that political transformations are not also equally epistemological in the strict sense. It is clear that a sexist bias, being a bias, is a strictly epistemological weakness. In fact, I argue that a real solution depends on perspectives that only the more marginalized—or explicitly politicized—epistemological work has opened up. But, as I hope to make clear, feminist epistemology has so far taken over conflicts of mainstream epistemology that remain independently of the politically relevant improvements.

These unresolved conflicts within epistemology have led to the second type of debate, between epistemologists and those who argue that epistemology as such is both futile and unnecessary. More extremely, one such claim is that the notion of epistemology has no substantive content at all. Donald Davidson and Richard Rorty are perhaps the most prominent of the antiepistemologists. Feminists seem to have focused less on this type of debate; but I shall argue that what is crucial to solving the problems that explicitly politicized epistemological efforts have made so urgently visible is a combination of the epistemological and antiepistemological positions. And more than this, I shall argue that these solutions also help resolve the still intractable conflicts that trouble mainstream positions *within* epistemology. That is, an acknowledgment of the force of antiepistemology is the basis for establishing a working and politically reasonable epistemology.

It should already be apparent that the logic here will be in some ways acutely paradoxical. It is in fact some of the political perspectives on epistemology that have made the necessity of this kind of paradox most apparent, as well as the need to rework what we think of as logic and sense themselves. As Donna Haraway writes, for example, feminists need "*simultaneously* an account of radical historical contingency for all knowledge claims . . . *and* a no-nonsense commitment to faithful accounts of a 'real' world," a combination that is "both contradictory and necessary."[6] Andrea Nye argues that logic itself is socially and historically conditioned, and she advocates finding "an understanding that logical analysis bound to consistency and univocality cannot."[7] And in Luce Irigaray's much more nuanced assessment, she argues that although what we understand as logic is all the logic we have, it is nonetheless tied to the functioning of a particular, patriarchal social order. Consequently it is necessary not to take its sense and validity for granted but to find a way of thinking paradoxically from both "inside" and "outside" logic at the same time.[8]

---

[6] Donna J. Haraway, "Situated Knowledges: The Science Question in Feminism and the Privilege of Partial Perspective," in *Simians, Cyborgs, and Women: The Reinvention of Nature* (New York: Routledge, 1991), 187.

[7] Andrea Nye, *Words of Power: A Feminist Reading of the History of Logic* (New York: Routledge, 1990), 5.

[8] Luce Irigaray, *This Sex Which Is Not One,* trans. Catherine Porter with Carolyn Burke (Ithaca, NY: Cornell University Press, 1985), 68–69.

I have noted the arguments for the possibility of legitimate logical contradiction in the Introduction (section 5). In this chapter I argue for the legitimacy and manageability of this particular contradiction as the discussion proceeds. This argument is in fact part of the central point of the chapter.

I first discuss the conflicts shared by mainstream and feminist epistemology, then a derivative conflict that is particularly acute for politically oriented approaches. I then sketch the antiepistemological view. Next I offer an example of the kind of situation to which feminist and other marginalized epistemologies are sensitive. This kind of situation motivates the solution I propose, with which I end.

2. Shared Problems

The perennial problems of infinite regress and ultimate circularity are very well known—so well known, in fact, that for the most part epistemologists seem to take them as irrelevant. There are no widely accepted solutions, yet the work of epistemology proceeds regardless. In a way, the very intractability of these problems cancels them out across all theories: any rival theory will suffer from the same problems, so the choice of the "best theory" is unaffected by the presence of these problems. In fact, it is because of these apparently intractable problems that antiepistemologists have rejected epistemology altogether.

Epistemologies based on correspondence theories of truth face the problem of infinite regress. Whatever given or datum is taken as a piece of the world "out there," to which assertions correspond, we still need a criterion for knowing that and how it "corresponds" with our beliefs and statements about it. This means that our knowledge of the correspondence must, in turn, correspond to some other datum, the fact or confirmation of the correspondence itself. And then we need a criterion for knowing that and how *that* datum "corresponds" with the belief about *it*. The result is an infinite regress. I described Davidson's account of this problem in Chapter 2: if we take as the link between our beliefs and the world "something self-certifying," such as our subjective experiences of observation, "it is so private as to lack connection with the sentences of the public language which alone are capable of expressing scientific, or even objective, claims. But if we start with sentences or beliefs already belonging to the public language (or what can be expressed in it), we find no intelligible way to base it on something self-certifying."[9]

In this section I limit myself to these brief comments on mainstream reservations about the epistemological solutions offered by the correspondence theory of truth, and to the brief comments that follow on the coherence theory, since the discussion of feminist concerns in the following section, and then the discussion of antiepistemology, will develop these reservations in a variety of ways.

Epistemologies based on coherence theories of truth for their part face the problem of circularity. The soundness of an assertion depends on its relation to all of the others in the system or web of relevant assertions. But the soundness of all of the others depends in part on their relations to the first assertion. In the end, the circle closes: each assertion is justified by assertions that are in turn justified by it. Differently put, the whole set of assertions, in their particular relations, is justified by the whole set of assertions in their particular relations, and nothing else. The mediation of justification through many assertions certainly performs a useful work of organizing the world, but the epistemological value of that work still rests on circularity. The weakness is made most visible in that more than one coherent set of assertions is conceivable, and if coherence is one's criterion of knowledge, there is no way to decide between them. Again, I noted Quine's comment on this issue in Chapter 2. As he points out, one need only adjust other parts of the web to cohere with a new assertion, and the new assertion is then equally justified with old, incompatible ones: "Any statement can be held true come what may, if we make drastic enough adjustments elsewhere in the system."[10]

Since feminist work has largely consisted in contributions to the first type of debate, that is, in attempts to improve, add to, or transform the way epistemology asks and answers the same questions it has traditionally asked, the same kinds of conflicts can be expected to appear there.

---

[9] Donald Davidson, "Empirical Content," in *Truth and Interpretation: Perspectives on the Philosophy of Donald Davidson,* ed. Ernest LePore (Cambridge, MA: Blackwell, 1986), 327.

[10] Willard Van Orman Quine, "Two Dogmas of Empiricism," in *From a Logical Point of View: Nine Logico-Philosophical Essays* (Cambridge, MA: Harvard University Press, 1961), 43.

3. A Derivative Problem in Feminist Epistemology

Feminist approaches have focused on identifying and attempting to correct the sexist biases in epistemological theory, or, alternatively, to make use of the perspectives illuminatingly opened up by gendered interests and standpoints. The possible loci of sexist biases in epistemological theory, to consider those for the moment, are various, ranging from a crude depreciation of women as thinkers and knowers to, as I have mentioned, the structure of logic as such. But while a sexist bias is certainly an epistemological problem, the decision that such a bias is present is itself a claim to knowledge and so itself subject to epistemological constraints. And as feminism itself has often worked to show, all epistemological approaches, including those of feminists, and including claims to knowledge about epistemology and about bias within it, are potentially or perhaps even inescapably subject to the biases of the interests motivating them. Alcoff and Potter, for example, write of "the political commitments and effects implicit in every philosophical position."[11] And as Sandra Harding notes about (what I believe is) the analogous case of sociological accounts of knowledge, such explanations, while valuable for what they achieve, "implicitly assume as grounds for their own account precisely the epistemology they so effectively undermine."[12] These problems of self-reference are exactly what have motivated paradoxical approaches such as Irigaray's.

Here the cogent and otherwise enormously helpful insight of various political epistemologists that the particularity of our perspectives is in fact helpful for gaining knowledge, and perhaps even necessary for it, does not resolve the problem. Harding, for example, explaining standpoint approaches, argues that one's social situation not only sets limits on but also *enables* what one can know. Standpoint theorists therefore regard examination of the roots of knowledge claims in specific social situations as a way of "maximizing objectivity."[13] But while the acknowledgment and use of our particular "biases" may allow us to avoid many of the weaknesses of a false "neutrality," and so in this respect may produce *better* epis-

---

[11] Alcoff and Potter, *Feminist Epistemologies*, 3.
[12] Harding "Is There a Feminist Method?," 24.
[13] Sandra Harding, "Rethinking Standpoint Epistemology: What Is 'Strong Objectivity?,'" in Alcott and Potter, *Feminist Epistemologies*, 54–55, 69. See also, for example, Haraway's "Situated Knowledges."

temologies than a commitment to neutrality can, this does not respond to reservations about the ways in which situated epistemologies are still subject to the *negative* features of particularity, to dimensions of *genuine* bias. For example, what, in the end, justifies situated claims to knowledge against *conflicting* situated claims? On this theory, we need another situated standpoint to adjudicate; but this new standpoint can have no privilege against the opposed claims of the standpoints it judges. We are back either to an infinite regress of adjudicating positions, or to taking one standpoint circularly to be the right one on the basis of that standpoint itself (or equally circularly taking both to be right, each on its own basis), or to abandoning the claim to knowledge altogether. As I discuss further below in connection with Kuhn's work on paradigms, it is not clear either that we can escape this kind of conflict or, given this kind of framework, that we can resolve it.

Returning to the issue of sexism: the very concept of sexism itself depends on various commitments that themselves are not simply given but are claims to truth, disputed by claims based on other commitments. As is well known, even the concepts of a "woman" and "women" are very troublesome to identify as a result of the role of interests in forming these concepts. In Denise Riley's words, the category of "'women' is historically, discursively constructed, and always relatively to other categories which themselves change." And she notes that "feminism has intermittently been as vexed with the urgency of disengaging from the category 'women' as it has with laying claim to it."[14]

Feminist critiques, then, have sharpened the relevance of the problems of ultimate circularity and infinite regress. And given these problems, feminist critique faces a dilemma. The very vigilance toward one's own biases that is one of the strengths of feminist epistemology problematizes the force of feminist critique. If bias is inescapable (this is not the universal feminist position; I shall explore further shortly), then feminist claims are ultimately no more justified than those of their opponents. But even if cruder forms of bias are escapable, or even if bias can be taken into account in ways that, for example, enhance objectivity, the problems of circularity and infinite regress ensure that, in the end, feminist claims are

---

[14] Denise Riley, *"Am I That Name?" Feminism and the Category of "Women" in History* (Minneapolis: University of Minnesota Press, 1988), 1–2, 3–4.

still no more justified than those of their opponents when opposing commitments are sufficiently different.

Thomas Kuhn's notion of incommensurability is relevant here. As Kuhn argues with respect to science, it is possible for competing scientific frameworks (in his word, paradigms) to differ with respect to their very criteria of evidence and of drawing conclusions, that is, with respect to what counts as evidence and valid inference. Consequently, "the choice [between paradigms] is not and cannot be determined merely by the evaluative procedures characteristic of normal science, for these depend in part upon a particular paradigm, and that paradigm is at issue. When paradigms enter, as they must, into a debate about paradigm choice, their role is necessarily circular."[15] Similarly, if logic itself can be put in question, being contextually constituted, if the formal structure of reasoning itself can be subject to accusations of partiality or bias, then conflicting positions need have no genuine criteria by which to legitimate their claims against each other. More to the point, in this situation positions cannot legitimate their claims *to themselves* against conflicting claims: they have no nonarbitrary grounds for rejecting the criteria of the conflicting positions, or at least no more grounds than the other positions have for rejecting theirs.

I use the word "legitimate" deliberately: the criteria that are lacking here are not merely criteria of persuasion but *epistemological* criteria. That is, they are the criteria by which one establishes the truth of one's claims, and it is those criteria that, given incommensurability of reasoning itself, fail to be valid for the other position(s). Consequently one cannot legitimately expect the other position(s) to accept one's claims. In fact the very basis for one's claims, that they meet the criteria for truth, is also the basis for the opposing claims, that they meet (different) criteria for truth. And since these are precisely the criteria for truth, they cannot be further justified without circularity; they themselves would have to

---

[15] Thomas S. Kuhn, *The Structure of Scientific Revolutions*, 2nd ed. (Chicago: University of Chicago Press, 1970), 94, my insertion. In his later work, Kuhn discusses ways of deciding rationally between incommensurable paradigms in the course of their development from one to another, but this does not affect the point I am making here, which concerns already completely given incommensurable frameworks. I briefly discuss this proposal of Kuhn's in Chapter 4, note 1.

be invoked in such justification. Given that the opposing claims retain their legitimacy, one also cannot simply avow the claims of one's own position oneself.

Here the political motive is at odds with the epistemological one, and if feminist approaches are to be based on truth and not simply on a dogmatic will to power, this divergence of truth and political concerns must be resolved.

One way to go here is to embrace relativism. Barbara Herrnstein Smith has offered a subtle account of relativism in which not "anything" would "go," because social conventions, our specific, socially given forms of justification, mandate some ways of reaching conclusions and not others.[16] The problem remains, however, that even if there are social constraints on knowledge claims, these are still not adequately *epistemological* constraints. They tell us what "we" allow ourselves to say, but this so far has no bearing on the truth of what we say, only on our conventions, even if, as Smith argues, all we have is our conventions. And, practically speaking, "we" are of course very divided, so we still have no means of establishing which criteria are the decisive ones.[17]

An alternative direction is to reject the idea that reasoning as such is gendered. While it is conceivable that feminist purposes would be served by such an approach, a great deal of productive work on the effects of gender-styled modes of inquiry would have to be abandoned. Perhaps more significant, the problems discussed above would remain unaffected in contexts like cross-cultural, historical, and racial comparison: and these contexts are central to feminism itself. As Alcoff and Potter note, "women, per se, do not exist. There exist upper-caste Indian little girls; older, heterosexual Latinas; and white, working-class lesbians."[18] The problem of incommensurability, and hence of ultimate circularity in justifying one's position, if it exists at all, is in many contexts common to all uses of rationality or to all truth-claiming discourses, even within a single culture.

---

[16] Barbara Herrnstein Smith, *Belief and Resistance: Dynamics of Contemporary Intellectual Controversy* (Cambridge, MA: Harvard University Press, 1997), 65, 54ff.

[17] For a critical discussion of "the disappearing 'we'" in connection with Richard Rorty, see Mark Kingwell, *A Civil Tongue: Justice, Dialogue and the Politics of Pluralism* (University Park: Pennsylvania State University Press, 1995), 36ff.

[18] Alcoff and Potter, *Feminist Epistemologies*, 4.

And even if we could find a way of showing that incommensurability ultimately does not exist, the equivalent problem would still exist for *practical* purposes. Many debates relevant to feminism are practically speaking irresolvable, given, for example, constraints on time and on willingness to engage reasonably or sympathetically with the opposing view. A familiar case would be debates between many pro- and antiabortion positions. The result is that even if genuine incommensurability does not exist, we would still need a way of negotiating conflicting truth claims each of which has some effectively incorrigible claim to justification.

Before investigating the notion of truth further, a sketch of antiepistemology will be helpful.

4. Antiepistemology

Richard Rorty has argued that epistemology is either an empty concept or a waste of time. The claim that it is an empty or meaningless (pseudo-) concept, having no substantive content, is really a sort of early approximation in his thought, and misleading in that it suggests that he could demonstrate something about a concept (its emptiness) once and for all, that is, that he can rely on a valid epistemology. In fact, his thinking later shifts to the claim that epistemology is simply not worth bothering with; there are more productive things to do. Nonetheless, I shall return to the claim of meaninglessness, which is still maintained by others, and is in any event helpful in its own right.

These rigorous rejections of epistemology supply the grounds for social epistemology, which without such grounds is not yet epistemology at all, for the reasons given above in connection with social conventions. Sandra Harding, again: such sociologies "implicitly assume as grounds for their own account precisely the epistemology they so effectively undermine."[19] As I argue after this section, however, the basic epistemological problems remain unless we find a way of coordinating traditional epistemology and antiepistemology, including in the latter social epistemology.

The later Rorty argues that epistemology is a waste of time because of the type of ultimate circularity I have discussed above. First, "the pragmatist [like Rorty] cannot justify . . . [our cultural] habits without circularity,

[19] Harding, "Is There a Feminist Method?," 24.

but then neither can the realist."[20] We cannot escape the limitations of our culture. And second, our criteria for establishing truth are interdependent with many other elements of our culture, including our language and our various conceptual networks. That is, in order to understand and make use of our truth criteria, we need to be part of a culture. "The only criterion we have for applying the word 'true' is justification, and justification is always relative to an audience."[21] It follows that any truth criteria that diverged from our own sufficiently to put them in real question would belong not simply to a different perspective but to an entirely different culture, with a language and conceptual "system" we could not understand. We are, then, restricted to what "people like us" say, and to pretend otherwise is just to spin our wheels making statements that have no purchase on anything we, in our culture and with our language and concepts, might mean by reality—or, simply, mean at all. Consequently there is no point in trying to ground—or criticize—our knowledge on ultimately justified criteria: we cannot get beyond what we happen to do and say. Any attempt to ground our knowledge ultimately depends circularly on what we happen to find ourselves doing or saying. Even "the pragmatist . . . cannot argue that [metaphysics] is inconsistent with a mass of our other beliefs. . . . All the pragmatist can do is . . . point to the seeming futility of metaphysical activity. . . . In the end we pragmatists have no real arguments against . . . [metaphysical] intuitions."[22] We have, in our culture, criteria for what, in our culture, we rightly call knowledge.[23] But these criteria are not ultimately justified (or unjustified); we simply learn them as part of becoming members of our society and its various subcultures.

Rorty argues earlier, however, for what is in one sense a more extreme position. As I discussed in Chapter 1, one of the resources he turns to here is the work of Donald Davidson, notably Davidson's paper "On the Very Idea of a Conceptual Scheme."[24] The partial (and extremely simplified)

---

[20] Richard Rorty, *Objectivity, Relativism, and Truth: Philosophical Papers, Volume 1* (New York: Cambridge University Press, 1991), 28–29, my insertions.

[21] Richard Rorty, *Truth and Progress: Philosophical Papers, Volume 3* (New York: Cambridge University Press, 1998), 4.

[22] Rorty, *Truth*, 42, my insertions.

[23] See, for example, Rorty, *Truth*, 73.

[24] Donald Davidson, "On the Very Idea of a Conceptual Scheme," in *Inquiries into Truth and Interpretation* (Oxford: Oxford University Press, 1984), 183–98.

gist of the argument is that if we cannot meaningfully speak of an alternative framework (or "conceptual scheme") to our own, we cannot meaningfully speak of our own framework either.[25] Talk of our own framework, which contrasts with no other framework, is just talk about how we are generally; it does not pick out any features of how we are. Since we cannot meaningfully speak of other frameworks, talk of our own framework does no work, identifies nothing, does not signify. In other words, the very idea of an ultimately or globally justifiable framework has no content. All there is, as Rorty's later argument also urged, is what we find ourselves doing and saying in particular circumstances. Consequently there is no content to the objection that what we do and say may be ultimately or globally flawed. While Rorty's later position might look like relativism, in this earlier version, as Rorty argues, there is nothing for our "framework" to be relative *to*,[26] and nothing we can speak of as a framework to be relative to anything.

It follows from this view, then, that epistemology is a mistaken enterprise, at least insofar as it asks foundational questions about the possibility of knowledge as such. Knowledge is an empirical or everyday matter, not a philosophical one. "The situation may be seen . . . as a matter of conditioning people . . . to hold certain sentences true under publicly observable conditions."[27] We have ways of getting knowledge that we have learned as members of our culture. What we need to do is to learn those ways, and they then give us whatever we might mean by knowledge. There are no further meaningful questions to be asked.

I turn now to an example of the kind of situation to which feminist and other marginalized epistemologies are sensitive, in order to illustrate the necessity for both the insights of the antiepistemological view and the conflicting insights of the pro-epistemological view.

5. An Example

Let us imagine a dialogue concerning contemporary feminists and women in earlier ages. If feminism itself depends on historical conditions (and it

---

[25] Ibid., 198.
[26] Rorty, *Objectivity*, 25–26.
[27] Davidson, "Empirical Content," 330.

must, if we take seriously the idea of the circularity and hence bias of all positions—including gendered bias, which goes both ways), we can ask whether it can make sense to say that men and women in earlier historical periods were sexist. One immediate response might be, perhaps we can say they were not sexist, whereas if we did the same things in our own historical period we would be. But, one might say, surely it makes no sense to say that men's dominating women is sexist now but was not so then? Surely it is the same act with the same parties?

A common response is that it is not in fact the same act with the same parties, since social structure constitutes both the parties and the acts as what they are, and in earlier periods both were differently constituted. But then, one might rejoin, what is the force of talking about "truth"? Everything, including *claims about* the social structure, becomes constructed or equally arbitrary. Diana Fuss notes (with the aim of arguing that social constructionism in fact depends on the idea of pregiven essences of things, and vice versa) that social constructionism avoids this by inconsistently treating "the social" as in effect an essence, as not itself constructed but as something simply given that explains everything else.[28] But if, as a consistent constructionism must take it, social structure constitutes everything, including claims about social structure, *no* socially intelligible claim is more justified than another, and in fact there is no substance to the notion of *justification* in this context at all. There is only how things happen to be constructed, and everything might as well be constructed arbitrarily one way as much as another. (This is a standard complaint against Foucault's reduction of everything to power, that he gives no reason to choose one form of power over another.)[29] This outcome leaves no principled or justice-bearing justification for feminism, even in justifying to *itself* that its claims are *true*.

---

[28] Diana Fuss, *Essentially Speaking: Feminism, Nature and Difference* (New York: Routledge, 1989), 6.

[29] Michael Walzer, for example, writes, "Foucault gives us no reason to expect that these [new power formations] will be any better than the ones we now live with. Nor, for that matter, does he give us any way of knowing what 'better' might mean." Michael Walzer, "The Politics of Michel Foucault," in *Foucault: A Critical Reader,* ed. David Couzens Hoy (Cambridge, MA: Basil Blackwell, 1986), 61, my insertion. As I discuss in Chapter 5, however, I do not believe that Foucault does reduce everything to power.

So we could try (and I urge the reader to bear with the following contradictions; I shall shortly try to show that they are not the end of the story): *then* it was not true to say that people were sexist in their consciousness and practice, but *now* it is true to say that even *then* it was true. In other words, truth as stated *in a particular context* remains coherently truth, remains universally constant, while that truth would be negated, equally universally and constantly, in a different context. Here the emphasis is on the constitution of truth by rhetorical context, the context of who is speaking to whom, and, considering relevant rhetorical features more broadly than my focus on the audience in Chapter 2, speaking when and for what purpose. A shift in rhetorical context would then involve a kind of dividing line on one side of which *everything* under discussion is one way and on the other side of which *everything* under discussion is another, incompatible way. This is a sort of line across which *the whole of truth* under discussion refracts, emerging differently.[30]

If this formulation achieves any sense at all (given arguments like Davidson's), it is of course self-contradictory. But before I address this contradiction, let me note something it does imply and something it does not imply. If any sense can be made of this kind of formulation—and it is my aim to show that a sense can be made of it—truth needs to be understood as a shifting (inconstant, fickle) terrain: now absolute, now relative, with, if anything, what Barbara Smith calls a "pidgin" status between.[31] The substance of relevant truth itself would shift depending on rhetorical context; logic and sense themselves would alter, in ways made determinate by

---

[30] Michael Williams has offered an approach to antiepistemology (or at least to restricting the limits within which epistemology is worthwhile) that goes some way toward the kind of formulation I am attempting. He argues, for example, that skeptical doubts are not meaningless but belong to a unique context, separate from that of our everyday concerns with knowledge, a context that we therefore need not take seriously in those everyday contexts. See, for example, Michael Williams, *Unnatural Doubts: Epistemological Realism and the Basis of Scepticism* (Princeton, NJ: Princeton University Press, 1996), e.g., 12. My own account differs by taking more seriously the problems of meaning across globally different contexts or frameworks, by proposing a mutual relevance of such mutually exclusive contexts, and by arguing for the value of the unrestricted scope of epistemological questioning for the contexts of our everyday concerns.

[31] Smith, *Belief and Resistance*, 68.

the specificity of the rhetorical contexts. And this set of formulations about truth is itself located within a specific rhetorical context. That is, there are also rhetorical contexts in which one is comparing *the rhetorical contexts* themselves, and the resulting formulations have their sense and truth only within those metacontexts. Assuming for the moment, then, that I can succeed in giving a sense to this role of rhetorical context, it would be right in some rhetorical contexts to say, for example, "those opposed to us are simply exclusively and absolutely wrong"; in other rhetorical contexts, "they are simply exclusively and absolutely right"; in others, "who is right is relative to the framework, or to the rhetorical context"; in others, "both parties are absolutely (exclusively) right"; and in others, "both parties are absolutely (exclusively) right *and* wrong."

If, again, these formulations can be given a sense at all, the contradictory alternatives are an artifact of the comparison between rhetorical contexts. That is *their* rhetorical context, a metarhetorical context, and necessarily requires a contradictory logic. But as I shall argue, the necessary contradictions are unique to this metacontext, and they *resolve* also as an artifact of shifting appropriately from this metacontext of comparison of rhetorical contexts. So these formulations do not imply that contradiction has free reign. Contradiction would occur only in metacontexts, and would lose its sense and relation to truth in any other contexts. That is, the role of contradiction here is limited by the very formulations that allow it.

It is worth noting that a description of such an account of truth would draw on a mixture of gender-evocative terms and evaluations. Truth becomes in one sense, as I have very briefly noted, fickle and inconstant; in another sense, truth is simply and stably what it is. More to the point, as will emerge below, its inconstancy is a condition of its constancy, and vice versa. Political oppositions become coordinations, in consequence of the coordination of epistemological oppositions, with interesting results for the gender-evocative presuppositions underlying the political debates.

6. *A Proposed Solution*

It is well known, if not necessarily formulated in this way, that rhetorical context alters the political force of an assertion or action. The political signification of a woman's opening a door for another woman is different from that of a man's doing so for a woman. A sexist statement in one context is a feminist, or at least a less significantly sexist, one in another. Political force, however, is not entirely independent of truth. That a statement has different political force entails that the statement means something different; and if it *truly* has different political force, then it states, at least to an extent, a different truth. So we have precisely the truth of the same statement being different in different rhetorical contexts. Conversely, conflicting statements can have the same or overlapping political force in different rhetorical contexts, with a related kind of result: what would be conflicting truths in the same context can bear the same truth in different contexts.

This opens up the possibility of conceiving truth, taken as the content of true statements, as something that varies (contradictorily) while remaining the same: the same content is conveyed, rightly, by a different content. One could object that the "same" content is in fact simply different in different contexts, since the contexts and not only the wording or significant actions constitute the content as what it is. But we can only state the content by stating the content: our very attempt to assert that the "same" content is different presupposes the same content. That is, the same contradictory variation of truth reemerges at the metalevel of any arguments we might make *about* it. We need, then, to conceive of truth-content as capable of being the same while being incompatibly different in the same respect at the same time. (On this issue of referring to the same thing in the contexts of incompatible conceptual structures, see also the quotation by Alasdair MacIntyre in section 4 of Chapter 1, and the discussions in the first sections of Chapters 8 and 9.)

I suggest that the idea of incommensurability, or what I shall also call truth incompatibility, allows such a conception. As I have noted, the idea of truth incompatibility or differences that affect truth itself is, at one contained level, self-contradictory. But let me stress that this does not immediately constitute grounds for rejecting it as senseless. My argument, like those of some feminist thinkers and, more generally, some postmodern thinkers, is partly that we need to conceive differently how sense itself can function (and I have offered some of the motivations for the need to do so). The different conception of sense I am about to propose therefore needs to be evaluated *before* the limitedly contradictory outcome can be validly rejected, and it needs to be evaluated *independently* of standard rejections of contradiction. To reject this outcome because of its elements of contradiction, before evaluating the different conception of sense on which it depends, and hence to reject it precisely on the basis of the global rejections of contradiction an alternative to which it seeks to explore is simply circular. One might be tempted to object that, if any contradiction is allowed, then no coherent evaluation of anything is possible.[32] But it is precisely this kind of conclusion that my proposed conception seeks to obviate. It is premature, then, to draw this conclusion right away.

As Rorty acknowledges, despite Davidsonian claims of meaninglessness, the argument for the sense of incommensurability is in fact still a possibility. Let me add to Rorty's general doubts about ultimately conclusive justifications of our claims that incommensurability is still arguably meaningful despite Davidson's arguments precisely because the lines of thought for and against the idea of incommensurability are themselves arguably incommensurable. That is, the argument against incommensurability depends on a decision about whether its own grounds are incommensurable with the opposing line of thought or not. In other words, it presupposes that it is arguing effectively with the other position, that it really is dealing with the same conception of the issues. And of course that decision presupposes the conclusion circularly. The argument against the sense of incommensurability, then, is far from conclusive.

Further, as I have mentioned, one of the central arguments against the sense of incommensurability is that, if such a thing applied, the parties involved would not even be able to understand each other. There would be nothing intelligible to have a disagreement about. And part of my own proposal depends on the kind of radical lack of content of incommensurable positions for each other that leads to that antiepistemological argument. But, as I discussed in Chapter 1, while our language would not allow us to grasp the other's language, we could presumably learn that other language as we first learned our own. Language cannot depend on the possibility of translation, otherwise we could not account for our learning a first language in the first place. Rorty himself has noted (although with

---

[32] This is part of a standard argument against the legitimacy of violations of the principle of noncontradiction. In the context of formal logic the argument is that anything at all follows from a contradiction: if one allows a contradiction, one can then say anything about anything. Again, however, on the possibility of legitimate logical contradiction, see the Introduction, section 5.

the aim of undermining the kind of point that is part of my own here) that "untranslatability does not entail unlearnability."[33] We can, then, learn to speak more than one language, each with its web of concepts and value commitments, and none of these languages and conceptual webs needs make sense in terms of the others.

These preliminary responses to antiepistemology do not remove the deeper contradiction of saying that truth itself (for example, truth about the same things in the same respect) is differently constituted in different positions or frameworks or contexts. They only suggest that the objections to the sense of incommensurability are so far inconclusive, and that *if* a sense can be made of the deeper contradiction it will not imply some of the self-refuting consequences that are often drawn in objection to it. I now turn to addressing the deeper contradiction.

My proposed solution is that, if we think of truth-affecting differences in rhetorical context as incommensurabilities of position or grounds, we can establish a way of making (a certain kind) of sense of juxtaposing epistemological with antiepistemological views. This in turn allows us to preserve the crucial insights of both. (Again, that these formulations are so far contradictory is not yet grounds for rejecting them. If such grounds emerge, they will do so legitimately—noncircularly—only in consequence of the following exploration of how sense might conceivably function, on which the sense of these formulations depends.) The guiding type of difference here is that between contexts in which truth-affecting differences are relevant and those in which they are not relevant at all. Where the disagreeing sides share relevant common grounds—and this of course is only established in the course of dialogue, not given in advance—truth-affecting differences do not occur. And here, as I shall try to show and as the antiepistemologists argue, we need no epistemology. But where there are no *relevant* common grounds—that is, grounds or criteria for truth, as opposed to common ground in many other respects, which may allow, for example, mutual understanding—epistemological issues become relevant.

A first advantage of conceiving things in this way is that deep epistemological issues *simply do not exist* for common-grounds situations. As Rorty argues, in talking with those "like us" (in this limited respect of sharing grounds for truth), we need have no doubts about the legitimacy of our

---

[33] Rorty, *Objectivity*, 48.

criteria for our claims, all else being equal, that is, if we meet our standards for responsible conclusions. No such deep *epistemological* doubts are relevant within the context of the discussion. As Davidson argues, in this context one cannot even speak meaningfully about one's own position *as a position*, and so no questions can arise about its ultimate grounds.

Second, in talking with those not "like us" in this sense, deep epistemological issues such as ultimate circularity and infinite regress are fully relevant. But the moment they become relevant, they also lose content, because the lack of common grounds for truth that makes them relevant also describes incommensurability of positions. As the antiepistemologists argue, incommensurability, or its practical equivalents I discussed above, entails that the claims and criteria of the other position are meaningless for or irrelevant to one's own (whichever one's own happens to be). But, again, the very ideas of issues like ultimate circularity and infinite regress depend on the perspective, claims, and criteria of the other position. Questions about the legitimacy of a position as a whole that produce ultimate circularity and regress cannot meaningfully come from within the position, since it can only be identified as a whole from the outside, that is, from the perspective of a contrasting position. Further, as Davidson argues, without the contrast of another position a position cannot meaningfully exist for itself in the first place as a whole position to be ultimately justified, and so as subject to these ultimate problems of justification. Since, however, this contrasting position is incommensurable with one's own, the same contrast of whole position that allows it to raise these issues also makes both the contrast and those issues meaningless for one's own position. If the reader will again bear with my apparent illogic for a moment, this means that the epistemological issues are consequently not a problem, since the very ideas of issues like ultimate circularity and infinite regress lose content the moment they become applicable. I discuss in a moment why it is an advantage that epistemological issues appear if it is also the case that they simultaneously disappear, but first I want to show—at last—why this self-contradictory statement is not simply an absurdity.

What makes this apparent illogic workable is conceiving it itself within the grid of incommensurable or truth-incompatible positions, taking these temporarily to be meaningful. (We have some grounds for at least allowing the possibility of their being meaningful; the outcome of exploring this possibility, I suggest, will resituate the objections to it in a way that strengthens those grounds. The meaningfulness of incommensurable positions here will then turn out to be not only a temporary heuristic device, but sometimes, though only sometimes, always true.)[34] We can, I suggest, apply this grid to the conflicting grounds for asserting the sense of incommensurability versus asserting its nonexistence themselves. I have already started to do this above in discussing the self-reference of this debate about incommensurability, its circular dependence on the decision it aims to support. And if we do apply this grid to this debate itself, there is a sense to speaking as I have both of the content of statements about a deeply different position and of the emptiness of content of such statements. In other words, first, we can view the very same phenomenon—the same assertions about the relation of deeply different positions—simultaneously both from the metaposition (with the web of concepts and meanings of that metaposition) that these assertions have content, on one side of the grid, and from the metaposition (with its different web of concepts and meanings) that they do not, on the other side of the grid. I argued in Chapter 1 (section 4) for the general legitimacy of basing our thinking on the starting point of two or more simultaneous incommensurable positions in this way. I argued there that this kind of basis and its resulting coordination of incompatible ways of making sense is at least as well founded as basing our thinking on the starting point of the single constellation of modes of sense we already inhabit and the "consistency only" logic that follows from that starting point. Second, this idea of the possibility of incommensurable positions itself makes room for a position incommensurable with it, the position that there are no incommensurable positions. In other words, the contradiction-producing position that there are incommensurable positions itself makes room for the position that it is not legitimate. It asserts itself, but it also makes a space for the legitimacy of not having to consider it at all. The apparent illogic of saying that the fundamental epistemological problems lose all content the moment they appear with content is not, then, unmanageable, though it puts very different constraints and freedoms on logic from those we are traditionally used to.

---

[34] I thank Jeffrey Ruff for drawing my attention to the way my own discussion's participation in the process of shifting meanings that it describes becomes clearly and (I hope) helpfully identifiable here. I also appreciate his help in improving the formulation of this and other passages in the book.

Again, we are not, at this point, occupying a particular position, but occupying more than one simultaneously. The epistemological problems arise for a position as we take into account the metaposition from which incommensurability is conceivable, and that *very same* metaposition entails that the claims and criteria of the contrasting position (since it is incommensurable with the first) are contentless for the first position: the problems disappear. As a result, one has returned to the rhetorical context of a single common-grounds position. At that moment, however, one has shifted on to the side of the grid for which incommensurable positions have no meaning. Consequently, even that metagrid itself of juxtaposed and simultaneous incommensurable positions no longer has bearing. The self-contradiction that results from the conception of incommensurability is then simply a self-contradiction, an incoherence that there is no reason to entertain, that is no longer given even the type of sense allowed by the grid. We can no longer speak with any kind of sense of truth-incompatible positions, and antiepistemology applies simply exclusively again. The specific kind of self-contradiction, then, that the conception of simultaneous incommensurable positions involves itself also produces the resolution of that problem.

In Chapter 8, I map out and explain the sense of the detailed process of these shifts of meaning and meaninglessness, there in the context of the structure of pluralist metaphysics.

I return now to the proposed advantage that deep epistemological issues become relevant in contexts where incommensurability of truth criteria is relevant, and *only* become relevant in such contexts, although they then also simultaneously vanish. Part of the advantage is that, as I have argued, the recalcitrant problems that mainstream epistemologies have been unable to resolve find a solution. As I have noted, they arise *as epistemological problems*, as we take into account the metaposition from which incommensurability is conceivable, and then they disappear, as that very conception of incommensurability entails their contentlessness. (Again, as Davidson argues, in this context even one's own position cannot be meaningfully considered *as a position*, and consequently there are no questions to be asked about its ultimate grounds.) That is, they do not simply fail to arise as epistemological problems at all, but they *emerge* and because of the context of that emergence they *also* disappear. Given that process, it is not the case that they were simply falsely understood to arise as conceivable problems, with the result that there is nothing for epistemology to do, but they are *formerly unresolved epistemological problems* for which *a solution has now been established*.

But another part of the advantage is that, in the process of exploring the epistemological issues (which of course will turn out to be contentless or, in a different rhetorical phase, simply senselessly self-contradictory), we establish in concrete ways, *for both or more sides*, the equivalent epistemological justification of *each* (or, in a different rhetorical phase, the equivalent lack of content of the requirement for such justification). This outcome must then transform the nature of the debate. First, we have established a framework within which we can account for the possibility of each side's coming to understand the other, despite the immediate senselessness of each side's claims for the other. Second, and consequently, each side is in a position to present its own justifications to the other(s) despite the barrier of immediate senselessness to the other—and, as important, to recognize that the other side may have justification despite the barrier of *its* immediate senselessness. Each side must, by the very principles by which it justifies itself or by which it legitimately rejects the need for such justification, recognize the equivalent status of the other side, and require the other side to do the same. Each side must then, by its own standards—to which the other sides can appeal—recognize the legitimacy of the other positions' conflicting claims, and, again, require the same of the other positions. Each is then required to learn to think in the terms of the other positions *simultaneously with its own*, and to find ways of negotiating that are not dependent on denying the truth either of the opposing claims or of its own, except where those claims are in conflict with the epistemological standards of the position from which they are made.

The political result is a kind of honoring of one's enemy without reducing the force and urgency of the conflict. Where all conflicting parties are doing this, I suggest that a lot of irresolvable debate would be obviated, and a very different type of dialogue, with hopes for surprising and constructive outcomes, made possible.

The rhetoric or language of "rhetorical positions," *as having purchase on the structure or constitution of truth*, itself only has content in rhetorical contexts in which truth-incompatible positions are at issue. The present account itself, then, loses content, becomes literally meaningless, in contexts in which truth incompatibility is rhetorically irrelevant.

As I have discussed above, there are many situations in which rhetorical context affects the truth of assertions. It follows that there are many, often quite ordinary situations in which incommensurability of grounds obtains. This may go some way to explain why sexists and feminists are so tragically divided from each other and among themselves, beyond mere disagreement, in ways that cut both sides to the existential quick. And it suggests that the kind of problem that this chapter tries to address has consequences well beyond engagements with epistemology as such.

4.   *The Logic of Genuine Political Pluralism and Oscar Wilde's Artificiality of Wit and Style*

I shall try to show in this chapter that Oscar Wilde's artificiality of wit and style exemplifies both the logic and method of genuine political pluralism, and that it does so in an unusually consistent and illuminating way. (His work is also pluralist in more wide-ranging ways, but here I want to focus on its political side. I focus on his metaphysical pluralism, for example, in Chapter 8.)

As I discuss, the well-known current approaches to political pluralism stop short of genuine pluralism in two ways. One kind of approach recognizes genuinely different standpoints: standpoints that are irreducible to each other, and so mutually exclusive of each other. But because mutually exclusive standpoints mean different things by the "same" concepts, these approaches disallow rational debate, or even coherent relations, between them.[1] (On the possibility of mutually exclusive standpoints' referring to

---

[1] See, for example, Alasdair C. MacIntyre, *Whose Justice? Which Rationality?* (Notre Dame, IN: University of Notre Dame Press, 1988); Charles Taylor, *Philosophical Papers, Volume 2: Philosophy and the Human Sciences* (Cambridge: Cambridge University Press, 1985), chapters 3–5. For a well-known version of this view of mutually exclusive standpoints in science, see Thomas S. Kuhn, *The Structure of Scientific Revolutions,* 2nd ed. (Chicago: University of Chicago Press, 1970). Kuhn argues that rational decision between incommensurable scientific frameworks is possible on the basis of criteria such as simplicity, accuracy, and breadth of applicability. In his later work, he acknowledges that any such criteria would themselves often mean something different in the different frameworks under discussion, but he argues that the shift to a new framework takes place incrementally over time, and that the rationality "of the conclusions requires only that the observations invoked be neutral for, or shared by, the members of the group making the decision, and . . . only at the time the decision is being made." At that time, he argues, only a small proportion of the relevant beliefs

the same things at all, so that there is genuine conflict to resolve, see the quotation by Alasdair MacIntyre in section 4 of Chapter 1, and the discussions in section 6 of Chapter 3 and in the first sections of Chapters 8 and 9.) These approaches have consequently been criticized for leaving us without a coherent way of thinking in terms of more than one standpoint at a time,[2] and so without *pluralism*. The other kind of approach allows different standpoints to be related to each other, but does so on the basis of shared principles, and so eliminates their mutual exclusivity, their genuine difference. This again eliminates genuine pluralism.

Both results are consequences of taking for granted the unrestricted and exclusive validity of classical noncontradictory logic and ideas of consistency, for which it is impossible to combine both mutual exclusivity of standpoints and a coherent relation between the standpoints.[3] But, as I shall try to show, in the context of pluralism classical consistency itself requires certain kinds of contradiction. And I shall argue that Wilde's artificiality of style and wit works with a recognition of this further developed understanding of consistency or logic, and as a result allows mutually exclusive positions to be related without obscuring their mutual exclusivity.

Specifically, I shall argue that Wilde's artificiality, without ceasing to be frivolous (in fact, *through* the way in which it *is* frivolous), presents the

---

and meanings is altered and made incommensurable by the ongoing shift to a new framework. Thomas S. Kuhn, *The Road Since Structure: Philosophical Essays, 1970–1993, with an Autobiographical Interview*, ed. James Conant and John Haugeland (Chicago: University of Chicago Press, 2000), 112–15. This seems to overlook, however, that ultimately the new framework will have developed sufficiently to pose the decision problem between the two frameworks each more or less as a whole, and so with each now covering and making incommensurable all or most of the relevant beliefs and meanings.

[2] As I discussed in Chapter 1, Davidson and Rorty criticize them for mistakenly thinking that we could have thought in terms of more than one fundamentally different standpoint in the first place, and so for misleading us into thinking in terms of this kind of pluralism at all. See, for example, Donald Davidson, "On the Very Idea of a Conceptual Scheme," in *Inquiries into Truth and Interpretation* (Oxford: Oxford University Press, 1984), 183–98; Richard Rorty, *Objectivity, Relativism, and Truth: Philosophical Papers, Volume 1* (New York: Cambridge University Press, 1991), 25ff., 215–16.

[3] For an account of some alternative, nonclassical logics, see Graham Priest, *An Introduction to Non-Classical Logic* (Cambridge: Cambridge University Press, 2001). On the possibility of legitimate logical contradiction, see again the Introduction, section 5.

very serious and unartificial possibility of things' being *essentially otherwise* than they are understood to be in any given standpoint. I shall characterize his aesthetic impact or import as a fresh opening of essential or constitutive or ontological spaces or standpoints. In light of the use of the word "oppressive" in phrases like "an oppressive atmosphere," his opening of constitutive spaces is a social and political intervention. I argue further, however, that this opening of spaces is thoroughly self-canceling, and so is *also* a validation of essential spaces exactly as they are. This validation involves self-canceling recognition of *mutually exclusive* "spaces."

In the following sections I first discuss some of the current approaches to political pluralism. I then develop, with reference to Wilde's work, a preparatory theoretical context for discussing his own approach. In the next section I present his pluralism in the light of that context. Finally, I discuss Wilde's idea of art in connection with the logic of his pluralism.

1. Current Approaches to Political Pluralism

There are several well-developed current approaches to political pluralism. I cannot begin to do justice here to the thoughtfulness that has gone into these approaches, but the following sketches will be sufficient to show the contrast with Wilde's approach. In fact, as it will turn out, Wilde introduces directions of thought that the current approaches do not consider, so that these approaches can only be properly evaluated, in this context, after Wilde's view has become clear. But a brief initial contrast will be helpful.

One approach, political liberalism, perhaps most prominently represented by John Rawls, argues that while it is historically clear that we cannot agree on substantive ideas of the ultimate good that should guide our lives, all of us can recognize that we cannot avoid living with each other and our inescapable ideas of the good. Given that we are stuck with living with each other, we need to try to do so in a way that allows us to live satisfying lives. Consequently we need to leave ideas of the ultimate good to the private sphere, while establishing public rights that will allow us each to pursue our goods within the constraints of living together productively.[4]

---

[4] See John Rawls, *Political Liberalism* (New York: Columbia University Press, 1993); idem, *A Theory of Justice* (Cambridge, MA: Belknap Press of Harvard University Press, 1999).

Political liberalism, however, has been criticized on the grounds that our ideas of the ultimate good cannot be sealed off so neatly from our views of appropriate rights and modes of living together, so that there is no neutral procedure, independent of ideas of the ultimate good, by which to decide rights.[5] In fact, it has been argued that political liberalism's stance of tolerating the private good itself is just a particular view of the good masquerading as a neutral position.[6] As Chantal Mouffe notes, Rawls's key "distinction between 'reasonable' and 'unreasonable,'" for example, is defined from a liberal standpoint in the first place, and so "helps to draw a frontier between the doctrines that accept the liberal principles and the ones that oppose them."[7] Political liberalism, then, while it allows debate between standpoints, does not really recognize the validity of genuinely different standpoints, but instead ultimately recognizes only one kind of rationality and so only one ultimate standpoint.

Another approach to pluralism is that of communitarianism, represented by, for example, Alasdair MacIntyre, Charles Taylor, and Michael Walzer.[8] Here the idea is that rationality—or sensemaking, including political sensemaking—is itself necessarily a product of cultural norms, not of abstract, potentially universal principles. As a result, there are different rationalities, and we need to find ways of deciding between them without relying on nonexistent shared principles and procedures of making sense and coming to conclusions. MacIntyre's proposal, for example, is that each tradition can be stimulated by others to criticize itself, by its own

[5] See, for example, Mark Kingwell, *A Civil Tongue: Justice, Dialogue, and the Politics of Pluralism* (University Park: Pennsylvania State University Press, 1995), 51ff.; Chantal Mouffe, *The Democratic Paradox* (New York: Verso, 2000), 22ff.; Georgia Warnke, *Justice and Interpretation* (Cambridge, MA: MIT Press, 1992), 2ff., 57ff.

[6] Kingwell, *Civil Tongue*, 73–74; Mouffe, *Democratic Paradox*, 24–26.

[7] Mouffe, *Democratic Paradox*, 24. Commenting on Rawls's statement that reasonable people "have realized their two moral powers to a degree sufficient to be free and equal citizens in a constitutional regime, and . . . have an enduring desire to honor fair terms of cooperation and to be fully cooperating members of society" (*Political Liberalism*, 5), Mouffe writes, "What is this if not an indirect form of asserting that reasonable persons are those who accept the fundamentals of liberalism?" (24), rather than, say, people who recognize the inescapable antagonisms belonging to any society.

[8] For instance, MacIntyre, *Whose Justice?*; Taylor, *Philosophical Papers*; Michael Walzer, *Spheres of Justice* (New York: Basic Books, 1983).

standards of rationality. Communitarianism too, however, has been criticized, on the grounds that, while it properly respects the plurality of standpoints, it gives no realistic means of allowing them to negotiate with other: rethinking one's entire tradition, for example, is at best enormously cumbersome, and in many or perhaps most cases need not lead to self-critical or even self-moderating results in its comparison of one's own tradition with others. Consequently, communitarianism can be unself-critically, brutally exclusive.[9] Communitarianism, then, while it recognizes genuinely different standpoints, allows little or no rational debate or decision making between them. What is more, as I suggested above, for the same reasons it gives us no way of thinking coherently in terms of more than one of them at a time, and so in fact does not allow us to conceive of a plurality of genuinely different standpoints.

A third approach is the more radical one of Ernesto Laclau and Chantal Mouffe, who take a step in the direction of the developed understanding of consistency that I believe Wilde exemplifies. Laclau and Mouffe, drawing on Marx, Lacanian psychoanalysis, and Derridean deconstruction, argue that "it is never possible for individual rights to be defined in isolation, but only in the context of social relations which define determinate subject positions."[10] That is, each person's rights and even her or his individuality itself are constituted in relation to all the other positions that make up the person's social context. Accordingly, any one position's nature, and therefore its rights, can only be established by *first* taking into account the other positions in the society. Laclau and Mouffe argue, therefore, for a "plural democracy."[11] But because each standpoint is defined in the context of the others, there is no independent, neutral standpoint that can serve as the pregiven foundation by which to assess the rationality of the others. What this plural democracy involves, then, is

> no longer a case of *foundations* of the social order, but of *social logics*, which intervene to different degrees in the constitution of every social identity, and which partially limit their mutual effects. From this we can deduce a

---

[9] Kingwell, *Civil Tongue*, 42, 120ff.; Warnke, *Justice and Interpretation*, 20ff.

[10] Ernesto Laclau and Chantal Mouffe, *Hegemony and Socialist Strategy: Towards a Radical Democratic Politics,* trans. Winston Moore and Paul Cammack (London: Verso, 1985), 84.

[11] Ibid., 184.

basic precondition for a radically libertarian conception of politics: the refusal to dominate—intellectually or politically—every presumed "ultimate foundation" of the social. Every conception which seeks to base itself on a knowledge of this foundation finds itself faced, sooner or later, with the Rousseauian paradox according to which men should be obliged to be free.[12]

And they point out that each kind of political struggle—homosexual, feminist, ethnic, workers', for example—"retains its differential specificity with respect to the others."[13]

But, on the other hand, they argue, if we take the differences, the mutual exclusivity, of standpoints as a foundation, we are really still thinking in terms of another kind of common ground: a single identifiable universal community of *differences*, each standpoint equally valued for its special particularity, so that we really have a shared standard of value (for example, the specialness of difference) as a common basis for our community as a whole. In this way we eliminate pluralism again:

> If each struggle transforms the moment of its specificity into an absolute principle of identity, the set of these struggles can only be conceived of as an *absolute system of differences*, and this system can only be thought as a closed totality. That is to say, the transparency of the social has simply been transferred from the uniqueness and intelligibility of a system of equivalences to the uniqueness and intelligibility of a system of differences. But in both cases we are dealing with discourses which seek, through their categories, to dominate the social as a *totality*. In both cases, therefore, the moment of totality ceases to be a *horizon* and becomes a *foundation*.[14]

Laclau and Mouffe are concerned, then, to allow for genuine pluralism, not by finding common ground but by taking the *absence* of common ground as a basis for the solution:

> Discursive *discontinuity* becomes primary and constitutive. The discourse of radical democracy is no longer the discourse of the universal; the

---

[12] Ibid., 183.
[13] Ibid., 182.
[14] Ibid., 182–83.

epistemological niche from which "universal" classes and subjects spoke has been eradicated, and it has been replaced by a polyphony of voices, each of which constructs its own irreducible discursive identity. This point is decisive: there is no radical and plural democracy without renouncing the discourse of the universal and its implicit assumption of a privileged point of access to "the truth," which can be reached only by a limited number of subjects.[15]

The step they do not take, however, and that I shall argue Wilde does, is to take into account the implications of this conception for its *own* statements. As Laclau and Mouffe themselves argue, the ways in which fundamentally, logically different positions understand themselves are at least in some respects meaningless to each other. Genuinely different standpoints ultimately do not share their basic meanings and sense of what is rational. Consequently, if one is to take genuinely different positions rigorously into account, without deciding between them on the basis of a neutral foundational position, one has to grant the validity of positions for which *this pluralist conception* itself is *meaningless*. Otherwise, it makes its own meanings the foundations for the thought of all standpoints. Precisely such a pluralist conception, then, must make spaces for positions in which totalities and universals are valid terms. This is required for the aim of positions *like* Laclau and Mouffe's, as well as supporting the standpoints opposed to theirs. As I noted in the first section of the Introduction, this problem is increasingly recognized by postmodern theorists. By not making room for nonpluralist positions, then, Laclau and Mouffe make pluralism itself the universal standpoint, and so once again eliminate genuine pluralism.

Mouffe's later work does note the dimension of paradox required for a properly democratic politics, in that we need both to aim at a cooperative, unified community overall and also to recognize the inescapability of irreconcilable differences within any community.[16] But she still does not apply her reflections to limiting the scope of her own standpoint as only one among others, with the result that, as she insists, the paradox is in no way resolvable.[17]

---

[15] Ibid., 191–92.
[16] Mouffe, *Paradox*, 56.
[17] Ibid., 16.

There exists a variety of further current approaches to political pluralism, but these either suffer from the same problem of undermining pluralism by advocating it in a universal way or else set an explicit limit to pluralism. James Tully, for example, shares the self-undermining problem. He insists that in the end, a just political constitution is "not grasped by a comprehensive representation," and that "there is not one . . . narrative that gives . . . unity, but a diversity of criss-crossing and contested narratives."[18] Analogously, though in a way that is closer to the more subtle account of Laclau and Mouffe, Jean-Luc Nancy argues for a "regime" that excludes the kind of "universality and . . . totality" that commitment to the principle of noncontradiction produces. This is the case even though he also insists that, not sharing the commitment to the principle of noncontradiction, this dispensation does not contradict that principle and so "the two regimes do not exclude one another." This is a dispensation that never forms "into the substance or higher power of a Whole"; we "understand only that there is no common understanding of community."[19] While William Corlett, among others, does argue for a place for exclusive and definitive standpoints in postmodern politics, these are always only provisional: again, "nothing 'adds up' and never did."[20] Similarly, Peter McLaren argues for a political conception of totality that is always only provisional.[21]

Among those pluralists who set explicit limits to pluralism is Charles Larmore, who argues that it is rationally neutral and common to all rational parties to recognize the need for all citizen groups of a state to live together peacefully.[22] Another is William Connolly, who insists, for example,

---

[18] James Tully, *Strange Multiplicity: Constitutionalism in an Age of Diversity* (Cambridge: Cambridge University Press, 1995), 183.

[19] Jean-Luc Nancy, *The Inoperative Community,* trans. Peter Connor, Lisa Garbus, Michael Holland, and Simona Sawhney (Minneapolis: University of Minnesota Press, 1991), 87, 89, 76, 69. See also the similar view of Maurice Blanchot, *The Unavowable Community,* trans. Pierre Joris (Barrytown, NY: Station Hill Press, 1988).

[20] William Corlett, *Community without Unity: A Politics of Derridian Extravagance* (Durham, NC: Duke University Press, 1989), 161.

[21] Peter McLaren, *Critical Pedagogy and Predatory Culture: Oppositional Politics in a Postmodern Era* (New York: Routledge, 1995), esp. 215ff.

[22] Charles E. Larmore, *Patterns of Moral Complexity* (New York: Cambridge University Press, 1987), chapters 3–5.

that for pluralists "it is extremely important . . . *how* people of diverse faiths hold and express their faiths in public space. . . . *Expansive pluralism supports the dissemination of general virtues across diverse faiths.*"[23] But to set these kinds of limit seems arbitrary in light of the possibility of deeply different, legitimate standpoints for which these limiting principles may not be justified, or may mean very different things from what they mean in these theorists' frameworks. It is certainly possible to argue thoughtfully against the idea that there could be such standpoints—in fact, I am about to argue, as I have done in previous chapters, for the sense and appropriateness of sometimes doing exactly that. But as I also argue here and elsewhere in the book, it is at least extremely difficult to do so without *also* fully acknowledging (contradictorily) the possibility of legitimate, deeply different standpoints. And this these approaches do not do. When deeply different standpoints are relevant, then, the approaches that set these limits in these ways are not engaging in rational politics but arbitrarily imposing their beliefs and values on others.

I turn now to the way in which Wilde's artificiality successfully relates mutually exclusive standpoints while respecting their mutual exclusivity.

2. Preparatory Ideas: Wilde's Concern with Constitutive Change and Difference

It will be helpful to begin by looking at how difference needs to be conceived in the context of radical or constitutive change from a current standpoint or set of circumstances.

A position that aims at constitutive change, change in the very nature of the things it deals with, aims to produce a position whose "natures" or meanings are incompatible with the ones it starts with, unthinkable in its own initial terms. That is, a position that aims for constitutive change aims to remove the conditions that make it meaningful. As Wilde writes in *The Soul of Man under Socialism*:

> It will, of course, be said that such a scheme as is set forth here is quite unpractical, and goes against human nature. This is perfectly true. It is unpractical, and it goes against human nature. This is why it is worth

---

[23] William Connolly, *Pluralism* (Durham, NC: Duke University Press, 2005), 48.

carrying out, and that is why one proposes it. For what is a practical scheme? A practical scheme is either a scheme that is already in existence, or a scheme that could be carried out under existing conditions. But it is exactly the existing conditions that one objects to; and any scheme that could accept these conditions is wrong and foolish. The conditions will be done away with, and human nature will change.[24]

A position that aims at constitutive change, in other words, aims to cancel itself. If it is to understand itself and present itself accurately, it must therefore take into account the self-cancellation of its own meanings. That is, it must take into account the meanings, incompatible with its own, of the aimed-at position it establishes in canceling itself.

But, since this self-cancellation is still to be achieved, the intervening position, the position that aims at change, must *also* be considered in the context of its *own* meanings, since these are still the meanings that constitute it. Now, as I have just argued, the position at which it aims is unthinkable in terms of these meanings. That is, while it remains true that the intervening position must take into account the meanings of the aimed-at standpoint, it is also true that the intervening position must be considered *entirely* on its own, without reference to its self-cancellation in favor of the other position. In other words, it must (also) be considered dogmatically. It rightly does not take into account, whether to criticize or justify itself, the terms of the position it is specifically opposed to, the position at which it aims in canceling itself.

Let me stress that in this context the meanings of the aimed-at position are *correctly* registered as not really being meaningful. That is, they are correctly registered as artificial, imaginary, unreal, trivial, frivolous, or superficial. The constitutively intervening position must rightly operate as dogmatically and closed-mindedly with respect to the position it aims at, as the most dogmatic of positions that refuse change or recognition of constitutive difference.

The intervening position, then, must *both* ignore the meanings of the aimed-at position in the context of the assumptions that make them real-

---

[24] Oscar Wilde, *The Soul of Man under Socialism*, in *Complete Works of Oscar Wilde*, ed. Vyvyan Holland (London: Collins, 1966), 1100. All further references to and citations of Wilde in this chapter are from the *Complete Works*.

istic *and also*, because it aims to cancel itself in their favor and establish them, take those same meanings into account.

In other words, accusations that thinking about fundamental social and political change is indulging in fairy tales are quite right. And what is more, thinking that aims at this kind of change is *itself* rigorous only when it also recognizes the truth of this description. But while this description is right, and excludes a description of profoundly interventive thinking as realistic, it does not *simply* exclude it. It is only one of two mutually exclusive, correct descriptions. And as I have just argued about mutually exclusive standpoints in general, they are meaningless in each other's terms. Consequently *each* of these descriptions is, paradoxically, the *exclusively correct* description.

While this formulation violates classical logic, it is a consequence of thinking out the nature of constitutive difference in standpoints by the principles of that same logic. That is, it is a violation required by classical logic itself. This is, in other words, one of the logical paradoxes that classical logic itself is well known to produce.[25]

If this is formulation is accurate, it shows that the paradoxical combination of mutually exclusive standpoints, without eliminating their mutual exclusivity, is sometimes logically required. It should help, then, to make sense of and redirect the focus of negotiation in a lot of otherwise apparently interminable contemporary political debates. Mutually exclusive standpoints can each be right while still also mutually excluding each other's being right.

Given the shifts that this formulation expresses between the reality and unreality of genuinely different standpoints in relation to each other, it should also help to show the direct relevance of nonrealistic artistic fantasy and sensibility to realistic pluralist political theory and practice.[26] As Wilde expresses the coordination of these incompatibles in *The Picture of Dorian Gray*:

---

[25] On the validity of these paradoxes, see, for example, R. M. Sainsbury, *Paradoxes,* 2nd ed. (Cambridge: Cambridge University Press, 1995), chapter 6.

[26] There is a long-standing current of Marxist and neo-Marxist thought, for example, that finds dimensions of truth in areas that are also furthest removed from sober concern with truth. Ernst Bloch, for instance, is a rigorous neo-Marxist who also emphasizes daydreams, fairy tales and folktales, wishes, and fantasy. See Ernst Bloch, *The Utopian Function of Art and Literature: Selected Essays,* trans. Jack Zipes and Frank Mecklenburg (Cambridge, MA: MIT Press, 1988). My proposal is that the principle of Wilde's thought and style offers a rigorous justification of this kind of combination.

But perhaps it had been only his fancy that had called vengeance out of the night, and set the hideous shapes of punishment before him. Actual life was chaos, but there was something terribly logical in the imagination. It was the imagination that set remorse to dog the feet of sin. It was the imagination that made each crime bear its misshapen brood. In the common world of fact the wicked were not punished, nor the good rewarded. (151)

Wilde makes room for incompatible standpoints and commitments in general in both his critical works and his purely fictional ones. He does so in both content and style. The dialogue "The Critic as Artist," for example, repeatedly diverts itself to lines of thought explicitly unrelated to and incompatible with what has just been very persuasively said. At one point, Gilbert disagrees with Ernest:

But I don't wish to destroy the delightfully unreal picture that you have drawn of the relation of the Hellenic artist to the intellectual spirit of his age. To give an accurate description of what has never occurred is not merely the proper occupation of the historian, but the inalienable privilege of any man of parts and culture. Still less do I desire to talk learnedly. . . . No; let me play to you some mad scarlet thing by Dvorak. (1015)

Later, he breaks off another argument (his own) with "But I see that the moon is hiding behind a sulphur-coloured cloud. . . . I am tired of my expedition into the dim, dull abyss of facts. There is nothing left for me now but the divine μονόκρονος ἡδονή [momentary pleasure] of another cigarette. Cigarettes have at least the charm of leaving one unsatisfied" (1019, insertion added). Then again, having proved his point with a wealth of historical evidence, he twists out of the binding backing of his own proof: "But, to get rid of the details of history, which are always wearisome and usually inaccurate, let us say generally, that the forms of art have been due to the Greek critical spirit" (1021). The art of the "critic as artist" makes room for constitutively alternative spaces at least to this extent.

Wilde's wit is often taken to express absurd, unmotivated divergences from sensible life, with no rational relation to the standpoints he addresses. But I suggest that it is instead characterized by both the logic and the humanity of making spaces for human possibilities. In *The Picture of Dorian Gray*, for example, he writes:

> As he looked back upon man moving through History, he was haunted by a feeling of loss. So much had been surrendered! And to such little purpose! There had been mad wilful rejections, monstrous forms of self-torture and self-denial, whose origin was fear, and whose result was a degradation infinitely more terrible than that fancied degradation from which, in their ignorance, they had sought to escape. . . .
>
> Yes: there was to be, as Lord Henry had prophesied, a new Hedonism that was to recreate life, and to save it from that harsh, uncomely puritanism that is having, in our own day, its curious revival. (104)

For

> it appeared to Dorian that the true nature of the senses had never been understood, and that they had remained savage and animal merely because the world had sought to starve them into submission or to kill them by pain, instead of aiming at making them elements of a new spirituality, of which a fine instinct for beauty was to be the dominant characteristic. (104)

And, he asks, "Is insincerity such a terrible thing? I think not. It is merely a method by which we can multiply our personalities" (112).

In fact, Wilde characterizes even this life-nurturing commitment in turn as belonging to only one standpoint, and so as not necessarily the final word: "Such, at any rate, was Dorian Gray's opinion. He used to wonder at the shallow psychology of those who conceive the Ego in man as a thing simple, permanent, reliable, and of one essence. To him, man was a being with myriad lives and myriad sensations" (112).

Edouard Roditi, for one, comments on the fact and degree of Wilde's rigor, "In all the confusion of late Victorian criticism . . . Oscar Wilde's ingenious, imaginative, and vigorous dialectical thought appears monumental."[27] He also points out that Wilde in fact works as much with traditional structures of careful thought as he departs from them:

> Wilde does not seem to have believed, moreover, that only new and confused art-forms could express the novelty and confusion of modern life. Like Baudelaire, he tended to adhere to traditional forms, even to revive them; he is more neoclassical, closer to Byron or even Pope,

---

[27] Edouard Roditi, *Oscar Wilde* (New York: New Directions, 1986), 4.

especially in his orderly handling of narrative, than Tennyson or Browning. . . . And this very art involves a complex body of critical beliefs which it illustrates more or less clearly.[28]

3. Wilde's Pluralism Proper

But Wilde is not principally concerned with aiming *at*, achieving, liberation from injustice, oppressive exclusion, and cruelty. He is principally concerned with having achieved it *already*, and so has no need to operate in the terms of the standpoints he opposes. As he writes in "The Critic as Artist,"

> Don't let us discuss anything solemnly. I am but too conscious of the fact that we are born in an age when only the dull are treated seriously, and I live in terror of not being misunderstood. Don't degrade me into the position of giving you useful information. Education is an admirable thing, but it is well to remember from time to time that nothing that is worth knowing can be taught. Through the parted curtains of the window I see the moon like a clipped piece of silver. . . . Let us go out into the night. . . . Who knows but we may meet Prince Florizel of Bohemia, and hear the fair Cuban tell us that she is not what she seems? (1015–16)

Analogously to the relation of an intervening position to its aimed-at position, but in reverse, in Wilde's *achieved* position the meanings of the contrasting intervening standpoint from which it has emerged do not exist for it as meanings to be taken seriously. The very idea of justifying itself with respect to that contrasting standpoint is consequently meaningless. Differently expressed, it is, again, rigorously or self-critically appropriate to be dogmatic with respect to that position.[29]

---

[28] Ibid., 3–4.
[29] A variety of leftist currents of thought have worked centrally with Kant's notion of the "(self-) critique of reason" (Marx's *Capital*, for example, is subtitled *A Critique of Political Economy*) specifically to avoid dogmatism and the consequent blind imposition of political ideologies. In that context, the critically appropriate lack of justification I discuss here might be called postcritical dogmatism.

But in the achieved position the *aim of getting there*—the *point* of occupying that position—is not given. In fact, in one's current, achieved standpoint considered entirely on its own, it makes no sense even to ask the question of how or why one got to where one already is. Without reference to a contrasting standpoint, a standpoint cannot even be thought of as a particular standpoint, and so as being a particular place one got to, or as having a particular existence that can consequently have a point. The aim or point of being there—the complete justification of one's standpoint—is *only* to be found in the preceding position that aimed at one's standpoint, or in a currently contrasting position that is still in the process of coming to understand one's own and so has not entered completely into it as understood from within.

But, as I have argued, that previous or genuinely contrasting position is unthinkable in the terms of the achieved one. As with the sense of intervening positions, then, the full sense of Wilde's work is given only with the sense of standpoints that have no meaning for his own. Accordingly, in order to understand his work, one has to locate not only the incompatibilities *in* his work but also the incompatibilities *with* his work, between what is thinkable in his terms and what is not.

The impact of the following typical passage, from *The Picture of Dorian Gray*, quite clearly shows this logic of the mutual relations and even dependence of mutually exclusive standpoints:

> Dorian was one of [Lady Narborough's] special favourites, and she always told him that she was extremely glad she had not met him in early life. "I know, my dear, I should have fallen madly in love with you," she used to say, "and thrown my bonnet right over the mills for your sake. It is most fortunate that you were not thought of at the time. As it was, our bonnets were so unbecoming, and the mills were so occupied in trying to raise the wind, that I never had even a flirtation with anybody. However, that was all Narborough's fault. He was dreadfully short-sighted, and there is no pleasure in taking in a husband who never sees anything." (134, insertion added)

The "bonnets right over the mills" idea starts off as a simple figure of speech, just an aptly extravagant adornment to a statement about the unrestrained desire of the lady's youth. Quite fluently and without comment it becomes, for no good reason, the prominent center of the following statement. And in that statement it is also said, but marginally—sandwiched between and so falling into the shadow of two or three strikingly unexpected statements—that the lady was extremely restrained in her youth ("I never had even a flirtation with anybody"). This second statement contradicts the first.

Now, the second, contradicting statement is given only a marginal status, while mitigating reasons that promise to make sense of it are given a central stress. But they, in turn, immediately cancel or contradict themselves as mitigating reasons. To say, for example, that the mills were raising the wind is also to say, "do not take this phrase as fulfilling the purpose it usually does in this grammatical context." The contradiction is made, mitigated, and unmitigated again, all in interweaving and immediately mutually interfering ways.

And, further, the two statements do not *simply* contradict each other. The functions and so the meanings of their organizing categories shift. At first, desire is offered as a motive force and the figure of speech that adorns it is marginal and trivial. Later, desire is marginal or trivial and what was formerly the accidental content of the figure of speech becomes the motive force. Center and margins, substance and ornament, switch places, so that in fact two standpoints are presented whose relevant sensemaking categories do not correspond. Given their respective meanings, what one standpoint must rightly take to be the serious, primary issue, the other must rightly take to be trivial and secondary. Beyond contradicting each other, then, they also transform the issue, so that they are no longer talking about the same thing at all.

But they have achieved this state of affairs, paradoxically, precisely *by* talking about the same thing and transforming it in relation to each other. (Again, on the possibility of mutually exclusive standpoints' referring to the same things at all, see the quotation from Alasdair MacIntyre in section 4 of Chapter 1, and the discussions in section 6 of Chapter 3 and in the first sections of Chapters 8 and 9.) That is, they *both* conflict with each other *and* shift the sense of the topic altogether out of the range of each other's meanings. And they do both of these incompatible things in the same act.

My suggestion is that this switching of basic categories—or, what comes to the same thing, of the whole standpoints structured by those categories—*the fact that* it occurs and so *can* occur as it does, is what gives this passage its peculiar impact. If so, what characterizes this impact is the sense of the *possibility of essential or constitutive change*, or the possibility of things' being essentially different from what they are currently rightly taken to be. This passage of Wilde's is, after all, as I have just argued, structured by constitutive change and difference of constitutive, sense-making categories.

Each region of meaning here *reconstitutes* the other's relevant meanings to accord with its own categories of what is meaningful, and so excludes the other's meanings from the available range of possible meanings. And in each case this reconstitution or alteration clashes with our appropriate expectations, so that the meanings are *also not* altered (otherwise the alteration would not strike us as incongruous: only our retaining the original meanings allows us to experience it so). And the passage as a whole contains both regions of meaning and both sets of "translations." The passage as a whole presents the components of rigorous recognition of essential or constitutive disparity of positions.

The content and tone of the passage also substantiate this suggestion, in that they constitute a self-canceling movement from the discussion of an agitating consideration ("she was extremely glad she had not met him in early life") to a transformation of the entire significance of the topic. And again, not only is the agitating factor eliminated, the category that makes the agitation possible in the first place, that of desire, is itself trivialized. And since this presentation of the possibility of fundamental difference or change is self-canceling, in that it moves through *nonsense*, it also presents the validity of things just as they were/are, *without* constitutive change or recognition of difference.

The extravagantly nonsensical element, the humor or absurdity, is the effect of the constitutive character of the difference and change. It is this constitutive difference between the positions at issue that makes the meanings clash in this extravagantly nonsensical way. Conversely, the extravagant character of the nonsense here is additional confirmation that the structure of constitutive change or difference really is in the passage, and really is conveyed by the passage. The extravagantly nonsensical element can retain its significance and impact only because the distortion of the relation between priorities across positions is still in effect and still felt.

And this distortion in turn can be in effect only because the sense of the first position's relation between trivial and important is still maintained in reaching the second position. That is, the sense of the first position's own viewpoint is still maintained in the second position's viewpoint.

These different constitutions of sense are simultaneous and dependent on each another. A description of the impact of this passage is incomplete without including both of them. But they are also incompatible. Each of them excludes the sense of the other. That is, they are both necessarily compatible and wholly incompatible. What makes them belong together is the character of the aesthetic impact of the passage. Wilde's aesthetic nonsense is how their incompatible fitting together is accurately conveyed.

The ending of "Lord Arthur Savile's Crime" also gives the aesthetic sense of this mutually sustaining relevant irrelevance of constitutively different or changed positions and meanings. The story is subtitled "A Study of Duty." It begins with a chiromancer, Mr. Podgers, favored by Lady Windermere, who predicts that Lord Arthur will commit a murder. Lord Arthur is horror-struck, but, wanting to marry his beloved, Sybil, with a clear future, he decides to get the murder over with and behind him. After failing repeatedly with various targets, he finally murders the chiromancer, and so can marry Sybil with hopes of living happily ever after. The story ends with a visit by Lady Windermere to the couple:

> "Do you remember that horrid Mr. Podgers? He was a dreadful imposter. Of course I didn't mind that at all, and even when he wanted to borrow money I forgave him, but I could not stand his making love to me. He has really made me hate chiromancy. I go in for telepathy now. It is much more amusing."
>
> "You mustn't say anything against chiromancy here, Lady Windermere; it is the only subject that Arthur does not like people to chaff about."

Lord Arthur arrives, and Lady Windermere questions him directly:

> "You don't mean to say that you believe in chiromancy?"
> "Of course I do," said the young man, smiling.
> "But why?"
> "Because I owe to it all the happiness of my life," he murmured. . . .

> "My dear Lord Arthur, what do you owe to it?"
>
> "Sybil," he answered, handing his wife the roses, and looking into her violet eyes.
>
> "What nonsense!" cried Lady Windermere. "I never heard such nonsense in all my life." (192)

The story begins, then, with a preposterously unrealistic, artificial pretext on the author's part: Lord Arthur is completely convinced by the chiromancer. This conviction reverses his initial romantic attitude that the world essentially works well:

> It was . . . the comedy of suffering that struck him; its absolute uselessness, its grotesque want of meaning. How incoherent everything seemed! How lacking in all harmony! He was amazed at the discord between the shallow optimism of the day, and the real facts of existence. He was still very young. (176)

But Lord Arthur nonetheless proceeds to behave on the basis of that abandoned attitude. The story comes full circle when he kills the chiromancer, and in so doing restores romance, exclusive of all horridness, once again. As Wilde describes their future, "For them romance was not killed by reality. They always felt young" (191). The catalytic incident that made room for the initial artificial pretext is then itself discovered to be—perhaps—artificial, a fraud: "that horrid Mr. Podgers . . . was a dreadful imposter." But what this incident artificially led to was pragmatically real. The catalytic artificiality becomes—perhaps—genuine. To which Lady Windermere, who was the one who introduced it as genuine, responds: "What nonsense! . . . I never heard such nonsense in all my life."

The artificial pretext reverses romance. This reversal in turn reverses itself: it becomes the means of establishing romance. This in turn reverses the chiromancer's lack of credibility, the very artificiality of the foundational artificial pretext itself, which as a result becomes undecidable as to whether it is artificial or genuine. Finally, this whole process, including the undecidability of its basis, reverses and displaces itself, keeping itself as it was, alongside its reversal ("What nonsense!," Lady Windermere says of the now inescapably genuine results), and with the impact of each sustaining that of the other. The result is a simple, humorous and joyous impact of undecidable nonsense that is even undecidable as to whether it is undecidable nonsense. It has the simply and clearly graspable outcome of a simply established love that is exuberantly nonsensical at the same time.

We are brought not to a position of pure artificiality, or to a position of simple pragmatic reality, but to an undecidability between them. And this undecidability does not, as in standpoints that *aim* at radical change or difference, primarily subvert all certainties of position (like the Maoist commitment to "perpetual revolution" or Lacanian psychoanalysis, for example). Instead, with full consistency, it is undecidable even as to its own being undecidable—its undecidability is not decidably what it *itself* is, so that in being *fully* undecidability it also undoes itself (while of course also still being itself). As a result, it *recognizes and celebrates* all certainties of position as much as it questions them. This includes, crucially, those that are not Wilde's.

This is a critically or undogmatically dogmatic stance, not acknowledging positions that it also acknowledges, and its logic is given in the very specific impact of Wilde's aesthetic nonsense. The simple, decidable coherence of the standpoint that *presents* this undecidability is itself given in the *specific comic impact* of the story. This impact and standpoint *are* the coherence or specificity of the story, in all its also-self-undoing undecidability, as the single, identifiable story it is. And this comic impact includes not only the unified effect of the incongruities of the story's content, but also the appreciation of the fact that such a radically self-incongruous story can and does successfully exist at all. In presenting the story, then, this undecidable position presents in the same act, and above all, the *simple fact* of its also-self-undoing undecidability. That is, in succeeding in presenting the story, it presents above all the principle that it itself is possible and graspable as a particular position.

This presentation of the simple fact of its own possibility is especially important. In general, recognition of the simple fact of one's own position, whatever it may be, as a *particular* position is already indirectly recognition that there are contrasting positions that are possibly valid. And once one constitutive difference or change is shown to be imaginable, as in this story, the idea of constitutive difference or change in general is shown to be imaginable. But since Wilde's particular position is already constituted as a coordination of fundamentally contrasting positions, recognition of the simple fact of *his* position in particular is a *direct* recognition of the principle that combinations of incompatible positions and meanings may be simply thought and lived.

And this includes again, of course, combinations other than Wilde's.

It is also significant that Wilde coordinates pure artificiality and pragmatic reality in constituting the same meanings in this story. As I have argued, what is primary, serious, and soundly practical for one standpoint can be secondary, trivial, and artificial for another, and an account of a situation involving both standpoints needs to include both incompatible construals of the same thing. As Cecily puts this kind of paradox in *The Importance of Being Earnest*, when Algernon has confirmed that he wants to discuss something "very serious": "In that case I think we had better meet in the house. I don't like talking seriously in the open air. It looks so artificial" (355).

Let me elaborate, a little, the importance for Wilde's position of standpoints for which his own is simply trivial, artificial, and negligible. Wilde does not *simply* repudiate the positions from which he essentially differs or moves away, positions in which constitutive difference or change is unthinkable (although, in keeping with the logic of relating mutually exclusive positions, he does *also entirely repudiate* them, *in addition* to accepting them). On the contrary, his work is defined by the juxtaposition of standpoints that maintain their mutually exclusive incompatibility. As a result, without reference to positions that wholly contrast with his own, his own standpoint disappears. This means that he must, and does, present his own position partly in the terms of the positions from which he is moving away or differs. That is, he must and does present his own position in terms that exclude his own, and so as artificial and negligible.

By presenting his position in the other position's terms—by presenting it as artificial—he articulates the fact of incompatibility simply as it is from the simple, nonparadoxical, nonpluralist viewpoint of that other position, since it is in that position's terms that he presents his own. And, since his own, contrasting position is in fact what he presents in the other position's terms, he *also* articulates the fact of incompatibility as it is from his own, paradoxical, pluralist viewpoint, as incompatibility combined with compatibility. That is, he not only articulates both standpoints simultaneously, he articulates *the relation (of incompatibility) between* the standpoints simultaneously from both standpoints' points of view, so both pluralistically and non-pluralistically. In other words, Wilde's pluralism is sufficiently consistent to make room for nonpluralistic standpoints that wholly exclude his pluralism.

Oscar Wilde and the Logic of Genuine Political Pluralism 123

The same logic of balanced incompatibility structures "The Sphinx Without a Secret." Gerald is in love with Lady Alroy, who lies to him: she secretly goes to a certain address at regular intervals, but denies it. Eventually he finds proof, confronts her with it, and insists on knowing what she does there.

> She stood up, and, looking me straight in the face, said, "Lord Murchison, there is nothing to tell you."—"You went to meet some one," I cried; "this is your mystery." She grew dreadfully white, and said, "I went to meet no one."—"Can't you tell the truth?" I exclaimed. "I have told it," she replied. (218)

As a result of this confrontation, he rejects her. Then he finds out she has died, goes to the address she used to visit, and is told by someone who opens the door:

> "She paid me three guineas a week merely to sit in my drawing-rooms now and then."—"She met some one here?" I said; but the woman assured me that it was not so, that she always came alone, and saw no one. "What on earth did she do here?" I cried. "She simply sat in the drawing-room, sir, reading books, and sometimes had tea," the woman answered. (218)

At the end, Gerald asks the narrator of the story, "Now, what do you think it all meant? You don't believe the woman was telling the truth?" "I do," replies the narrator. "Then why did Lady Alroy go there?" Gerald asks.

> "My dear Gerald," I answered, "Lady Alroy was simply a woman with a mania for mystery. She took the rooms for the pleasure of going there with her veil down, and imagining she was a heroine. She had a passion for secrecy, but she herself was merely a Sphinx without a secret."
> "Do you really think so?"
> "I am sure of it," I replied.
> He took out the morocco case, opened it, and looked at the photograph. "I wonder?" he said at last. (218)

The "I wonder" at the end positions the tale perfectly. Either she really did have a secret, or the bare fact that she would go to such lengths to pretend to have a secret is itself a mystery or secret. In the end, each position is the same as the other, but with a reversal of meanings: of the fullness or emptiness of the content of the secret, of what is mundane and what is remarkable (Lady Alroy's mundane or merely imaginary activity itself becomes what is remarkable), of what is significant and what is signified (her doing nothing significant becomes what is significant, rather than signifying a further mystery), and of what is marginal and what is central (her mundane time in the room becomes central, in place of other activities to which it would be incidental). And Wilde leaves us poised exactly with both options, with the impact of both, and also of the unresolved choice of either or both of these options.

4. Wilde's Idea of Art and the Logic of Pluralism

I suggest that this recognition and celebration of the certainties of all positions, including their exclusions of the certainties of other positions, is, for Wilde, the meaning of art. In *The Soul of Man under Socialism* he insists that "Art is the most intense mood of Individualism that the world has known." And the beauty of a work of art "comes from the fact that the author is what he is. It has nothing to do with the fact that other people want what they want" (1090). The ideal he presents here is that society should be structured so that *everyone* can live without concern for other people's incompatible wants. That is, his position involves exclusion of the certainties of other positions *and* affirmation of their rightful exclusion of the certainties of his own position. The possibility of doing this, he believes, is found in art.

He also describes art itself in mutually exclusive ways. In *The Picture of Dorian Gray*, for example, he writes, "All art is quite useless" (17), but in "A Few Maxims for the Instruction of the Over-Educated," "Art is the only serious thing in the world," to which he adds, "the artist is the only person who is never serious" (1203). I have been arguing that there is a logical necessity in statements of this kind, the realistic logic of the kind of thought and society that Wilde believes are true to human existence. The engagement of art with the world, whether it is a political, moral, theoretical (or, for that matter, a lunch) engagement, does not lie in art's having a simply realistically effective dimension but in the realistic significance of its pure artificiality. For, on the one hand, given the mutual exclusion of the meanings of different standpoints, each rightly construes the meanings of the others as purely artificial, nonsensical. But given that they nonetheless also coexist, and that each has as much or as little right as the others to be taken as the starting point and so as the standard of meanings, the very same pure artificialities switch over into being genuine and in fact basic meanings. In the relations and negotiations between genuinely different standpoints, then, pure artificiality, *as* pure artificiality, engages with reality as a profoundly logical pragmatism, *purely exclusive* of artificiality.

This self-incompatible Wildean kind of statement, to the extent that it is justified by the logic of pluralism, requires the nature of logical necessity itself to be rethought. In this context, this necessity is not simply: necessary and not frivolous. It is not simply: necessary despite its frivolity. It is: both of these; *and*, necessary *and* as it happens frivolous; *and*, necessary *because* it is frivolous; *and*, frivolous despite *and* because of its necessity.

Wilde's kind of art both presents and *is* the critically justified logic or sense of suspending one's (or equally the other's) critical rigor, of thoughtfully presenting oneself (or equally the other) dogmatically, without concern for one's potential uncertainties, without justification or attention to one's presuppositions. Where standpoints are constitutively different, the other standpoints that might meaningfully question one's ultimate standards of sense and truth are, when *undogmatically, critically*, taken into account, meaningless or purely artificial for one's own achieved standpoint, and vice versa. And without such contrasting standpoints, there is no meaningful question about one's ultimate standards of sense and truth: one's own standpoint would *rely* on those standards even in asking that kind of question. One is self-critically justified, then, in not reflecting self-critically on one's point of view.

The impact/import of Wilde's kind of art, then, both contains the justified fact of simply being who one is, without need for justification—that is, it expresses that one's existence is truly its own justification—and carries that principle through to the incompatibly justified fact of conflicting others' simply being who they are, without need for justification. "The true personality of man," he writes in *The Soul of Man under Socialism*,

> will not be always meddling with others, or asking them to be like itself. It will love them because they will be different. And yet while it will not meddle with others, it will help all, as a beautiful thing helps us, by being what it is. (1084)

Part of the impact of Wilde's work, then, lies in the absence of justification for it outside of its own being what it is. There is no adequate reason for his having structured, for example, "Lord Arthur Savile's Crime" precisely as he did. Its structure did not follow logically from any way of making narrative sense that preceded it, and so the sense and justification of that structure could only be considered after it had already come into existence. In other words, it opened up a new constitutive or essential space. And that it came about for no adequate reason in this way, and works in ways that had no adequate reason until they came into existence as themselves the ways of providing such a reason, is the chief beauty and marvel of it. And as a marvel, as resulting in an utter, incomparable freshness in relation to what precedes and surrounds it, that it came about for no adequate reason is its full justification.

Wilde's aesthetic presents the simple coherence or specificity of this self-incompatible principle, pragmatic and artificially imaginative, justified and justifiably unjustified, and yet also simply single by virtue of the single aesthetic impact that its undecidable artificiality makes. Wilde expresses the structure of the coherent, single impact of this nonsensical artificiality, undecidably opening spaces for meanings that the current meanings exclude, in "The Young King":

> "Where is this dreamer of dreams?" they cried. "Where is this King, who is apparelled like a beggar—this boy who brings shame upon our state? Surely we will slay him, for he is unworthy to rule over us."
>
> . . .
>
> And the young King came down from the high altar, and passed home through the midst of the people. But no man dared look upon his face, for it was like the face of an angel. (233)

To reemphasize the other side of this self-incompatible coin: explicit critical awareness is also required for this critical dogmatism to come about. In "The Critic as Artist," Gilbert says, "it is the critical faculty that invents fresh forms. The tendency of creation is to repeat itself. It is to the critical instinct that we owe each new school that springs up, each new mould that art finds ready to its hand" (1021). According to him, the antithesis between the unself-questioning creative and the self-reflective critical faculties is "entirely arbitrary. Without the critical faculty, there is no artistic creation at all worthy of the name" (1020).

But, again, attention to one's own presuppositions—the appropriate entry into the often inappropriate activity of rigorous questioning and debate—belongs to the kind of position that *aims for* something, or *aims to* understand a different position. The kind of position that *achieves* what the former aims for is in this respect constitutively other than that former position, and must include in some sense a constitutive absence of such attention, a dogmatism. And since both mutually irrelevant kinds of position are required to understand either, they must, again, be thought paradoxically, simultaneously in both a thoroughly critical and a thoroughly dogmatic style.

The following description from *The Picture of Dorian Gray* shows again how elaborately Wilde situates himself in this kind of context. He writes of "loving for their mere artificiality those renunciations that men have unwisely called virtue, as much as those natural rebellions that wise men still call sin" (101). The opposition of the evaluations considered here is both sharply maintained and thoroughly undone, and in a way that depends on simultaneously thinking the contrasting positions that give those evaluations their meaning. The "renunciations" are "mere artificiality," and "unwisely called virtue." These descriptions of the Christian renunciations come from a position opposed to that in which they are wise and sober, and so, in fact, in which they are *renunciations*, in the Christian meaning, at all. The "natural rebellions," on the other hand—where to value "natural" positively in this context is a modern, post-Christian idea, a reconstituted understanding of passions—are "wisely" still called "sin." These descriptions belong to the Christian position, opposed to that in which these "natural rebellions" are what *they* are.

The second statement reinstates the Christian position, understood in its own Christian terms. The first statement already upheld the modern position in its own modern terms. And these confirmations emerge from a position in which *both* positions are upheld *simultaneously* each in the other's terms. The Christian position is upheld for its artificiality, the modern position for its sin.

The reader is put in both of the familiar positions, each exclusive of the other, since each retains its own meanings. The reader is also placed in each position as it is reconstituted in the other's terms. And the reader is also placed somewhere entirely new, in a position that can *recognize* both these particular standpoints in their mutual exclusion. As a result, the reader can also recognize the possibility of new, unforeseen, constitutively different standpoints in general, and, further, the possibility of their relating to one another without eliminating their mutual exclusivity.

In short, as Wilde expresses it in "Phrases and Philosophies for the Use of the Young," "The well-bred contradict other people. The wise contradict themselves" (1205).

5. Foucault's Pluralism and the Possibility of Truth and of Ideology Critique

> But need we dispense for ever with the "*oeuvre*," the "book," or even such unities as "science" or "literature"? Should we regard them as illusions, illegitimate constructions, or ill-acquired results? . . . What we must do, in fact, is . . . recognize . . . that they require a theory . . . And I, in turn, will do no more than this.
> I have no wish at the outset to exclude any effort to uncover and free . . . "prediscursive" experiences from the tyranny of the text.
> —Michel Foucault[1]

Michel Foucault's work involves a pluralism of conflicting but equally legitimate truth frameworks or "regimes of truth," each of which has its own standards for truth. On a standard set of interpretations of his work, his pluralism eliminates the sense of the concept of ideology as a politically motivated system of ideas that claims to be true but in fact is false, since in his view there are no standards for truth independent of the particular system of ideas and their associated practices. Consequently, his work also makes the practice of identifying and questioning ideology—that is, ideology critique—meaningless. In other words, if his insights are valid, they remove any meaning from the notion of criticizing and so of justifiably rejecting or endorsing the systems of ideas under which we live our lives. As a result, our concerns for political justice and responsibility turn out to be largely and perhaps entirely meaningless.

Although ideology critique is primarily a Marxist concept, related concerns are also essential to liberal and non-Marxist radical frameworks,

---

[1] Michel Foucault, *The Archaeology of Knowledge*, trans. A. M. Sheridan Smith (New York: Pantheon, 1972), 26, 47.

which require genuineness and hence the exposure of systematic distortions of truth. Further, in addition to the problem Foucault's work presents specifically for ideology critique, the reasons for which he seems to undermine this concept are standardly taken also to eliminate the concept of the truth of our statements and insights as in some sense an accurate transcription of reality. On these interpretations of his work, then, Foucault presents a direct challenge to all political theories and practices that base themselves on some form of reason and/or, more flexibly, reasonableness.

I shall argue that these interpretations are mistaken, and that Foucault's work in fact gives a more rigorous foundation for the distinction between truth and ideology, and hence for ideology critique, than do frameworks that more obviously support these notions.

As I have argued in the previous chapters, where there are fundamentally different frameworks for sense and truth—and there is good reason to think that there are such frameworks—they cannot legitimately simply assert their own criteria for truth against those of the other frameworks. If they do so, they are arbitrarily and dogmatically imposing their not yet established *claims* to truth on a standpoint with competing and at least equally legitimate claims to truth. In these contexts, then, frameworks that do not recognize the kind of pluralism with which Foucault's work deals are in fact treating baseless claims as truth. And without a thoughtful awareness of fundamental differences of framework, they also do not have the kind of perspective and conceptual resources that would allow them to recognize and establish the difference, in these contexts, between unjustified assumptions, including ideological ones, and truth.

I shall argue, in company with some of Foucault's critics, that because Foucault tries to justify his standpoint—in other words, to make a case for its truth—the part of his reasoning that makes him seem to dismiss ideology critique in fact requires him to endorse the presuppositions about truth that make this kind of critique possible. But I shall also argue that the standard set of interpretations is mistaken, and that Foucault already integrates ideology critique and its presuppositions into his framework. I shall argue that his analysis runs deeper than the frameworks that more obviously support ideology critique, in a way that gives these frameworks themselves both a far more rigorous justification than they themselves offer and a corrective context that they need in order to fulfill their own aims.

It remains true that Foucault challenges the frameworks that *immediately* support ideology critique. His challenge, however, does not eliminate them, but displaces them to a different, less deep level of analysis. My key point is that Foucault's is a framework of frameworks, a metaframework—what one might describe, very cautiously, as a transcendental or metaphysical framework. Accordingly, his claims, for example about the variability of truth, do not have immediately obvious implications for truth *within* any particular framework. In fact, as I argue, one of his contributions is precisely to articulate (develop a rhetoric for) a metaframework within which the possibly ideological criteria for truth in any given particular framework can be debated *without* simply eliminating the meaningfulness of truth claims, which retain their full sense within the particular frameworks. That is, he avoids the problems of relativism without also giving in to the possible (and politically significant) dogmatism of standard ideology critiques.

Let me give some brief, provisional textual support here for this claim that Foucault establishes this kind of metaframework that has no commitment to any particular truth but also does not undermine truth within the particular frameworks of which it is a metaanalysis. He explains, for example, that he aims to articulate "what might be called a *historical a priori* . . . an *a priori* that is not a condition of validity for judgements, but a condition of reality for statements. It is not a question of rediscovering what might legitimize an assertion, but of freeing the conditions of emergence of statements."[2] Again, "the description of the episteme," or knowledge-producing framework, does not give us "a form of knowledge" but "what, in the positivity of discursive practices, makes possible the existence of epistemological figures and sciences."[3] This is not to deny that concerns with validity have a place but rather to contextualize them: "this *a priori* . . . has to take account of the fact that discourse has not only a meaning or a truth, but a history."[4] What is more, this a priori context not only does not eliminate truth in the particular frameworks that it contextualizes, it partly *depends* on the forms it takes there: "this *a priori* . . . is defined as the group of rules that characterize a discursive practice: but these rules

[2] Ibid., 127.
[3] Ibid., 191–92.
[4] Ibid., 127.

are not imposed from the outside on the elements that they relate together; they are caught up in the very things that they connect."⁵

Again, "What are described as 'systems of formation' do not constitute the terminal stage of discourse, if by that term one means the texts (or words) as they appear, with their vocabulary, syntax, logical structure, or rhetorical organization. Analysis remains anterior to this manifest level, which is that of the completed construction."⁶ But this analysis outside given frameworks is also not simply independent of them: "Behind the completed system, what is discovered by the analysis of formations is . . . multiple relations . . . that . . . characterize certain levels of discourse, that . . . define rules that are embodied as a particular practice by discourse."⁷

Foucault establishes the need for this metaframework and develops the metaframework itself, first, by challenging the competence of any given truth-permitting particular framework to allow rigorous and so fair discussion at the level of the support for its own bases. Second, he articulates a rhetoric that, suited to this metalevel, functions as a medium for negotiation between frameworks without either denying or precommitting to the truth of any one framework. As I shall argue, this metanegotiation can allow indirect but, since it is external, properly noncircular support for the bases of truth-permitting frameworks.

Foucault does not seem to me to offer any substantial argument that this framework of truth about truths is genuinely possible. He seems not to take into account the possibility, for example, that the deep paradoxes on which his approach very noticeably relies might render it conceptual nonsense. Whatever the case with its ultimate possibility and sense, however, I believe that this metaframework is what he articulates. If he is wrong it is because this metaframework fails, and not because the conception he proposes involves, if it succeeds, the elimination of truth and ideology critique. As the other essays in this book show, I do believe that this kind of metaframework is coherent and deeply cogent. But that is an argument I shall leave to those chapters. Here, since Foucault himself does not seem to offer that kind of justification, I aim to show only that his work is best understood as exemplifying this kind of metaframework.

⁵ Ibid., 127.
⁶ Ibid., 75.
⁷ Ibid., 76.

One paradox or potential conceptual nonsense that it will be helpful to note here, however, is that because this metaframework taken as a whole consists in mutually exclusive truth claims and rejects none of them, it is meaningless as a set of descriptive statements. I argue in the other chapters of the book that a framework that is structured in this way is not simply meaningless but self-canceling, so that its meaninglessness is compatible with and in fact produces meaningful statements. This in turn allows us to see both how this kind of framework is logically legitimate and how it is possible for it to connect with straightforwardly meaningful frameworks and so function as a medium for negotiation between them.[8]

Again, Foucault himself does not make this point about self-cancellation and so does not justify the logical possibility of his framework in this respect. He does, however, present this general framework as something like self-canceling in the way I argue it is. He presents the domain of his general account as having no stable quality in general, as shifting into incompatible and equally impermanent characters, in other words as not an "it." He writes, for example, "We are now dealing with a complex volume, in which heterogeneous regions are differentiated or deployed, in accordance with specific rules and practices that cannot be superposed."[9] Again, the kind of description this framework produces "is a constantly moving set of articulations, shifts, and coincidences that are established, only to give rise to others."[10] In his later work he describes his general explanatory term, "power," similarly: "Power's condition of possibility . . . is . . . force relations which . . . constantly engender [particular] states of power, but the

---

[8] Bruno Latour argues very neatly for this mediating function of meaningless language, though, like Foucault, without giving an account of its logical possibility: conventional sociologists, he writes, "are keen to produce precise, well chosen, sophisticated terms for what they say the actors say. But then they might run the risk of confusing the two meta-languages—since actors, too, have their own elaborate and fully reflexive meta-language." Latour advocates instead "what could be called an *infra-language*, which remains strictly meaningless except for allowing displacement from one frame of reference to the next. In my experience, this is a better way for the vocabulary of the actors to be heard loud and clear"; Bruno Latour, *Reassembling the Social: An Introduction to Actor-Network-Theory* (New York: Oxford University Press, 2005), 30.

[9] Foucault, *Archaeology*, 128.

[10] Ibid., 192.

latter are always local and unstable." Power in general "is simply the overall effect that emerges from all these [local, particular] mobilities, the concatenation that rests on each of them. . . . One needs to be nominalistic, no doubt."[11]

I do not want to suggest that Foucault's work consistently presents the metaframework I suggest. Like any of us, he is likely to fall short of his own thought on occasion, and, for that matter, there may be more than one "Foucault." What I shall argue is only that he does, and, for his purposes (or the purposes of this "Foucault"), *must* present this metaframework, whether he keeps to it consistently or not.

In the first section I outline both the standard construal of Foucault's challenge to frameworks that immediately support ideology critique, and some crucial problems for Foucault's own framework (in this standard construal) that this challenge seems to present. En route, I suggest some ways in which his analysis increases the rigor and scope of ideology critique even in the light of the standard set of interpretations of his work. In the second section I argue that Foucault's framework, properly understood, not only solves the problems that appear to emerge in his challenge but also indirectly and rigorously grounds ideology critique and its attendant frameworks rather than simply opposing them. (That is, it does oppose them, but because of his framework's self-canceling character it also supports them unqualifiedly at another level of its meaning for them.)

1. The Challenge to the Concept of Truth and Resulting Problems

Practitioners of ideology critique understand ideology to be a truth-claiming discourse or a set of beliefs that is in fact false and misleadingly serves interests other than the purported one of expressing truth. This concept of ideology depends on a distinction between discourses that capture truth and those that betray it. It also presupposes that truth can be established, presented, and lived in a way that is not primarily constituted by other interests. Foucault is routinely taken to reject—and, at one level, but only one level, *does* reject—both this distinction and this presupposition.

---

[11] Michel Foucault, *The History of Sexuality* (Harmondsworth: Penguin Books, 1978), 93, my insertions.

First, the idea that we can decide between true and false discourses presupposes a foundation in truth on the basis of which we can make that decision. But in Foucault's view any foundation we might claim is itself given sense in the context of language and particular practices and institutions. It is therefore always only one possible foundation among differently, but equivalently, contextualized alternatives. "What reason considers its necessity or much more what various forms of rationality claim to be their necessary existence, has a history. . . . They rest upon a foundation of human practices and human faces, because they are made they can be unmade."[12] It seems that there is therefore no foundation in truth on whose basis to decide between true and false discourses. Second, since claims of truth are always given their sense in particular social contexts, it seems that no truth claims can be separated from this particularity and so from the partiality and hence interests they serve. On this interpretation, Foucault is taken—at one level rightly—to conclude that concern with the accuracy of truth claims as disinterested transcriptions of reality, and the corresponding concern with ideology, are pointless. "The notion of ideology appears to me to be difficult to make use of. . . . I believe that the problem does not consist in drawing the line between that in a discourse which falls under the category of scientificity or truth, and that which comes under some other category."[13] Attempts to identify and correct ideological biases, then, are meaningless. In contrast, a meaningful concern is the effects truth claims, as a kind of power, have on people's lives (Foucault writes, for example, of "the fundamental point: the effects proper to true discourses"[14]).

But even at this level of analysis the standpoint Foucault offers as an alternative to focusing on the contrast between truth and ideology has positive implications for the aims the concept of ideology is believed to underpin. Foucault identifies and focuses on what he calls disciplinary and normative strategies of power. These are effects and functions of truth-claiming discourses and practices in which they *internally constitute* agents

---

[12] Michel Foucault, *Foucault Live (Interviews, 1966–1984)* (New York: Semiotext(e), 1989), 252.

[13] Michel Foucault, *Power/Knowledge: Selected Interviews and Other Writings 1972–1977* (New York: Pantheon, 1980), 118.

[14] Ibid., 131.

as what they are. "One has to arrive at an analysis which can account for the constitution of the subject within a historical framework."[15] That is, agents are constrained to understand and experience themselves, others, and the world in certain ways, and, since agents *are* subjects of experience, they are consequently constrained to *be* in certain ways. The result is that agents are constituted so as to govern their *own* awareness and behavior along lines that have been imposed upon them. They do not, as subjects, begin in a position to go along with or fight the imposition. Their very awareness is constituted by this imposition, so that their reflection and commitment presuppose it. For Foucault, then, discourses and practices that claim truth have powerful material effects on agents, constituting their subjectivity and hence the parameters in which they experience and live. And these discourses include what is otherwise thought of as ideology.

Foucault's framework, then, allows a very thoroughgoing analysis of what is otherwise thought of as ideology, as an instrument and in fact a kind of power. His analysis explains exactly how discourse and institutions, social phenomena, can be effective at the individual level. And it shows how thoroughly discourse and social practices, including what is otherwise thought of as ideology, can be effective at the individual level. That is, he shows that ideologies, systems of ideas, are themselves a dimension of power, a dimension that is as material, and therefore as significant, as any other material feature of existence, including economic conditions. "A regime of truth . . . is not merely ideological or superstructural; it was a condition of the formation and development of capitalism."[16]

But, as I have discussed above, in Foucault's framework there can be no truth-claiming discourse or practice that does not function as ideology in the sense of having non-truth-related, material effects. "Truth isn't outside power, or lacking in power. . . . Truth is a thing of this world: it is produced only by multiple forms of constraint. And it induces regular effects of power. Each society has its regime of truth."[17] *Any* truth-claiming discourse has effects of interested constitutive power. And such discourses can be analyzed *only* with respect to these interested effects: there is no foundational discourse that allows us to assess them with respect to their

---

[15] Ibid., 117.
[16] Ibid., 133.
[17] Ibid., 131.

truth as a transcription of reality. Consequently, as many of Foucault's critics have pointed out, we cannot even justify some effects as morally or politically better than others. As Michael Walzer puts it, Foucault does not "give us any way of knowing what 'better' might mean."[18] Crucially, this includes Foucault's own discourse and *its* effects. Insofar as Foucault makes truth claims, whether with respect to states of affairs or to moral or political values, his work is subject to his own critique.

And Foucault does claim that his framework is in the service of knowledge, freedom, and human possibility. For example, he describes the object of his work as a whole as "to learn to what extent the effort to think one's own history can free thought from what it silently thinks, and so enable it to think differently."[19] But his framework so far seems to make this aim pointless. On his account, his framework can function only to have power effects, emptily renamed "truth" (here, what we have "learned"). And there is no justification for aiming at "freedom": "freedom" is just a name for another power effect, no better or worse than any other. His framework, then, seems to be self-defeating.

Accordingly, as those of his defenders who address this problem understand him, he disclaims any relevance of traditional truth or falsity to his work.[20] The problem that all truth-claiming discourse has interested power effects is only a problem when understood on the basis of the distinction between truth and falsehood taken as accurate and inaccurate transcriptions of reality. For Foucault, this understanding of truth, and the concerns that are based on it, are meaningless and so utterly irrelevant. "The problem," in his view, consists in "seeing historically how effects of truth are produced within discourses which in themselves are neither true nor false."[21] Again, what *is* meaningful and significant is the way in which truth-claiming discourses have effects on subjectivity.

If we follow this understanding of Foucault, then, we are not in a position, but we also do not find it an aim that makes any kind of sense, to

---

[18] Michael Walzer, "The Politics of Michel Foucault," in *Foucault: A Critical Reader*, ed. David Couzens Hoy (Cambridge, MA: Basil Blackwell, 1986), 61.

[19] Michel Foucault, *The Use of Pleasure* (New York: Pantheon, 1985), 9.

[20] See, for example, Barry Allen, *Truth in Philosophy* (Cambridge, MA: Harvard University Press, 1993), 180–81.

[21] Foucault, *Power/Knowledge,* 118.

defend or refute the validity of truth-claiming discourses and the practices and institutions they are taken to justify, whether these discourses and practices are Foucault's or those opposed to his. And we are also not in a position, and do not find it an aim that makes sense, to justify or deny the validity of aiming to achieve particular *effects* by means of discourse and institutions, whether these aims are Foucault's or those opposed to his. As Ian Hacking puts it (although making a different point), "At present rhetoric about the good life is almost always based on some claim to know the truth about desire, about vitamins, about humanity or society. But there are no such truths to know."[22]

This understanding of Foucault (which at one level is right) offers an alternative to truth-versus-ideology-oriented strategies. Precisely *because* truth-claiming discourses constitute subjectivity rather than accurately reflecting its preexisting nature, agents can *reconstitute* their own subjectivity by reconstituting truth-claiming discourses: "we have to promote new forms of subjectivity through the refusal of this kind of individuality that has been imposed on us."[23]

At this deeper level of analysis too, Foucault's framework has an important positive relation to ideology critique. While on this understanding of his work, ideology critique is meaningless as an attempt to recover truths that have been distorted or hidden by ideology, it is all the more significant as part of an attempt to destroy some truths in order to *create* new truths (or at least to create new realities and forms of life). For example, "relations of power-knowledge are not static forms of distribution, they are 'matrices of transformations.'"[24] And, the "essential political problem for the intellectual is . . . that of ascertaining the possibility of constituting a new politics of truth."[25] These new truths, like the old, are given their warrant as truth by being materially efficacious for agents, offering them freedom in the form of creating themselves.

---

[22] Ian Hacking, "Self-Improvement," in *Foucault: A Critical Reader*, ed. David Couzens Hoy (Cambridge, MA: Basil Blackwell, 1986), 239.

[23] Michel Foucault, "Afterword," in Hubert L. Dreyfus and Paul Rabinow, *Michel Foucault: Beyond Structuralism and Hermeneutics,* 2nd ed. (Chicago: University of Chicago Press, 1983), 216.

[24] Foucault, *History of Sexuality*, 99.

[25] Foucault, *Power/Knowledge,* 133.

Further, ideology critique, reconstituted in this framework, has a range of application that extends to *all* truth-claiming discourse and practices. I can no longer say of some truth-claiming discourses and their attendant institutions and practices that they are unjustified; this claim is meaningless, since it contrasts with no alternative. But I *can* say of *any* truth-claiming discourse and its practices and institutions that it has no self-evident, unquestionable claim on me, that I am free to consider and explore refusing to situate my subjectivity within it. And I can use the strategies of ideology critique to help remove the efficacy of the imposing discourse. Much of Foucault's work can be seen as just this, the "unmasking" of operations of power, so that their real operation can be distinguished from how they are misleadingly presented. For example, "a historical problem arises . . . of discovering why the West has insisted . . . on seeing the power it exercises as juridical and negative rather than as technical and positive."[26]

Ideology critique here can no longer be guided by the recovery of truth; rather, it must be guided by the creation of truth. Because this shift involves substituting truth as a transcription of reality with truth as effects that constitute reality, we would need to—and we can—reunderstand the theory of ideology critique in the context of an understanding of the mechanism or operation of this alternative notion of truth.

But there are problems with this understanding of Foucault, too. We still have no way to decide what new truths to create, or which, as Walzer puts it, are "better," worth aiming to create in the first place. In this light, as well, it seems inconsistent that Foucault's work consists enormously in his offering various kinds of empirical evidence for the truth of his claims. Insofar as truth is now seen only as something one creates, something that has effects, why should anyone, including Foucault himself, undertake the labor of marshalling this evidence to create the truth about her- or himself (to affect her- or himself) so that she or he becomes someone who believes Foucault's claims? Why, again, is this an effect worth aiming for? And why is it *evidence* in particular that helps to achieve this effect? Additionally, Foucault distinguishes freedom from power effects, a distinction his framework so far does not permit. "If there are relations of power throughout every social field it is because there is freedom everywhere. . . . One cannot impute to me the idea that power is a system of domination which . . .

[26] Ibid., 121.

leaves no room for freedom."[27] In fact, he also speaks about truth itself not as another name for power effects but as something in various kinds of relation to power effects, and therefore as at least partly distinct from them. His framework so far does not permit that either. Even on this sympathetic interpretation of the standard construal of Foucault, then, his framework is not only still self-defeating but also incoherent.

What is more, the argument that truth as an accurate transcription of reality is irrelevant to Foucault's framework, so that he does not need to take it into account, is viciously circular. Foucault's main project, on this reading, is to show that truth is always a function of power, that it always depends on local historical norms, and to show the implications of this fact.[28] Precisely what he needs to justify, then, is his abandoning of truth as accurate transcription of reality. His whole project depends on it, and so to say that he need not address the issue of truth because it is irrelevant to his project is to say that he has shown the irrelevance of truth because his project has already succeeded before it started. That is, he *assumes* without first having shown the irrelevance of truth. On this understanding, then, Foucault's framework does not even get off the ground. It is, so far, simply fiction.

Part of this argument sympathetic to the standard construal of Foucault is that justification is irrelevant, since it depends on a non-Foucauldian concept of truth, and consequently fiction is fully a matter of truth in the only sense "truth" can have. But that claim too still waits to be justified. Without that paradoxical justification of the irrelevance of justification, we have the same vicious circularity in this claim as well. And without the resulting specification of the nature of this irrelevance, we are also left without clues as to why Foucault's framework is not self-defeating and incoherent.

---

[27] Quoted by David Halperin in *Saint Foucault: Towards a Gay Hagiography* (New York: Oxford University Press, 1995), 191, n. 1, from Raul Fornet-Betancourt et al., "The Ethic of Care for the Self as a Practice of Freedom: An Interview with Michel Foucault on January 20, 1984," *Philosophy and Social Criticism* 12, nos. 2–3 (1987): 123–24.

[28] See, for example, Allen, *Truth in Philosophy,* 143.

2. Foucault's Deeper Contextualization of Truth

Foucault's claims and reasoning seem to me to make perfect sense when understood in the following way. He does not *simply* oppose the idea of truth as accurate transcription of reality, he does not *simply* oppose the requirement of justification, and he does not *simply* present the model of the constitution of human subjects by power as the fact of what happens. Foucault himself insists, "How is it that thought . . . insofar as it has a relationship with the truth, can also have a history? That is the question posed. . . . All those who say that for me the truth doesn't exist are simple-minded."[29] I suggest that he operates at two levels simultaneously: one level outside all particular frameworks, where he does make all of these claims, and another within particular frameworks, where he opposes all of them. He attempts "not a history that would be concerned with what might be true in the fields of learning, but an analysis of the 'games of truth,' the games of truth and error through which being is historically constituted as experience; that is, as something that can and must be thought."[30]

This statement about the two levels is not a contradiction. Although, as I argue in other chapters, the interaction of these two levels does in the end involve contradictions (which I also argue are workable), there is no contradiction immediately present in the formulation I have offered. If the level where he does make these claims is outside all particular frameworks, then the functioning of those statements has to be very different from what it would be within a framework. That is, those statements do not function as simple truth claims, since a truth claim presupposes a framework that gives it sense. Consequently these statements do not contradict, at least not in any immediate or obvious way, the apparently opposed claims he makes when situating himself within a framework.

As a first move toward supporting this interpretation, I suggest reading Foucault as being exact in his more central rhetorics. He typically uses the word "knowledge" (*savoir* or *connaissance*) or "knowledges" rather than equivalents of "belief," and he does not typically qualify this usage with equivalents of "purported knowledge" or "claimed knowledge."

---

[29] Foucault, *Foucault Live*, 294–95.
[30] Foucault, *Use of Pleasure*, 6–7.

This suggests that he wants to retain the sense of authenticity that attaches to that word. And he typically uses this word in connection with frameworks for which his theory of knowledge as a power effect could not be meaningful. Further, Foucault's emphasis is on taking seriously the terms of each knowledge-producing framework ("episteme," in his earlier work) without judging it in the terms of another framework. "There is always something ludicrous in philosophical discourse when it tries, from the outside, to dictate to others, to tell them where their truth is and how to find it, or when it works up a case against them in the language of naive positivity."[31] It seems very unlikely, then, that Foucault uses the word "knowledge" to indicate only the authenticity of the constitutive power effects of discourse; this particular construal of authenticity belongs only to a few frameworks, like his own. Foucault also uses the word "truth," and not equivalents of qualified versions like "purported truth" or "claimed truth," and the same considerations apply.

Beyond the more specifically rhetorical dimensions of Foucault's work, he explicitly claims that his analysis is not "a skeptical or relativistic refusal of all verified truth."[32] He is clear that truth is given by specific criteria, which, as much of his work aims to demonstrate, belong to particular frameworks: "by truth I . . . mean . . . 'the ensemble of rules according to which the true and the false are separated and specific effects of power attached to the true.'"[33] And, "I deal with practices, institutions and theories . . . and I look for the underlying knowledge (*savoir*) that makes them possible."[34]

These declarations have at least two relevant implications. First, even if truth is ultimately an effect of power and is ultimately interesting only because of the effects it has as power, what counts as truth is nonetheless given by criteria that Foucault does not link directly to power. In other words, to whatever degree power is relevant here, it is mediated by criteria specific to truth and in some sense independent of power. To approach the same point differently: the object of his analysis, truth, must first be iden-

---

[31] Ibid., 9.

[32] Michel Foucault, "The Subject and Power," in Dreyfus and Rabinow, *Michel Foucault*, 212.

[33] Foucault, *Power/Knowledge*, 132.

[34] Foucault, *Foucault Live*, 2, translator's parenthesis.

tified in its own terms, and only subsequently related to power, whether as power's effect or its effector ("and specific effects of power *attached to* the true," my emphasis). As Arnold Davidson notes,

> many of these rules [of production of discourse] will only be intelligible when one takes a standpoint internal to the development of [the] knowledge. The level of discursive practices must maintain its theoretical independence.... Foucault never denied that scientific knowledge is "endowed with its own rules for which external determinations could not account—its own structure as discursive practice."[35]

Foucault, then, does not abolish the notion of truth as accurate transcription of reality—the "rules" are typically criteria for exactly that. Rather, he re-situates truth with respect to its status and to the questions one might ask about it, while *retaining it exactly as it is already understood in the frameworks that give rise to it*. For example, in challenging the "repressive hypothesis" of power and sexuality, he writes,

> let there be no misunderstanding: I do not claim that sex has not been prohibited or barred or masked or misapprehended . . . but it is a ruse to make prohibition into the basic and constitutive element . . . All these . . . elements . . . which the repressive hypothesis groups together . . . are doubtless only component parts.[36]

Second, if truth is given by criteria located within particular frameworks, then, when Foucault positions himself to talk about a variety of frameworks, each in its own terms, he is not, at this level, making or required to make truth claims at all. (As I have noted, some of his supporters identify this level with his whole framework.) At this level he is not in a framework at all, and there are no criteria of truth to give sense to truth claims. He is not a relativist when comparing frameworks because he is saying nothing about truth at all. "We must make the intelligible appear

---

[35] Arnold Davidson, "Archaeology, Genealogy, Ethics," in *Foucault: A Critical Reader*, ed. David Couzens Hoy (Cambridge, MA: Basil Blackwell, 1986), 227, my insertions. Davidson is quoting Foucault in Paul Rabinow, ed., *The Foucault Reader* (New York: Pantheon, 1984), 337.
[36] Foucault, *History of Sexuality*, 12.

against a background of emptiness.... We must think that what exists is far from filling all possible spaces."[37]

I suggest that his talk of power-in-general and of truth-in-general is a rhetorical device that operates at this level to allow a just discursive and practical passage from one meaningful kind of talk and practice of truth to others, whether existing or possible. His claims about power, on this interpretation, are not statements that describe or refer to something named "power" but tropes that, like metaphors, function to articulate attention to two or more meaningful frameworks at once, relating them. For example (talking about his early *The Order of Things*, which offers a kind of analysis that does not disappear from his later work on power), "I wanted to establish the transformations necessary and sufficient for passing from the initial form of scientific discourse, that of the 18th century, to its final form, that of the 19th."[38] Much later, in *The History of Sexuality*, he writes, "Power's condition of possibility ... is ... force relations which ... constantly engender [particular] states of power, but the latter are always local and unstable." As he explains, power does not "embrace" everything, "but comes from everywhere." It

> is simply the over-all effect that emerges from all these [local, particular] mobilities, the concatenation that rests on each of them.... One needs to be nominalistic, no doubt: power is not an institution, and not a structure; neither is it a certain strength we are endowed with; it is the name that one attributes to a complex strategical situation in a particular society.[39]

I suggest that his claims that truth in general is nothing but, or only interesting as, an effect or effector of power occur at this metalevel. That is, he is not describing truth but performing an operation *on* truth, for example, rigorously comparing more than one kind of truth. He uses words like "strategy" to describe how truth appears *as a result of* or *exclusively within* his own, very specifically constrained approach. For example,

---

[37] Foucault, *Foucault Live*, 209.
[38] Ibid., 16.
[39] Foucault, *History of Sexuality*, 93, my insertions.

the analysis of discursive practices made it possible to trace the formation of disciplines (*savoirs*) while escaping the dilemma of science versus ideology. And the analysis of power relations . . . made it possible to view them as open strategies, while escaping the alternative of a power conceived of as domination or exposed as a simulacrum.[40]

Necessarily, a comparison between incommensurable frameworks cannot itself fall into the category of a truth claim. Since truth claims presuppose a framework that establishes truth criteria, if this kind of comparison does make truth claims, it has illegitimately—by any rational standards—already committed itself either to one of the frameworks in question or to yet another framework that cannot but impose its own irrelevant criteria on the frameworks in question. That this is the case is what the vast body of Foucault's own work shows. Foucault's analysis, then, has the merit of recognizing and addressing real problems of rational negotiation between frameworks with different truth criteria.

One kind of objection sometimes made here is that one *can* compare very different frameworks without this kind of paradox and complexity, the evidence being that we do it all the time, and that people like Foucault himself do it perfectly intelligibly.[41] But the point is not that making and understanding these comparisons is a rare and formidable achievement. The point is that we do not necessarily understand all of what we are doing when we make them. An adequate explanation of an easy action may be very complicated. I am suggesting that Foucault's claim is partly that we misunderstand much of what we are doing in comparing different epistemic frameworks, with the result that we are often irresponsible when a fuller understanding is required.

That Foucault's talk about power, and about truth in general, cannot itself consist in truth claims means that the criteria for its rigor can only be those of the particular frameworks being discussed.[42] As I quoted in the

---

[40] Foucault, *Use of Pleasure*, 4–5.
[41] See, for example, Donald Davidson on Thomas Kuhn in *Inquiries into Truth and Interpretation* (Oxford: Oxford University Press, 1984), 184.
[42] Sheldon Wolin criticizes Foucault for opposing "totalizing" political theory with a "power-laden conception of theory which is the equal of the claims made by any theory-intoxicated totalizer of the past." He argues instead for a conception "in which, as it were, theory self-destructs. Thus Plato's dialogue is always incomplete

introductory section, the a priori rules that "characterize a discursive practice" but are not themselves concerned with validity "are not imposed from the outside on the elements that they relate together; they are caught up in the very things that they connect."[43] Similarly, Gilles Deleuze, who also takes the radical difference in levels as fundamental in Foucault, notes that, while "the [ontological] conditions do not vary historically . . . they do vary *with* history": "the conditions are never more general than the conditioned element, and gain their value from their particular historical status."[44] This is also evident in the quotes about power from *The History of Sexuality* above.

The test of Foucault's metadiscourse, I suggest, is precisely that it does allow each framework to be understood in its own terms. The test, to repeat, is not that it accurately describes power in general or truth in general. And Foucault's work does allow each framework to be understood in its own terms. When he discusses psychoanalysis, for example, there is no incompatibility between his description of it and its self-description. In its own terms, it establishes certain truths; in his terms, precisely the successful establishing of those truths demonstrably has the kinds of effects he notes. Writing of repressive discourses, he comments, "one might argue that the purpose of these discourses was precisely to prevent children from

---

and the issue is never closed. Hegel and Marx both understood theory dialectically . . . Self-consuming theory—to use Stanley Fish's term—preserves the playful, self-derisive mien of theory without surrendering its potential contribution to decentered politics"; Sheldon S. Wolin, "On the Theory and Practice of Power," in *After Foucault: Humanistic Knowledge, Postmodern Challenges,* ed. Jonathan Arac (New Brunswick, NJ: Rutgers University Press, 1988), 200, 199. On the interpretation I propose here, especially bearing in mind my comments about self-cancellation in the introductory section, Foucault offers exactly the kind of conception Sheldon asks for. It is possible that Sheldon's interpretation of Foucault is in fact the right one. For his part, however, Sheldon does not seem to understand the difficulties in claiming that a theory can both be genuinely self-eliminating and also preserve its meaningful contribution.

[43] Foucault, *Archaeology*, 127.

[44] Gilles Deleuze, *Foucault* (Minneapolis: University of Minnesota Press, 1988), 114, my insertion. Deleuze seems to me to underestimate the importance of truth criteria's operating only within frameworks. He seems to treat the metalevel as descriptively true throughout his book, so that its truth then invalidates the truth of frameworks opposed to Foucault's.

having a sexuality. But their *effect* was to din it into parents' heads that their children's sex constituted a fundamental problem . . . and into children's heads."[45]

The question he raises is not whether psychoanalysis is true or false but whether, *granting its truth,* it is a truth worth its effects in comparison with other kinds of truth established by other frameworks (and these other truths need never invalidate the psychoanalytic ones). As John Rajchman writes,

> Foucault argued that it is not the case that where power is exercised, our true nature is alienated, and nothing true can be said about us. Our critical question should rather be: Why are there some truths about ourselves and not others at a time and place? And what are the costs and consequences to ourselves and our society that there exist these sorts and not others?[46]

How does one make this kind of decision? As Foucault's work emphasizes, that one can think at all, including think of making a decision, means one is already at least partly in a framework. If one is troubled by one's framework, or intrigued by possibilities of another—and work like Foucault's, or like ideology critique, may produce this result—then one is already implicitly engaged in the alternative framework(s) that allow the perspective on one's initial one. Then the only reasonable way to decide is to find, if possible, a way of balancing the frameworks without precommitting to either (perhaps, for example, through the kind of existential decision I discuss in Chapter 1, section 5, or through the self-canceling negotiation and the justified resituating that results from it that I discuss in that and other chapters, and which is really a different side of the same thing). One's decision will then be (epistemologically) noncircular and (ethicopolitically) unbiased. Foucault's contribution, I suggest, is to offer one such way.

The point of allowing each framework to be understood in its own terms is to avoid theoretical and practical bias given by the very truth-criteria that are under discussion. "We have learned to put the words of men into yet unformulated relationships stated by us for the first time, and

---

[45] Foucault, *Power/Knowledge,* 120, emphasis in original.
[46] John Rajchman, *Truth and Eros: Foucault, Lacan, and the Question of Ethics* (New York: Routledge, 1991), 124.

yet objectively exact."[47] In other words, Foucault is trying to carry out precisely the rational or reasonable commitment to truth as accurate transcription of reality, in the name of justice, that motivates, among other things, ideology critique. But he does so more rigorously, taking properly into account that different interpretations of what counts as truth and reality themselves are what are most fundamentally at stake. And his version of critique does not let even itself off the hook. "If people are willing to . . . make use of [my books] . . . to . . . disqualify systems of power, including even possibly the ones my books come out of, well, all the better."[48]

Foucault's work, then, does not aim to eliminate truth as accurate description or to establish power effects as the descriptive truth of what happens. On the contrary, he aims to articulate a rhetoric that allows truth-conferring frameworks to be put in question without the result that this general questioning itself eliminates the meaningfulness of truth. He does this by operating simultaneously at two levels, one within particular frameworks, where truth is straightforwardly truth, and one outside of all particular frameworks, where truth is irrelevant. The coherence of this metaframework-and-frameworks analysis lies in the complete irrelevance of the metadiscourse to the object discourses. The metalevels and object levels do not conflict with each other because the apparently equivalent terms (like "truth") used disparately at each level are performing unrelated functions.

A last point: it is implicit in this justification of Foucault that when frameworks like psychoanalysis or those that give immediate sense to ideology critique (Marxism, liberal theories) simply assert their truth against frameworks with different criteria for truth itself, they are being arbitrary and irresponsible. Foucault's challenge shows why, in such contexts, they must, if they are to be genuinely committed to their own aims of establishing truth without bias, enter into the kind of rigorous rhetorical medium that Foucault's work exemplifies. In fact, the reasons for Foucault's framework of frameworks and its characteristics show that they *do* enter into that rhetorical medium, but that they mistake their own claims for those given sense *within* a particular framework. Consequently they do, at

---

[47] Foucault, *Foucault Live*, 21.

[48] Quoted in Halperin, *Saint Foucault*, 52, my insertion, from a quotation in Didier Eribon, *Michel Foucault et ses contemporains* (Paris: Fayard, 1994), 237.

those points, exactly what they often accuse Foucault of doing: they produce mere rhetoric, unrigorously and irresponsibly, mistaking it for truth—conceptual nonsense playing the role of ideology.

And they do so because they do not acknowledge the multiple self-disparities of which *rationality itself,* as Foucault recognized, is capable ("I do not speak of a bifurcation of reason. Rather I speak of multiple bifurcations. I speak of an endless prolific division").[49]

> Nothing is more inconsistent than a political regime that is indifferent to the truth; but nothing is more dangerous than a political system that claims to prescribe the truth. . . . The task of speaking the truth is an infinite labour: to respect it in its complexity is an obligation that no power can afford to short-change, unless it would impose the silence of slavery.[50]

---

[49] Foucault, *Foucault Live,* 243.
[50] Ibid., 308.

6. *How to Be Properly Unnatural*

The Metaphysics of Heterosexual Normativity and the Importance of the Concepts of Essence and Nature for Pluralism

> I want a queer studies that allows for attachments that are not necessarily politically consistent and acknowledges the incalculability of the subject. . . . More devotion to the fundamental perplexity of all lives—rather than contempt for those who appear *only* to reproduce norms—seems particularly urgent at the moment. . . . A flat anti-normativity is not necessarily the most efficacious political or conceptual challenge to the forms of constraint and abjection we face.
>
> —Biddy Martin[1]

With qualifications that I discuss below, sexuality and gender theorists have largely rejected the concept of "nature," and the similar concept of "essence," except when understood as constructed by social and historical processes. I argue in this chapter that for reasons involving both the sense of these concepts at the metaphysical level and, connected with it, their liberatory political significance, we desperately need to reclaim *construction-free* natures or essences, *and* that we need to think of them as ultimately constructed, *and* that these views are irreconcilably contradictory. I propose what I shall argue is a viable contradictory, or genuinely "unnatural," logic that allows us to reclaim the independent value of these conflicting ideas. In the course of this discussion, I briefly suggest the relevance of this logic to the concept of nature in environmental thought in connection with the work of Bruno Latour. Finally, I explore some of the implica-

---

[1] Biddy Martin, *Femininity Played Straight: The Significance of Being Lesbian* (New York: Routledge, 1996), 14–15.

tions of this logic for our experience, practice, and relation to others whose ways of making sense are not our own.

It is commonly felt in our cultures that heterosexuality is normal as a matter of course, that it should be taken for granted as the right way to be. One way of expressing this is that gendered creatures are heterosexual by "nature." Queer theory has labeled this attitude and the practices and institutional pressures that produce and express it "heterosexual normativity," or, more compactly, "heteronormativity."[2] Like any way of thinking about reality, this idea, attitude, and system of social practices can exist only under particular assumptions about what makes sense in general and about the ultimate nature of reality. In other words, this idea is based on a logic and a metaphysics. (As I shall argue, it is important for the sake of queer theory itself to note that this *is* true of all ways of dealing with reality. Even if, as in the case of many sexuality theorists, the "metaphysics" is a view that there is no, or no valid or worthwhile, metaphysics, this is still a view about the ultimate truth of reality, and that is what a metaphysics *is*. The "no metaphysics" view, then, really only rejects *competing* metaphysics, which take reality to include something beyond historical, social, material reality.) One dimension of the heteronormative metaphysics and logic that I would like to explore here is its widely recognized understanding of homosexuality (in particular, though not uniquely) as not belonging to the way things truly, unquestionably, and inescapably are, or, in other words, as "unnatural."

Over the last few decades, sexuality and gender theorists have increasingly responded to this heteronormative view by rejecting the idea of a "nature," of an inescapable way that things are, independent of historical change and social construction. This has been the gist of much of the debate between constructionism and essentialism.

It is true that there have also been substantial attempts on the "antiheteronormative" side of that debate to make room for natures or essences. Eve Kosofsky Sedgwick, for example, writes with respect to "essentialist and constructivist . . . accounts of gay identity" that "there are certainly rhetorical and political grounds . . . for underwriting continuously the legitimacy of both. . . . And beyond these, there are crucial reasons of

---

[2] See, for example, Michael Warner, ed., *Fear of a Queer Planet: Queer Politics and Social Theory* (Minneapolis: University of Minnesota Press, 1993), xxi–xxv.

respect."³ Ann Cvetkovich similarly argues against the assumption that "the queer [or "what is without fixed identity"] and the lesbian [an essential identity] . . . are mutually exclusive—that the queer, for instance, is the undoing of the identity politics signified by the category lesbian, or that lesbian culture is hostile to queer formations."⁴ And Biddy Martin points out that "postmodernism, for its rhetorical attention to otherness and difference, enacts its own form of othering, of anything that looks too stable, too fixed, too certain."⁵ But I argue that these attempts have consistently been made in ways that do not recognize that the essentialist and constructivist conceptions are so deeply contradictory that they are in fact entirely mutually exclusive. As a result, these attempts either give no account of how the relation between these two conceptions is possible (as is the case with the three authors I have just quoted), or in the end turn out really to subordinate natures or essences thoroughly to construction.

Against the responses that endorse the legitimacy of both conceptions but do not give an account of its possibility, I want to try to show the *cooperative* value of their *excluding* each other's sense, of their *not* making room for each other. This is of course also a contradiction, but, as I have done in other contexts, I shall argue that this particular kind of contradiction is a workable one. That there is this kind of contradiction is, again, a central theme of my account. Against the responses that do offer an account of the relation between the two conceptions but in doing so subordinate natures to construction, what I want to show is that, on the one hand, this thoroughgoing ultimate rejection of a "nature" of things cedes too much to the victimizers: too much that is of value, and in fact that is more than just valuable, but essential (a term whose sense I try to justify here) to our lives. And I want to show, on the other hand, that this thoroughgoing rejection requires too little of us who reject heterosexism, makes us too liable to repeating related kinds of injustice ourselves.

The discussion of "nature" here is also relevant to the concept of nature as it is taken up in and troubles environmental thought. I discuss this as-

---

³Eve Kosofsky Sedgwick, *Epistemology of the Closet* (Berkeley: University of California Press, 1990), 27.

⁴Ann Cvetkovich, *An Archive of Feelings: Trauma, Sexuality, and Lesbian Public Cultures* (Durham, NC: Duke University Press, 2003), 11, my insertions.

⁵Martin, *Femininity Played Straight*, 15.

How to Be Properly Unnatural 153

pect of its relevance briefly below, in connection with Bruno Latour's contribution to the debate between nature and social construction.

I approach these issues of essence or nature by revisiting the essentialism versus constructionism debate. In recent years many theorists have come to dismiss this debate as irrelevant, often because one or the other version of the now familiar attempts to reconcile the two views is taken to have succeeded, so that the debate is "old news." But I want to argue, first, that these attempts have not in fact succeeded, and second, that there is still a great deal of politically relevant insight to be gained from these views in their specifically antagonistic forms.

I begin by sketching the logic of the metaphysics of "natures" and its close connections with the logic of essences. I then argue that the essentialist versus constructionist debate, in working with and against that logic, has been caught up in unrecognized and insoluble contradictions. I argue that these contradictions are another way of expressing the problem of ceding too much and taking too little responsibility that I mentioned above. I then try to show that the solution to both these forms of the problem lies precisely in working with those *unresolved and unresolvable* contradictions.

I shall propose an alternative logic to both those of heterosexism and those so far relied on, as it seems to me, by sexuality and gender theorists. This will be a contradictory logic, and will underpin a contradictory metaphysics. Again, I try to show that these particular kinds of contradiction make viable sense, and so are capable of being helpful in the ways I claim for them.[6] I also discuss some dimensions of what this logic concretely requires of us and offers us in practice, with respect both to our own lives and to our relations with others whose ways of making sense are very different from our own.

While a lot of feminist and queer work, especially some versions of "French feminism," has already developed frameworks that accept contradiction, and has even developed logics of contradiction, these frameworks and logics, as I discuss, go only so far.[7] The frameworks that simply accept

---

[6] On the general possibility of legitimate logical contradiction, see again the Introduction, section 5.

[7] Sedgwick, for example, writes against the idea that there is "any standpoint of thought from which the rival claims of [various different] understandings of sexual definition could be decisively arbitrated as to their 'truth.' Instead, the performative

contradiction typically do not show either how we can successfully conceive contradiction or how it can be managed. And while the logics of contradiction do give this kind of account, they remain consistently—noncontradictorily—contradictory. As a result, they still really preclude the sense of a nature or essence, which is characterized by being entirely without contradiction, by being simply and changelessly what it is. In fact, they themselves (contradictorily, as one would expect from standpoints that consist in contradiction), in pursuing contradictions that are *only* or noncontradictorily contradictions, are still too committed to the idea of an unwavering self-consistency in the case of contradiction itself. That is, they are still committed to the idea of a "nature" or unvarying essence *of contradiction*. (This remains true even if they acknowledge *other, separate* aspects of things that are not contradictory.)

Since the logic I want to explore partly (or, more accurately, sometimes always, although only sometimes always) violates the logic that belongs to thinking of things (and logics) as having natures, as being simply self-identically what they are and are meant to be, I think of it as a logic of "the unnatural." My hope is that this "unnatural" logic will contribute to resolving some of the more recalcitrant problems we encounter in experiencing and dealing with heteronormativity.

1. The Logical Characters of Nature, Essence, and Construction

The heterosexist reaction to homosexuality as unnatural is an especially extreme form of normativity. For this reaction, there are things that are not merely statistically normal, not merely conveniently or comfortably standard and so, by default, preferable for the (by definition) standard majority, but are *natural*, are the way that belongs to them without any possible or conceivable question, the only way they can conceivably be. As a

---

effects of the self-contradictory discursive field of force created by their overlap will be my subject"; Sedgwick, *Epistemology*, 9, my insertion. And Teresa de Lauretis argues for a "movement between the . . . discursive space . . . made available by hegemonic discourses and the space-off, the elsewhere, of those discourses. . . . To inhabit both kinds of spaces at once is to live the contradiction which . . . is the condition of feminism here and now"; Teresa de Laretis, *Technologies of Gender: Essays on Theory, Film, and Fiction* (Bloomington: Indiana University Press, 1987), 26.

result, anything that conflicts with what is natural is literally inconceivable, contradicting sense and the only way that things can be.

Roland Barthes, for example, notes about the role of the "myth" of nature, in the case of bourgeois ideology, that it "transforms . . . History into Nature . . . man as represented by it is universal, eternal . . . bourgeois ideology yields an unchangeable nature."[8] Similarly, Rosalind Coward and John Ellis write that this kind of ideology is "effective precisely for the reason that it appears as 'natural,' 'the way things are'": so, "for example the existing relations of power are . . . perceived precisely as the way things are, ought to be and will be."[9] Because the concept of nature is that of things as the only way they can be, it makes the idea of accounting for "natural" things literally meaningless. If something cannot be conceived to be otherwise, there is no meaning to asking how it got to be that way. The question contrasts its present way of being with some other, and no other way of being is conceivable for it. In Barthes' words, this concept of nature "refuses explanations," and, in the case of human reality, "produces the . . . image of an unchanging humanity, characterized by an indefinite repetition of its identity."[10]

The politically relevant result, of course, is that those things that are understood as natural, such as heterosexuality, have no conceivable alternatives. They are the unique and unquestionable standard by which all related things are measured, and the idea that things might be different from what they legislate is not merely false but utterly incoherent. As Barthes, again, puts it, "ideology is . . . constituted by the loss of the historical quality of things: in it, things lose the memory that they once were made."[11] In fact, they (in this case, heterosexuality as a "natural" norm) lose the sense that they are the kinds of things that could even be thought of as having been made, and so of course also the sense that they could even be thought about with a view to being remade.

---

[8] Roland Barthes, *Mythologies,* trans. Annette Lavers (London: Granada, 1972), 141–42.
[9] Rosalind Coward and John Ellis, *Language and Materialism: Developments in Semiology and the Theory of the Subject* (London: Routledge & Kegan Paul, 1977), 67.
[10] Barthes, *Mythologies,* 142.
[11] Ibid., 142.

Closer to home, however, as Coward and Ellis argue, "what is produced in ideology is the very basis of the [human] subject's activity . . . and the coherency of that subject."[12] This implies two things that are important here. The less radical one is that one's sense of being a person is subject to the concept of the natural. As a result, if one does not conform to what is usually taken to be part of being a person, one is unnatural, and it is clear that this now means that one is inconceivable, without an identity (that is, without logical coherence, without sameness with oneself), and so not part of reality at all. As Judith Butler writes, "The cultural matrix through which gender identity has become intelligible requires that certain kinds of 'identities' cannot 'exist'—that is, those in which gender does not follow from sex and those in which the practices of desire do not 'follow' from either sex or gender. . . . Indeed, precisely because certain kinds of 'gender identities' fail to conform to those norms of cultural intelligibility, they appear only as developmental failures or logical impossibilities from within that domain."[13] More simply, Michael Warner refers to "the assumption that this group [queers] . . . does not or should not exist."[14]

The second, more radical implication of the idea that "the coherency of the subject" is produced by the ideology of the natural is that *the very idea of being a person, a human subjectivity, at all*, is born out of this concept. And this means that *any* sense of being a person is subject to the extreme normativity that it involves. As a result, many gender and sexuality theorists have argued that if we want to avoid being entrapped by politically motivated normativities, we need to reject being persons, identities, subjects, at all. Butler, for example, is troubled by putting herself forward under *any* category: "To write or speak *as a lesbian* . . . is . . . to come out or write in the name of an identity which, once produced, sometimes functions as a politically efficacious phantasm." For, she argues, "identity categories tend to be instruments of regulatory regimes," even when they are

---

[12] Coward and Ellis, *Language and Materialism*, 67–68, my insertion.
[13] Judith Butler, *Gender Trouble: Feminism and the Subversion of Identity* (New York: Routledge, 1990), 17.
[14] Warner, *Fear*, xxv, my insertion.

"the rallying points for a liberatory contestation of . . . oppression."[15] Similarly, Denise Riley notes that "feminism has intermittently been as vexed with the urgency of disengaging from the category 'women' as it has with laying claim to it."[16] And John Champagne follows Foucault in arguing that although "one cannot *not* be a subject," we need to "resist the continuing practices of subject formation and . . . work strategically towards a 'freeing' of the subject from subjectivity."[17]

The result of this kind of response has often been the articulation and endorsement of a kind of "unnaturalness" as a sort of "anything but nature," as the opposite, and only the opposite, of what is natural, of what is simply given as what the thing simply is. Mark Blasius, for instance, discusses how "lesbians and gay men virtually invent a way of life through which they create and re-create the self continually" in ways that "have, of course, nothing to do with any intrinsic qualities of homosexuals."[18] Eve Sedgwick writes that one value of the term "queer," in contrast with the "univocal whole" that "sexual identity" refers to, is that it can name "the open mesh of possibilities, gaps, overlaps, dissonances and resonances, lapses and excesses of meaning when the constituent elements of anyone's gender, of anyone's sexuality aren't made (or *can't be* made) to signify monolithically."[19] Similarly, Steven Seidman embraces postmodernism as a "standpoint that aims to decenter or destabilize unitary concepts of the human subject, foundationalist and objectivist views of knowledge, and totalizing perspectives on society and history."[20] Leo Bersani, again, argues for a "'self-shattering' . . . anti-identitarian identity."[21] Reflecting

---

[15] Judith Butler, "Imitation and Gender Insubordination," in *Inside/Out: Lesbian Theories, Gay Theories,* ed. Diana Fuss (New York: Routledge, 1991), 13–14.

[16] Denise Riley, *"Am I That Name?" Feminism and the Category of "Women" in History* (Minneapolis: University of Minnesota Press, 1988), 3–4.

[17] John Champagne, *The Ethics of Marginality: A New Approach to Gay Studies* (Minneapolis: University of Minnesota Press, 1995), xxvii.

[18] Mark Blasius, *Gay and Lesbian Politics: Sexuality and the Emergence of a New Ethic* (Philadelphia, PA: Temple University Press, 1994), 192.

[19] Eve Kosofsky Sedgwick, *Tendencies* (Durham, NC: Duke University Press, 1993), 8.

[20] Steven Seidman, *Difference Troubles: Queering Social Theory and Sexual Politics* (New York: Cambridge University Press, 1997), 109.

[21] Leo Bersani, *Homos* (Cambridge, MA: Harvard University Press, 1995), 101.

on Jean Genet's celebration of being an "outlaw," an outcast from all norms, a status that Bersani takes as one fruitful model of this kind of "identity," he notes that "the question becomes: how do you get rid of an essence?"[22] And in an extreme but by no means unique formulation, Gregory Bredbeck asserts that even "'sense' itself is form of cultural fascism that seeks to pin down, label, constrain, control, and dismiss in a way that is undermined by history itself."[23]

And the theorists of subjectivity (or antisubjectivity) mentioned above certainly do not want to settle for any form of unquestioned or unchallenged subjectivity, or "having a nature." As Cathy Griggers, for example, notes, "In the lesbian cultural landscape of postmodernity, essentialist arguments about feminine identity are more defunct than ever."[24]

But there are problems with this purely antinatural or antiessentialist stance, problems in fact often recognized by these same theorists in connection with the conflict between "essence" and "construction."

2. The Incompatibility but Necessity of Both Essence and Construction

While, as we have just seen, many sexuality and gender theorists now completely reject the concept of a nature or essence, many others have come to see a need for something like this concept in a viable sexual politics, and have developed a variety of ways of accommodating it to the alternative idea of social construction. In either case, the respective theorists have largely come to regard the debate between essence and construction as settled, and so no longer relevant. In this section, however, I want to show *both* that we cannot dispense with either the concept of an essence or nature or that of construction, *and* that the familiar ways of accommodating them to each other have not succeeded, and logically *could not* have succeeded. The problem, then, is still very much with us.

---

[22] Ibid., 173.

[23] Gregory W. Bredbeck, *Sodomy and Interpretation: Marlowe to Milton* (Ithaca, NY: Cornell University Press, 1991), xii.

[24] Cathy Griggers, "Lesbian Bodies in the Age of (Post)mechanical Reproduction," in *Fear of a Queer Planet: Queer Politics and Social Theory,* ed. Michael Warner (Minneapolis: University of Minnesota Press, 1993), 184.

As the discussion has already indicated, there are close connections between the assumptions that underlie the visceral reaction to the "unnaturalness" of homosexuality and the theoretical language of essences that has played such a large role in analyses of homophobia and the ways to fight it. The concept of an essence in fact neatly translates the concept of a nature. It too is the final and fixed answer to the question of what something is, beyond which there are no questions to be asked. And as a result, it is inconceivable here as well that anything with an essence could have genuinely different variations, or that it could (and still less should) change in any fundamental way. As Barthes makes this connection between nature and essence, in his discussion of the "myth" of the natural, "The world enters language as a dialectical relation between activities, between human actions; it comes out of myth as a harmonious display of essences."[25]

Because these concepts are closely related and also play a closely related political role, the reasons for fighting the concept of essence are identical to those for fighting the concept of nature. They both belong to a logic and metaphysics of a given, exclusive sense and identity of things. Butler and Diana Fuss, among others, have elaborated some of the politically relevant problems with this logic and metaphysics.[26] Essences, being the ultimate answer to what things are, and constituting their fixed identity, allow for no fundamental change, development, or deep differences between people who share an identity understood as an essence. The idea of essences also denies social responsibility for how groups are categorized. And beyond these problems, this idea puts an unjustified and unjustifiable end to explanations and analysis, so that the standpoints based on this kind of concept are ultimately arbitrary.

The alternative concept is, of course, social construction, or the production of what things are by specific historical circumstances. But, as I mentioned, it has become increasingly apparent to many in these debates that we cannot do without either concept. This has emerged as the case not only because both are necessary in order to allow a viable politics but, more fundamentally, because both are also *logically* (and in fact also

---

[25] Barthes, *Mythologies,* 142.
[26] Butler, *Gender Trouble,* 12ff.; Diana Fuss, *Essentially Speaking: Feminism, Nature and Difference* (New York: Routledge, 1989), 2ff.

metaphysically) necessary. That is, both concepts are also necessary to sense or meaning itself (not, I think, in Bredbeck's sense of a "fascistic," controlling "making sense of things," but) in the sense of *having* meanings, and articulable connections between them, *at all*.[27]

With respect to political concerns, essences without construction present the problems I have mentioned just above. And, with respect to sense or meaning itself, without construction, that is, without genuine historical production and change, there would be no escape or separation from the absolutely unchanging given that would make it possible to put it in relation to anything else, and so even to refer to it, let alone reflect on it. If each thing were really an eternally self-same essence, one could not alter one's state (oneself also being an essence) to relate oneself to it, and more generally there could be no "relating" of anything "to" anything else, only simply being the thing or simply not being the thing, always in exactly the same way. There could be no transformations of anything, no processes, including the shifts or movements of consciousness involved in making statements, still less modifiable statements, about anything.

But, on the other hand, constructions without essence would be continuous production and transformation. With respect to sense or meaning, this would allow nothing to be graspable *at all,* nothing to be *that specific thing that is* constructed or *those specific things that are* constructed *from,* or anyone in particular for whose sake one is thinking about these issues in the first place. It would allow us to have no specific meanings, and so to say nothing specific—not even to mean anything in particular when we deny that "essences" exist. Neither the words and ideas one would use in discussing this process that is reality nor the actions one would take in participating in it would have any coherence, would *be* any particular words or any particular actions.

We need to recognize that the essences required here are essences *entirely unqualified* by construction, what I shall call pure essences. It is incoherent to think of construction *itself* without something simply given, not-to-be-explained and so ahistorical, in some form, that the construction can work *on* and that the process of construction can already *be*. Other-

---

[27] For an extended discussion of this literature, see Fuss, *Essentially Speaking*. See also Bredbeck, *Sodomy*, 237–38; Butler, *Gender Trouble;* Riley, *"Am I That Name,"* e.g., 99ff.

wise every part and aspect of the process and materials of construction must be conceived as being constructed before any construction can begin. That is, construction must take place to make it possible for it to take place: construction must happen before it is possible for construction to happen.

In fact, as Fuss points out, social constructionist explanation as it exists already relies on a pure essence: the idea of the "social," itself not requiring, and insusceptible of, explanation.[28] Because construction is performed by the social conditions, the "social" is what is doing the explaining. It is consequently *presupposed* by this kind of explanation, and so necessarily remains unexplained by it. And that at least something that is doing the explaining must necessarily remain unexplained is another way of arguing the inescapable reliance of sense or meaning in general on pure essences, on a simply given starting point.

Butler makes another kind of argument for the reliance of "nonessential" thought on essences or simple identities, noting, for one example, that when Julia Kristeva adopts the (obviously tempting) strategy of developing an opposition "between the principle of multiplicity that escapes the charge of non-contradiction and a principle of identity based on the suppression of that multiplicity. . . . that very principle of multiplicity . . . operates in much the same manner as a principle of identity."[29] Contradictory multiplicity, by being stably opposed to and contrasted with identity and singleness, gains a self-same, unified consistency, a simple identity. The same problem, I suggest, applies to the consistent kind of logic of contradiction explored by thinkers like Luce Irigaray, who writes, for example, that "woman . . . enters into a ceaseless exchange of herself with the other without any possibility of identifying either."[30] The idea of contradiction itself is usable only because it *has a given, self-same sense.* (And if there is genuinely no essence here, the problem I discussed above applies: because there is *only* contradiction, we are no longer saying anything identifiable at all.)

---

[28] Fuss, *Essentially Speaking*, 6.
[29] Butler, *Gender Trouble*, 89.
[30] Luce Irigaray, *This Sex Which Is Not One*, trans. Catherine Porter with Carolyn Burke (Ithaca, NY: Cornell University Press, 1985), 31.

On the political side, as Fuss puts it in the course of a general argument that constructionism and essentialism depend on each other, politics itself is unthinkable without some sense of a self-identical phenomenon in its own right.[31] One cannot mobilize on behalf of "homosexuals" or "women" without a sense that these categories refer to something sharing stable traits with others of its kind.[32] And for the same reasons that sense requires something simply given, it is not enough to regard these categories as historically assembled, temporary stabilities. (As Butler, for example, argues we should, proposing "the reconceptualization of identity as an *effect,* that is, as *produced* or *generated*";[33] or as Alison Stone has more recently argued along different lines, in the course of proposing that we should reject even the concessions that have so far been made to essence in these debates.[34]) Again, what these categories were assembled *out of,* and something about the process *by which* they were assembled, needs to be *simply given* in some form if the process of assembly can be coherently conceived at all. Otherwise, again, neither the words one uses in discussing this process nor the actions one takes in participating in it have any coherence, *are* any particular words or actions.

As I discuss in the next section, the concept of essence in fact has positive value in its own independent right. Here I am restricting myself to the ways in which it and construction are both simply necessary, in order to show the nature of the logical problem they present.

Lately, as I mentioned above, many theorists have taken these developments to show that the debate is now pointless. Seidman (who in fact only sees a point in constructionism, and not in essentialism at all) makes this point forcefully: "the arcane polemics between constructionists and essentialists has evolved into a sterile metatheoretical debate increasingly devoid of moral and political import."[35] But, while both concepts are necessary, as the history of this debate has succeeded in showing, they are also, as I am about to argue, incompatible, and in fact irreconcilably con-

---

[31] Fuss, *Essentially Speaking,* xii.

[32] Ibid., 24ff.

[33] Butler, *Gender Trouble,* 147.

[34] Alison Stone, "Essentialism and Anti-Essentialism in Feminist Philosophy," *Journal of Moral Philosophy* 1, no. 2 (2004): 135–53.

[35] Seidman, *Difference Troubles,* 109.

tradictory. Consequently we are caught in a real contradiction to which we so far have no solution.

The theorists who have attempted to reconcile these concepts do not, of course, see them as incompatible in this way. Fuss, for example, refers to "a largely artificial (albeit powerful) antagonism between them."[36] But the idea of construction as a basic explanation denies the possibility, or any sense to the very idea, of being simply *given,* without a history of being produced, which partly defines an essence. And the idea of essence, as the related concept of nature brings sharply into relief, denies any sense to its being constructed *in any way.* What counts as an explanation for the one simply is not an explanation, is not even coherent as a statement about the matter, for the other. As a result the attempts so far made to reconcile them have failed, I believe, and necessarily so.

Both Fuss and Butler, for example, while explaining the necessity for both views, in the end do not, it seems to me, give them both equal weight. While clearly trying to make a place for essentialisms, they nonetheless still think about how to combine them with constructionist insights from within what is really an entirely constructionist perspective. Fuss, for her part, writes that "we need both to theorize essentialist spaces from which to speak and, simultaneously, to deconstruct those spaces to keep them from solidifying. Such a double gesture involves once again the responsibility to historicize, to examine each deployment of essence . . . in the complicated contextual frame in which it is made."[37] But this does not really do justice to the concept of an essence. From a genuinely essentialist standpoint, essences are *not historical at all.* Consequently, they are also not the kind of thing that can be "deployed"—they just *are,* they are just given as the core of what is real, not strategically selected from among alternative possibilities of thought. And, as I argued above along the lines introduced by these theorists themselves, it is just *this* sense of "essence"—that it just *is,* that it is simply given—that we need if either politics or sense itself are to be possible.

Butler, similarly, proposes to understand identity as, exactly, an historically constructed effect, and notes that this view "opens up possibilities of 'agency' that are insidiously foreclosed by positions that take identity

[36] Fuss, *Essentially Speaking,* 119.
[37] Ibid., 118.

categories as foundational and fixed.... Construction is not opposed to agency: it is the necessary scene of agency." As a result, "The critical task for feminism is not to establish a point of view outside of constructed identities" but rather to participate in "those practices of repetition that constitute identity and, therefore, present the immanent possibility of contesting them."[38] This preferential reliance on constructionism is easy to understand: a view of social reality as deeply historical, that is, as deeply changeable and therefore full of contrasts, seems readily to account not only for phases of history that continuously or pervasively undergo fundamental change but also for phases that contrast with those by having become temporarily stable, circumstantially constellating something like an essence or identity or nature. But, again, in the essentialist view "social" reality is not ultimately historical, or ultimately social, at all. And essences are not the kind of thing one contests. They are the basis of reality and sense, and so are that which gives sense to contestation, that on the basis of which one contests. If one were to try to contest them, one would be relying on them entirely in doing so, and contestation would lose its meaning.

Bruno Latour offers a subtle and elegant attempt to reconcile nature and social construction in the context of science studies rather than sexual politics, and so with a particular focus on the relation between the "objectively given" natural world and our artificial, "fabricated" theoretical constructions and technology.[39] Latour argues that there is no opposition between fabrication and given objectivity, and that we and our activities, on the one hand, and the environment and its processes and things, on the other, are simply different elements in one and the same network of relations. What is more, which is which, object or subject, what initiates action or what is passively acted on, depends on the context. "Of quasi-objects, quasi-subjects, we shall simply say that they trace networks. They are real, quite real, and we humans have not made them. But they are collective because they attach us to one another, because they ... define our social bond by their very circulation. They are discursive however; they are narrated, historical, passionate, and peopled with actants [actors, whether hu-

---

[38] Butler, *Gender Trouble*, 147.
[39] I thank Irene Klaver for pointing out Latour's importance for this discussion.

man or nonhuman] of autonomous forms."⁴⁰ Out of this unstably defined networking between many diverse elements, stable configurations emerge that we can identify as fixed and given things or as free agents. The distinctions between elements in terms of which we usually think are valid, but "*at the end* of the process, not at the beginning. Once the institutions of the collective have stabilized these distributions of roles and functions, we shall in fact be able to recognize subjects and objects, an externality, humans, a *cosmos*."⁴¹ For Latour, then, there is no conflict between "construction" and "essence" or "nature"; they are phases of a continuous process.

His reconciliation of the two conceptions rests, however, on an idea very similar to Butler's: he conceives essence or nature as a generated effect. Essence is, again, the "provisional conclusion" of a process: "there are indeed essences, but these are obtained by institution at the end of an explicit process that gives them durability and indisputability."⁴² But as I have argued, an essence is not the kind of thing that can be produced, or that can be continuous with a process of production, and in fact any such process would presuppose the original sense of essence. Latour's account really misses what the concept of essence expresses, and reconceives it in constructionist terms.

Unlike Butler, Latour does recognize that "the two orders are not only different, they are incommensurable" (in this case, the orders of politics and nature).⁴³ In fact, he works out the consequences of this and other incommensurabilities brilliantly, in a dazzling variety of contexts. But when he tries to give a general account of how these incommensurable orders can be related, he does so by proposing a way in which the incommensurability and so the contradiction between them can be eliminated. "Worlds appear commensurable or incommensurable only to those who cling to measured measures. Yet all measures, in hard and soft science alike, are also measuring measures, and they construct a commensurability that did not exist

---

⁴⁰ Bruno Latour, *We Have Never Been Modern*, trans. Catherine Porter (Cambridge, MA: Harvard University Press, 1993), 89, my insertion.

⁴¹ Bruno Latour, *Politics of Nature: How to Bring the Sciences into Democracy*, trans. Catherine Porter (Cambridge, MA: Harvard University Press, 2004), 90.

⁴² Ibid., 241.

⁴³ Ibid., 30.

before their own calibration."[44] But he does not address the logic by which these commensurabilities can be constructed. Surely, if we recalibrate our measures, that is exactly what we have done: we are no longer dealing with the original worlds but with a rewriting of them into a mode of sense that is neither their own nor consistent with their own. Rather than making further sense of the subject, we have changed it. Latour argues in the same passage that "nothing is, by itself, either reducible or irreducible to anything else. Never by itself, but always through the mediation of another." Even if this is so, surely the "mediating measures" by which it accounts for itself prior to our recalibrating account of it are entitled to a voice, and simply replacing them with conflicting mediating measures is in no way working with what *they* legitimately express. In fact, Latour's own rewriting of the concept of essence in the terms of construction described in the previous paragraph is an example of this same unacknowledged replacement of the original subject with a different one that works according to a different logic. Latour, then, does not reconcile the incommensurabilities between the two conceptions but instead avoids contradiction by subordinating the one to the mode of sense of the other.

To the degree that theorists who want to retain constructionism also want be logically coherent, then, they cannot accommodate the concept of essence. Despite these kinds of attempt at harmonizing the two views, they remain irreconcilably contradictory.

And this is where, I believe, a logic of the unnatural can help us: a logic that is incompatible with itself, contradictory, not self-identical, and in these specific ways not coherently conceivable. As I shall discuss, because it is *genuinely* contradictory, contradicting even itself *as contradiction,* it can make legitimate room for what it (also) excludes, for what is *absolutely not contradictory* but is simply and unquestionably what it is: essences and natures.

3. The Character and Value of a Logic of the Unnatural

In this section I first sketch the character of a logic of the unnatural—its basic elements and how they fit together. Then, in the light of the discussion above of essences, I discuss the problems that, at the start of the chapter, I suggested arise from abandoning the concept of nature to heteronorma-

[44] Latour, *We Have Never Been Modern,* 113.

tivity. I then outline some of the ways in which this unnatural logic responds to those problems. The problems involve not only the issue of contradiction between necessary concepts that I have just discussed, but also positive dimensions of "nature" or "essence" that, I claimed, we have ceded at our own political and moral cost. (In the next section I try to show in more depth that this logic makes viable sense, and discuss some aspects of what it concretely requires of us and offers us in practice.)

I suggest that the logic that we need is one that can work with a certain kind of unmitigated contradiction, work with it not only as a flaw that needs to be resolved but (also) as part of how sense, and so reality, work. That is, we need to be able to work with a particular kind of breakdown of sense itself, a specific kind of incoherence or inconceivability, without eliminating it. And this is exactly what a thoroughgoing concept of the "unnatural" involves. As I have discussed, the idea of a nature involves the inconceivability of any alternatives to the sense that things have in its context. Consequently, the idea of the unnatural, in *this* context, is exactly an idea of what is inconceivable, what is beyond the boundaries of sense.

But this is not the unnatural as "anything but nature" or "anything but stable sense." These ideas, as I have argued, are defined by a stable contrast with "nature" and stable sense, and therefore really have a "nature" and sense of their own. Instead, this is the unnatural as *genuinely* contradictory and genuinely without a nature: an also *self*-contradictory alternative to nature and sense. Because it is properly self-contradictory, it can *also* make room, paradoxically, for what it excludes, that is, for the concept of a self-identical nature. This is an unnatural that contradicts itself even as contradiction, to make room for natures, that is, for sense that is entirely independent of it and entirely unqualified and unchallenged by it. Differently expressed, it makes room for sense to which it is simply meaningless and irrelevant.

This is why it can (contradictorily) allow us to work with the contradiction between standpoints without either simply eliminating the sense of one or both of the standpoints altogether, or evading the force of the contradiction.

In the case of essentialism and constructionism, each of these, as I have argued, depends on the other as the other is entirely independently of it, completely unqualified by it. We need *pure* essences (otherwise, again, we would have nothing that we could grasp), for which change is simply not conceivable. And we also need to think of *real* change as built into things (otherwise, again, we could not even have the shifts of consciousness and relation necessary to refer to anything), and for this the idea of something whose nature excludes the very sense of change is simply incoherent. That is, what each of these standpoints depends on, in the other, is an understanding of things for which the alternatives it itself presents are inconceivable, literally have no sense. And this is the idea of a nature.

We have, then, two incompatible ideas of what is natural, and the need for both. A logic of the unnatural, if it is possible at all, makes room for the sense of both and so for the contradiction between them, *and* for their simple, independent inconceivability or meaninglessness to each other. That is, it makes room both for the contradiction between them and for the meaninglessness or irrelevance of the contradiction to each of them. It connects them and it keeps them disconnected in the same act.

Now, if we *can* have both construction and essence, as we have established we *must* (meaning and sensemaking themselves require it, and consequently logic requires it), then we *can* think both together while accepting each one's understanding of reality as entirely excluding the very sense of the other's understanding of reality. That is, more generally, we can think two or more incompatible "natures" *and* the literal non-sense that each is to the other. We can consider and maintain incompatible views together, as simultaneously *both* of them *exclusively and entirely* true (and false).

This is not an idea of relative truths but rather an idea of *more than one absolute* truth. That is, this is an idea of more than one truth each of which excludes the possibility of any other truth.

In short, then, as human beings, whatever our politics, we *need* to take certain things for granted (though not necessarily the same things as others do); we *do* take certain things for granted; and we are *right* to do so. Differently said, because we are human—that is, not out of self-indulgence but because of what is *true* about being human—with our human limitations, including limitations on our responsibilities for reality, we are entitled to be sometimes deeply at ease, to relax, to be at peace with ourselves.

There is a growing number of voices in queer theory that recognize, independently of the particular metaphysical and logical issues I explore here, the need to respect uncritical, simply lived dimensions of our lives. I have already mentioned Ann Cvetkovich and Biddy Martin.[45] Biddy Martin in particular offers, I think in the same impressively many-sided and fair-minded spirit as Eve Kosofsky Sedgwick, a wonderful account of the human depth of "norm-following." In addition to the quotation I have used as the epigraph to this chapter, Martin writes, for example, "Part of the critique of totalizing views requires that we also keep alive not only transgressive desires but also emotional attachments, pleasures, fascinations, and curiosities that do not necessarily reproduce, reflect, or line up neatly with political ideologies or oppositional movements."[46] And Sedgwick makes a related case for "reparative reading": for example, "camp is most often understood as uniquely appropriate to . . . mocking exposure of the elements and assumptions of a dominant culture," but it is equally legitimate to consider and celebrate "the degree to which camping is motivated by love" of "the culture surrounding it."[47]

Let me stress here that my main thesis is that we can, unnaturally, have more than one such unquestioning sense of the nature of things. So in arguing for the validity of our own sense of nature, I am not implying that we should or are entitled to subject everyone to our own normativity. I am only arguing that we are wrong to make *no* room for our own sense of nature. And, as I argue below, where there is more than one such nature to consider, this unnatural logic allows us also to question our unquestionable "natural" meanings and practices.

We also need the concept of what is natural to give genuine respect, to do justice, to ourselves and our sense of our own reality, and also to others' sense of their own realities. For example, part of the problem with the vocabulary of "sexual preference" or "choice of one's sexuality" is that it ignores the ways in which, in being false to oneself, one betrays oneself, is untrue to *who one really is*. And that experience of self-betrayal or, alternatively, of being true to oneself, is surely not sufficiently expressed by saying, "in another social formation I could have been otherwise." *This* "I,"

---

[45] See notes 4 and 5 to this chapter above.
[46] Martin, *Femininity Played Straight*, 14.
[47] Eve Kosofsky Sedgwick, *Touching Feeling: Affect, Pedagogy, Performativity* (Durham, NC: Duke University Press, 2003), 149.

one could reasonably argue, could not have been otherwise without simply being some other person, and not myself at all.

Again, if one really treats oneself or others as living in a constructed reality, one does not give what they (or oneself) take to be reality the status of reality, but rather the status of a *version* of reality, a sort of "almost the real thing." But surely it is insincere or false to treat someone's reaction to the death of their lover, or to the legal exclusion (or, by contrast, recognition) of their own personhood, as having only a restricted claim to reality, as being just one version of the reality of what they are feeling and of what they are responding to, among other ultimately equivalently constructable alternatives. Surely this disrespects, trivializes, evades, is false to, their experience, part of whose force is, precisely, that it is an unquestionably real confrontation with something unquestionably and exclusively real.

And, finally, this kind of unself-critical unfairness directly harms our own lives, in itself. In its uncritical certainty about the role and value of critical concepts like construction, it is a form of deep dishonesty, not only with respect to our immediate thinking and activities, but also with respect to our status as epistemically and morally fallible human beings. In this way it divides us from our own reality, that is, from ourselves, and as a result deprives us of full presence and participation in our own lives. And it cuts us off from the possibilities of growing beyond our current depth of insight, and developing in new and unanticipated directions. (I discuss these possibilities further below in connection with the unnatural logic.)

The possibility of fundamental difference between "natures" is important not only for confrontations between bigotry and liberatory perspectives but also for dealing fairly and with fidelity to truth with deep differences among liberatory perspectives themselves. In the context of an "unnatural" logic, various deeply conflicting liberatory frameworks can *all* be valid without resolving any of the conflicts.

This does not mean that the debates between them lose their point. Each still needs to uphold its own sense of things, to come to understand the perspectives of the others, and to question itself in the light of the insights of the others (while also, in this contradictory context, recognizing the irrelevance of the others). And all of this requires the mutual struggle of justifications and explanations. But it does mean that one can recognize and respect why another standpoint, given its ways of sensemaking, thinks one's own standpoint is clearly wrong, while still having no doubt, given one's own ways of sensemaking, that it is the other one that is clearly wrong.

In the bigger picture, I think we need to recognize that being in a situation predominantly structured by ideologies that distort sense and reality—and this is what requires a theorized struggle for justice in the first place—means that we are already in a situation predominantly characterized by contradiction. (And this is the kind of contradiction that is *simply* opposed to what is "natural.") Consequently, if we are to fight all of what is wrong in this situation, we can only do so by adopting a variety of contradictory stances. Given that an "unnatural" logic allows us to see how this is approach is viable, it follows that it is appropriate and constructive that we have a variety of unresolvedly contradictory standpoints.

(In a still bigger picture, it is arguable that just being human is contradictory in the "unnatural" sense, so that we need this logic among ourselves even where there are no political concerns at issue. But that is not a line of thought I shall pursue here.)

A logic of the unnatural, then, gives us the means of satisfactorily and completely *justifying* our general standpoints (if not particular issues within them) without committing the injustice of reserving that complete justification for ourselves, and without the self-disservice of preventing growth and change in our general sense of things.

Because this logic validates concepts of *nature,* that is, ways of sensemaking to which there are no meaningful alternatives, it validates bases of thinking that cannot be meaningfully questioned. Questions within a natural order presuppose those bases to make sense at all, to be the questions they are, while questions outside it are literally senseless. This logic, then, allows the possibility that there are things we can *legitimately* take for granted. It justifies our having a sense of simple reality.

And because this logic, in being a logic of contradiction, *also* makes room for us to consider a nature outside its boundaries of sense, in (contradictory) relation to another or others, it enables our moving outside its bases altogether, to the entirely different bases of a different sense of "nature." As a result it also allows radical criticism of a position as a whole, including our own, and so allows for deep responsibility, and for deep social and personal growth.

Finally, since this logic justifies the concept of the natural, it allows us, again, to deal with heterosexism in a way that does not repeat the constitutionally unself-critical and so constitutionally unjust exclusions made by the heterosexist version of the natural. Instead it lets us find ways of acknowledging heterosexism's own sense of itself, while also fully endorsing our own. And, as I have suggested, it allows the same in our attitudes to and dealings with each other, within the field of attempts to oppose heterosexism.

In the next section I try to show in a little more depth how the type of contradiction in this unnatural logic makes viable sense, and I discuss some dimensions of what this logic concretely requires of us in practice.

4. *The Sense and Some Practical Dimensions of an Unnatural Logic*

One line of thought that helps, despite itself, to show the sense of this concept of the unnatural occurs in Richard Rorty's discussion of relativism. Part of Rorty's argument is that we cannot coherently conceive a way of making sense that is completely inaccessible to our own ways of making sense, a way that is inconceivable for us. That idea, if it makes sense to us, can only be part of our own way of making sense. Consequently it cannot to refer to something excluded, by definition, from our way of making sense.[48] The result is something like what I have discussed as the concept of what is natural: there is no conceivable alternative to our way of construing things.

But this argument works only if one *starts*—so far arbitrarily, as I discuss further below—with the assumption that only a self-identical, never-contradictory logic or way of making sense is possible. This is what makes it simply inconceivable that we could step outside our way of making sense, that there could be alternative ways of making sense that contradict our own. We could, instead, begin (so far no more arbitrarily, though also no less so) with the assumption that sense itself is not always self-identical, that there are contexts in which the senselessness of contradiction has a place in the structure of sense itself. On this assumption, that sense does not always coincide with itself, we sometimes *start* in two logically incompatible places at once: we are sometimes *already* simultaneously inside and

---

[48] Richard Rorty, *Objectivity, Relativism, and Truth* (New York: Cambridge University Press, 1991), 25ff.

outside our way(s) of making sense. In that case we can and often do simultaneously work with contradictory ways of making sense, and we can come to learn an entirely new way of making sense (as we all in fact did as infants in learning our present ones).

It would remain true that, as Rorty argues, and as I have maintained in the context of unnatural logic, each of our ways of making sense would be inconceivable to (would fall outside the boundaries of sense of) the others. But, on the assumption of this contradictory logic, there would be no problem granting *both* that we cannot conceive one way of sensemaking from within another *and* that we can inhabit and come to inhabit more than one such sensemaking framework.

Now this, of course, is just to start with the assumption that I am supposed to be justifying, the possibility of a contradictory, "unnatural" logic, and so is uselessly circular. But Rorty's kind of argument does exactly the same thing. It only works on the *assumption* that this kind of contradiction (conceiving what is beyond what we can conceive) is *not* possible: but that, again, is exactly what it is supposed to be justifying. His argument depends equally uselessly on the "natural" logic it is supposed to be justifying as mine depends on the "unnatural" logic *it* is supposed to be backing. As a result, there is no logical reason to begin with one of these assumptions rather than the other.

It follows that there is nothing to prevent our legitimately *exploring* a logic of the unnatural. And, in exploring that logic, we have seen a variety of reasons why it is necessary. And even more than this, an unnatural logic can recognize and deal with exactly *this* situation, the illegitimacy of making a general decision between logics, which natural logic cannot do.

In fact, as I have argued, unnatural logic, which allows for its *own* contradiction and so for its own simple senselessness, can *justify and endorse* beginning with the assumptions of natural logic, in contexts where one is already working within a particular standpoint. Within a standpoint, that is, considering that standpoint on its own, one can only make sense by pursuing its ways of sensemaking. If one does not, one is simply not making sense, with nothing further to be said about it. Here only the logic of the natural has a claim to meaning.

But when claims to a different way of making sense enter the picture, there *is* good reason to make room for at least the possibility of moving beyond one's current boundaries of sense, and so for the senselessness and inconceivability of self-contradiction as made room for by the standards of sense and as contributing to the further establishing of sense. And here the logic of the unnatural is the appropriate starting point.

The logic of the unnatural, then, legitimates contradiction, or senselessness, but does so only in specific and limited contexts, when one is making room for the possibility of alternative ways of making sense. When, for whatever reasons, this possibility is no longer relevant (a satisfactory outcome has been negotiated; an existential decision as to life choice has been made; some other issue that is not affected by the conflict of sense frameworks is now the issue under consideration; one has done the best one can and no longer has the resources to pursue negotiations), natural logic and noncontradiction, that is, sense, are the only legitimate possibilities.

But it is also *only* when unnatural logic *is* relevant, when we *do* need to take into account contrasting "natures," that we can justify, through this logic's establishing its own irrelevance, our resting on a standpoint's *natural* logic.

All of this really expresses the not very strange insights that, first, we need to be open to the possibility of learning new ways of making sense, which means learning what for us, now, is inconceivable. Second, we can legitimately require that others equally be open to the possibility of our own present ways of making sense, however unassimilable they may be to those others. And third, it expresses the insight that all parties should be open to the possibility of the simple, unavoidable, genuine reality of their own and others' experience.

And being prepared to succeed in grasping new ways of making sense means being prepared to be surprised by sensemaking possibilities we could not have foreseen, including unforeseeable possible ways of negotiating our own standards of sense with these conflicting ones, and of finding resolutions in those negotiations.[49]

---

[49] Apart from the suggestions in the other essays in this book, I explore the possibility and nature of these kinds of negotiation in detail in Chapter 8, and also in Jeremy Barris, "The Convergent Conceptions of Being in Mainstream Analytic and Postmodern Continental Philosophy," *Metaphilosophy* 43, no. 5 (2012): 592–618; *The Crane's Walk: Plato, Pluralism, and the Inconstancy of Truth* (New York: Fordham University Press, 2009); *Paradox and the Possibility of Knowledge: The Example of Psychoanalysis* (Selinsgrove, PA: Susquehanna University Press, 2003).

In experiential terms, encountering ways of making sense that are currently inconceivable for us, and working toward grasping them, necessarily means dealing with periods of confusion, of being unable to make sense of what or whom we encounter, being unable to find our bearings, stumbling blindly about, not seeing clearly what does and does not make sense. These are experiences that we need to learn to welcome, and actively develop our receptivity to, as part of coming to recognize and understand unfamiliar ways of making sense. For that matter, we also need them as part of acquiring perspective, through now having these other standpoints for comparison, on our *own* general standpoints. As I have argued, without that comparison, we have no way of knowing whether our *own* standpoints really make sense, or are justified, or do for us what we think they do.[50]

The other side of this confusion and surprise, then, is that this process is what allows us legitimately and genuinely to have *clear sight,* and legitimately to rely on the simple coherence and consistency of sense, *within* any framework. As a result of undergoing this process we have not simply assumed and so arbitrarily imposed the claims of our "natural sense," given in our framework, as the only relevant "natural" claims, but we have also not simply eliminated the "natural" character of our sensemaking. Here, then, we have simple sense and clear sight that we can rely on as genuine. We have established, as well, that they are also not blind injustice to other

---

[50] There have been several recent explorations in queer theory of the importance of various kinds of being thrown, incapacitated, or failing for responsible and transformative insight. See, for example, Cvetkovich, *Archive*, 237: "trauma" can be "the provocation to create alternative life worlds"; Judith Halberstam, *The Queer Art of Failure* (Durham, NC: Duke University Press, 2011), 129–30: since "mastery, pleasure, and heroic liberation" are defined in terms belonging to "the normative regimes against which" liberatory movements struggle, "maps of desire that render the subject incoherent, disorganized, and passive provide a better escape route"; Heather Love, *Feeling Backward: Loss and the Politics of Queer History* (Cambridge, MA: Harvard University Press, 2007), 163: "grief, regret, and despair. . . . It would be . . . impossible to imagine transformative politics without these feelings"; José Esteban Muñoz, *Cruising Utopia: The Then and There of Queer Futurity* (New York: New York University Press, 2009), 176–77: "Failure and hopelessness" and the "sentiments associated with despondence contain the potentiality for new modes of collectivity, belonging in difference and dissent . . . that become transformative behaviors"; Sedgwick, *Touching Feeling*, 37: "shame . . . is the place where the question of identity arises most originally and most relationally."

positions, or to the tentativeness that, when other "natures" have claims, is part of the only way we can honestly approach ultimate or foundational truths. (And the need for this tentativeness holds even if the ultimate truth we claim is that there are no foundational truths. This too is a particular view among other possibilities, and so must be open to question and further thought.)

Certainly, there will be truths that we have never had occasion to notice have alternatives in other frameworks of what is natural, that we have not achieved a legitimating perspective on. But here our willingness to *come* to notice that we might have to make room for a conflicting version of sense allows others the possibility of justice from us, and allows us the possibility of learning better. This willingness, then, is the moral equivalent of the legitimating achieved perspective.

A third important aspect of the kind of positive confusion and lostness that living out this unnatural logic involves, is that sometimes being at a loss *is* itself a clarity we have achieved. Where incommensurable ways of making sense are simultaneously relevant to the same things or events, the reality we are dealing with is itself incoherent. Logic or the structure of sense, after all, as I argued in the Introduction, is the structure of the sense of things, and not simply a calculus referring only to itself. Where two mutually exclusive ways of making sense both apply, the reality they express is correctly described in mutually exclusive ways, and is consequently itself logically incoherent. This happens precisely in the kinds of cases I have been discussing here, when we encounter ways of making sense, or "natures," that are not our own and a resolution has not yet emerged. I would argue that elements of nonconscious (or not directly conscious) reality also sometimes evolve into forms incommensurable with their previous ones, for example when societies shift into new meaning structures, or when life emerges, as perhaps it does, from inorganic structures. The point of transformation can then too only be described in terms of two mutually exclusive conceptual orders or ways of making sense. In cases like these, then, our being confused and unable to find our bearings is an accurate registering and representation of the nature of the reality we are considering.[51] It is itself an achievement of insight, and because the con-

---

[51] In this connection, John Dewey, for example, argues that "indeterminate situations ... are disturbed, troubled, ambiguous, confused, full of conflicting tendencies,

text is one of grappling with the foundations of sense itself, it is a particularly deep insight.

In this light, I suggest that one way of expressing the problem with the attempts to reconcile essence and construction that I have criticized in this chapter is that they share an assumption that logical sense involves a thoroughgoing or continuous clarity of connection, a clarity that would allow an overview of all the relevant elements in some kind of stably graspable relation with each other. In contrast, however, this continuous clarity is exactly what incommensurable ways of making sense of the same things precludes. In order to make room for the relevant shifts in sense, the approaches I have described would have to be able occasionally to render themselves meaningless in the terms to which they next proceed. That is, they would have to be self-canceling in the manner of "unnatural logic."

It is not that we cannot have continuously clear overviews. The statement rejecting overviews that I have just made, if it is to be consistent with its own commitments, must *also* be capable of rendering itself meaningless, and so of making way for the legitimacy of simply clear, stable overviews. The problem is with *simply* continuous consistency, in contrast with "sometimes always" continuous consistency. To the extent that the approaches I have discussed do not violate their own criteria for sense and specific application, they are all in some contexts—but only in some contexts—entirely and unqualifiedly right.

I shall discuss the simply taken for granted logic of continuous consistency and its limitations further in the following chapter, on what I argue is a central problem with Martin Heidegger's understanding of interpretation.

(It may seem odd to connect a discussion of heteronormativity with Heidegger's thinking about ultimate reality. If we understand "authentic" to mean "true to one's own nature," Giorgio Agamben comments

---

obscure, etc. It is the *situation* that has these traits. *We* are doubtful because the situation is inherently doubtful. . . . The notion that in actual existence everything is completely determinate has been rendered questionable by the progress of physical science itself. Even if it had not been, complete determination would not hold of existences as an *environment*. For nature is an environment only as it is involved in interaction with an organism, or self"; John Dewey, *Logic: The Theory of Inquiry* (New York: Henry Holt, 1938), 105–6.

on Heidegger's thought in a way that helps to suggest its connection with my discussion here of being "properly unnatural": "*Authentic existence has no content other than inauthentic existence; the proper is nothing other than the apprehension of the improper . . .* mastering an alienation and becoming attentive to a distraction." Again, "Human beings do not originally dwell in the proper; yet they do not . . . inhabit the improper and the ungrounded. Rather, *human beings are those who fall properly in love with the improper, who . . . are capable of their own incapacity.* This is why . . . the free use of the proper is the most difficult task."[52])

5. Conclusion

In the spirit of opposition to heterosexual normativity and the metaphysics of which it is one expression, let me suggest what I think of as, and I think genuinely is, a rightly perverted principle of knowledge and truth. Our uncomprehending struggle with a new sensemaking framework leads us to the surprise of a sense we can necessarily only discover well after it was already being made. If we can recognize it, we must already, before we came to be aware of it in that way, have been initiated into it to some substantial degree; otherwise its sense could not yet *be* sense to us. As a result, we might say, revising the norms and expectations in whose context we usually think of truth and inquiry, that it is often in the nature of truth to take us from behind.

In this light, we need a new sense of what dignity, empowerment, and insightful conduct can involve.

As Emerson, for one example, wrote about our relation to the nature of things, all the more fittingly because it was in his essay "Self-Reliance": "Who has more obedience than I masters me."[53]

---

[52] Giorgio Agamben, *Potentialities: Collected Essays in Philosophy*, ed. and trans. Daniel Heller-Roazen (Stanford, CA: Stanford University Press, 1999), 197, 204, italics in original.

[53] Ralph Waldo Emerson, "Self-Reliance," in *The Best of Ralph Waldo Emerson: Essays, Poems, Addresses,* ed. Gordon S. Haight (New York: Walter J. Black, 1941), 134.

7. *The Necessary Inconclusiveness of Heideggerian Interpretation of Metaphysics and the Undecided Nature of Essential or Logical Connection*

> Because of... this ultimately radical undecidability, all interpretations are, in the last resort, delusive or illusionary. Interpretations are fundamentally accidental and inessential, although not in the terms of what would normally be considered the essence or truth of the text. Interpretations have the status of examples. They are in essence of the order of the particular.
>
> —Rodolphe Gasché[1]

Martin Heidegger's mode of reading or interpreting the history of metaphysics has been very widely influential in contemporary continental philosophy. One aspect of his approach is his frequent assertion of *decisive* or definitive understandings of the history of metaphysics, a kind of assertion that much contemporary continental work fairly typically echoes, both explicitly and in tone. (I give some examples shortly below.) In this chapter I try to show, however, that there is a central problem with Heidegger's understanding of interpretation, a problem that much of contemporary continental philosophy consequently shares. This problem does not affect the possibility of Heideggerian interpretation as such, but it does undermine the possibility of this kind of decisive understanding of metaphysical positions and their history, precluding all readings that conflict deeply with it. (As I explain below, this is not to say that no decisiveness is possible, but only that it is not possible on the basis of Heidegger's interpretive framework.)

---

[1] Rodolphe Gasché, "Introduction," in Andrzej Warminski, *Readings in Interpretation: Hölderlin, Hegel, Heidegger* (Minneapolis: University of Minnesota Press, 1987), xxvi.

I shall also try to show that this problem has its source in a particular, and questionable, understanding of the coherence of concepts or of the logic or essential nature of connection between the different items, elements, and dimensions of the world. This is the kind of logic I identified in the last chapter as a "simply continuously consistent" logic (which in Heidegger, as I discuss, and in much of postmodern thought often turns out to produce continuously consistent paradox or logical "strife"), in contrast with the "sometimes always continuously consistent"—or "unnatural"—logic for which I have argued.[2] The profoundly thoroughgoing form in which Heidegger thinks this simply continuously consistent logic through has itself also been widely influential in contemporary continental philosophy. It is central, for example, to the work of philosophers of various understandings of "immanence," among them Gilles Deleuze, Jean-Luc Nancy, and (I think equivocally, because more deeply thought) Giorgio Agamben.

It is true that one feature of Heidegger's interpretive framework is that at a fundamental level it offers a kind of permanent openness or non-decisiveness of understanding, in the light of the central importance that our finitude has in his thinking. Iain Thomson, for example, writes, "Heidegger believes that the radically pluralistic, postmodern age will be the 'last' age . . . in so far as it constitutes a permanent openness to other possible interpretations, and so to the future."[3] But Heidegger presents this nondecisiveness itself in turn as decisively and finally the right view. As a result, at this level his thinking shares the same problem I have argued characterizes most postmodern thought and most contemporary pluralism: it does not apply its assertions of universal limitation and indeterminacy to themselves, so as to limit *their* truth. If it did, it would, as I have argued, on occasion emerge again as unqualifiedly definitive (or "unlimitedly determinate"), but now in ways that are produced in cooperation with equally unqualified nondefinitiveness, instead of simply excluding and being excluded by it. In criticizing Heidegger's tone of decisiveness,

---

[2] See the quotation from Giorgio Agamben I gave toward the end of the last chapter to help suggest the connection between Heidegger's thought and the discussion there of being "properly unnatural."

[3] Iain D. Thomson, *Heidegger, Art, and Postmodernity* (New York: Cambridge University Press, 2011), 9, note 4.

then, I am in fact also trying to make room for genuine kinds of decisiveness or definitiveness that his version precludes. I discuss some of these in the course of the chapter.

In fact, this failure to carry consistency through self-reflexively, to the point where it applies to its own bases, is not only a problem for postmodernism and pluralism. It is also a problem for standpoints that are not paradoxically self-conflicting, standpoints committed to a univocal mode of sense, such as Davidson's and Rorty's. As I argued in the Introduction, the self-reflexive problem of pluralism is rooted in and an offshoot of the basic concerns of "big question" philosophy generally. I have argued in subsequent chapters that these big question considerations require deep thinking generally to make room for what its own sense excludes. What postmodernism, including Heidegger's thought, and deep pluralism typically exclude is uncomplicated, nonparadoxical definiteness of meaning and truth, with nothing further to say; in contrast, what the kind of thought committed to univocal modes of sense typically excludes is self-undermining, undecidable paradox. But I have argued that in either case, sense and consistency themselves, or the undermining of sense and inconsistency themselves, come to require and endorse the legitimacy of the other, whose legitimacy they (also continue to) exclude.

The logic of simply continuous consistency that I discuss in this chapter, then, is not only the source—or perhaps, rather than a source, one very basic characterization—of the problem of decisiveness I propose in Heidegger's thinking but also of the problems I have discussed in connection with the other standpoints I have criticized in these essays. I suggest that both Heidegger and these other thinkers inherited it from a widely prevalent tradition of modern thought. Here, however, I discuss it in the context of Heidegger's thinking. This, I hope, will be illuminating not only with respect to his influential mode of interpretation but also with respect to some of the particular themes that he made his focus and that have been taken up in much subsequent continental thought. But if it is illuminating with respect to Heidegger, it should also cast light on some features of the wide variety of other contemporary standpoints that draw on the same logic, including on the ways in which they too take for granted the legitimacy of definitively asserting or relying on their fundamentals.

Returning to Heidegger's decisiveness, then, here are a few examples of his assertions of decisive understanding, taken at random. Heidegger, discussing Kant's view of the relation between concepts and intuition, writes: "When pure concepts are initially apprehended as notions, the second element of pure knowledge is by no means obtained in its elementary form. On the contrary, it is deprived of the decisive moment of its essence, namely its relation to intuition."[4] Again, writing on Nietzsche: "Metaphysical thinking rests on the distinction between that which truly is and that which by comparison does not constitute true being. But what is decisive for the *essence* of metaphysics does not lie by any means in the fact that this distinction appears as an opposition between the super-sensible and the sensible. Instead, this distinction . . . remains the first and sustaining one."[5] In a less textual context, discussing the contemporary power of calculative thinking, Heidegger writes, "the battle for the dominion of the earth has now entered its decisive phase."[6]

Heidegger understands interpretation as necessarily involving a kind of "violence," a kind of distortion. In the context of Heidegger's thinking, however, this is not ultimately a problem for interpretation. As I discuss, in his view this dimension of distortion is integral to the nature or working of truth, and therefore does not simply vitiate truth, whether in the context of interpretation or elsewhere. That is, in the Heideggerian understanding, truth includes a kind of variance from itself, of which the violence of interpretation is therefore a true expression. Far from this violence or distortion simply clashing with truth, then, it is part of and necessary to its expression and pursuit. I shall try to show, however, that this kind of violence in fact necessarily involves the ineliminable possibility of simply clashing with the truth of interpretation, in the classical sense of distorting its truth. That is, it is always at least *possible* that this "self-variance" of truth, although integral to truth, also involves simple error about the truth, in the classical sense of "error." As a result, within this Heideggerian mode of interpreting the history of philosophy,

---

[4] Martin Heidegger, *Kant and the Problem of Metaphysics*, trans. James S. Churchill (Bloomington: Indiana University Press, 1962), 60.

[5] Martin Heidegger, "The Word of Nietzsche: 'God Is Dead,'" in *The Question Concerning Technology and Other Essays*, trans. William Lovitt (New York: Harper & Row, 1977), 105.

[6] Martin Heidegger, "The Nature of Language," in *On the Way to Language*, trans. Peter D. Hertz (New York: Harper & Row, 1971), 105.

there can be no *decisive* understandings of the truth of the history of metaphysics.

Differently expressed, Heidegger distinguishes a deep conception of truth as essentially self-varying, or, in his language, as a "concealing-revealing," from a shallower conception of truth as simple correctness. But I argue here that truth as essentially self-varying in Heidegger's sense necessarily includes and is partly subject to the constraints of truth as simple correctness, and with it, correspondingly, necessarily includes and is partly subject to the possibility of falsehood as simple incorrectness.

I first trace Heidegger's view of the relation between truth and the violent dimension of interpretation. Since Heideggerian interpretation occurs largely as interpretations of the history of philosophy, this relation has direct and explicit bearing on reading the history of metaphysics. I then illustrate the problem by looking at a particular example of this kind of interpretation of the history of metaphysics. Here, perhaps a little dizzyingly, I shall *defend* the possibility of sustaining Heidegger's view of Plato (as having a more *traditionally* conceived place in the history of metaphysics) against John Sallis's Heidegger-informed but contrasting interpretation of Plato's thinking (as in fact more akin to *Heidegger's* own "beyond of metaphysics"). My aim here is not to show that Heidegger is right but to show that the outcome of this kind of disagreement of interpretation is necessarily inconclusive. I end by exploring the understanding of logical or essential connection that I believe Heidegger's kind of decisiveness assumes, and some of the implications for "sometimes always truth" of the lack of decisiveness that his own thought nonetheless, as I hope to show, necessitates.

1. *Truth and the Violence of Interpretation*

A path can be traced from Heidegger's occasional comments on interpretation to his interpretation of truth itself. Since this interpretation occurs largely as interpretations of the history of philosophy, the path can be pursued from there to readings of the history of metaphysics in Heidegger's manner. As the exploration of that path concerns interpretation as such rather than particular interpretations, I shall attempt it by way of a few exegetically light indications. If Heidegger's comments on interpretation are equivocal, as I hope to show they are, then his interpretation of truth will share that equivocity. And this in turn should lead us to some insight regarding what Heidegger expresses as the destruction—and Derrida as the deconstruction—of the history of metaphysics, within the context of Heidegger's thought as well as much of the thinking it has influenced.

In *Kant and the Problem of Metaphysics,* Heidegger writes, "It is true that in order to wrest from the actual words that which these words 'intend to say,' every interpretation must necessarily resort to violence. . . . The interpretation must be animated and guided by the power of an illuminative idea. . . . The directive idea itself is confirmed by its own power of illumination."[7] What is the status of "violence" here, to which every interpretation must necessarily resort? Clearly, this provocative statement cannot be taken to mean that there are no constraints on illumination, that one is free to make what one wishes of a text or philosophical standpoint or issue. His own readings are in many respects models of careful and comprehensive attention to detail, context, and the necessary implications of the standpoints to which the texts commit themselves. Heidegger makes other comments that are explicit about the need to be guided by what one thinks about. In "The Onto-Theo-Logical Constitution of Metaphysics," Heidegger writes, "the matter requires thinking to stay with it in its own manner of being, to remain steadfast toward that manner of being, answering to it by sustaining the matter to its completion."[8] And in *Schelling's Treatise on the Essence of Human Freedom,* he writes: "the matter must prescribe its own kind of procedure."[9]

But his comment equally clearly cannot be taken to mean that one leaves the text or philosophical position simply as it initially was. Of course, it is Heidegger of all people who opens up the question of the inner relation between truth and distortion (the appropriateness of the word "distortion" will become clear as we proceed). So, for example, "the open site for and ground of *error*" is "errancy," which "is the essential counter-essence to the primordial essence of truth. . . . As leading astray, errancy at the same

---

[7] Heidegger, *Kant and the Problem of Metaphysics,* 207.

[8] Martin Heidegger, "The Onto-Theo-Logical Constitution of Metaphysics," in *Identity and Difference,* trans. Joan Stambaugh (New York: Harper & Row, 1969), 46.

[9] Martin Heidegger, *Schelling's Treatise on the Essence of Human Freedom,* trans. Joan Stambaugh (Athens: Ohio University Press, 1985), 62.

time contributes to . . . the possibility that, by experiencing errancy itself and by not mistaking the mystery of Da-sein, he *not* let himself be led astray."[10] That is, for Heidegger, error is a *dimension* of truth, and not simply opposed to it. (It is not necessary here to explore his *grounds* for linking truth and error. The issue I am exploring concerns only the *implications* of this influential Heideggerian understanding of the connection between truth and error. I take no stand here on its legitimacy in its own right.) Now, given this inner relation between truth and "leading astray," it is unclear what it means to say that the text or standpoint is left as it was or not, distorted or undistorted. With this inner relation in mind, there are important Heideggerian senses in which distorting the interpreted thought *is* leaving it undistorted. But his use of the word "violence" sustains a meaning for something like distortion, a sense in which the text or thought is drastically different after its interpretation from what it was before, in a way which conflicts with its former state. All of this is, again, in keeping with Heidegger's interpretation of truth itself as involving, or rather being, an essential or inner "strife" ("truth is the primal strife").[11]

Nonetheless, there is perhaps room for alternatives even in a unity of, on the one hand, following the directions required by a careful reading of a text as it stands, and producing a text very different from the one with which one began, on the other: Heidegger's assertion is still perhaps equivocal in important ways. On the one hand, it can mean that one has to enact the inner strife of truth itself, in such a way that one allows the truth to speak through one. This is not the truth of the text or standpoint taken on its own, since the text or standpoint has no truth on its own, is merely an abstraction when considered as a reality existing outside a relation to interpretation. That is, there is no text or standpoint outside interpretation. Meaning is not "present at hand." Rather, the truth of the text *is* its being taken up in a careful interpretation, which, as it were, activates its essential relation to, and hence its existence *as*, interpretation and, equivalently, transformation.

---

[10] Martin Heidegger, "On the Essence of Truth," trans. John Sallis, *Basic Writings*, ed. David F. Krell (New York: Harper & Row, 1977), 136.

[11] Martin Heidegger, "The Origin of the Work of Art," trans. Albert Hofstadter, in *Basic Writings*, ed. David F. Krell (New York: Harper & Row, 1977), 180.

On the other hand, it can be, and (together with the substance of Heidegger's actual readings) has been, taken to mean that Heidegger is warranting a tendentious reading on his own part. This kind of reading would, in the classical sense, distort the interpreted standpoint, though perhaps so as to give genuine insights warranted not by the interpreted standpoint but by Heidegger's own thinking, as it exists independently of that particular interpretation. This too is, if ultimately problematically, in keeping with the unity of reading the text as it stands and producing a different text, but at a different level and so with diverging consequences. On this alternative, one cannot help but distort the interpreted text because one has one's own place in history (taking "history" as essential to one's being and meanings) from which one inevitably reads; but that one has this place in history is itself part of the working of truth. "The metaphysics of *Dasein* is in no sense an 'organon' fixed and ready at hand. It must constantly be reconstructed by the transformation which its idea undergoes because of the development of the possibility of metaphysics."[12] The original text (on this interpretation we can rightfully speak of the original text, independent of our particular reading of it) was itself an interpretation of the issues dependent on its historical place, and given the *essential* historicity of the original text, its *own* truth is different in a different historical place.

The inner strife of truth here occurs at a level less intimately connected to the text or standpoint as it initially stands. As a result of this lesser intimacy, while the unity of "the text as it stands" and "the different, interpreted text" still occurs here, a sense is left open in which the interpretation is not true to the text in its own terms. Heidegger explicitly makes room for such a sense: "what is essential in all philosophical discourse is not found in the specific propositions of which it is composed but in that which, although unstated as such, is made evident through these propositions."[13] One can then distinguish between the different interpretations that are the original text and the interpreted version, a distinction that ultimately vanishes if the inner strife of truth is more intimately connected with the specific text or standpoint. For the more intimate connection, there is no specific text or thought outside its interpretation; for the less intimate connection there is such a text or thought, distanced from the interpreting

---

[12] Heidegger, *Kant and the Problem of Metaphysics*, 239.
[13] Ibid., 206.

thought by the relation between different historical epochs. And here violence occurs at least at one level as a distortion of the original text.

This second alternative is problematic in that, in the end, as one thinks through the essential connections between thought standpoint and historical epoch, and between historical epoch and historical epoch, one ends up with the first alternative, that the inner strife of truth has no distance from any of them. One has artificially abstracted each of these moments from the others, but a proper thinking through undoes that artificial separation at the level of essence. With this in mind, interpretation involves no distortion of the text in the classical sense of "distortion."

It is this point that I wish to question. Now there is no question, I believe, that within the framework or closure of Heidegger's standpoint a properly rigorous interpretation involves no distortion, in the classical sense, of the interpreted text. What the interpretation brings out is the inner meaning of the interpreted thought, as proffered by that thought itself. While there is a transformation of the text, insofar as what was in a sense implicit is made explicit, that is just another, if perhaps inadequate, way of phrasing the truth strife essential to the text. (There is a legion of demons lurking in this rendition of the movement from implicit to explicit, and I shall return to at least one of them.) Consequently, if, as I want to show, there is indeed a problem with saying that there can be no distortion of the text in properly rigorous interpretation, then there is a problem with the whole of Heidegger's standpoint. That the problem would be so comprehensive is immediately clear in that everything in Heidegger turns precisely on the essential connections between truth and distortion, or, rather, on the occurrence of truth and distortion only given the essential connection. This is not, of course, to say that such a problem would mean that the "destruction of metaphysics" should be discarded. What it would say is that, to the extent that Heidegger had something to say about truth, this problem bears directly on the nature of truth.

Even from a standpoint outside Heidegger's framework or closure of thought, I do not mean to suggest that his readings are mistaken or distortions. (They may be, on more careful readings even within his standpoint, of which he is only one protagonist, but that is irrelevant to my point.) What I want to show is that they are not, and cannot be, sufficient *to establish that they are not* distortions in the classical sense, at least not without restricting oneself uncritically to the closure of his thought. They may not be distortions, but they themselves do not establish whether or not they are. And given the essential relation between Heidegger's view of interpretation and his view of truth, the kind of insufficiency I am suggesting will inevitably require us to rethink the character of truth and of philosophical assertion or textuality (the essential "hanging together" or "belonging with" of concepts: the essence of logic).

A note of caution here: it is not sufficient to think, on the grounds that Heidegger undoes the distinction between classical distortion and classical truth, that his readings do not need to establish that they cannot be distortions. His undoing of that distinction depends in large part on his readings; it is only if they are not classical distortions that they work to undo the distinction. They are what must establish that undoing, rather than presupposing it.

My aim is to show that there is in truth a problem with saying that rigorous interpretation cannot distort the interpreted text or standpoint. But the real concern of this discussion is broader: I want to show that much of the contemporary reworking of the history of metaphysics presupposes the kind of guiding logic of essence that Heidegger pursues so profoundly, and consequently shares the same problem. In order to show the problem, I shall reflect on a few extremely limited aspects of well-known interpretations or types of interpretation.

2. Heidegger versus Sallis on Plato

Heidegger has read Plato as inaugurating the metaphysical tradition (that Heidegger is trying to overcome and move beyond) by establishing the domination of presence in the concept of truth. That is, truth is a "visible form," what shines in and as the light, and excludes what is hidden and in shadow. "The essence of the idea consists in its ability to shine and be seen.... This is what brings about presencing ... coming to presence is the essence of being."[14] Truth, and true being, then become a matter of the intelligible, which is fully present in a fully self-consistent way, in contrast with the sensible (what is registered by our senses), which is neither fully present nor fully self-consistent. The sensible is not the locus of truth pre-

---

[14] Martin Heidegger, "Plato's Doctrine of Truth," trans. Thomas Sheehan, in *Pathmarks*, ed. William McNeill (Cambridge: Cambridge University Press, 1998), 173.

cisely *because* it is not properly present. The unthought here is the status of presence itself as a measure of truth. By contrast, Sallis has argued that Heidegger himself is reading Plato through the lenses of the tradition he believes he finds in Plato. Instead, Plato exhibits the essential connection between the sensible and the intelligible, via the sensible images of the intelligible which his texts constantly invoke and which his texts themselves, as dialogues that enact their subject matter, manifestly *are*. We cannot speak of or conceive the intelligible without making use of sensible images, and so we cannot mean anything by it that is ultimately independent of such images. The lack of presence that sensible images involve is accordingly essential to anything we can mean by the intelligible. For example, in reading the *Cratylus*, Sallis notes that "what is introduced is not [intelligible, fully present] being itself in distinction from images of being, but rather . . . an image of the distinction between original [being] and image."[15] On this reading, Plato is being ironic when he radically distinguishes the sensible from the intelligible, and in fact he falls outside the tradition which that distinction inaugurates.

Here I want to reflect on what is at stake in deciding between these interpretations, not to choose the right reading but to illustrate a point about reading in general. To this end, I focus on a very limited area of interpretation, an aspect of the relation in Plato between the somatic and the psychic.

For Sallis, when Plato suggests that one can have knowledge entirely beyond the confines of the body, it is a comical suggestion, and the text requires one to read it that way. In reading the *Republic*, for example, Sallis writes of "the discussion of the distribution of studies . . . which amounts to an attaching of the upward movement [of insight, character, and political regimen] to the stages of human genesis, hence, a limiting of it by . . . the body—following this discussion, the comedy is more transparent than ever."[16] For Heidegger, in contrast, Plato's suggestion is seriously meant, and indicates Plato's turn to a concept of truth as fully self-present, which can only occur beyond the body and the bodily. Heidegger is seeing in the text an embodiment of an early phase of the metaphysical tradition. Sallis

---

[15] John Sallis, *Being and Logos: The Way of Platonic Dialogue* (Atlantic Highlands, NJ: Humanities Press, 1986), 300–301, my insertions.
[16] Ibid., 451, my insertion.

is seeing in the text an embodiment of something that in a sense falls outside that history of metaphysics. Now, to approach this very generally for the moment: these are, precisely, interpretations of *a metaphysics* or something in a sense beyond even metaphysics (since it may precede the entire history of metaphysics and so may not be subject to the limitations of what can be meant by that term and within that history). They are not interpreting what the text says about this or that: they are interpreting what the text says about truth as such, and being as such. That is, they are interpreting what the text says about *how to interpret anything, including itself*: what the text determines as what is proper to see in it. Consequently, for each of them *the text is different*. The very being of the text, and of the elements of the text, is itself determined by an interpretation of being, and precisely what we have here is two different interpretations of being. We cannot turn to the text to help us decide between them: we have two different texts. More properly, since this entire discussion depends for its meaning on our talking about the same text, as Andrzej Warminski puts the issue of reading (he distinguishes reading from interpretation, but it is his reflection on interpretation that leads to reading as its more general economy): "the entire process ... is a viciously (i.e., and yet asymmetrically) circular story: simultaneously same and different with no possibility of mediating the two."[17]

I confess to a degree of accidental mischievousness here, in that Heidegger, of course, reads Plato in order to overcome the kind of metaphysics he reads there, and Sallis approaches Plato within the context of Heidegger's overcoming of that metaphysics. The result of treating Heidegger as working within a traditionally Platonic metaphysics and Sallis as working within a Heideggerian at-the-limit-of-metaphysics is therefore dizzying. But I think the point holds, and the possibility of making it in this way compounds the seriousness and difficulty of the problem. One can ask what exactly is happening even when Heidegger identifies a classical metaphysics in the first place: what establishes the truth of *that* interpretation, and is it not, for example (and putting it crudely), an artifact of his identification of a limit to metaphysics? Further, what happens when *any* philosophers identify a metaphysics or metaphysics and its history?

[17] Andrzej Warminski, *Readings in Interpretation: Hölderlin, Hegel, Heidegger* (Minneapolis: University of Minnesota Press, 1987), xxxiv.

I am deliberately not pursuing otherwise essential distinctions between essence and that of which it is the essence, and distinctions *within* essence or primordiality. Clearly, there are distinctions between, for example, what Heidegger names the merely ontic, the ontological, and the register of beyng. But these distinctions make no difference to the problem at hand. To the extent that we are concerned with the essential truth of the text, less primordial differences can have no purchase. If we were, indeed, concerned with the text as, say, a system of propositions distinct from a deeper interpretation of them, the problem would be worse, and less philosophically interesting. For here there is immediately a sense to speaking of distortion of the text in the classical sense, and if we could speak at this level without reference to more essential levels, the necessity of interpretive violence could only mean that we are bound to miss the truth of the text, which is then (also) given through these "propositions of which it is composed." But if we take the distinctions within the essence of truth to allow *this kind* of external separation between the merely ontic and the more essential, we would also have stopped thinking with Heidegger. If we do think the *truth* of such propositions with Heidegger, the problem leads us back to the essential truth of the text, and the distinctions within essence can provide no solution to a problem exhibited in essential truth as such.

Another note of caution: it is not sufficient to think that Sallis's standpoint, or ultimately Heidegger's, for that matter, is, in enacting a beyond to metaphysics, already essentially open to the otherness of the other's reading. Nor is it sufficient to think that they are not frameworks or closures of thought to which there could be a beyond on the grounds that, again, they are already open to their "beyond." Of course, if this were sufficient, the entire present discussion would be redundant, or misconceived from the start. It is true that this openness to otherness is inherent in both their standpoints. But, first, just because this openness is *essential* to them, they foreclose standpoints for which that specific openness is not essential, in which the distinction between "within" and "beyond" is either simply affirmed or simply irrelevant. Such standpoints can only be incoherent for them once they are read essentially: a specific notion of essence, as it is essential to them, guides their reading, and does so in advance of their reading. Closures of thought that claim a different notion of essence are then ruled out in advance: such closures are the classical "others" of "always already open" modes of interpretation.

Second, this closure of thought "at the end of metaphysics" itself is an interpretation of being, or of the history of being. Consequently it itself is subject to the constraints essential to interpretation: that is, its decisiveness needs to be shown *on the basis of interpretation*, rather than being presupposed in interpreting interpretation. This is precisely why Heidegger's comments on interpretation relate essentially to his interpretation of truth. We are in the same situation in interpreting being or the history of being as we are in exploring the small point of Plato interpretation under discussion.

Returning to Plato, we can approach the small issue more specifically. Let us say that Heidegger is, as Sallis argues, reading through the lenses of the history of metaphysics, with its distinctions between the sensible and the intelligible. Accordingly he is reading Plato in a traditional way, seeing the relevant distinctions in Plato as seriously meant as they function in the text. On this reading, when Plato talks about images, he is talking about steps on a ladder to truth that can be discarded. And when Plato writes dialogues, he is indeed presenting an image, but one that can be used as a step and transcended, just like the images in the text. The Socrates of the dialogues is expressing Plato's viewpoint, again as an image that can be transcended by learning the discipline of thought, explained in the dialogues, which takes one beyond images. There is no disagreement about whether Plato is using images or not; the disagreement is about the being of those images and its meaning, whether, on the one hand, in not being fully self-present, they are unlike the true realities or, on the other, they complicate that traditional distinction between presence and absence and its relation to the truth or nature of reality. Now, there is nowhere else in the text to go to decide how to read the status of the images: the images *are the text*. Reading the images *is* reading the text, which means that we cannot decide how to read the text except by making a decision about how to read the images. More accurately, we cannot read the text at all without already having made a decision about how to read the images.

One way to make that decision is to argue, on the basis of the text, that it is incoherent to think of knowledge outside the limits of the human body and sensibility, in which case the text itself mandates one's seeing its own statements to the contrary as ironic. (A version of this strategy will appear again below, in connection with Heidegger's reading of Kant.) But that argument in turn depends, again, on how one interprets the status of the images of the text: one has to decide in advance whether the use of images functions comically to undermine the statements that one can transcend them, or whether they function to show a way beyond them. By way of illustration, let us say that Plato holds the traditional distinction between the sensible and the intelligible. And let us think with that distinction, say in the manner of the Stoics. Here one has a metaphysics in which human minds are continuous with, crudely, the divine mind, the *Logos*. Continuing to think with this metaphysics, there is no incoherence in the idea that one can transcend the limits of the body: one has already transcended them. If there is incoherence here, it is in the whole metaphysics. Now, if one is to show that Plato's text is incoherent in the respects in which it appears to endorse knowledge transcending the human body, one has to show that the metaphysics as a whole is incoherent: there is no incoherence on this point *within* the closure of the metaphysics. And *that* demonstration again depends on how one understands the status of the images of Plato's text. *If* Plato (or the thought he expresses) is really committed to Stoic-type metaphysics, his images already have the status of approximations to thought that has means of moving beyond them. If he is not so committed, his images have a different status. And, again, reading his text *is* reading his images. In order to decide, one has to choose how to read the images. The problem, again, is that, at a new level, we are interpreting a metaphysics, or beyond: the being of that which we depend on for our interpretation is itself determined by the results of our interpretation.

It follows that what warrants either Sallis's *or* Heidegger's readings is a particular interpretation of metaphysics and of what can be coherent in a metaphysics. And again, and for all the same reasons, that interpretation is not warranted over and against the alternative interpretation by an appeal to any deciding factor outside itself. As Warminski puts it, "If the philosophical interpretation . . . constitutes itself by a leap . . . then to repeat that (same and other) leap, backward as it were, is not to deconstitute it (or to reconstitute its origins) but to tell still another story, (re)write still another (and the same) supplementary text."[18]

Here is where we rejoin the issue of Heidegger's own practice of interpretation and the reworking of the history of metaphysics in contemporary philosophy.

[18] Ibid., xxxiv.

3. Heidegger and Rereading the History of Metaphysics

Heidegger's mode of reading occurs in the context of specific developments in the history of philosophy. Here I can offer no more than a sketch of this context, but the historical points are easily recognized and uncontroversial. Late nineteenth-century romantic thought developed a view of reality as an organically connected unity. The philosophies collectively known as German Idealism emerged as a deeply thoroughgoing thinking through of this intrinsic unity of things, and the most influential of these philosophies was Hegel's. The philosophical tradition that has learned positively from Hegel, and that Heidegger inherited, understands the coherence of concepts as founded in this kind of intrinsic unity. With specific reference to the body/mind problem addressed above, it understands the concepts of these two realms of being, and hence the realms of being themselves, as capable of being connected only if they are already essentially connected. That is, they can be brought into relation with each other only if they are in some sense expressions of a deeper unity. Further, this philosophical world understands concepts in general as essentially already in relation to the matter of which they are concepts. Language, thought, the world, and different aspects of the world are not *essentially* distinct realms of being.

This is, of course, a form of the logic that I have described as a "simply continuously consistent" logic. As I have noted, it is only one among a variety of inherited forms of this logic, each with its own history. But this one has its own peculiar characteristics, and it is, I believe, the one that Heidegger inherited.

In the context of philosophy, the setting for the comprehensiveness of this view of concepts, comprehensive in the sense that *all* concepts deeply thought must be brought to their primordial unity, is really established for the modern Western world most prominently by Kant. Kant situated knowledge strictly within the human context (a "Copernican revolution" in thinking, as he described it),[19] and hence as everywhere irretrievably marked by, for example, the limits of the body and the structures that organize it. As he famously argued, while sensory intuitions without con-

---

[19] Immanuel Kant, *Critique of Pure Reason*, trans. Norman Kemp Smith (New York: St. Martin's Press, 1929), B:xvi.

cepts are blind, a concept without sensory intuition is empty.[20] But it is Hegel who formalized and made fully comprehensive the logic of general a priori connection to which Kant gave prominence. (Not only does Kant not argue for this comprehensiveness, he maintains—I believe to his credit—a number of central logical disconnections to which both Hegel and Heidegger object.) Given that explicit comprehensiveness, once one accepts that concepts cohere only if they are already internally, that is essentially, related, one is committed to the kind of standpoint with which Heidegger ultimately emerges (and on whose basis, as I shall try to show, he perhaps misreads Kant).

First, everything we can think is marked by the constraints of human finitude, since any concepts we can reach must be essentially related to the concept of ourselves, and hence to our finitude. "Pure concepts can be determined as ontological predicates only if they are understood in the light of the essential unity of finite pure knowledge."[21] Second, the essential thing has to be the essential relation, not the individual concepts, since individual concepts, being expressions of a deeper, essential unity of the concepts and elements of the world, no longer have an essence on their own. But since what are related in this relation are often incompatible concepts, essence itself must be self-divided, and truth is essentially strife. Hans-Georg Gadamer puts this general regression to a unifying source nicely: "that conception of 'truth' which Heidegger seeks to formulate in his thought as the 'event of being' and which opens up the space for the movement of reflection, as well as for all knowledge, in the first place."[22]

But all of this is itself a particular closure of thought. This closure cannot tell us whether its own conception of logic is appropriate, since it depends on that conception of logic. And here we are in the same position as in trying to interpret the fundamentals of Plato: any decision we make is dependent on our always already having made the decision. But, as with Plato, it is possible to make other decisions. This, for example, is part of the gist of Jean-François Lyotard's *The Differend*, in which he pursues Wittgenstein's notion of language games in Lyotard's own version of phrase

---

[20] Ibid., A:51; B:75.
[21] Heidegger, *Kant and the Problem of Metaphysics*, 61.
[22] Hans-Georg Gadamer, *Hegel's Dialectic: Five Hermeneutical Studies*, trans. P. Christopher Smith (New Haven, CT: Yale University Press, 1976), 96.

regimens and genres of discourse, precisely in order to find an alternative to the hold of predecided logics. "A wrong," he argues, "results from the fact that the rules of the genre of discourse by which one judges are not those of the judged genre or genres of discourse. . . . A universal rule of judgment between heterogeneous genres is lacking in general."[23]

Consequently, when, for example, as Heidegger, Derrida, and other postmodern thinkers do, one reworks the metaphysical tradition on the basis of thinking through its own necessities to the point at which they disrupt each other, one is reading these necessities in accordance with one possible notion of logical necessity, of essential connection. That is, it is unclear that one is not simply distorting them, in the classical sense. Again, I am not saying that one *is* distorting them, only that it is unclear whether or not one is. This possibly distorting reading is what mandates Sallis's seeing the continuity of sensible and intelligible in Plato, as well as Heidegger's seeing the unthought in Plato. All of this suggests the possibility of another side of the coin of the "destruction" or "deconstruction" of metaphysics. The possibility emerges that one can distinguish the logic to which the traditional texts are committed from the post-Hegelian logic applied to them. And with that emerges the possibility of reading post-Hegelian work and textuality from the standpoint of logics for which it is not mandatory that all aspects of the domains of being and truth must belong together essentially. As R. G. Collingwood argues, for example, because the presuppositions of a metaphysical framework are absolute in the sense of being the starting points for all justification, and so are not discussable on the basis of anything else, "the literary form of a treatise in which a metaphysician sets out to enumerate and discuss the absolute presuppositions of thought in his own time cannot be the form of a continuous argument. . . . It must be the form of a *catalogue raisonné*, as in the fourth book of Aristotle's *Metaphysics* or in the *Quaestiones* of a medieval metaphysician."[24]

But, more important, there emerges the possibility simply of different coins: even the possibility of speaking *unproblematically* of a metaphysics or of a history of metaphysics, the possibility of the lack of purchase of such

---

[23] Jean-François Lyotard, *The Differend: Phrases in Dispute*, trans. Georges Van Den Abbeele (Minneapolis: University of Minnesota Press, 1988), xi.

[24] R. G. Collingwood, *An Essay on Metaphysics* (Oxford: Clarendon Press of Oxford University Press, 1940), 67–68.

(non)concepts as the essential strife of truth, undecidability, the trace. Because of the lack of warrant for decisiveness in these matters, the possibility, and hence in careful reading the necessity, always remains of thinking a mere separation of meanings (or constraints on meaning) between and within closures of thought, a separation not recuperable into an essential relation, whether dialectically, or by thinking the primacy of the relation (or dif-ference) between terms, or via an undecidable trace, all of these deriving their purchase from a specific closure of thought. They are insufficient to be decisive in this respect. Putting this more sharply: the possibility emerges of a *decisiveness* that the decisiveness of post-Heideggerian reading forecloses, the possibility that a thing simply is what it is in the classical sense. And further, the possibility emerges of *more than one* such decisiveness, that Kant, Hegel, Descartes have the right be convinced by their own thinking in their own reading of it (were conceivably simply right in what they stated) and to reject the readings and thinking of others, including ours (who are conceivably simply wrong). Perhaps one can say that the paradox that is the essential strife of truth emerges, of course paradoxically, in a variety of unpredictable, unrelated, and even opposed forms and directions.

A general consequence of these considerations is that it is not sufficient to speak decisively of a single history of metaphysics, or even of histories as a plurality that can be described or articulated in one essentially gathered phrasing (such as "histories"), a single mode of textuality (such as a statement or a narrative), or one coherent mix of propositions (in whatever singular sense, however complicated, of "coherent"). One or more additional phrasings that are simply incompatible with the description or articulation they are added to will be necessary at least. Of course, this applies too, as it must, to the phrasings offered here.

The possibility always remains, then, of a merely external, rhetorical relation between the terms of a discourse that engages more than one closure of thought, more than one fundamental interpretation. For example, one can use language to describe a framework of thought, as Heidegger describes Platonic metaphysics, without any necessarily essential relation between that language and the "same" language one *also* uses to describe a framework sufficiently different to be in what Heidegger would understand as an essential strife with the first. Thus there is no *necessity* to the relation between the hidden (unstated) and the unhidden (stated) in Heidegger's senses of these terms, no necessity, then, that truth be an essential strife. A reading of such a necessity already presupposes a logic of essence that is not decisive.

Similarly, there is no necessity that images, and the being of images, must mark the intelligible and its being. (Here, in contrast to the discussion of Heidegger's contrast with Sallis above, we restore to Heidegger his own closure of thought, and defend the classical metaphysical tradition against both of them.) The relation can be a rhetorical one, in which images are *merely* external metaphors, in the classical sense, for the realities, simply external and distinct from them.

Heidegger's reading of Kant is instructive in these respects. Heidegger brings the thought of the first *Critique* to a fundamental unity that, as Heidegger acknowledges, significant parts of the text deny. As Heidegger accordingly notes, "the following interpretation . . . must go beyond the architectonic which governs the external succession of the problems and their presentation in order to bring to light the internal development of the problematic which led Kant to adopt this form of presentation."[25] In fact, he goes so far beyond the given architectonic that he describes Kant's extensive revisions in the second edition, which Kant of course understood as clarifying his problematic, as "Kant's recoil from the ground which he himself revealed, namely the transcendental imagination."[26] There is a decision here: which areas of the text are truly in keeping with and the guide to the fundamental problematic?

Heidegger's grounds for this decision, in summary, are expressed in this statement: "Placed as it is at the beginning of the *Critique of Pure Reason*, the transcendental aesthetic is basically unintelligible. It has only an introductory character and can be truly understood only in the perspective of the transcendental schematism [in which the transcendental imagination is given its grounding role]."[27] Here we find again the strategy, which I imputed to Sallis' reading of Plato, of establishing incoherence in the text as indicated by the sense of the text. But, as we have already seen in the case of reading Plato, there is a problem with this strategy when it comes to deciding between alternative *fundamental* problematics.

---

[25] Heidegger, *Kant and the Problem of Metaphysics*, 72.
[26] Ibid., 222.
[27] Ibid., 152, my insertion.

I have already quoted the following comment from Heidegger: "what is essential in all philosophical discourse is not found in the specific propositions of which it is composed but in that which, although unstated as such, is made evident through these propositions."[28] That is, the fundamental problematic is found *through* the stated propositions, including those of the transcendental aesthetic. And Heidegger is quite clear about the bearing of this kind of comment in this context: "It is not a question of eliminating the transcendental aesthetic as a provisional statement of the problem but of keeping its problematic while, at the same time, rendering it more precise."[29] All of this means that the "only introductory" and "unintelligible" character of the transcendental aesthetic, as it stands, has to be established partly *through* the propositions of the transcendental aesthetic merely made more precise and not eliminated as a "provisional" statement (may I translate: "not taken as only introductory and unintelligible in that role?"). It is crucial that these propositions not be taken as merely introductory, still less as unintelligible in that role, precisely because the fundamental problematic can only be established through them. Nevertheless, once the fundamental problematic is established, Heidegger does take these initial propositions to be unintelligible and merely introductory. That is, they are now read in the light of a problematic *different from* that which initially made sense of them. It is not merely a case of uncovering the hidden problematic through the "external succession" of the stated propositions but, as Heidegger's own vacillation in commenting on his interpretive procedure suggests, a case of shifting commitment from one sense-conferring problematic to another. At this level of *essential* reading, the transformation from implicit to explicit is not, as I suggested it is at the start of the first section, simply a matter of rephrasing the truth strife of the text or standpoint, still less of simply bringing out what was already there. At *this* level it is a matter of establishing a different essence of truth, and hence an essentially different text or standpoint.

Putting this in terms of general and summary principle, the problem is that the unstated which is found through the propositions constitutes the propositions as the propositions they are. The propositions are essentially related to the unstated. The propositions do not then in the end provide

[28] Ibid., 206.
[29] Ibid., 54.

decisive warrant for uncovering the unstated: the unstated is presupposed in reading the propositions at all, and hence circularly provides its own warrant. Unless, of course, there is only one possible unstated for the propositions to lead to: and that is precisely what interpretation, in principle, or essentially, does not allow to be established. The decision as to which problematic, in whose light one must read the text or grasp the standpoint, is truly fundamental, then, cannot be made on textual grounds. It occurs independently of reading the text.

In the case of Kant, the possibility remains that the essential connections do in truth simply stop short at a certain point, that Kant has put his finger on the point at which the relation between disparate spheres becomes external. Nothing warrants Heidegger's reading, in contrast with the thinkable alternative, except his precommitment to the type of logic of essence he pursues. And nothing, given the thinkable alternative, requires Kant's text to conform to that logic. Heidegger argues that "the faculties of the mind involved" in the "regression to the source-ground," rather than being "explicitly and primordially defined in the light of this transcendental function," are, "throughout the course of the laying of the foundation and even in its conclusion . . . presented according to the provisional conception of the first point of departure."[30] It remains possible that the "provisional," "external succession" of Kant's presentation is the fundamental problematic, that the relevant faculties of the mind (the understanding and sensibility) at a certain point can be conceived as ultimately thoroughly distinct, simply external to each other, that even the absolute reality that is the in-itself can in truth be indicated metaphorically, without a deeper incoherence resulting. Here it would be Kant who thought truth through more deeply, and not Hegel or Heidegger, who, on this reading, "recoil" from the brute and thinkable limits of the logic of essence itself as those limits are presented plainly by Kant.

Similar considerations apply to Cartesian and other dualisms. Precisely because an essential externality (taking "essence" here in a broader sense, a family of externally related senses in some of which "inner" is not tied to "essential") is thinkable, we can think as logically appropriate the classically, merely metaphorical relation between logically disconnected and independent spheres. The logical legitimacy of this kind of relation needs

[30] Ibid., 206.

a further accounting for only if a post-Hegelian logic of essence is presupposed as the ubiquitous decisive necessity. Similarly, again, with Nietzsche: it is easy to see, I believe, that Heidegger brings him to a fundamental unity that, while it is perhaps not of the type Nietzsche protested against, nonetheless forecloses the indications in Nietzsche's aphoristic style and in his emphasis on metaphor that he might have been proposing a direction divergent from any type of consistent or systematic unity. As I have argued, systematicity in general is only a specific way of conceiving unity or coherence of thought and not definitive of unity of thought as such.

I discuss the nature of these kinds of external relations between conceptually different spheres further in the Coda.

The issue, again, is not that Heidegger's reading is wrong but that truth is not necessarily confined to the closure of Heidegger's logic of essence. If we can speak about truth at all—and this whole discussion occurs only within the context of talking about truth, so that even putting in question whether we can talk about truth occurs only in the context of already talking about it—then, clearly, Heidegger, like Hegel, has a great deal to say about truth. But the point is that there is more to be said, and whatever it is, it cannot, without arbitrarily prejudging its character, be said within the closure of Heidegger's thought, or within that of the more general contemporary reworking of the history of metaphysics that follows on his thought.

One way to proceed with this, however, is to continue to think with Heidegger: the essence of truth must account for and therefore in some sense organically (essentially) include what is inessential, what has no great cogency or significance, connections that are more or less superficial, what is thoughtless.[31]

In fact, I have argued that these superficial, external, in some contexts "merely" rhetorical relations are, in an incompatible and self-canceling coordination with essential, internal relations, what can offer a legitimate foundation for the simply or purely essential truth articulated by logics that, like Heidegger's, (also sometimes always legitimately) exclude these external relations.[32]

---

[31] I think this is one way of describing the path Jacques Derrida has taken in relation to Heidegger.

[32] I discussed the rhetorical dimension of these relations in Chapters 2 and 3.

8. *The Formal Structure of Metaphysics and* The Importance of Being Earnest

In this chapter I try to show that the climactic moments of Oscar Wilde's *The Importance of Being Earnest* are structured in a way that displays the formal structure or logic of a central and perhaps the deepest type of metaphysical thinking. This structure, I argue, is fundamentally pluralist in the way I have presented in the other chapters. (In other words, its pluralism is also self-canceling, and in this way, as is appropriate for a genuine pluralism, makes equally fundamental room for nonpluralism.) I do not aim to show that the play *is* metaphysics, or that it *justifies* this formal structure as appropriate to metaphysics, but only that it parallels and displays this structure in its own way.

In the first section I sketch what I mean by the formal structure of this type of metaphysics. In the second section, I show how the play maps this structure. As my discussion of the play proceeds, I explain further details of the corresponding structure or process of metaphysical thought, and try to justify these details as truly and legitimately characterizing metaphysics.

1. A Preliminary Sketch of the Formal Structure of Metaphysics

One well-represented aim of metaphysics is to account for the world as a whole. While not all metaphysics pursue this aim, for those that do it is a familiar insight, in a variety of philosophical perspectives—among others, ordinary language, pragmatist, Wittgensteinian, existential—that metaphysics, in trying to account for the world as a whole, has to use language in a way that is different from any of its particular applications *within* the world. Karl Jaspers, for example, notes, in connection with his own philosophical work, that "for the clarification of . . . the Encompassing, we have used words and concepts which had their original meaning for definite things in the world; now however they are used to go beyond the limits and are not to be understood in their original sense."[1] That is, the language of metaphysics does not share the meanings of language as used *in any context within the world*. In other words, it is meaningless with respect to the entirety of our familiar language. When metaphysics succeeds, then, in providing an account of the world as a whole, it makes itself entirely meaningless and so irrelevant to anything we might mean, in any language but its own, by what it accounts for.

A well-known extreme version of this idea is that metaphysical language, or attempted talk from a vantage point on reality as a whole, simply has no meaning at all.[2] As will become clear, this is not what I am proposing here.

On the other hand, it is also true that metaphysical grounding and explanation arrives at its language *through* the use of our familiar language. It transforms our familiar language into its own, produces its own language on the basis of familiar language. Consequently, familiar language itself goes through a process in which *it makes itself* meaningless and irrelevant. As Jaspers comments, "transcending thought ... in its form of thinking the unthinkable ... always seems to be canceling itself."[3]

We can conceptualize this as an all-embracing circle of meaning becoming two entirely separate all-embracing circles of meanings, wholly closed off to and irrelevant to each other. In this respect, the process by which metaphysical thought establishes itself is exactly analogous to the process by which globally different standpoints would have to relate to each other's sense.[4]

---

[1] Karl Jaspers, *Reason and Existenz: Five Lectures*, trans. William Earle (Milwaukee, WI: Marquette University Press, 1997), 111.

[2] This is, for example, Wittgenstein's later view: so, "if the words 'language,' 'experience,' 'world,' have a use, it must be as humble a one as that of the words 'table,' 'lamp,' 'door'"; Ludwig Wittgenstein, *Philosophical Investigations*, 2nd ed., trans. G. E. M. Anscombe (Oxford: Blackwell, 1958), 44e, no. 97. As I have noted in the other chapters in connection with the idea of a perspective on our own framework as a whole, Donald Davidson gives another well-known argument for this extreme version in his "On the Very Idea of a Conceptual Scheme," in *Inquiries into Truth and Interpretation* (Oxford: Oxford University Press, 1984), 183–98.

[3] Jaspers, *Reason and Existenz*, 112.

[4] For extended discussions of metaphysical or global philosophical systems as constituting separate and conflicting domains of meaning, or as systematically giving different meanings to all the "same" facts, see R. G. Collingwood, *An Essay on*

Metaphysics, in this context, has the structure of two globally different domains of meaning, meaningfully interacting with each other. By "meaningfully interacting" I mean relating to each other specifically with respect to each other's meanings: in contrast, for example, with simply ignoring what the other has to say and dealing with that other by means of unilateral force. Because these are *global* domains of meaning, they are the ultimate contexts in which questions about and concepts of reality and truth have their sense. They therefore give the most basic structure of anything we might mean by anything, including what we might mean by reality and truth themselves.[5]

Metaphysics (Oxford: Clarendon Press of Oxford University Press, 1940); Everett W. Hall, *Philosophical Systems: A Categorial Analysis* (Chicago: University of Chicago Press, 1960). On philosophy as in fact logically presupposing more than one, all-embracing framework, and on the acceptability of this contradiction, see Henry W. Johnstone, Jr., *Validity and Rhetoric in Philosophical Argument: An Outlook in Transition* (University Park, PA: Dialogue Press of Man and World, 1978), e.g., 45, 114ff.

[5] This idea, although, like all fundamental issues in philosophy, controversial, is one way of expressing one of the impulses behind much of what used to be practiced as conceptual analysis, as well as, in a modified form, the more recently favored combinations of philosophy of language, mind, and action. Wittgenstein, for example, argued that *"the limits of my language* mean the limits of my world"; Ludwig Wittgenstein, *Tractatus Logico-Philosophicus,* trans. D. F. Pears and B. F. McGuinness (London: Routledge & Kegan Paul, 1961), 56, prop. 5.6. And he noted that his discussion of the limits of language "has to do with the Kantian solution of the problem of philosophy"; Ludwig Wittgenstein, *Culture and Value,* trans. Peter Winch, ed. G. H. von Wright and Heikki Nyman (Chicago: University of Chicago Press, 1980), 10e. In his later work he argued for resolving all philosophical problems in terms of "language games" and the social practices they involve. J. L. Austin, in pursuing a very different approach but sharing the same general impulse to resolve even fundamental philosophical problems in terms of language, noted, "It is essential to realize that 'true' and 'false,' like 'free' and 'unfree,' do not stand for anything simple at all; but only for a general dimension of being a right or proper thing to say as opposed to a wrong thing, in these circumstances, to this audience, for these purposes and with these intentions"; John L. Austin, *How to Do Things with Words* (Cambridge, MA: Harvard University Press, 1962), 144. More recently, Paul Horwich, for example, has argued for a theory of truth that, although "minimalist," is partly rooted in a theory of meaning. Paul Horwich, "The Minimalist Conception of Truth," in *Truth,* ed. Simon Blackburn and Keith Simmons (New York: Oxford University Press, 1999), 244–45. As Blackburn and Simmons note, even "deflationist" theorists of truth find it very hard "to

And since metaphysics in our sense has precisely the structure of meaningful interaction between globally different circles of meaning, the formal or essential structure of metaphysics in this sense, its logic, is the same as the formal or essential structure, or logic, of meaningful interaction between globally different circles of meaning.

As I shall try to show in the main body of the chapter, the climactic moments of *The Importance of Being Earnest* display the formal structure or logic of meaningful interaction between globally different circles of meaning. This is worth exploring and laying out in its own right, and in this respect the logic I explore here may be of interest even to those who do not pursue the type of metaphysics I claim that it characterizes, or who, for that matter, do not accept that claim. But, while the play is concerned with interacting circles of meaning, and not with reality and truth each as a whole, the formal structures of the two concerns are the same. As a result, in displaying the formal structure of this interaction of meaning circles, Wilde also displays the formal structure of metaphysics in the sense of an account of the world as a whole.

Returning to this structure or logic: in fact, we can only speak of a circle of meaning when there is another circle to contrast with it. In other words, it is not at first the case—or not at first correctly expressed to say—that a circle of meaning becomes two circles. Until the second circle is there, there is no sense to speaking of any circles at all. (This is not to say that we cannot talk about our *meanings*, but that we cannot genuinely speak about meaning as a *complete whole or "circle,"* in comparison, say, with a kind of meaning wholly different from the entirety of our meanings. We would not know what we meant there by the phrase, "wholly other kind of meaning.") Consequently, it is only at the moment when two contrasting circles of meanings occur, when the new set of meanings has become established, that we can say, retrospectively, that our familiar language constituted one set of meanings among possible others, rather than simply constituting meaning as such, period.

Before metaphysics succeeds, then, we have an absolute range of meanings, with nothing meaningful to be "relative" to. Similarly, *within* the new circle, because it is a circle by virtue of being all-embracing, alternative

---

avoid engagement with the notion of a proposition, or that of a judgement or idiolect or language" (*Truth*, 28).

"meanings" simply do not exist. Consequently, within the new circle we also have an absolute range of meanings, the only meanings there can conceivably be. That is, within the new circle, again, it is not a circle; there are no other, contrasting circles to give this concept a meaning. But at the point of transition between no circles and two circles, or at the point at which two such circles try to communicate with each other, we have a moment of relative meanings and so of relative truths. (For example, if an Aristotelian comes to understand a Leibnizian, before going about making the decision as to which of them is right, she will need, if she does not want to beg the question by deciding which is right in advance, to be able to think of an object like this page both as truly not extended in space but a coordination of sizeless, mutually independent monadic perceptions, each aware of the entire universe, and also as truly extended in space and composed of an organic integration of impercipient form and matter, neither of these components containing in itself any relation to most of the rest of what surrounds it. These interpretations of the "same" thing will then be relative to the respective metaphysical frameworks.) But, again, the moment we can conceive these circles as circles at all (and this is the *same* moment as the moment of transition or attempted communication), they are, being circles, closed and so absolutely meaningless and irrelevant to each other. As a result, this is a relation between, a relativity of, two *absolute* meanings and truths.

This is, of course, a paradox, involving a contradiction. But it is a paradox that, for the reasons I have been giving, I believe accurately describes the situation of global metaphysics.[6] As a result, it is a paradox that metaphysics needs to accept and work with.[7]

This paradox has certain inescapable consequences. As I have argued, the circles of meaning have absolutely nothing to do with each other, and

---

[6] As I mentioned in the Introduction, Jaspers, again, also argues that it is necessary for thinking at its deepest and most comprehensive to accept the contradiction of conceiving more than one absolute position. He describes our existence as coming to stand "before its final limits: that there are many truths in the sense of existential absolutes" (*Reason and Existenz,* 100). And he elaborates, "Through reason I catch sight of something which is only communicable in the form of contradiction and paradox. Here a rational a-logic arises, a true reason which reaches its goal through the shattering of the logic of the understanding" (112).

[7] On the necessity of this paradox, see also notes 4 and 6; on the general possibility of legitimate logical contradiction, see again the Introduction, section 5.

yet *also* can be in relation to each other. This paradox is resolved in that, as I have noted, the circles *cancel themselves* as soon as they emerge as relatable circles. That is, because these circles can only be said to exist by contrast with each other, and yet as soon as they exist are absolute and meaningless to each other, they come into existence at the same moment and for the same reasons that they become meaningless to each other. In other words, they can only be said to come into existence at the same moment as they can no longer be meaningfully contrasted, and consequently also can no longer be meaningfully said to come into existence. Again, then, the moment at which metaphysics, and also mutual recognition of globally different standpoints, succeeds, it cancels the meaning of the process by which it was established or grounded, and also cancels its own meaning for and relevance to the world, or cancels the meaning of the different standpoints for each other.

The result, and the value, of this self-canceling kind of thought is that we then have access to a *type* of insight that was not available to us before.[8] This self-canceling moment of thought is itself a grasp of reality itself as a whole, or, for example, of truth itself as a whole, or sense or meaning themselves as a whole.[9] It also leaves us with a new global understanding *of all the particulars* of our world: we see them all as they are in a certain light. And it

---

[8] Wittgenstein makes an analogous point about self-canceling thought: "The results of philosophy are the uncovering of one or another piece of plain nonsense and of bumps that the understanding has got by running its head up against the limits of language. These bumps make us see the value of the discovery" (*Philosophical Investigations*, 48e, no. 119).

[9] Wittgenstein argues for a version of this: "The solution of the problem of life is seen in the vanishing of the problem"; and "My propositions serve as elucidations in the following way: anyone who understands me eventually recognizes them as nonsensical, when he has used them—as steps—to climb up beyond them. (He must, so to speak, throw away the ladder after he has climbed up it.) He must transcend these propositions, and then he will see the world aright" (*Tractatus,* 73, prop. 6.521, 74, prop. 6.54). See also F. H. Bradley: "But in this very point of failure . . . lies the way to success. . . . Truth claimed identity with . . . all reality. And when we had to see how truth fails, as truth, in attaining its own end, we were being shown the very features of difference between truth and reality. . . . Hence, being the same as reality, and at the same time different from reality, truth is thus able itself to apprehend its identity and difference"; F. H. Bradley, "On Truth and Copying," in *Truth,* ed. Simon Blackburn and Keith Simmons (New York: Oxford University Press, 1999), 37.

can enable us to recognize *different* global understandings of these particulars. In doing these things, it renews our appreciation of the world (or reality, or life) in general, and it allows dialogue between different global understandings. We cannot gain such global appreciations and understandings without this global and so self-canceling separation of our thought from the particular understandings of things with which we start.

Another result is that we get a deeper, more thoroughgoing kind of objectivity than is available, say, to the sciences. (I take radical shifts in scientific frameworks to be the results of philosophical, and specifically metaphysical, thinking undertaken by scientists. But if we take this kind of thinking to be properly scientific, then my discussion will apply to that particular kind of scientific thinking as well as to global metaphysics in the context of philosophy.) At this level, because our thinking can cancel itself, it can, so to speak, get itself out of its own way, and leave the world it thinks about entirely free of its own effects and possible distortions.

Because this process by which metaphysical thinking gets itself out of its own way departs entirely from our familiar meanings, and then cancels its own meanings, it makes itself entirely redundant, entirely unnecessary. In other words, it is a purely artificial activity. But its pure artificiality, its self-canceling character, is precisely what allows us to gain and establish insights into the nature of reality itself as a whole. That is, this artificiality is the basis for our sense of nature in general. And that grasp of the sense of the nature of reality in general is the context in which all particular insights into reality get their own sense. Consequently, this pure artificiality is not only a legitimate kind of justification, it is the kind of justification on which all others ultimately depend.

Metaphysics, then, just as it is traditionally understood to do, sets out both to establish and express the truth of things more deeply and fully than other forms of knowledge do, and to be itself more fully established as true, as revealing its objects without distortion, than other forms of knowledge are.

A central feature of the self-canceling moment of metaphysical thought is a moment of undecidability of meanings. Both sets of incompatible meanings apply and do not apply to the same (and therefore also not the same) thing in the same respect and at the same time. (For additional discussion of why the differently meant thing is still also the same thing, see the quotation by Alasdair MacIntyre in section 4 of Chapter 1, and the discussions in section 6 of Chapter 3 and in the first section of Chapter 9.) For example, there is the "same" page understood simultaneously in the Leibnizian and Aristotelian frameworks, which I briefly discussed above. Each construal of the page depends on its own independent framework of meanings, Aristotelian or Leibnizian, *as will any contrasting construal*: and there is no page we can speak of "outside" of this kind of framework, to make any of them the right or wrong one. For that matter, even "rightness" itself only has meaning and so is only decided within the context of a framework of sense. It is important to note, however, that rightness *does* have its specific meaning *within* a framework and so, when the framework's criteria are sufficiently clear in a given case, *is* decided there. Consequently—and this is just another way of expressing the same paradox we have been discussing—each construal is right or wrong depending on which framework one is drawing on, and each is right *and* wrong when one is drawing on both frameworks simultaneously.[10] But this moment of undecidability, like everything else in this context, cancels itself, in this case into two entirely separate and so decidable, incompatible sets of meanings.[11]

(It follows, for the reasons I have given for this account of global metaphysics, that the historical record of actual metaphysical systems needs to be understood as a collection of this kind of wholly separate and incompatible sets of meaning that *also* interact with each other in a self-canceling confusion of meanings.[12])

Because this process or logic involves a partly unintelligible moment or phase of self-contradiction and undecidability of meanings, both the insight in which it consists and the knowledge or recognition of it itself cannot be purely conceptual. But this unintelligible phase is part of the logic by which the nature of meaning in general (among other global "natures") is made graspable and is established. It must therefore have some kind of graspable relation to intelligible concepts. I suggest that this is a kind of knowledge or insight characterized by an awareness that the whole of things includes the *questions* about the *sense* of the whole of things, so that

---

[10] On the legitimacy of this kind of formulation, see, again, notes 4, 6, and 16.

[11] I discuss this self-cancellation of undecidability in detail below, but see also Chapter 2, section 6.

[12] For extended discussions of existing metaphysical and global philosophical systems in a similar light, see Collingwood, *Essay*; Hall, *Philosophical Systems*.

an insight into the whole *is* partly these questions, the *lack* of insight and intelligibility. It is, perhaps, an insight characterized by a sense of the insecurity and impermanence of its own meaning.

And I suggest that one of the ways in which this grasp occurs is as the impact of the contradictions of certain kinds of humor. I shall try to show that one of these is Wilde's.

More specifically, I argue that the climactic moments of Wilde's *The Importance of Being Earnest* are structured as a kind of detailed map of this insight-granting process of the self-cancellation of a global range of meanings. That is, as I said at the start of the chapter, I shall try to show that they express the formal structure or logic of legitimate metaphysical thinking.

2. The Importance of Being Earnest *and the Formal Structure of Metaphysics*

The plot so far is as follows. When Jack Worthing is in London, he pretends that his name is Ernest. But when he is in the country, with his ward, Cecily Cardew, he pretends he has a wicked brother Ernest who lives in the city. While in London, Jack has fallen in love with Gwendolen Fairfax, and she has accepted him. But she loves him for his name, Ernest. He therefore returns to the country to undo the pretense, by declaring his fictional brother dead and having himself rechristened Ernest.

Meanwhile, his friend Algy, having discovered Jack's secret, and wanting to meet Cecily, has already arrived at Jack's country home. He passes himself off as Ernest, Jack's fictional brother. But he finds that Cecily is already in love with him because of his name, Ernest. He therefore also arranges to be rechristened Ernest.

While Jack and Algy are off making their christening arrangements, Gwendolen arrives at the country home looking for Ernest, the name by which she knows Jack. There she meets Cecily, of whose existence she has so far been unaware, and for whom the name Ernest refers to Algy.

The scene is therefore set for the kind of situation I have described in connection with metaphysics: two different general understandings of things (*so* general that they also give the meaning and nature of our relation to truth itself: I shall return to this shortly), in the context of which the same words—in this case, a name—can only mean completely unrelated things. While this is not a *global* difference in understandings, it will be enough to parallel and so to exhibit the structure of the process that occurs when the differences *are* global. As I mentioned at the start of the chapter, my aim here is not show that Wilde's play *is* metaphysics, or that it justifies this formal structure as appropriate to metaphysics, but only that it shares and displays it.

As the discussion of the play proceeds, however, I shall explain further details of the corresponding structure of metaphysical thought itself, and try to justify these details as truly and legitimately characterizing metaphysics, and there I shall do so in the terms that *are* appropriate to global thinking. In fact, at first I need to offer much more metaphysics and much less Wilde, in order to establish the details of the philosophical context. But, if the reader will bear with me, that proportion will gradually change as the discussion continues.

I should remind the reader here that, as I discussed near the start of the previous section, because we are dealing with global domains of meaning (or elements of the play that share their ways of functioning), we are dealing with what gives the most basic structure of what we might mean by anything, and this includes what we might mean by reality and truth themselves.[13] And, since metaphysics in our sense is the account of reality and truth themselves, each as a whole, and has, as I argued, precisely the structure of meaningful interaction between globally different circles of meaning, the formal structure of metaphysics in this sense is the same as the formal structure of meaningful interaction between globally different circles of meaning. As a result, while the play is concerned with interacting circles of meaning and not with reality and truth each as a whole, when it displays the formal structure of the interaction of meaning circles it also displays the formal structure of metaphysics in the sense of an account of the world as a whole.

I should note again, too, that the formal structure of meaningful interaction between globally different circles of meaning is worth exploring and laying out in its own right, so that the logic I explore here may be of interest even to those who do not pursue global metaphysics, or who do not accept my characterization of it.

The stage is set, then, to display the structure of metaphysics, of the self-canceling movement that occurs between mutually exclusive global ranges of meaning.

---

[13] In this connection, also see note 5.

Gwendolen enters:

CECILY (*advancing to meet her*): Pray let me introduce myself to you. My name is Cecily Cardew.
GWENDOLEN: Cecily Cardew? (*Moving to her and shaking hands.*) What a very sweet name! Something tells me that we are going to be great friends. I like you already more than I can say. My first impressions of people are never wrong.
CECILY: How nice of you to like me so much after we have known each other such a comparatively short time. Pray sit down.
GWENDOLEN (*still standing up*): I may call you Cecily, may I not?
CECILY: With pleasure!
GWENDOLEN: And you will always call me Gwendolen, won't you?
CECILY: If you wish.
GWENDOLEN: Then that is all quite settled, is it not?
CECILY: I hope so.[14]

Gwendolen immediately and fully presents her position, and an initial, clear relation between their standpoints is established. This is a *decidable* relation: there is no apparent conflict of meanings to make the two positions mean incompatible things by the same terms.

This initial relation, however, is based on a misunderstanding of basic terms that are not yet explicitly relevant. As I discussed in the previous section, the meaning of terms is established by the framework(s) of sense within which the terms occur, frameworks that consist partly in other terms whose connections and contrasts with the relevant terms contribute to giving them their meaning, and in this case the relevant frameworks are not yet recognized. As a result each position here wrongly understands something (what "Ernest" truly names in Gwendolen's and Cecily's respective lives) as it is given meaning by the other's framework of sense. In fact, this kind of misunderstanding is logically unavoidable in the relation of positions ("circles") with wholly mutually exclusive ranges of meanings. They do not initially have access to meanings other than their own, and so can *only* take the other position's meanings as the same as their own. It

---

[14] Oscar Wilde, *The Importance of Being Earnest*, in *Complete Works of Oscar Wilde*, ed. Vyvyan Holland (London: Collins, 1966), 361–62. Unless otherwise noted, all further references to and citations of Wilde in this chapter are from this book.

follows that the establishment of their true relation *requires* the movement, not simply from ignorance to knowledge, but also from unavoidable or well-founded *misunderstanding* to knowledge. Initial misunderstanding, then, is a valid and in fact logically necessary part of the process of establishing knowledge of wholly unfamiliar ranges of meaning.

Because this misunderstanding is logically necessary in establishing truth, a positive relation to truth, as conceived by the *right* understanding, is part of the *meaning* of this misunderstanding. Certainly, at the very least, it and the relevant truth strictly entail each other. That is, the misunderstanding, *as it stands*, captures an element of the relevant truth, or in other words, is, *as it stands*, in some way *also true*. I return to this point to justify it in more detail as the discussion proceeds.

Now, *throughout* this process, both when the misunderstanding is in force *and* when the true relation is known, there are two disparate positions, each the locus of a range of meanings incompatible with that of the other. And in the case of positions that consider and account for the whole of things, there is no "outside" standpoint to offer a neutral set of meanings. Consequently, if we are genuinely considering the relation between the standpoints, and not simply ignoring one in favor of the meanings of the other, the terms that occur in the interaction or relation between the positions can only be understood throughout in terms of both incompatible sets of meanings. That is, these terms can only be understood throughout in ways that are simultaneously both *wholly true* in the one context *and wholly false* in the other. (That individual terms, including names, can be true or false in this context, rather than simply being applied in different ways, follows from the all-embracing character of each range of meanings: they each *exclude even the possibility* of any applications of terms that fall outside their all-embracing range.)

But when the true relation is known, when the misunderstanding is no longer in force and it has been established that the two sets of meanings are separate, the truth and falsity of the grasp of the terms can be sorted out into the two different standpoints. These incompatibly valued understandings are then each limited to a context for which the other understanding and its context literally have no meaning and so no relevance. In this sense, the understanding of the terms is, at that point, *decidably* both true and false. In contrast, when the misunderstanding is still in force, no separation between the two sets of meanings has been established. At that

214 *The Formal Structure of Metaphysics*

point the grasp of the terms is therefore *undecidably* both true and false. But at that point it has also not been established that there is an issue of different meanings at all, so that this undecidability is only implicit.

The required movement to establish the true relation of the two standpoints, then, is in fact from an understanding of the terms that is not simply false, but implicitly and undecidably both true and false, to a knowledge that is not simply true, but explicitly and decidably both true and false. Or, more fully expressed, it is a movement from the terms' initial implicit undecidability but explicit or clear and harmonious decidability to their full and explicit but separate and incompatible decidabilities. As will shortly become clear, in this process the initial implicit undecidability is transformed into two decidabilities precisely by, and in its own activity in bringing about, the becoming explicit of the difference between the two positions.

Now, the initial explicitly decidable relation, the clear relation between the positions and terms that is not yet explicitly based on a misunderstanding, is a result of exactly the same relation of positions that ultimately makes each understanding of the relevant terms both decidably false *and decidably true*. This initial clear and decidable relation, then, despite being implicitly based on a misunderstanding, is again, *as it stands*, in some sense partly simply (decidably) true.

The movement from unavoidable or well-founded misunderstanding to knowledge occurs through a shift from one range of meanings to another. More specifically, it will become clear below that once the movement from the initial clear decidability begins, the implicit misunderstanding gradually becomes explicitly relevant to that initial relation, but that because it is an implicit dimension *of what that relation itself is*, as it becomes relevant *it transforms the explicit meaning* of that relation. But the original explicit meaning of the relation is in some sense *true as it stands*. Consequently, in transforming the initial explicit meaning of the initial relation, the misunderstanding becomes relevant to the initial relation *as the initial relation truly was not* when the misunderstanding was only implicit. The relation's original meaning is not just more fully expressed in being made explicit, it really is not the same meaning.[15]

---

[15] Bertrand Russell notes of the relation between the implicit content of statements and the explicit version of this content produced by analysis that, in general, "you never get back to the acorn in the oak.... It will not really be the same as the

Because, then, the treatment of the issue shifts to a semantic area that will allow correction of the misunderstanding, the misunderstanding, while corrected, is *not simply* corrected. The corrective shift in semantic area *also* transforms the meaning of the issue so that it is not what the misunderstanding is correcting any more. The correction itself retroactively changes the meaning of what it was supposed to correct, so that it really passes it by. The correction of the misunderstanding necessarily proceeds by establishing a new misunderstanding, a misunderstanding of the misunderstanding itself.

But this retroactive transformation of the meaning of the initial relation between the standpoints is a stage of this overall process of thought that itself happens in stages. And in the context of a metaphysical or global understanding, it is logically necessary that it do so. For an all-embracing standpoint, there simply *is* no meaning that is not already available to it, that it does not already include or that cannot be constructed from its current range of meanings. Consequently, if a different standpoint offers it a term with a meaning wholly unrelated to any of its own, it cannot register that meaning *as* a meaning. It can only register it as a series of deflections and distortions of its current meanings by the other standpoint, until those meanings are sufficiently reworked and redirected to produce the new meaning. Similarly, although contradictions and undecidabilities endemic to its *own* meanings can set up the conditions to produce a new meaning, not yet available to it, it also cannot initially register *that* new meaning, but only the progressive reworking and redirecting of its meanings that those conflicts produce.

And, in this stage just as in the overall process, it is again necessary that this process reach the point where the global standpoint reworks *its initial understanding* of the very issue itself, the meaning that it first understood the issue to have. In other words, it is *logically necessary* that the movement from misunderstanding (or, within a *single* global standpoint, from a sense-

---

thing we started from because it will be so much more analytic and precise"; Bertrand Russell, "The Philosophy of Logical Atomism," in *Logic and Knowledge: Essays 1901–1950*, ed. Robert Charles Marsh (London: George Allen & Unwin, 1956), 188–89. This is a version of the "paradox of analysis." (On this paradox, see, for example, Pascal Engel, *The Norm of Truth: An Introduction to the Philosophy of Logic*, trans. Pascal Engel and Miriam Kochan [Toronto: University of Toronto Press, 1991], 100, 137f.)

216 *The Formal Structure of Metaphysics*

disturbing conflict of meanings) to knowledge (or to reestablishing sense) involves a shift of semantic areas, and so also a misunderstanding of the misunderstanding itself. The standpoint cannot resolve the instabilities in its meanings until it has reached their source in the wholly new meaning. And, as a global standpoint, it can only reach that source by reworking *all* its relevant meanings. But these include those involved in the whole process it has gone through in reworking its meanings. For that re-working itself occurs in the context of the position's available meanings, and so is just a change among those available meanings. Consequently, the issue cannot be resolved until the whole *process of resolving it* itself, including the meaning of the very issue that motivated that process, has been reworked, and in fact canceled in favor of the wholly new, unrelated meanings.

Now, the standpoint's *first* attempts to rework even the issue's initial meaning can still only be in terms of the meanings already available to it, can still only be constructed from its *own* meanings. This is not yet the point, then, at which the wholly new meaning itself, and so the misunderstanding of meanings, have become explicit. But, still, the point at which it reworks the issue's initial meaning into a *different* one of its own meanings (and not just into a variation or distortion of a single meaning) is the point where it can become recognizable that a *difference in meaning* is what is at stake in this particular issue.

This moment is reflected in *The Importance of Being Earnest* by a retroactive reworking of the meaning of the initial relation between Cecily and Gwendolen. And the stages of the process are also reflected in this reworking.

First, the misunderstanding becomes explicitly relevant to the *current, ongoing* relation between the positions and terms, without yet having any explicit significance for understanding the way the relation began, and also without yet being explicit itself. (It has explicit effects, but the cause of those effects is still hidden from view.)

>   CECILY: Yes, I am Mr. Worthing's ward.
>   GWENDOLEN: Oh! It is strange he never mentioned to me that he had a ward. How secretive of him! He grows more interesting hourly. I am not sure, however, that the news inspires me with feelings of unmixed delight. (*Rising and going to her.*) I am very fond of you, Cecily; I have liked you ever since I met you! But I am bound to state that now that I

The Formal Structure of Metaphysics 217

know that you are Mr. Worthing's ward, I cannot help expressing a wish you were—well, just a little older than you seem to be—and not quite so very alluring in appearance. In fact, if I may speak candidly—
CECILY: Pray do! I think that whenever one has anything unpleasant to say, one should always be quite candid.
GWENDOLEN: Well, to speak with perfect candour, Cecily, I wish that you were fully forty-two, and more than unusually plain for your age. Ernest has a strong upright nature. He is the very soul of truth and honour. Disloyalty would be as impossible to him as deception. But even men of the noblest possible moral character are extremely susceptible to the influence of the physical charms of others. Modern, no less than Ancient History, supplies us with many most painful examples of what I refer to. If it were not so, indeed, History would be quite unreadable.
CECILY: I beg your pardon, Gwendolen, did you say Ernest?
GWENDOLEN: Yes.
CECILY: Oh, but it is not Mr. Ernest Worthing who is my guardian. It is his brother—his elder brother.
GWENDOLEN (*sitting down again*): Ernest never mentioned to me that he had a brother.
CECILY: I am sorry to say they have not been on good terms for a long time.
GWENDOLEN: Ah! that accounts for it. And now that I think of it I have never heard any man mention his brother. The subject seems distasteful to most men. Cecily, you have lifted a load from my mind. I was growing almost anxious. It would have been terrible if any cloud had come across a friendship like ours, would it not? Of course you are quite, quite sure that it is not Mr. Ernest Worthing who is your guardian? (362–63)

Gwendolen is completely reassured, but on the basis of a complete misapplication of the name "Ernest" as Cecily is using it. Cecily proceeds on the basis of the misunderstanding, however, and as a result, the effects of the term's misapplication become further developed.

CECILY: Quite sure. (*A pause.*) In fact, I am going to be his.
GWENDOLEN (*inquiringly*): I beg your pardon?

> CECILY (*rather shy and confidingly*): Dearest Gwendolen, there is no reason why I should make a secret of it to you. Our little country newspaper is sure to chronicle the fact next week. Mr. Ernest Worthing and I are engaged to be married.
>
> GWENDOLEN (*quite politely, rising*): My darling Cecily, I think there must be some slight error. Mr. Ernest Worthing is engaged to me. The announcement will appear in the "Morning Post" on Saturday at the latest.
>
> CECILY (*very politely, rising*): I am afraid you must be under some misconception. Ernest proposed to me exactly ten minutes ago. (*Shows diary.*)
>
> GWENDOLEN (*examines diary through her lorgnette carefully*): It is certainly very curious, for he asked me to be his wife yesterday afternoon at 5.30. If you would care to verify the incident, pray do so. (*Produces diary of her own.*) I never travel without my diary. One should always have something sensational to read in the train. I am so sorry, dear Cecily, if it is any disappointment to you, but I am afraid I have the prior claim.
>
> CECILY: It would distress me more than I can tell you, dear Gwendolen, if it caused you any mental or physical anguish, but I feel bound to point out that since Ernest proposed to you he clearly has changed his mind.
>
> GWENDOLEN (*meditatively*): If the poor fellow has been entrapped into any foolish promise I shall consider it my duty to rescue him at once, and with a firm hand.
>
> CECILY (*thoughtfully and sadly*): Whatever unfortunate entanglement my dear boy may have got into, I will never reproach him with it after we are married. (363)

And as a result of this development of the misunderstanding's effects, in turn, Gwendolen becomes outraged, and moves to redefine their relationship.

> GWENDOLEN: Do you allude to me, Miss Cardew, as an entanglement? You are presumptuous. On an occasion of this kind it becomes more than a moral duty to speak one's mind. It becomes a pleasure.
>
> CECILY: Do you suggest, Miss Fairfax, that I entrapped Ernest into an engagement? How dare you? This is no time for wearing the shallow mask of manners. When I see a spade I call it a spade.
>
> GWENDOLEN (*satirically*): I am glad to say that I have never seen a spade. It is obvious that our social spheres have been widely different. (363–64)

The Formal Structure of Metaphysics 219

Now Cecily is also outraged, and also moving to redefine their relationship, on the basis of the same misunderstanding.

> GWENDOLEN: You have filled my tea with lumps of sugar, and though I asked most distinctly for bread and butter, you have given me cake. I am known for the gentleness of my disposition, and the extraordinary sweetness of my nature, but I warn you, Miss Cardew, you may go too far.
>
> CECILY (*rising*): To save my poor, innocent, trusting boy from the machinations of any other girl there are no lengths to which I would not go. (365)

And at this point the misunderstanding (still without yet having become explicit itself) also becomes explicitly relevant to (has explicit effects on) the *initial* relation between them. That relation itself comes *always to have meant* something different. It comes to have been a different clear and decidable relation:

> GWENDOLEN: From the moment I saw you I distrusted you. I felt that you were false and deceitful. I am never deceived in such matters. My first impressions of people are invariably right. (365)

The tone of Cecily's response also eliminates the meaningfulness of any earlier sentiments of friendship:

> CECILY: It seems to me, Miss Fairfax, that I am trespassing on your valuable time. No doubt you have many other calls of a similar character to make in the neighbourhood. (365)

The initial gestures of friendship remain in content exactly as they were. But because the context or criteria for their meaning have changed, they now retroactively become, not gestures of friendship, but false versions of those gestures: perhaps defenses or guardednesses or manipulations.

The clarity and consequent apparent stability and security of the initial relation itself allows and encourages a development to a new set of issues. This development results in the explicit relevance to the positions' current relation, of the (itself still implicit) misunderstanding involved in the initial relation. And this relevance then brings about a shift from the new set of issues back to an explicit awareness of the relevance of the (itself still implicit) misunderstanding to the initial relation. And, in turn, in virtue of this explicitness of the misunderstanding's relevance, the initial relation is retroactively shifted away from having been what it was.

The initial relation between Cecily's and Gwendolen's positions in its old meaning was clear and decidable, and that initial relation in its *new* meaning is also clear and decidable. But these two relations are incompatible. And the initial relation must be understood in terms of *both* meanings. For at this point both simply *are* parts of the situation, of the relation between positions, we are trying to understand, and in the context of a global understanding there is still no neutral range of meanings to justify a decision to invalidate one meaning in favor of the other.

In fact, in that context, the old meaning in each position is what has *produced and justified* the new, corrected meaning, and it and related meanings *alone* have done so, since in a global standpoint there are no other, neutral meanings. Consequently whatever truth the new meaning has is based entirely on a process governed by the old and related meanings. That is, it *only* has whatever truth it has *if the old meaning is*, in some sense, *also true, as it stands*. In other words, this is a kind of liar's paradox (as in "I am lying": it is so if, in saying I am lying, I am telling the truth. In other words, it is so if it is not so—and only because it is not so—and it is also not so if and only because it is so).

And this paradox applies equally when the process has gone far enough to eliminate the misunderstanding altogether and establish the wholly unqualified true meaning of the contested term for each position. Again, then, as I argued earlier, the corrected or misunderstood meaning is a logically necessary part of the establishment of the true meaning, and so as it stands captures some element of the truth, or in other words *is* in some sense *also simply true*, as it stands.

During the *transition* from the initial decidability to the later decidability, when the misunderstanding became explicitly relevant to the *ongoing* situation (that is, not yet to the initial situation), the meanings exchanged between Cecily's and Gwendolen's simultaneous positions were undecidable. They applied simultaneously to the same thing without a neutral meaning to allow a decision between them. But now that the misunderstanding is also explicitly relevant to the *initial* situation, the undecidability is also located in—partly shifted or displaced to—the meanings in the *sequential* relation between the earlier version of the initial decidable relation between their positions and the later version of the initial decidable relation between their positions.

This means that the undecidability of meanings—or, more precisely, an undecidability of a different set of meanings that is its effect—now occurs *within* each position. When the undecidability of meanings was located *between* the positions, they had no access to the contrasting meaning that produced it, and so could not recognize that an undecidability of meanings, and so a misunderstanding between equally valid but incompatible meanings, might be at issue. But now an undecidability that is explicitly relevant to the conflict between them occurs *within* them, where they can recognize it as an undecidability, or, in other words, as a *contradiction that is true*.[16] As a result, they can for the first time recognize that the meanings on which the conflict turns might themselves be conflicted in a way that would not only require a change among familiar meanings but a change that those meanings cannot cope with, that they are not sufficient to produce.

That is, the positions now for the first time have the resources of meaning, first, to conceive that their relevant range of meanings might *not cover* the whole possible range of meanings but that, instead, entirely unfamiliar meanings might be in some unfamiliar way conceivable. And, second, because the undecidability is also explicitly relevant to this particular conflict, they can also recognize that this kind of possible unfamiliar meaning might be what is at issue in this case. They have taken another step toward coming to recognize the other position's meaning, and so making the misunderstanding itself explicit.

Let me stress that, until the process has reached this point, there is literally no meaning, for a global standpoint, to the idea of a meaning beyond its range. In other words, it is not that the standpoint came to recognize something it was simply missing before, but that *there was nothing meaningful for it to recognize* before. It is only as a result of the process of moving toward the unfamiliar meaning that this meaning comes into existence for

---

[16] On the formal admissibility of true contradictions, see, for example, Manuel Bremer, *An Introduction to Paraconsistent Logics* (Frankfurt am Main: Peter Lang, 2005), 16, 19ff. And again, on the general possibility of legitimate logical contradiction, see the Introduction, section 5.

the standpoint. And since the standpoint is *global*, covering the world and meaning as a whole, this is the same as saying that the meaning simply did not exist before.

But, on the other hand, once the new meaning *is* conceivable, the range of meanings that excluded it is not global any more. As a result, there is no longer any meaningful context in which the new meaning did *not* exist before. In other words, like the meanings on either side of any of the undecidabilities here, the global standpoint's meanings *before* they correct themselves are *true as they stand* (there is nothing that can meaningfully qualify them), and the meanings of the *corrected* standpoint are *also* true as they stand.

Consequently, although these stages of the movement toward metaphysical knowledge or knowledge of different global standpoints cancel themselves, the truth they have is not qualified. It is either *the wholly exclusive truth* or *wholly canceled as simply having no meaning*. And at the moments of transition between the relevant ranges of meaning it is *both*. At these moments what each of them establishes to be true by its own criteria is either explicitly and decidably both true and false, or implicitly and undecidably both true and false.

All of these sets of alternatives, however, occur only in the context of establishing or considering the difference between two ranges of meaning, each existing as a global whole of meaning in its contrast with the other. And this means that they really *all* occur as parts of the moment (any of the moments) of transition, and in fact as stages of it. For just as *the whole conflict* between these alternatives of meaning and truth has no meaning for the old global range of meanings, as we move into a new global range the old range and with it the whole conflict lose all meaning.

This *whole process*, then, including all the stages and distinctions and conflicts of truth I have discussed in it, ultimately and necessarily cancels itself into meaninglessness. Even *discussion* of the process, including my own, cancels its meaning, since discussion of it is itself metaphysical, dealing as it does with vantage points on the whole of things, and so itself necessarily consists in a transition between global ranges of meaning.

But each of these stages of the process is again fully meaningful as soon as one returns to reengage in its part of the establishment of metaphysical insight. And what truth it has is then again the unqualified and exclusive truth.

To return, then, to our discussion of the development of the process. We have now reached the point at which the initial meanings, through the stages of an interaction with each other that is in logically necessary ways mistaken, alogical, and guided by non sequiturs and tangents, have brought about their own reworking, until each has itself come to open the possibility that it needs to be replaced by a wholly unrelated meaning, a meaning for which it itself is meaningless. That is, they have begun to cancel themselves, each in favor of a wholly new meaning.

And consequently they are now in a position to take that final step and establish explicitly what the relevant new meaning is.

Enter JACK.
GWENDOLEN (*catching sight of him*): Ernest! My own Ernest!
JACK: Gwendolen! Darling! (*Offers to kiss her.*)
GWENDOLEN (*drawing back*): A moment! May I ask if you are engaged to be married to this young lady? (*Points to* CECILY.)
JACK (*laughing*): To dear little Cecily! Of course not! What could have put such an idea into your pretty little head?
GWENDOLEN: Thank you. You may! (*Offers her cheek.*)
CECILY (*very sweetly*): I knew there must be some misunderstanding, Miss Fairfax. The gentleman whose arm is at present round your waist is my guardian, Mr. John Worthing.
GWENDOLEN: I beg your pardon?
CECILY: This is Uncle Jack.
GWENDOLEN (*receding*): Jack! Oh!
Enter ALGERNON.
CECILY: Here is Ernest.
ALGERNON (*goes over to* CECILY *without noticing anyone else*): My own love. (*Offers to kiss her.*)
CECILY (*drawing back*): A moment, Ernest! May I ask you—are you engaged to be married to this young lady?
ALGERNON (*looking round*): To what young lady? Good heavens! Gwendolen!
CECILY: Yes! to good heavens, Gwendolen, I mean to Gwendolen.

ALGERNON (*laughing*): Of course not! What could have put such an idea into your pretty little head?

CECILY: Thank you. (*Presenting her cheek to be kissed.*) You may. (ALGERNON *kisses her.*)

GWENDOLEN: I felt there was some slight error, Miss Cardew. The gentleman who is now embracing you is my cousin, Mr. Algernon Moncrieff.

CECILY (*breaking away from* ALGERNON): Algernon Moncrieff! Oh!

The two girls move towards each other and put their arms round each other's waists as if for protection.

CECILY: Are you called Algernon?

ALGERNON: I cannot deny it.

CECILY: Oh!

GWENDOLEN: Is your name really John?

JACK (*standing rather proudly*): I could deny it if I liked. I could deny anything if I liked. But my name certainly is John. It has been John for years.

CECILY (*to* GWENDOLEN): A gross deception has been practised on both of us. (365–66)

The difference in meanings between Gwendolen's and Cecily's positions, and so the incompatibility between them, is finally clarified.

And this in turn resolves the *sequential* undecidability *within* their positions, between the earlier and later meanings of their initial relation. Where the implicit undecidability *between* the positions had earlier been shifted or displaced into the explicit, sequential undecidability *within* them, the conflicted meanings responsible for those undecidabilities are now separable into the explicitly established contexts of differently meaning positions that produced them. As a result the conflict is now shifted back again to the now explicit, *decidable* clash in meanings *between* them.

The problem was an unrecognized incompatibility of simultaneous positions. It became a recognized sequential incompatibility. And this in turn allowed it to become a recognized or understood simultaneous incompatibility.

And, consequently, the initial relation between the positions is now reestablished in its first meaning of mutual understanding, but this time on the basis of each position's understanding of the key terms each *in its separate region of meaning*. That is, the truth of their initial relation too is now fully and explicitly established, and as being *exactly as it initially explicitly stood*, as a mutual understanding. The misunderstanding, then, is no longer relevant, either implicitly or explicitly, even to *that first understanding of the initial* relation between the positions. The misunderstanding has utterly canceled itself, retroactively, by its own efficacy. As a result, the entire process that it produced, and that culminated in the new understanding, has lost all meaning. It is as though nothing relevant to the relation between the positions had ever been understood otherwise than it is in the new understanding.

> GWENDOLEN: My poor wounded Cecily!
> CECILY: My sweet wronged Gwendolen!
> GWENDOLEN (*slowly and seriously*): You will call me sister, will you not?
> (366)

In fact, because the truth of the initial relation between the positions has been established *as it stood*, it now turns out to be the case that *that initial relation never did involve a misunderstanding*. That is, it is now the case that there never was the misunderstanding that set the whole process going. Now, this emerges on the *basis* of the misunderstanding, so that the misunderstanding and its process *also retains its truth*. This is what we can meaningfully say, and to be accurate must say, in describing the transition to the completed process. But in this postprocess stage, in this *new region of meanings*, that truth literally has no meaning. It is now retroactively, even though also for the first time, the case that the misunderstanding between the positions never meaningfully existed.

As this last paragraph illustrates, again, my own discussion, in describing this movement from process to completed process or post-process, shifts from being located in the context of comparison or transition between regions of meanings to being located only in the post-process region of meanings. As a result, what my own statements can and must mean about the same or "same" things shifts.

This absurd cancellation of the very existence of the issue, *by virtue of the existence* of that issue, is just another expression of the fact that we are describing the transition or relation between (at least) two entirely separate regions of meaning that, each being all-embracing, *also cover all the same or "same" things*. Consequently, it is necessarily the case that all the meanings involved in this transition or relation are replaced by different meanings, including the meaning of the misunderstanding of meanings itself *as a misunderstanding*. And again, on the far side of the process, when one moves into the context of a new all-embracing range of meanings, it is necessarily the case that anything outside that range, including the process that got one there (and that therefore occurs outside the range), loses all meaning, and so all meaningful existence. At that point there literally *is* no meaning to the idea that things were ever understood otherwise.

Now, however, the *new* meanings having been established, it is possible to explore those meanings, and on their basis to proceed in directions that could not have been anticipated in the context of the old range of meanings. And the key term that carried the formerly misunderstood meaning, and so structured or organized the whole process of thought that brought us to this point, is now present only as empty verbiage, as an entirely artificial concern (that is, no longer as importantly or metaphysically artificial), as simply trivially tangential to anything meaningful in the relations between the positions. (In the case of metaphysics proper, in contrast with relations between globally different positions in general, this might be the relations between metaphysical and everyday meanings *or* between different metaphysical positions.)

> CECILY (*rather brightly*): There is just one question I would like to be allowed to ask my guardian.
>
> GWENDOLEN: An admirable idea! Mr. Worthing, there is just one question I would like to be permitted to put to you. Where is your brother Ernest? We are both engaged to be married to your brother Ernest, so it is a matter of some importance to us to know where your brother Ernest is at present.
>
> JACK (*slowly and hesitatingly*): Gwendolen—Cecily—it is very painful for me to be forced to speak the truth. It is the first time in my life that I have ever been reduced to such a painful position, and I am really quite inexperienced in doing anything of the kind. However, I will tell you quite frankly that I have no brother Ernest. I have no brother at all. I never had a brother in my life, and I certainly have not the smallest intention of ever having one in the future.
>
> CECILY (*surprised*): No brother at all?

> JACK (*cheerily*): None!
>
> GWENDOLEN (*severely*): Had you never a brother of any kind?
>
> JACK (*pleasantly*): Never. Not even of any kind.
>
> GWENDOLEN: I am afraid it is quite clear, Cecily, that neither of us is engaged to be married to any one.
>
> CECILY: It is not a very pleasant position for a young girl suddenly to find herself in. Is it? (366–67)

The play then presents a suitable phase of adjustment to and consolidation of the startlingly new meanings and understandings.

> GWENDOLEN: Let us go into the garden. They will hardly venture to come after us there.
>
> CECILY: No, men are so cowardly, aren't they?
>
> *They retire into the garden with scornful looks.*
>
> JACK: Pretty mess you have got me into.
>
> ALGERNON *sits down at tea table and pours out some tea. He seems quite unconcerned.*
>
> What on earth do you mean by coming down here and pretending to be my brother? Perfectly monstrous of you!
>
> ALGERNON (*eating muffin*): What on earth do you mean by pretending to have a brother! It was absolutely disgraceful! (*Eats another muffin.*) (367)

Now, given the recognition that two sets of meanings are at issue, it is not *only* that a new, differently meaning position has become meaningful but also that this self-canceling process of relating incompatible meanings itself has been brought into relation to meaning. Consequently it is not just new meanings that are available to each standpoint but also the possibility of a *different kind of relation to meaning*, a different kind of understanding, one distributed simultaneously across different and mutually exclusive contexts of meaning. And this kind of understanding, as a result of its being distributed in this way, is also one that can *reflect on the conditions and possibilities of meaning themselves*.

And in this kind of context, where the pertinent meanings are established and distributed between their separate contexts of meaning, and (as a result) their possibilities can also be reflected on, the formerly troublesome key term or terms themselves can now come to function differently.

228   *The Formal Structure of Metaphysics*

They are no longer a problem for understanding and responsible conduct. Instead, they can be used without difficulty for their original simple purposes, in the full knowledge of the interaction or compresence of incompatible ranges of meaning.

> GWENDOLEN *and* CECILY (*speaking together*): Your Christian names are still an insuperable barrier. That is all!
> JACK *and* ALGERNON (*speaking together*): Our Christian names! Is that all? But we are going to be christened this afternoon.
> GWENDOLEN (*to* JACK): For my sake you are prepared to do this terrible thing?
> JACK: I am.
> CECILY (*to* ALGERNON): To please me you are ready to face this fearful ordeal?
> ALGERNON: I am!
> GWENDOLEN: How absurd to talk of the equality of the sexes! Where questions of self-sacrifice are concerned, men are infinitely beyond us.
> JACK: We are. (*Clasps hands with* ALGERNON.)
> CECILY: They have moments of physical courage of which we women know absolutely nothing.
> GWENDOLEN (*to* JACK): Darling.
> ALGERNON (*to* CECILY): Darling!
> *They fall into each other's arms* (371–72)

As is the way of such transformations of meaning generally, the category confusion in the term "Ernest" has produced a transformation of attitude and concomitant practices that reconstitutes this confusion itself into a simple separateness and simultaneity of meanings. That is, the problem of incompatible meanings has itself become the answer, the true clarity of single, exclusive meanings it was originally thought to be.

This occurs not by eliminating the incompatibilities, but by acknowledging them, as they stand, together, as the (self-canceling) given on whose *basis* one can proceed.

After the christenings, the situation at the end is exactly as each position independently took it to be at the beginning. That is, nothing has changed. And this is exactly what one would expect in the case of all-embracing standpoints, in which alternatives to, and so changes of, the range of meanings with which they start can simply have no meaning. Problems and resolutions can only meaningfully occur *within* the existing range of meaning, and simply nothing occurs outside that range. As Wittgenstein writes, if something alters the world, it cannot alter "what can be expressed by means of language. In short the effect must be that it becomes an altogether different world. It must, so to speak, wax and wane as a whole."[17]

And so, in the end:

> LADY BRACKNELL:. . . My nephew, you seem to be displaying signs of triviality.
> JACK: On the contrary, Aunt Augusta. I've now realised for the first time in my life the vital Importance of Being Earnest. (384)

3. Conclusion

Aristotle makes the following comment in his *Poetics*:

> poetry is something more philosophical and more worthy of serious attention than history; for while poetry is concerned with universal truths, history treats of particular facts. By universal truths are to be understood the kinds of thing a certain type of person will probably or necessarily say or do in a given situation; and this is the aim of poetry, although it gives individual names to its characters.[18]

That is, Aristotle argues that the fictional or artificial, what does not or need not express any actual circumstance of our world, is better suited to expressing universal truths than are accounts of actual circumstances. Universals, in his view, however, are also *what alone express* the nature and truth of actual things: they describe the essences of the things. There is a hint in Aristotle, then, that the artificial, what has or need have no

---

[17] Wittgenstein, *Tractatus,* 72, prop. 6.43.

[18] Aristotle, *On the Art of Poetry,* in *Classical Literary Criticism: Aristotle Horace Longinus,* trans. T. S. Dorsch (Harmondsworth: Penguin Books, 1965), 43–44.

relevance to the specific meanings of any particular, actual circumstances in our world, is what gives us access to the *essential truth* of those actual circumstances.

As Wilde wrote, "One should always be a little improbable." For, "if one tells the truth, one is sure, sooner or later, to be found out."[19]

---

[19] Oscar Wilde, "Phrases and Philosophies for the Use of the Young," in *Complete Works of Oscar Wilde*, ed. Vyvyan Holland (London: Collins, 1966), 1205.

9. The Logical Structure of Dreams and Their Relation to Reality

Dream narratives are very often thought to be full of contradictions—for example, of shifts in identity as one thing suddenly turns out to be another—and of non sequitur leaps in continuity. These are the most basic ways of being illogical, of violating the conditions for making sense. Although, as I discuss below, a lot of dream researchers and theorists defend dream thinking as not typically violating sense in these ways, I endorse the view that dream narratives do often contain contradictions and non sequiturs. In doing so, however, I am not accusing dream narratives of the kinds of irrationality from which those theorists aim to defend them. For I propose, first, that dream narratives are nonetheless perfectly logically valid, and that they are so not despite but *in* these violations of sense. More accurately, I shall try to show that these violations are logically valid in dream narratives at least in some respects, leaving open whether there are not also ways in which these narratives are simply nonsensical. Second, I shall try to show that these violations of sense are logically valid because they accurately express the logic of certain very deep kinds of issues, and that dreams involving these otherwise illogical dimensions sometimes deal precisely with these kinds of issues. I shall argue that these issues are those of dealing not with this or that aspect of our selves, our lives, or the world but with ourselves as a whole, our lives as a whole, or with the sense of reality as a whole.

In the rest of this chapter, I refer to dreams rather than dream narratives. This may give rise to two sorts of objections. First, it is true that there are all sorts of possible problems, both epistemological and semantic, with the idea of dreams' existing independently of our reports of them. So far, however, this debate is far from concluded, and reference to dreams themselves is still certainly defensible.[1] In any event, it does not affect my claims or argument here if we replace "dreams" with "dream narratives." If dream reporters can identify with or become caught up in the attitudes and feelings articulated in the narratives they present, then what I have to say about dreams applies just as well to those narratives of dreams. (This has the result that narratives of other kinds, like artistic fictions or even other people's dream reports, can have exactly the same status for these purposes as a person's own dream reports. I see no problem with that result.)[2] If, then, the reader is convinced that reference to dreams themselves is illegitimate or too problematic, she or he may take my use of the term "dream" as convenient shorthand for "dream report" without affecting the purport of the discussion.

The second possible objection is that, for those who are committed to the idea that logical relations characterize only collections of propositions and not the world of events and things, the claim that dreams are contradictory or contain non sequiturs is incoherent, since dreams are events or perhaps "thing"-like experiences or states. These readers too may replace the references to dreams with references to dream narratives without affecting the gist of the argument. It is not, however, clear to me that dreams are simply objective events or states, rather than consisting partly in a point of view on things. A point of view, presumably, *can* be contradictory or involve non sequiturs. Further, as I argued in the Introduction, I do not in any event believe that this very widespread view of the field of application of logic is tenable.[3]

My claim that there are logically valid violations of sense may give rise to another possible immediate objection, that in principle or by definition

---

[1] See, for example, the essays responding to Norman Malcolm's seminal book on this issue in Charles E. M. Dunlop, ed., *Philosophical Essays on Dreaming* (Ithaca, NY: Cornell University Press, 1977). Malcolm's book is *Dreaming* (London: Routledge & Kegan Paul, 1959).

[2] Calvin Hall has commented, conversely, that if we dismissed dreams because they are hallucinations, "we would have to dismiss all of the great works of art, of literature, and of music, everything in fact that has been created out of the mind of man. For dreams, too, are creative expressions of the human mind. They are the portals through which we can view the workings of the mind"; Calvin S. Hall, *The Meaning of Dreams* (New York: McGraw-Hill, 1966), 9.

[3] See the Introduction, section 4.

contradictions cannot contribute to or be a form of making logical sense. But as I have noted in other chapters, this is no longer uncontroversially the case even in formal logic.[4]

I now return to my thesis. As I mentioned, I propose that this paradoxical logic of legitimate violations of sense not only characterizes dreams, it also characterizes certain very deep kinds of issues. In fact, as I shall argue, it characterizes the deepest, most meaningful dimensions of our sober waking reality. I propose that dreams involve this type of logic because they accurately express and work with the logic of those real and deepest dimensions of our lives. These are the dimensions in which, as I suggested above, we deal, not with this or that aspect of ourselves, our lives, or the world, but with ourselves as a whole, our lives as a whole, or with the sense of reality as a whole.

Currently, there are both an influential postmodern and, as I have discussed in other chapters, an influential pragmatist and neo-Wittgensteinian skepticism about the sense of the idea of "things as a whole" or "oneself as a whole," and so of a view of things or oneself as a whole. Both schools of thought, however, also include defenders of the genuine sense of this idea, such as Thomas Nagel and Jacques Derrida.[5] The view Derrida expresses in this connection is central (as he insists repeatedly throughout his work) to the entire project of his version of "deconstruction": that traditional metaphysical concepts like that of the "totality of things" are essential, although they are not the last word. Consequently, Derrida's version of postmodernism is what he calls a "double writing," always *both* a "most faithful" reading "inside" the metaphysical tradition *and* a reading "outside" it.[6] On the sense of an idea of "things as a whole" or "oneself as a whole" specifically in connection with dreams, see, for example, Bert States, who writes, "my dream . . . is the pulse and direction of my existence. . . . Just as a child cannot possibly detect the moment at which it became aware of the world . . . the dreamer cannot detect the beginning of his dream because

---

[4] Again, on the possibility of legitimate logical contradiction, see the Introduction, section 5.

[5] Thomas Nagel, "The Absurd," in *Mortal Questions* (Cambridge: Cambridge University Press, 1979), 11–23; for example, Jacques Derrida, *Positions,* trans. Alan Bass (Chicago: University of Chicago Press, 1981), 6.

[6] Derrida, *Positions,* 6.

for that interval the dream is all of his consciousness that exists. The dream is the center and the horizon of his world."[7] Another dream theorist, Eugene Gendlin, points out that we may have a need "to grow *as a whole*" when it is not enough to "keep trying to fix only the situation."[8] J. J. Valberg focuses specifically on this dimension of dreaming, and actually uses the all-embracing "horizon" of dreams to demonstrate the necessity of the idea of a view of the world or one's life as a whole.[9]

Taking the idea of a view of "things as a whole" as legitimate, then, the kind of situation in which we deal with ourselves or our lives as a whole arises when, for example, we grow in an overall way, our entire sense of ourselves becoming transformed, or when we lose our sense of ourselves. And we deal with our sense of reality as a whole when, for example, we encounter, in other people or cultures or subcultures, ideas about reality that do not fit with our sense of what reality can include. (I should note that the fact that ideas that do not make sense in our terms belong to a different culture or subculture does not automatically make them valid. They may in fact be simply and absolutely nonsense. But an encounter even with mistaken ideas about reality that do not fit with our own overall ways of making sense can produce, by their contrast with our sense of reality, an awareness of that sense of reality in general, or as a whole.)

I argue, then, that dreams express and work with the logic of gaining a sense of and a relation to ourselves, our lives, or our sense of reality as a whole. These three senses of things as a whole have in common that they are self-inclusive, or self-reflexive. For example, the sense that we might have of reality as a whole is itself included in reality as a whole: this sense is therefore, in at least some respect, partly a sense of *itself*. I shall try to show that, because of this self-inclusion, the logic of these senses of things as a

---

[7] Bert O. States, *The Rhetoric of Dreams* (Ithaca, NY: Cornell University Press, 1988), 85.

[8] Eugene T. Gendlin, *Let Your Body Interpret Your Dreams* (Wilmette, IL: Chiron Publications, 1986), 188, italics in original.

[9] J. J. Valberg, *Dream, Death, and the Self* (Princeton, NJ: Princeton University Press, 2007), e.g., 69–70. I am grateful to Steve de Wijze for drawing my attention to this intriguing book.

whole, in waking reality as in dreams, is validly one of contradiction and non sequitur.[10]

As I mentioned at the start of the chapter, there are researchers or theorists who argue that dreams are no less logical than waking life, and who show how the apparently bizarre logic of dreams can be translated into the logic of waking life. Corrado Cavallero and David Foulkes, for example, argue that "dreams are not, in general, wildly implausible, vaguely experienced, or full of nonsensical images or image sequences. They are, rather, reasonable projections of what we might expect if waking cognition were operating under the somewhat dissociated circumstances generally accompanying sleep."[11] Bert States makes a similar argument from the point of view of dreams as storytelling.[12] But insofar as I do not take waking life to be always essentially describable on the basis of the criteria of standard logic, I do not think these views are necessarily incompatible with my own.[13] I agree that dreams show the same basic logic as everyday life, but I also think that everyday life involves dimensions that are only and legitimately describable in contradictions and non sequiturs. Consequently, while dreams do share the same logic with waking life, it is partly a logic

---

[10] On the theme of the relation between self-reference and true contradiction, see Paul M. Livingston, *The Politics of Logic: Badiou, Wittgenstein, and the Consequences of Formalism* (New York: Routledge, 2012); Graham Priest, *Beyond the Limits of Thought* (Oxford: Oxford University Press, 2002), e.g., 4.

[11] Corrado Cavallero and David Foulkes, eds., *Dreaming as Cognition* (London: Harvester Wheatsheaf, 1993), 11.

[12] Bert O. States, *Dreaming and Storytelling* (Ithaca, NY: Cornell University Press, 1993), especially chapter 1.

[13] Erich Fromm argues that dreams do operate with a logic that would be bizarre in waking life, but that this logic is appropriate for the context of nonaction that goes with sleep. In that context, there are no consequences of my thoughts for what I could realistically do to or with the things I think about, so that many kinds of constraints crucial for waking thinking are irrelevant. Erich Fromm, *The Forgotten Language: An Introduction to the Understanding of Dreams, Fairy Tales, and Myths* (New York: Grove Press, 1951), 28. This view is more unambiguously in conflict with my own proposal.

Very briefly in response: since the inactivity of sleep is registered within the waking perspective, and the events of dreams mostly do not occur within that perspective (except very ambiguously in lucid dreaming, and as remembered *but no longer occurring* upon waking), it is not clear to me that the inactivity of sleep has any bearing on the logic appropriate to the activity or otherwise that occurs within dreams.

of legitimate violations of sense. In any event, I think these theorists can agree that there are at least some dreams that involve genuine contradictions and non sequiturs. With that restriction, I would be content to argue that, while many dreams may reflect the standard logic of everyday life, the illogical dreams at least sometimes or in some part express the deeper, paradoxical kind of logic that I have proposed belongs to the sense of our lives as a whole.

Even if there is real and intractable disagreement between these theorists and myself, however, I do not wish to say that they are wrong. I find their arguments persuasive and thought-provoking. I am only proposing a possible way of making sense of dreams and a possible role they play in our lives, with, I hope, enough justification to show that this proposal is worth exploring further. There is room here to explore conflicting explanatory proposals without deciding which of them is right.

I shall not explore here whether there are in fact valid methods of dream interpretation. I take it as at least arguable that some of the widely used methods (say, Freudian, Jungian, Gestalt, or Focusing methods) are valid, so that dreams possibly express something at least in *some* way meaningful for the dreamer's life. What I shall really try to show, then, is that *if* dreams can be interpreted at all, *if* they have any meaning at all, then they are logical in this paradoxical way. This assumption may of course be wrong, but it is not obviously or uncontroversially so.

In the first section, I explain why, in those waking situations that involve dealing with our lives or reality as a whole, logic, or the way sense works, must be contradictory and discontinuous. (I discuss dealing with our selves as a whole in the second section, as part of an illustration from an actual dream.) In the second section I try to show that dreams do deal with these situations. In the third section I briefly discuss how it follows from this proposal that dreams are not only expressions of a sense of our lives or reality as a whole but are at the same time dynamic transformations of our lives or our relations to reality as a whole. In other words, they are a form of what we might call existential practice. In the final section I try to show that some of the classical theories of dream interpretation offer partial or indirect support for my proposal.

1. The Same Logic in Waking Life

To start with an easily recognizable example, when we are depressed, everything in the world is felt in keeping with that low mood. The blue sky and sunshine are annoying because they remind me how depressed I am, they rub it in that I cannot enjoy the beautiful weather. The piece of good news brings into relief how unsatisfying everything else in my life is, and even makes me feel worse because I cannot enjoy it properly. When, on the other hand, I am in a good mood, everything in the world is felt in keeping with my cheerfulness. The gray, rainy weather makes a nice cozy contrast to the warmth inside; the bad news is a challenge to be overcome, or is only one part, not especially important, of a basically likeable world.

Now, if we want to explain how one shifts from one of these moods to another, or how one might debate the truth or value of these two views of reality, we cannot point to anything in the world. *Everything* in the world, all of reality, reality itself, is understood as miserable in the one mood and as lending to or at least not harming cheerfulness in the other. Each of these two overall senses of things includes all the same entities and events, and interprets *all* of them in opposed ways. As Wittgenstein pointed out, "the world of the happy man is a different one from that of the unhappy man"; in moving from one to the other it "becomes an altogether different world."[14] There is no way, then, to have a rational debate between these senses of reality, or to undergo a rationally motivated transformation of one into the other. *Anything* one might refer to in the debate or in motivating the change is already understood by each sense of reality to the exclusion of the other. As a result, as soon as one refers to or specifies what one means, the "debate" is already decided. The contrasting version of things one wants to justify is already excluded as senseless, as not part of the world, as unreal by definition. And there is no neutral ground that either sense of reality needs to or can acknowledge. They each already include everything, reality as a whole. There is nothing left over to be neutral ground.

But one mood *does* become transformed into another. And the person in each mood can be (and usually is) aware that the sense given by the other

---

[14] Ludwig Wittgenstein, *Tractatus Logico-Philosophicus*, trans. D. F. Pears and B. F. McGuinness (London: Routledge & Kegan Paul, 1961), 72, prop. 6.43.

mood exists, that she or he has felt before and can feel again in ways that are not accessible to her or him at the moment. But it still remains true that the two moods grasp the *whole* of reality differently, and that there is therefore nothing left out of each sense of reality. As a result, the awareness that both moods are possible can only consist in understanding exactly the same thing—the world as a whole—in different, and in fact in mutually exclusive ways, at the same time. In other words, this awareness involves contradiction and discontinuity.

The fact of the transition itself from one mood to another is also significant here. This transition can only consist in one sense or understanding of things *itself* giving rise to an incompatible one. There is nothing left out of each sense of the world, so that one sense of reality can only give rise to the incompatible one out of itself. In other words, it itself gives rise to the sense it also excludes. In this situation, transformation too, then, involves contradiction and discontinuity.

It may be objected, and rightly, that standpoints that grasp the whole of reality differently in this way cannot conflict with each other and therefore cannot contradict each other. Such standpoints cannot mean and so share the "same" things to disagree about. But, because I am arguing that in this kind of situation of understandings of the whole of things contradictions are both necessary and true, this point is not an objection to what I am saying but part of it. One way of expressing my proposal is that wholly mutually exclusive standpoints *both* have nothing in common at all *and* are standpoints on all the "same" things. In other words, the objection is true *and* the contradiction of it is true. (I give concrete context and support to flesh out this abstract principle below.) Wholly mutually exclusive standpoints are not about the same things and so cannot contradict each other, and yet they also are and do. As I have argued, first, since we understand the whole of everything in each of the two mutually exclusive ways, *this,* the whole of everything, is at least in some sense exactly the same thing we are understanding in each case: there is nothing left over, nothing *else,* we can be reunderstanding. Second, such standpoints do become transformed into each other: the unhappy world *itself* becomes transformed into the happy world. Again, there is nothing else, nothing left over, to undergo this transformation. It is a shift of one and the same thing into the new sense of it. Consequently, while the two standpoints cannot refer to the same things, and so cannot conflict with each other, they also cannot but refer to the same things, and so cannot but conflict with each other.[15]

This metacontradiction, then, about the occurrence of contradiction in cases involving understandings of the whole of things is one expression of the type of contradiction I am defending in general here.

It may be objected even more fundamentally that it is simply not meaningful to compare two such different ways of making sense *at all*, so as to say they are in some sense interpretations of the same thing. Consequently it is literally without meaning to say that they can conflict with and so contradict each other. But if this comparison is literally without any meaning at all, it is equally meaningless to make both this objection and the argument supporting it, since their topic (the comparison) literally has no meaning. First, any substantive statement about the comparison then contains a meaningless part and so itself has no meaning. Second, an entirely meaningless "topic" has no content on whose basis to make inferences and so *justify* an objection. (For a detailed exploration of these arguments and of the implications of their outcome, see Chapter 1.)

Let me note, then, that if I am wrong about the possibility of contradiction in this kind of situation, it is not because we already know that "incommensurable" standpoints (as Thomas Kuhn influentially called them)[16] cannot contradict each other. I know this too, and am insisting on it. If I am wrong about the relation between these standpoints, it is because I fail to demonstrate that this contradiction, *as well as not occurring, also, in contradiction to what we know, does occur* in this case. And that needs to be judged on the basis of the discussion supporting it in this section, not on the basis of preconceptions about what can be said on this issue that miss or fail to engage with the point this discussion defends. In fact, even

---

[15] For additional discussion of the possibility of incommensurable frameworks' referring to the same thing, see section 6 of Chapter 3 and the first section of Chapter 8. See also Alasdair MacIntyre, whom I quoted on this topic in Chapter 1: "each community, using its own criteria of *sameness* and *difference*, recognizes that it is one and the same subject matter about which they are advancing their claim; incommensurability and incompatibility are not incompatible"; Alasdair MacIntyre, "Relativism, Power, and Philosophy," in *Relativism: Interpretation and Confrontation*, ed. Michael Krausz (Notre Dame, IN: University of Notre Dame Press, 1989), 190.

[16] Thomas S. Kuhn, *The Structure of Scientific Revolutions,* 2nd ed. (Chicago: University of Chicago Press, 1970).

if these presuppositions were relevant, I have already given explicit reason to question them in the discussion of contradiction above; there is no justification for taking them for granted here.

To move from moods to the world of ideas and developed knowledge, it is a familiar argument in philosophy of science, in political philosophy, and in treatments of disagreements between whole philosophical systems that conflicting understandings of what reality itself is, of what reality can include, cannot rationally debate with each other on this issue.[17] These kinds of understandings or frameworks do not only see this or that piece of reality differently but see reality *itself and in general* differently. Consequently, as with moods, anything they might point to, in order to resolve the debate, is already understood differently in the other framework. More specifically, it is understood in the context of the other framework's sense of what reality can include, so that each piece of evidence already depends on the decision about reality that the debate is supposed to decide.

One cannot appeal either to the broad rules of logic or sensemaking to decide between the frameworks. These rules can only work with meanings as they are given to them, and here the meanings are exactly what are in conflict, exactly what need to be decided. And, in any event, the rules of sensemaking themselves can differ between very different frameworks of the sense of things.

For example, in debates between evolutionists and creationists, evolutionists tend to have a view of reality as consisting in matter and energy, and of the reality outside our bodies as having basically reliable connec-

---

[17] In philosophy of science, see, for example, Paul Feyerabend, *Against Method*, 3rd ed. (London: Verso, 1993), especially chapter 16; Kuhn, *Structure;* Ludwig Wittgenstein, *Remarks on Frazer's Golden Bough*, trans. A. C. Miles (Atlantic Highlands, NJ: Humanities Press, 1979). In political philosophy, see, for example, Jean-François Lyotard, *The Differend: Phrases in Dispute*, trans. Georges Van Den Abbeele (Minneapolis: University of Minnesota Press, 1988); Alasdair C. MacIntyre, *Whose Justice? Which Rationality?* (Notre Dame, IN: University of Notre Dame Press, 1988); Charles Taylor, *Philosophical Papers, Volume 2: Philosophy and the Human Sciences* (Cambridge: Cambridge University Press, 1985), esp. chapters 3–5. With respect to philosophical systems, see, for example, Robin George Collingwood, *An Essay on Metaphysics* (Oxford: Clarendon Press, 1940); Everett W. Hall, *Philosophical Systems: A Categorial Analysis* (Chicago: University of Chicago Press, 1960); Henry W. Johnstone, Jr., *Validity and Rhetoric in Philosophical Argument: An Outlook in Transition* (University Park, PA: Dialogue Press of Man and World, 1978), e.g., 114.

tions with our senses. Creationists, by contrast, tend to have a view of reality as including divine revelation and spiritual dimensions, in comparison with which our senses and independent human reasoning are entirely fallible. Now, it is logically impossible for scientific method to prove that there is matter and energy, since the sensory observations that are essential to its method *depend* on there being a material world that can make them *sensory observations at all* (rather than, say, self-produced dream images). And it is logically impossible for revelation to prove the spiritual world exists, since it *depends* on the reality of that world to give it any meaning as *revelation* in the first place (rather than, say, a result of chemical imbalance).

But whether or not either or both of these views is true, we are capable of understanding both. And, as in the case of understanding the possibility of conflicting moods, this means we understand *exactly the same thing*—the world as a whole or in general—in mutually exclusive ways at the same time. Further, we are rationally *required* to gain an understanding of both views (assuming both are at least intelligible by their own criteria): we cannot decide which is true without entertaining both of them. Consequently, at least one phase of rational thinking about these issues requires us to think about the same things in mutually exclusive ways at the same time. Again, then, this is a necessary kind of awareness that involves contradiction and discontinuity.

In fact, as I have discussed in several of the other chapters, one cannot have even *one* understanding of or perspective on reality as a whole without automatically also having the idea of possible contrasting alternatives.[18] The idea that reality as a whole is to be understood one way implies a contrast with other possible ways of understanding it, ways that it rejects. Otherwise the "one way" is not distinguished from any other, and so has no particular content. And since these are contrasting ways of understanding the sense of things *as a whole*, they are mutually exclusive. Any single perspective on reality as a whole, then, implies a contrasting perspective that it wholly excludes. Consequently, even a single perspective on or sense

---

[18] Donald Davidson, "On the Very Idea of a Conceptual Scheme," in *Inquiries into Truth and Interpretation* (Oxford: Oxford University Press, 1984). As I have discussed in earlier chapters, Davidson takes this point in the opposite direction from mine. I return to this below.

of reality as a whole necessarily involves logical contradictions to or discontinuities with itself.

These kinds of situation are not simply a matter of entertaining conflicting possibilities about the same thing. In that case there would be no contradiction, since possibilities, by definition, do not assert themselves as the unique state of affairs: they make room for conflicting alternatives. Here, however, in the context of perspectives on reality as a whole, there is no sense to the ideas either of an actual thing or its possibilities apart from each interpretation. As a result, in each case we are understanding the thing *with* all its possibilities—in fact, everything that might be meant by that thing—in mutually exclusive ways. We are understanding the "same" thing simultaneously in ways that exclude each other even as *possible* ways of understanding "it." Or, to put the same point differently, because reality itself, as a whole, is what is differently understood in these two frameworks, with nothing left out in each case, each interpretation of reality *is* the unique state of affairs, allowing no meaning to the idea of conflicting alternatives.[19]

The idea that such different understandings of reality are really possible has often been challenged, perhaps most powerfully by Donald Davidson and Richard Rorty, whose work in this connection I discussed in Chapter 1. Apart from my own response to their views, the debate is still running strongly, so there is at least that much warrant for continuing to explore the idea that such different frameworks *are* possible. But in the context of the issues my presentation has raised in this chapter, I would like to add a brief comment to my discussion in the first and in some of the later chapters.

Very roughly, Davidson's argument is that it is self-contradictory to claim to conceive contrasting understandings of reality as a whole, since

---

[19] For descriptions and accounts of the detailed structure of the partly nonsensical (or, as I have described it here, contradictory and involving non sequiturs) relation between different perspectives on reality as a whole, or of the process of shifting from one to another, see Chapters 4 (especially the last few pages, on Wilde's *Dorian Gray*) and 8, and also Jeremy Barris, "The Convergent Conceptions of Being in Mainstream Analytic and Postmodern Continental Philosophy," *Metaphilosophy* 43, no. 5 (2012): 592–618; *The Crane's Walk: Plato, Pluralism, and the Inconstancy of Truth* (New York: Fordham University Press, 2009); *Paradox and the Possibility of Knowledge: The Example of Psychoanalysis* (Selinsgrove, PA: Susquehanna University Press, 2003).

any conception *we* have can by definition only occur within *our* understanding of reality as a whole—and this includes conceptions of contrasting understandings of reality as a whole. I acknowledge that this is a quick and very roughly approximate description of his view, and as a result, any conclusions I draw from responding to it can only be very provisional and tentative. It is the kind of objection, however, that other theorists raise, and that it is natural to raise against a proposal that endorses contradiction. My response is therefore worth making even if it ultimately misses Davidson's own point.

Clearly, this kind of objection is ultimately based on the principle that logical contradiction is always unacceptable. In that light, any idea that leads to endorsing logical contradiction, as the idea of such different frameworks does, must have something wrong with it. But, as I have noted, the exclusive principle of noncontradiction cannot be taken for granted in this way. And as I have argued, this principle is not, itself, something that can be defended by the kind of logic that endorses it: that kind of logical argument *depends* on it. This principle is one of the standards for sensemaking on which it relies in order to *produce* its arguments, including its justifications of the principle itself.

In other words, the exclusive principle of noncontradiction is part of just another one of those ways of understanding the sense of reality as a whole and in general, that cannot rationally debate with contrasting frameworks. This principle on its own, then, cannot justify rejecting a framework that is based on accepting some kinds of contradiction. And since the argument that we need such a framework is partly based, as I hope I have illustrated, on implications of noncontradictory sensemaking itself, there is reason for adherents (or, more accurately, inhabitants) of the no-contradiction framework to make room for the legitimacy of at least exploring the viability of the some-contradiction framework.

Now, assuming that different understandings of reality itself are possible, or even that one can have a single understanding of reality as a whole (and as I have argued, these come to the same thing), engaging with such understandings is not just a matter of intellectual vision. Since the self that is doing this understanding is part of reality as a whole, if this self understands reality as a whole in a certain way, then it automatically understands its own reality in a certain way. And since a self *is* partly an awareness (this is still the self *as a whole* that is partly an awareness: while it may also partly be other things, it would not be a self at all without that awareness) and therefore partly is its understanding, it then also *exists,* as a whole, partly in that certain way in which it understands itself. Now, as I have argued, an understanding of reality as a whole necessarily involves contradictions (in fact, contradictory understandings of reality). Consequently, the self that has this kind of understanding automatically also understands itself, and so exists, as a whole, in a way that involves contradictions. (This is also and more obviously true, of course, if the conflicted understanding is of the self's life as a whole, rather than of reality in general as a whole.) That is, the sense of itself as a whole, and so it as a whole, is automatically caught up in the contradiction.

2. The Logical Structure of Dreams

I shall now try to show that dreams express and work with this kind of situation of dealing with our selves, our lives, or reality as a whole. If this is true, then at least part of their contradictory and non sequitur character expresses the legitimate logic of some kinds of real situations.

Like different moods or different global understandings of reality in relation to one other, dreams and waking life deal with *all the same* particular events and entities as each other, and consequently grasp them differently only as a whole. The old problem raised by skeptics, of how we can know whether we are dreaming or awake, is very hard if not impossible to answer, exactly because we can take everything in waking life to be equally part of a dream.[20] And when we are dreaming, we can and often do take everything in our dreams as waking reality. In other words, *no part* of dream life establishes that it is different from waking reality, and vice versa. If we want to pinpoint what makes dreams different, then, we need to look at dream life and waking life with respect to their sense of the whole of things. And this means that dreams do involve a sense of the whole of things.

Even some of the kinds of logical impossibilities that are commonly taken to be parts of dream life that distinguish it from waking reality are,

---

[20] Valberg rejects this version of dream skepticism but defends an alternative version that still results in the view that dreams involve a different sense of the world as a whole from that of waking life. Valberg, *Dream,* 105–108.

as I have argued, also found in waking life. (Whether or not they express the *same* situations as those in waking life is a separate issue, which I am only now in the process of discussing.) And Medard Boss, as I discuss in the final section, argues that *all* the apparent oddities of dreams are equally present in waking life.[21]

But even without these arguments, it is clear that dreams need not, and often do not, contain any oddities of sense at all, and yet (at least as we think of them on waking) would still be radically different from waking life. As a result, even if the presence of illogic *could* establish that they are dreams, their dream character is independent of it. There is still no particular part of dream life, then, that explains its difference from waking life. The difference must lie in the sense it makes of things as a whole.

Perhaps this is a way of understanding Fechner's description, made famous by Freud, of dreams as occurring in a "different scene of action."[22] There is no other setting or place beyond the settings or places in waking life: if there were, it would be just another place included among the places in waking life. But dream settings are clearly not locatable in the waking world of places. And dreams deal with all the same events and entities that we find in the waking world. As a result, the setting of dreams can only be the *same whole* world of settings and places as the waking world, experienced differently.

In principle, then, dreams must be understood to be another view or experience of reality as a *whole*, or of a life as a whole.

But let me give a concrete illustration of this kind of sense of a whole, and of its contradictory and non sequitur logic, in this case *within* an actual dream of my own. One of the paradoxes inherent in the contradictory and non sequitur character of a relation to the whole of things is that one can engage with the whole even while still in many ways being within it. As I argued in the previous section, even a perspective on a single "whole of things" involves logical discontinuities with itself. Differently expressed, the sense of the whole involves something like its being outside itself. That is,

---

[21] For example, Medard Boss, *The Analysis of Dreams,* trans. Arnold J. Pomerans (London: Rider, 1957).

[22] Sigmund Freud, *The Interpretation of Dreams,* trans. James Strachey (Harmondsworth: Penguin Freud, 1953), 112.

since it is outside *itself*, its very inside is outside itself. Consequently, one can engage with the whole even while still in many ways within it.

Equally, one can and consequently, when one engages with them, does engage in the same paradoxical way with limited wholes within the greater whole, each having its own integrity as a whole because it is logically discontinuous in the relevant respects with the rest of the whole.[23]

Here, the dream involves the case I have not discussed very much so far, the self's relation to itself as a whole. I dreamed that someone was sneering at me, being confidently judgmental. I became angry in the dream, and successfully rejected the appropriateness of his attitude. When I woke, I realized that I was angry with myself for a recent failure that was a result of circumstances beyond my control, and that the dream was expressing my feelings in the context of this situation.

It is not important for our purposes here whether or not this particular interpretation is accurate. It is a kind of interpretation that is often made of dream images and events, and, on the assumption that there are valid ways of interpreting dreams, it is therefore enough to illustrate the logic that typically belongs to them.

If the combination of the person who is judging and the person who is judged expresses my being angry with myself, then each person expresses myself. And if it expresses my self, it expresses my whole self. It is not, in this case, that part of myself is angry with another part of myself, but that I am angry with my *self*—that is, with my self as a whole. Otherwise there is no reflexive, self-referring anger but instead the *different* case of one part

---

[23] A distinct conceptual or semantic area constitutes a limited whole in this sense. The concept constitutes or frames the whole of the sense of its content, of that semantic area. This is evident in that grasping the concept means acquiring something new and unique, and to describe its content entirely in terms of other concepts is to engage in conceptual confusion, or category mistakes. The shift from understanding something in terms of one conceptual order to understanding it in terms of another, then, shares the same violations of logical sense as a shift from one comprehensive framework to another. (Conversely, both also share the violations of sense belonging to category mistakes.) As a result, gaining a new perspective on an element of one's life, where that perspective involves acquiring a new concept, is a passage partly consisting in these violations of sense. I suggest that these partly nonsensical transitions are often part of what happens in dreams, as in waking life. See note 19 above for references to accounts of the detailed structure of these kinds of passages.

of a person's being angry with another part, or of one person's being angry with another, separate person. But where the dream figures express my actually being angry with *myself*, they express one and the same thing—my self as a whole—as two different things, two different ones of myself as a whole.

And, as I shall try to show, they do so rightly. They express a situation in which one and the same thing really also *is*, in the same respects, two different things.

Now, it is certainly possible for a part of the self to be angry with other, different parts of the self. One could, for example, be angry with oneself only for a specific issue, and then be angry with oneself only for feeling that anger. In these cases there is no self-including conflict (one is not angry with the very anger one is feeling right then and there) to give rise to contradictions or incompatible identities. But these are not the cases we are dealing with. It is still possible to be angry with *oneself*, and not just with specific aspects of oneself. And my proposal is that it is *those* kinds of situation that make sense of the contradictions and incompatible identities we find in dreams.

That, on this interpretation of the dream as being about anger with myself, it is right to understand the dream figures as in some sense fully expressing the whole self in each of the two selves can also be seen by reflecting on the logic of the possible interactions between the two persons in the dream. If, for example, I had quailed in the face of the judging person's rejection, I would have been enacting the substance of that very rejection. To give a parallel, if I condemn myself, and accept the validity of the condemnation (for example, I feel bad because of it), both the condemnation and the acceptance of it are the same act of condemnation. They are both *my* attitude, and they are both the *same* attitude, and they are about the *same* subject, myself. They are, then, simply different expressions of one and the same thing. In this case, since it is *my* act of rejecting *my same self*, and equally *my* quailing in the face of *my same self*, my quailing is my *carrying out* of that *same* rejection: my quailing is continuous with and expresses that very same act of rejection.

Similarly, if I as the judged self had rejected or condemned the judging self as a whole for condemning me (rather than just rejecting its condemnatory attitude), then my rejected or condemned self would have been again, or still, rejecting or condemning *itself*. It would have been carrying out the very activity of condemnation of itself that it was reacting to in the "other" person. This activity would not just have been the same *as* the other's, it would have been *one and the same* activity.

This continuity between the different expressions of the same self as a whole applies in waking life as well as in dreams: the same examples and arguments I have just given apply equally in both contexts. But because of this real continuity between the expressions of the self, there is a real contradiction—again, in waking life as well as in this kind of dream—when a self is in conflict with itself as a whole. For example, the attitude of rejecting or condemning the worthiness of the self as a whole is itself included in the self as a whole, that is, what it rejects includes itself, so that the attitude rejects its own worthiness to reject. And for the same reasons of self-inclusion or self-continuity, a self that is in conflict with itself as a whole is rightly understood contradictorily as one and the same thing that is also two different things. Each side of the conflict includes the whole, and as a result leaves nothing out to be another "thing." And yet, since it is a conflict, there *are two sides* to it, *each* consisting in the one and only "thing." Here, then, we have logically necessary—that is, valid—contradictions, of exactly the kind that dreams express.

Now, in resolving the situation in which a self rejects itself, it cannot accept itself as a whole if it rejects its self-rejection, since its self-rejecting attitude is part of itself. Consequently, if it is to resolve the situation, it must shift to self-acceptance without rejecting its self-rejection. What is more, since it is rejecting itself as a whole, it excludes self-acceptance altogether. For both reasons, it must therefore shift to an understanding of itself the possible sense of which its current understanding entirely excludes. And here we have a logically necessary moment of non sequitur, expressing the logic of real situations in which we do in fact shift our attitudes toward ourselves as wholes (just as our moods do in fact change).

There is another relevant side to this kind of resolution. In achieving that shift to acceptance, the self must accept all of itself; and this, as I have noted, includes accepting its rejection of itself (to achieve acceptance of itself). The non sequitur, then, also involves another kind of contradiction.

In fact, a week later I had a dream in which I was appreciatively delighted by someone's silliness. Here, if this dream expressed self-acceptance (and, again, this is a typical kind of interpretation, and in that way is enough to illustrate the point), the accepting self judged the accepted self as silly, a judgment that is a form of rejection, or is at least in some sense negative. But I was appreciatively *delighted* by that silliness. And, following the sometimes contradictory logic of a self as a whole, since I was accepting *myself,* that is, myself as a whole, which includes the various attitudes of the accepting self, I was accepting my act of negative judgment too. I was accepting myself together with my silliness *and* my judging myself as silly.

At least part of the contradictory and non sequitur logic of dreams, then, is a valid expression, enactment, and reworking of our sense of ourselves as a whole, or, as the first part of this section argued, of our sense of reality as a whole.

In the next section I explain why I use the language here of "enactment" and "working."

3. Dreams as Simultaneously Expression and Transformation

In this section, I shall try to show that if my proposal is right so far, it follows that dreams are not only expressions or reflections of a sense of our lives or reality as a whole, but are at the same time dynamic transformations of the sense of our lives or of our relations to reality as a whole. In other words, they are a form of what we might call existential practice.

As I argued at the end of the first section, if different understandings of reality as a whole are possible, then, since the self that is doing the understanding is part of reality as a whole, if this self understands reality in contradictory or otherwise conflicting ways then it automatically understands *itself,* as a whole, in contradictory or otherwise conflicting ways. (This is also and more obviously true, of course, if the understanding is of the self's life as a whole, rather than of reality in general as a whole.) That is, the sense of itself as a whole, and so *it* as a whole, is automatically caught up in the contradiction or conflict. This in turn automatically means that this self is actively engaged, as a whole, in challenging the sense or meaning of its own nature and in the struggle of that challenge. In other words, this kind of understanding is in itself an active *unsettling and resettling,* a *reworking,* of the sense and nature of the self that is doing the understanding. This reworking consists, for example, either in a transformation of the self or in gaining a fresh relation to itself as its old self.

In fact, as I have argued, even a *single* awareness of things as a whole automatically involves awareness of alternative views that it also entirely excludes, and so engages the person, as a whole, in a contradiction, in an unsettling and reworking of her or his sense of things. Differently put, registering our existing sense of things *as* a particular sense of things, rather than as just a perception of how things simply are, is already an unsettling of it. Even if we then come to accept our existing sense of things as the right one again, we now hold it with a deeper perspective on it. There is transformation of one's standpoint even if its substantial content remains entirely unchanged.

If dreams also involve this kind of understanding, they too are not simply passive ways of seeing, of being a spectator to, these challenges to and transformations of our sense of ourselves or of things as a whole. They are also active *processes of establishing* or *enactments* of this reworking understanding and its logic; they are acts and processes of unsettling and reworking the dreamer's self as a whole or her or his relation to the sense of reality as a whole. That is, they are in themselves transformations of ourselves or of our relations to the sense of reality as a whole.

If my proposal is right, then, dreams, whatever else they may be, are ways of asking and dealing with what are sometimes called existential questions. And this means that dreams are in themselves a practice of philosophy. They establish and express insight into the sense that our lives as a whole have or existence as a whole has for us. And in achieving that insight, they are in themselves an activity, a practice, of orienting, situating, or resituating ourselves in our relation to our lives or to existence as a whole.[24]

As Harold Alderman writes, "The dream . . . is one horizon through which the dreamer comes more securely—or insecurely—into the presence of his world. To interpret a dream is to act as a Socratic midwife,

---

[24] I explore philosophy or deep thought as at once both enactment or activity of being and straightforward, stable descriptive statement (in the way of the coordination of sometimes always true alternatives whose logic I discuss in this book) at length in *The Crane's Walk*, esp. part 1, idea 2, but also throughout. Chapter 7 of the present book, which deals with a fundamental limitation of Heidegger's conception of truth as enactment of being, also offers a detailed account of a closely related version of this coordination of conflicting alternatives in the course of pursuing its own focus.

assisting at the birth of the dream and at the re-birth of the dreamer's world."[25]

4. Partial and Indirect Support in Some Classical Theories of Dream Interpretation

That dreams have this kind of logical structure finds partial and sometimes indirect support in some of the well-known theories of dream interpretation.

In Freud's framework, the dream as we experience it, with its mixture of sense and nonsense, consists in what he calls the manifest dream thoughts. But these are a compromise between perfectly intelligible latent dream thoughts and perfectly intelligible waking thoughts that exclude or censor the latent ones (or that exclude the entirely intelligible unconscious wishes that the latent thoughts express or with which they engage). "Two separate functions may be distinguished . . . during the construction of a dream: the production of the dream-thoughts, and their transformation into the content of the dream. The dream-thoughts are entirely rational. . . . On the other hand, the . . . product, the dream, has above all to evade the censorship."[26] The censorship is our commitment to blocking away from our awareness what our waking thinking or attitude regards as unacceptable. The irrationality of dreams, then, is the result of combining incompatible ways of making sense of or evaluating the same things.

The conflicting ways of making sense in Freud's framework, however, are not necessarily ways of understanding reality or oneself as a whole. In the cases he discusses, consciousness generally rejects a particular idea of a piece of reality for reasons that emerge from its particular experiences. This rejection of particular things is contingent. It could have been otherwise: it is not part of or a result of the ultimate sense of things—that is, the sense of things as a whole—itself. As a result, there is no *logical* necessity (that is, no necessity following from the very sense of the ideas involved) to its incompatibility with the latent thoughts or unconscious wishes, and so no logical necessity to the resulting incoherence.

---

[25] Harold Alderman, "The Dreamer and the World," in *On Dreaming: An Encounter with Medard Boss,* ed. Charles E. Scott (Chico, CA: Scholars Press, 1977), 118.
[26] Freud, *Interpretation of Dreams,* 649–50.

Freud's model, then, only partly coincides with my proposal. But it does support the view that the illogic of dreams is really a combination of two (or perhaps more) logical sets of ideas, rather than simply having no connection with coherence at all. And for the rest, the particular focus of the censorship, and Freud's procedures and model for working with it, are not incompatible with the framework I am suggesting. There is no difficulty understanding the two types of conflict, global and particular, between modes of thought as simply different dimensions of dreams, neither interfering with the occurrence of the other.[27]

Jung, by contrast, does see dreams as most deeply expressing and working toward the coherence of the self as a whole. "The ego-conscious personality is only a part of the whole man, and its life does not yet represent his total life."[28] Through the analysis of dreams there is a process of "assimilation of unconscious contents" that "finally reaches completion in the restoration of the total personality."[29]

On the other hand, he does not see dreams as ultimately structured as or expressing a contradiction in the dreamer's sense of things. (This is not the case for some more recent Jungians; I discuss their work briefly below.) It is true that for Jung the total personality includes a balance of contradictory opposites, including a balance between rationality and irrationality. Development of any one side of one's personality will necessarily be accompanied at another level by the development of its opposite.[30] But, first, these opposites are included in the same "total personality," making up its opposite poles. As a result, the contradiction is contained within a bigger picture, and so is not a contradiction of or in the ultimate sense of things. Second—and, really, another expression of the same issue—there is a balance *between* "rationality" and "irrationality," and not an "irratio-

---

[27] In *Paradox and the Possibility of Knowledge*, however, I argue that Freud's (and also Jacques Lacan's reconceived Freudian) procedure, if not the models and content he derives from it, works rigorously in keeping with the logic of interaction between conflicting ways of understanding reality or oneself as a whole that I explore here.

[28] Carl G. Jung, *Dreams,* trans. R. F. C. Hull (Princeton, NJ: Princeton University Press, 1974), 78.

[29] Ibid., 108.

[30] Carl G. Jung, *Two Essays on Analytical Psychology,* 2nd ed., trans. R. F. C. Hull (London: Routledge & Kegan Paul, 1953), 71.

nality" *of* "rationality" itself.[31] Finally, Jung's idea of balance here is not that of a balance between conflicting understandings of the whole of things but between different dimensions of what he takes to be the one and only whole. As a result, while his approach involves the self as a whole in relation to reality as a whole, it really does not properly raise the issue of the sense of the whole but takes for granted the exclusive validity of one particular construal of that sense, which it then explores.

His theory does, however, give a kind of indirect or implicit support to the view that dreams express an ultimate contradiction in consciousness. There is a central element of incoherence or contradiction in his theory, though as far as I know not recognized as such by Jung or, often, by Jungians, that flows necessarily from the idea that dreams engage with a sense of the self as a whole. That the self has to *achieve* the wholeness of *itself* means that it is not yet itself. That is, it is not yet what it is: it does not coincide with itself. And this is a contradiction. (I should clarify that in my view we *can* meaningfully speak of achieving and of not yet having achieved "the whole of ourselves," so that this is what I have been arguing is a valid contradiction: but it is still a contradiction.)

This contradiction emerges in his theory in a variety of ways. For example, the self communicates the achieved sense of its wholeness to itself, in the form of motifs like the mandala image, and it does so prior to achieving that sense of its wholeness. Jung describes these motifs as "'images of the goal,' as it were, which the psychic process, being goal-directed, apparently sets up of its own accord, without any external stimulus."[32] And in his framework the self *must* communicate with itself in this way, so that it can know to move toward itself, and know that it is genuinely itself that it is moving toward. In other words, it knows, and must know, where to go and what it is before it (the "itself" it is communicating with) knows where to go and what it is.

Jung does point out that the self communicates this sense of itself to a part that is artificially separated from it, the persona, or the fragment of ourselves that we falsely identify with as our self. There is therefore no real contradiction: the whole communicates to a part of itself, which need not coincide with or know everything in the whole. But it is also Jung's

[31] Ibid., 71.
[32] Jung, *Dreams*, 295.

view that the whole is the real thing, from which the persona arises as only a *fake* separate entity, one that we take, "altogether wrongly, for something individual."[33] And this view is *necessary* to his framework, since the goal is to work toward the wholeness *of* the parts: the self is the wholeness or self *of the persona*. If this were not so, the persona could not find and would have no need to find its own completion in the self. This means that the whole is *necessarily* the *true reality* of the persona, which therefore necessarily has no genuinely separate reality. But if the whole is the only real thing, the contradiction reemerges in a different way. The self *itself* has produced a part of itself that is discontinuous with and not privy to itself. This is equivalent to going about hiding something in a place one does not know about.[34]

My own proposal might help to articulate and explore the validity of this contradiction implicit in Jung's framework. But it would also result in undermining the nature of classical Jungian dream therapy. The goal of that kind of therapy is to be guided by the coherent sense of the self that awaits and unfolds. "The archetype is, so to speak, an 'eternal' presence," that "only *appear[s]* more and more distinctly and in increasingly differentiated form."[35] On the view that there is a real and central contradiction in what dreams express, however, this coherent sense of the self is necessarily capable of being understood in contradictory ways. That is, that particular sense of the self is necessarily only one among conflicting senses of the self as a whole, none established in advance as more legitimate or more real than the others. The goal of dream analysis would then be to hold in suspense and balance the contradictory senses of self in order to find out, after the fact, which one turns out to be (or, perhaps better, turns out to have been) the self's commitment. The persona, for example, might need to be reunderstood as possibly one of the alternative, legitimate senses of the self in its full reality and in all its wholeness. And all the archetypal motifs might need to be reunderstood as signifying and enacting points of decision, or phases of decision, between different and potentially

---

[33] Jung, *Two Essays*, 276.

[34] On the contradictions in Jung and their reemergence, see also Ludwig Binswanger, "Dream and Existence," in *Being-in-the-World: Selected Papers of Ludwig Binswanger,* trans. Jacob Needleman (Riverdale, NY: Baen Books, 1963), 246.

[35] Jung, *Dreams*, 295.

equally legitimate understandings of oneself or of reality, rather than as signposts to or communications from the pregiven, right understanding of oneself or reality. (Although *after* one has made the decision or found out who one is, and so, as it may then be right to say, who one has always been, it is perhaps or sometimes true to say, for example, that the archetypal motifs were signposts to the pregiven right understanding.)

Differently expressed, where Jung takes individuation into selfhood to be the solution to the problem of our relation to ourselves and to existence as a whole, I take it to be a first, more or less complete articulation of the problem. To put the kind of contradiction I have discussed differently, in the process of settling our relation to ourselves and to existence as a whole, we stand outside the whole of which we are part. In the case of our relation to ourselves, achieving our identity with a previously unknown self would be the kind of thing that would allow us to recognize, by contrast, the contradiction or incoherence in our previously *not* having achieved that identity, *not* having been what we have always been. It would allow us to see that part of the nature of being a self is that it is possible for us not to be what we are, and, for that matter, that in some ways we also have been or are actually not what we are. This is an element of incoherence that eludes settled understanding and that only properly *emerges* in establishing one's selfhood or, analogously, one's sense of the whole of things.

As I mentioned above, there are some more recent Jungian analysts and theorists who do see the psyche, and therefore its dreams, as ultimately structured by contradiction, and these views consequently give explicit support to my proposal, at least in this respect. Stanton Marlan, for example, discusses a number of such recent writers who argue that, even though the Jungian Self is thought of as a wholeness that balances all opposites, the same principle of balance requires that there be a balance to balance and wholeness themselves: a "No-Self" that is "both complementary and antagonistic to Jung's idea of the Self."[36] Among others, Marlan cites Jungian analyst Niel Micklem as emphasizing "the importance of paradox rather than unity," and quotes Micklem's explanation: "When we talk of paradox, we mean the presence of any two conflicting truths present at

---

[36] Stanton Marlan, *The Black Sun: The Alchemy and Art of Darkness* (College Station: Texas A&M University Press, 2005), 182.

the same time in consciousness."³⁷ Similarly, Marlan notes James Hillman's insistence that the genuine Jungian unity of opposites includes "incommensurabilities" and consequently "is more like an absurd pun or the joy of a joke than the bliss of opposites transcended."³⁸

Medard Boss, in his phenomenological framework for understanding dreams, maintains as I do that dreams reflect and engage the deep structures that constitute the sense of our life or our world as a whole. "Man when dreaming, no less than when awake, always exists in his relationships with things and with people," relationships that "go to make up his entire existence,"³⁹ and that express "the total and original essence of things as such."⁴⁰

Phenomenology aims to describe the structures of our experience as we live it, without arbitrarily giving one dimension of it or any particular basis for explanation greater weight or validity than another. For example, when we feel close to someone who is physically far away, that person is *both* physically far *and* emotionally close, and neither needs to be the truer or more basic state of affairs, or the one in terms of which the other is explained. Consequently, if we dream, for instance, that a person who was far away is suddenly next to us, this is not a distortion of the nature or truth of distance but an accurate expression of one dimension of its reality: we suddenly feel close to that person.⁴¹

Boss notes the varied kinds of sense that phenomenological description identifies as structuring our world, and argues that our dream experiences consist in this *variety* of sense structures, rather than in senselessness. And because these are the structures that give the senses of our world, that is, that constitute its meanings, phenomenological (or, as Boss calls it, existential) analysis, as it occurs through dream interpretation, can lead to "a new and true relationship with the essence of all things."⁴²

---

³⁷ Ibid., 150, 151. The quotation is from Niel Micklem, "I Am Not Myself: A Paradox," in *Jung's Concept of the Self: Its Relevance Today*, ed. Niel Micklem (London: BAP Monographs, 1990), 8–9.

³⁸ Marlan, *Black Sun*, 155. The discussion he cites is in, for example, James Hillman, "Silver and the White Earth, Part Two," *Spring* (1981): 21–63.

³⁹ Boss, *Analysis of Dreams*, 122.

⁴⁰ Ibid., 101.

⁴¹ Ibid., 88–89.

⁴² Ibid., 121.

On the other hand, Boss does not account for the contradictory and non sequitur features of dreams. In fact, he denies that they have these features, since dreams share the deepest sensemaking structures of waking life. The logic of dreams only appears mysterious, in his view, because these structures are "possibly hidden in daily life," so that we may not initially recognize their sense when dreams force them on our attention.[43] But as I have argued, the waking awareness of "the total and original essence of things as such," which he argues dreams share, is itself necessarily and legitimately contradictory and logically discontinuous.

And while Boss does see dreams as expressing the structure of our sense of reality as a whole, he focuses only on their expression of particular dimensions of that structure, rather than on their expression of the sense of the whole of things simply and in its own right. These two kinds of focus, however, are at least not incompatible. There is no difficulty in understanding them as just giving insight into different, and in fact closely related, dimensions of dreams.

Still, in this respect my proposal is closer to Ludwig Binswanger's understanding of the existential analysis of dreams. In his view, for example, "the dream . . . is nothing other than a particular mode of human existence in general," and "our whole existence moves within the meaning matrix" of the dream.[44] Binswanger, however, is like Boss in seeing no need to account for the contradictory character of dreams. And while he does see dreams as involving conflict, it is a conflict between the sense of things as a whole and a *lack* of that sense,[45] and not between alternative senses of the whole of things. Consequently, his view allows only a limited variety of ways for the details of dreams to be significant (as Boss also

---

[43] Ibid., 89.

[44] Binswanger, "Dream and Existence," 227, 223. Heidegger, however, criticizes Binswanger for carrying out his analysis in a way that, roughly speaking, does not in fact step outside its own presuppositions and so does not really involve a sense of existence as a whole. Martin Heidegger, *Zollikon Seminars: Protocols—Conversations—Letters,* ed. Medard Boss, trans. Franz Mayr and Richard Askay (Evanston, IL: Northwestern University Press, 2001), e.g., 188–92. I think Heidegger is in important ways clearly right; but see also my comments on the necessary limitations of Heidegger's interpretation of metaphysical thought in Chapter 7.

[45] Binswanger, "Dream and Existence," 247.

points out, in a different connection).[46] For Binswanger, there is only one sense of things as a whole that dreams can express, and they only express it in the form of a contrast with the lack of that kind of sense.

In conclusion, I propose that we need to acknowledge and account for the distinctly nonstandard kind of logic found in dreams, and that we need to do so not simply to identify and work with what characterizes dreams but to identify and work with their significance for waking reality.

[46] Boss, *Analysis of Dreams*, 82–83.

Coda

Overviews

In this concluding chapter, I explore what it is to have an overview or a general sense of the kind of situation in which there are simultaneously relevant but wholly mutually exclusive frameworks of sense.[1] What does it mean to grasp these coordinations of mutually exclusive frameworks or conceptual structures? I explore this not only as an issue of intellectual grasp but also with respect to what it requires of us and offers us to recognize and live with these kinds of coordination. I have discussed this kind of overview and what it involves at length elsewhere.[2] Here I aim only to give some brief, general ideas of what it might mean. I shall do this by looking at a few of the types of context in which they occur.

Let me set the scene for this discussion by noting a connection between the framework I argue for and a standard line of thought in some prominent areas of contemporary philosophy. It is well established in some areas of contemporary philosophy informed by Wittgenstein and ordinary language philosophy, for example, that, while things and states of affairs and concepts do have essences (or, alternatively expressed, properties that are internal to them), what they essentially are is often incompatibly different from context to context. The logical structure or "grammar" of what we can say and mean about something shifts between "language games" or

---

[1] I am grateful to Paul Turner for making me aware of the need for a concrete, lived sense of what this "sometimes always" outlook might mean, and for occasioning my trying to get clear about it in many of the specific contexts I discuss in this chapter.

[2] Jeremy Barris, *The Crane's Walk: Plato, Pluralism, and the Inconstancy of Truth* (New York: Fordham University Press, 2009), esp. part 2, chapter 1.

"contexts of usage" of the relevant forms of expression. In this tradition, the key is not to reconcile these ways of talking but simply to recognize that they arise in different contexts, so that the questions appropriate to a concept in one context of its meaning simply do not arise in other contexts. In an important sense, meaning, and with it what we mean by reality, is often discontinuous from one kind of context to another. These discontinuities do not need to be reconciled because they require reconciliation only if we can compare their different contexts of meaning. But meaning is given only by the grammars of particular contexts, and comparisons between contexts would be located outside all particular contexts and so outside all grammars and the meaning they provide. As a result, that kind of comparison, and with it the reconciliation it would call for, literally has no meaning. Reconciliation of the differences in meaning, then, simply does not arise as a meaningful issue. To give just one example, Raimond Gaita makes the following argument:

> If someone were to say that I should ... declare whether I believe evil to be a reality or whether I do not, then I would say ... there cannot be an independent metaphysical inquiry into the 'reality' of good and evil which would underwrite or undermine the most serious of our ways of speaking. I would say: now you may see why someone should speak of the reality of evil, and now you may see why the same person might say that Good is the only reality. We are likely to misunderstand ... if we try to press him into acknowledging that he is contradicting himself. It would be better, at least in ethics, to banish the word 'ontology'.[3]

This kind of view clearly has strong affinities with the idea for which I have argued, that truth can be incompatibly but legitimately different from sense framework to sense framework.

There are prominent equivalents of this line of thought in other traditions of contemporary philosophy as well, although they have not all become part of established philosophical procedure. For example, Collingwood argues that "you cannot tell what a proposition means unless you know what question it is meant to answer," so that statements have no meaning in general, taken outside the specific contexts of specific questions that

---

[3] Raimond Gaita, *Good and Evil: An Absolute Conception*, 2nd ed. (New York: Routledge, 2004), 190.

they answer.⁴ Gadamer also argues that "the meaning of a sentence is relative to the question to which it is a reply," with related consequences.⁵ Again, Dewey understands the results of inquiry essentially to resolve specific situations of doubt.⁶ Quine hybridizes this pragmatist idea with the more linguistically framed "meaning depends on contexts of usage" line of thought to produce a similar general perspective on philosophical questions. So, for example, "the arbitrariness of reading our objectifications into the heathen speech reflects not so much the inscrutability of the heathen mind, as that there is nothing [outside the constraints of particular languages, so that theirs has no privilege over ours] to scrute."⁷

As the quotation from Gaita illustrates, however, this kind of view denies that these grammars or sense frameworks need to or even meaningfully can be brought together. As a result, they do not produce the kinds of contradictions, and still less their self-cancellation, for which I have argued. But I have tried to show that there are many situations in which it is inescapably true that such incompatible frameworks are in fact simultaneously relevant. For example, I have argued that sometimes one such framework emerges from another, and as a result, at some point in that transition both frameworks apply to and structure the sense of the same world and the same elements of that world.⁸ Again, interactions of mind and body are describable with full recognition of the possibly essential and logically incompatible differences between them, and it would be very hard to argue that there is no meaning at all to statements about these interactions. We also think of people (perhaps falsely, but still meaningfully) as essentially in relation to others and to their environment, as what they are in virtue of those relations, but also as affected by what is not themselves in

---

⁴R. G. Collingwood, *An Autobiography* (Oxford: Clarendon Press of Oxford University Press, 1978), 33. See also R. G. Collingwood, *An Essay on Metaphysics* (Oxford: Clarendon Press of Oxford University Press, 1940), 23–25.

⁵Hans-Georg Gadamer, *Truth and Method*, 2nd ed., trans. Joel Weinsheimer and Donald G. Marshall (New York: Continuum, 1995), 370. Gadamer acknowledges Collingwood's contribution here.

⁶John Dewey, *Logic: The Theory of Inquiry* (New York: Henry Holt, 1938), e.g., 3–4.

⁷W. V. O. Quine, "Speaking of Objects," in *Ontological Relativity and Other Essays* (New York: Columbia University Press, 1969), 5, my insertion.

⁸I argued this in most detail in Chapters 4, 8, and 9.

their environment, and, contrariwise, as essentially responsible for their own individual actions, that is, in a way that is independent of the activity of what surrounds them. It is also easy to think of circumstances in which we understand people as essentially both of these simultaneously.

I have also tried to show, principally through the example of Davidson's work, that this prominent contemporary view that there is nothing meaningful to say about sense outside particular contexts, or, alternatively expressed, about sense in general or as a whole, cancels itself. It is itself, after all, an attempt to say something about what is possible for sense as a whole. Analogously, as I quoted from Putnam in that discussion, "if we agree that it is *unintelligible* to say, 'We sometimes succeed in comparing our language and thought with reality as it is in itself,' then we should realize that it is also unintelligible to say 'It is *impossible* to stand outside and compare our thought and the world.' . . . In this case to say that it is impossible to do '*p*' . . . involves a '*p*' which is unintelligible."[9] Because this line of thought cancels itself, then, it is built into it itself that a general view or coordination of these conflicting grammars that it excludes is also a legitimate possibility.

In fact, this self-cancellation is expressed indirectly in this widespread line of thought itself, in that it is really not entirely without an attitude toward the fundamental sense of the world. Instead, it generally has what is perhaps a kind of ascetic attitude toward it. It does not fail to offer an answer to the great questions of the meaning of life and of the sense of the world that are traditional to philosophy, but offers the answer that the questions themselves are an illusion, and that we consequently do not need the satisfactions they seem to provide. This is a genuine answer, and not just an arbitrary abandoning of the big questions: this line of thought gives a thoroughgoing account of why these questions have no meaning and so are not in fact questions at all. As a result, we can recognize that there truly are no questions to answer, and we can be at justified peace with what those questions aimed to raise. As Wittgenstein writes, "the clarity that we are aiming at is indeed *complete* clarity. But this simply means

---

[9] Hilary Putnam, *Words and Life*, ed. James Conant (Cambridge, MA: Harvard University Press, 1994), 299.

that the philosophical problems should *completely* disappear. The real discovery is the one . . . that brings philosophy peace."[10]

That this line of thought actively cancels itself in some respects means that this kind of philosophy often carries out the kind of logic and procedure for which I argue in this book, although typically without recognizing what it is doing.[11]

In terms of this line of thought, then, what I try to do in this book is to show the necessity of coordinating these mutually meaningless grammars, and to give an account of the possibility and nature of these kinds of coordination. One result of doing this, as I have argued, is that we can offer a justification of the legitimacy of this kind of current philosophy in a thoroughgoing way that is not available to it purely in its own terms, as we also can analogously for its alternatives in other traditions.

Now I turn to looking at the nature of an overview or general sense of these sorts of coordination.

A general point about situations where mutually exclusive sense frameworks or conceptual structures are simultaneously relevant is that even in these situations direct clashes between these frameworks occur only sometimes, in the very particular circumstances where they simultaneously have focus on precisely the same elements of the world. When these direct clashes do not occur, the extreme nature of the disparity of the frameworks itself helps to grasp the frameworks simultaneously: because they are meaningless, and so completely irrelevant to each other, they present no obstacle to each other's general construal of things.

There are, however, occasions when or respects in which they are directly relevant to the same issues, and consequently directly clash. On those

---

[10] Ludwig Wittgenstein, *Philosophical Investigations*, trans. G. E. M. Anscombe (Oxford: Blackwell, 1958), 51e, no. 133.

[11] I discuss this in detail with reference to what used to be called conceptual analysis and is now, in a modified form, widely practiced in Anglo-American philosophy as a combination of philosophy of language, mind, and action, in Jeremy Barris, "The Convergent Conceptions of Being in Mainstream Analytic and Postmodern Continental Philosophy," *Metaphilosophy* 43, no. 5 (2012): 592–618. I also try to show there that this Anglo-American line of thought has this in common, again in a typically unrecognized form, with much of postmodern continental philosophy and, in particular, with Heidegger (although, as I argue in Chapter 7, this is not what Heidegger's work ultimately carries through).

occasions, one possibility is that it might fit the sense of the situation for us to have no views about the issue in those conflicted respects at all, to have no sense of how it might or might not make sense in those respects, in the way of the ascetic view I described above. As Gaita notes, if we try to press the issue to gain more than the understanding we already have of the clashing sides each on its own, we are likely to misunderstand. We then need to engage in the discipline of simply not understanding and not pursuing understanding.

Sometimes, however, we have to enter into the conflict because it affects issues that need to be sorted out. It then fits the sense of the situation for us to be confused and at a loss as to how to proceed. But since, as I have argued, the situation itself is confused and incoherent, this experience of confusion *is* in fact an accurate and clear grasp of the situation. In addition, this kind of confusion or senselessness is self-canceling: our confusion will resolve itself into unqualified kinds of clarity. But it is also part of its self-cancellation that we can recognize the confusion itself as already constituting a successful grasp of the sense of the situation, and this recognition is also part of that resolution. In these cases we need to engage in the discipline of accepting confusion and being at a loss, and delivering ourselves over to the process by which sense variously emerges from the working of that confusion or loss of sense itself.

As I noted, these alternative possibilities apply generally to situations involving mutually exclusive structures of sense. One pressing specific question about these sorts of coordination, however, is how we can live with other people or cultures whose views we recognize as unqualifiedly true while also recognizing that those views unqualifiedly exclude the truth of our own. How are we to understand the kind of attitude we should have toward those others, toward ourselves, and toward truth, when balancing these mutually exclusive recognitions? As I have argued, this contradiction is self-canceling and so resolves itself, in a several-faceted way. Further, however, I suggest that even with respect to that part of its resolution that consists in the recognition of its unresolved incoherence or confusion as itself a legitimate and successful grasp—what we might call its "resolvedly unresolved" aspect—a kind or measure of straightforward overall grasp is possible.

I have argued that the truth of each view, ours and theirs, is partly a matter of these views' being rooted in the truth of our and their respective being.[12] (As I noted in arguing this, our being is not just a brute entity, meaningless in itself and so incapable simply on its own of offering a contribution to truth beyond the fact of itself. For one thing, our being consists partly in a meaningful awareness, so that it is in itself in some sense inherently connected with what it reflects on. For another, constituted as our being is by our sense framework, it is partly conceptual, consists partly but essentially in meanings, which in turn are constituted as the meanings they are partly by their relations to systems of other, connected and contrasting meanings. That is, our being is conceptually or logically connected with, among other meanings, the contrasting and also in many ways connected meanings of its contexts.) This truth to the being of the one committed to the view is one of the conditions for any truth (even while its contribution can, certainly, conflict with those of other conditions). The other person's or culture's view is certainly simply wrong from our perspective, but if it is an honest view it is rooted in the truth of that person's being, as our honest view is rooted in the truth of ours. As a result, since this rootedness is one of the conditions of any truth and so is common to all truth, their view is, *more deeply* than the conflict between the views, *of the same truth* as ours: the truth that is the truth to being itself or being as such. Even though the particular being to which the views are true is different in each case, the principle of truth to being itself is the same. Consequently we can and should respect their view simultaneously as wholly wrong but as nonetheless *legitimate*. We can see this in commonsense terms, in that we can see the sense of respecting the integrity, intelligence, and responsibility of someone who, when she wholly disagrees with us, is honest to what she thoughtfully cannot but believe, and consequently of respecting her view because it is the view of that honest and responsible kind of person.

An important variety of this kind of relationship is that between people who are reflectively aware of their own frameworks and assumptions, or at least of the possibility that their views are informed by larger assumptions that may be questionable, and people who do not have this awareness. It is more particularly important in the context of this book that this is a relationship between people who can take the idea of "sometimes always" logic seriously (at least to contemplate before dismissing it), and people for

---

[12] See, for example, Chapter 1, section 5.

whom this idea simply cannot have any meaning. There are two possibilities here that I would like to discuss.

First, it is arguably possible that people for whom this idea cannot have any meaning are not lacking something but are legitimately taking for granted truths that should be taken for granted. That this kind of taking for granted can be legitimate is in fact part of the force of the ascetic line of thought I outlined above. According to its account, there is no sense outside particular contexts of meaning, and there is consequently no sense to the idea of reflecting on those contexts so as to justify them. If this account is appropriate for the people who do not have a reflective awareness of their own frameworks, then the reflective position has no privilege of thoughtfulness or depth over the nonreflective one. The conflict between these two kinds of standpoint is then not essentially different from conflicts in general between frameworks.

Second, however, it is arguably possible that the nonreflective person does in fact lack the capacity to think his framework through as thoroughly as the other, and so is comparatively limited or shallower. In this case, the nonreflective person, because he does not think things through as thoroughly as they meaningfully can be thought through, is ultimately dogmatic in an arbitrary way, and consequently deeply unjust. His knowledge claims are ultimately unfounded, and his attitudes and actions arbitrarily exclude the concerns and sense of reality of others in advance and without appeal.[13] (Of course, people who are deeper in this sense can also be unjust, by failing to live out their awareness fully or because of other kinds of limitations. But that is a different, more limited and more straightforward type of problem.) Even if this is true, however, I think that if the person is genuinely incapable of thinking things further, then that limitation is part of his own being, to which he is honestly true. As a result, while deeper or reflective people are certainly unqualifiedly justified in identifying his injustices as injustices and as shallowness and in defending themselves against them, it is *also* true in this kind of case that that person himself is unqualifiedly reasonable and just. What is more, reflective peo-

---

[13] As I mentioned in section 3 of the Heidegger chapter, this kind of problem is, for example, the concern of Jean-François Lyotard's *The Differend: Phrases in Dispute*, trans. Georges Van Den Abbeele (Minneapolis: University of Minnesota Press, 1988).

ple who do take "sometimes always" logic seriously must, by their own principles, recognize both descriptions, since it is part of their reflectiveness to make room both for the meaningfulness of the other person's standpoint and for the rootedness of truth in the person's being, which in this case relevantly includes his honest limitations.

This case is really also essentially the same as relationships between mutually exclusive standpoints in general. It just has an additional layer of twisty-turny. As a result, we can grasp and negotiate it in the same kinds of ways.

Another variety of this kind of paradox in relationships with others is that, because mutually exclusive principles of sense are both relevant, it can happen that the way to carry out a principle is by carrying out its opposite. So, for example, if someone lives by a principle according to which it is appropriate to disrespect conflicting views, then those who live by principles of respecting conflicting views can respect that view by disrespecting it: this respects its principle. In fact, they not only can do so, they are disrespectful if they do not do so. Purely to carry out their principle of respect is to disrespect the principle they aim to be respectful toward. Where people or cultures are nasty as a principle or in a way that is essential to who or what they are, being nice to them is also being nasty or deeply disrespectful to them, at the deeper level of the principles that shape their attitudes and conduct.

On the other hand, simply carrying out one's own principle of being nice to them and in this way being nasty to them is still being nasty to them, and so in turn respects their nasty principle. But that is what it is doing: it is not simply being nice to them, it is also disrespecting them. And it is doing so in an especially deep way, since it is directly disrespecting their principle itself: it actually ignores their principle of disrespect as a principle to be considered at all, as even to be recognized as a possible principle of conduct.

I suggest, then, that the choice we have in these particular kinds of situations is not between respecting and disrespecting the other framework, or between being nice and being ugly to it, but between being respectful of it on the surface and as a result disrespectful at the deeper level of its principle, and being disrespectful of it on the surface and as a result respectful at the deeper level of its principle.

These alternatives describe the significance of our actions for the other framework. We also have to balance these kinds of significance they have for the other framework with the significance they have for our own. In being deeply respectful to the other framework by its lights, for example, we are deeply disrespectful to it by our own, and we strain or perhaps sacrifice our own principle of respect in the sense it has purely in our own framework. We may not find it right to make that sacrifice.

The same kinds of considerations apply to dealing with frameworks for which self-serving violence is legitimate, or for which hate is a self-justifying attitude. In responding to these kinds of frameworks, violence can be the action that respects the other framework's principles and so carries out the principle (perhaps our own) of nonviolence, and similarly, hate can be the attitude that carries out the principle of love.

To resolve these kinds of situation, again, we need to submit to the confusion that is appropriate to them and allow it to cancel itself into sense. Again, as I have discussed, part of this resolution may lie in our truth to our own being, in the existential decision in which we establish (in a sense we decide, but in a sense we find, since the deciding emerges from and as what we are) what we are honestly committed to and what we can honestly find to make sense.[14] The confused, self-canceling, and emerging sense of these situations, then, includes the sense of ourselves, which is part of what these sense frameworks frame. As a result, our own truth emerges together with and in the same way as that of the other relevant elements of the situation, and in resolution-contributing connection with them. We ourselves undergo confusion and emerge into clarity, and this is not just an unfortunate byproduct of the process of establishing a resolution, but a necessary part of its working.

This peculiar logic of relations between mutually exclusive structures of sense does not create only difficulties for thinking about our relationships with other people and other cultures. It also offers ways of making

---

[14] In Chapter 2, for example, I mentioned Johnstone's argument that the self resolves the problem of negotiating between mutually exclusive frameworks, since it exists as the tension involved in standing both inside and outside one's position at the same time and in the same respect; Henry W. Johnstone, Jr., *Validity and Rhetoric in Philosophical Argument: An Outlook in Transition* (University Park, PA: Dialogue Press of Man and World, 1978), 60–61, 120ff.

sense of these relationships, and in fact of making sense of aspects of our relationships even when they are within a shared framework of sense.

For example, it helps us to understand why certain kinds of impersonality, indifference, and even dislike need not qualify in any way the fully devoted and intimate bond we share with those we love. An impersonal critical distance from a friend, for example, is part of a genuinely caring friendship, but involves seeing her independently of our personal commitments to her. This is still more sharply true of actively opposing our sympathies for the other person and rigidly refusing to accommodate her perspective when, say, we are dealing with an alcoholic, whose self-destructiveness is no longer within the area of her choices. The same paradox occurs in less intimate relationships, too. For example, impersonal clinical distance in a therapist or doctor is a way in which concern for the specific person's interests is carried out. (Interestingly, the reverse is also true: an impersonal, principled, even bureaucratic way of dealing with others with whom one has no personal relationship, say in a professional role, is connected to a commitment to their personal well-being, although this is true as part of the nature of the principle rather than out of explicit concern for or attention to this specific person.)

Each of these is part of caring for the other person or at least looking out for her; but they are successful as caring for the person in, and only in, being indifferent to and even actively excluding that person as someone we care for. Differently expressed, each is wholly internal to our personal bond with or concern for the other person, while also being wholly external to it.

More extremely, a genuine bond with another allows for us sometimes to take her for granted, and at a deep level requires us to do so. If we wonder whether we can rely on a friend when we are in difficulties instead of just assuming it, we insult the other person and even put the friendship in question. But it is also true that if we do not greatly appreciate her reliability and her willingness to help, we also fail fully to appreciate and respect the friendship. Both of these mutually exclusive attitudes are appropriate simultaneously and in the same respects. Similarly, a genuine bond allows for us (at least up to a point) to make hurtful mistakes, to be annoyed, even unreasonably, and to have genuine conflicts with the other person. It allows these not just as acceptable exceptions to the bond but as part of it. It belongs to the sense and health of the bond itself that, up to a point, one is free to work against it, that there is room for these kinds of conflicts with it.

I argued in Chapter 6 (section 4) that sometimes sense does not coincide with itself. Here we can see that intimacy in some respects itself essentially consists in a coordination of itself with what it wholly excludes.[15] In those respects or contexts, it is not only that different conceptual structures legitimately describe it simultaneously but that its own character as intimacy consists in that self-incongruent coordination: what it excludes belongs to its own sense. It is what it is by not being the same as itself. Or, rather, this is sometimes always true, since this nonself-identity or nonself-coincidence in turn also does not fully coincide with itself, and partly consists in what it wholly excludes.[16] This nonself-identity is sometimes always (but only sometimes always) the case with all the things, states of affairs, or issues that the logic of these kinds of coordinations describes. This includes the nature of this "sometimes always" logic itself, as its name indicates, since it is also one of the things it describes.

In the case of intimacy, the confusion or incoherence that is part of the coordination of incompatible appropriate attitudes resolves itself in the same self-canceling way I have discussed. But here the "resolvedly unresolved" aspect of that resolution, in which the confusion is recognized and

---

[15] This modifies what is involved in the kind of absolute respect that, for example, Emmanuel Levinas argues we are obliged to have for others. It is not that we need not have that kind of respect but that what we understand by it needs to include in some contexts not being true to it. Conversely, this idea also modifies what is involved in what Nancy, for example, argues is the state of already being essentially connected with others: "the essence of Being is only as coessence.... In fact, coessentiality cannot consist in an assemblage of essences.... If Being is being-with, then it is ... the 'with' that constitutes being"; Jean-Luc Nancy, *Being Singular Plural*, trans. Robert D. Richardson and Anne E. O'Byrne (Stanford, CA: Stanford University Press, 2000), 30. My argument, on the contrary, is that it is part of deep coessentiality itself that there are nonessential, simply external, trivial relations between things, that these are already included in the "with." While what Nancy is trying to show in this context is, I think, right and profound, and is right even as explaining an essential dimension of the very kind of separateness of things for which I myself am arguing, I think it also needs to make room for what its own rigor cannot encompass (or, in my language here, room for its own complete self-cancellation).

[16] On the affinities of this self-canceling logic with that of Taoism and Zen Buddhism, see the Introduction, note 19.

retained as in itself being an insight, is perhaps part of our sense of the deep mystery of friendship and of love generally.

Along the same lines, we can see how an ethics based on compassion and an ethics based on impersonal duty or calculation can be simultaneously right, and in fact can be parts of each other, not because they can be shown ultimately to share the same sense of what is at stake in ethics, but despite and partly because of their unqualified mutual exclusiveness.

Similarly, we can see how, although the obligations of compassion often cannot be satisfactorily limited, even then the limitations of our capacity for compassion and, for that and other reasons, the limitations of what we can offer or of what we can afford to offer, as the limited beings we cannot help being, sometimes also need not qualify in any way the significance of what we *can* offer. This can be true both in our relationships with others in general and in our intimate relationships. And in some ways, again, as I discussed in connection with our caring relationships, these opposed and mutually exclusive aspects or concerns of our relationships can actually belong to each other's sense and so can be parts, and even essential parts, of each other.

As I commented in the Preface, it is not that there are no definitive answers to philosophical questions or questions about essential reality, but that there are many, mutually exclusive definitive answers.

Another context of these coordinations I would like to look at is that of our relations to ourselves: our personal identity or integrity as persons. For example, someone who is typically pleasant and thoughtful can be unpleasant and unfair because she is unusually stressed, hungry, or vulnerable. Her conduct is still her responsibility: she is fully responsible for her unpleasant behavior in the stressed circumstances. But this need have no bearing on her nature, her appropriate self-conception, when she is in more typical conditions. Fair treatment of her still involves not characterizing her as what she is in the anomalous conditions: we reasonably regard her as essentially a pleasant person. Nonetheless, she is responsible for her anomalous unpleasant conduct even when she is in the mood that typically characterizes her. She is the same person in both contexts. As a result, she is always both the person who is capable of being unpleasant in that kind of way (she is responsible for it) and also someone who is simply not that kind of person (she is appropriately regarded and trusted as someone who does not behave in that kind of way). The phrase "it was out of character" helps to carry out this coordination: it was this person, but it was not this person.

Similarly, in the case of conflicts with oneself, defenses against awareness of oneself or rejections of aspects of oneself are also acknowledgments of what they exclude. If they were not, they could not target it as what needs to be pushed away. As a result, defenses and self-rejections are at once both barriers to what they defend against in oneself and connections with it, both separate from and continuous with it. In fact, what they defend against is *of* the defense itself or internal to its own being, since an acknowledgment or recognition is the specific awareness it is only as an awareness of its particular object. Without that object the acknowledgment is not itself. Because of this continuity or connection, defenses and self-rejections, as psychotherapists are usually aware, can often be a gateway to integration with what they defend against. In fact, they are often the *necessary* path to integration, since they are often necessary defenses with respect to what the person can manage emotionally. I suggest that, as essentially (or wholly) self-contradictory structures, they cancel themselves, through moments of confusion, incoherence, and lost bearings, into including what they exist to exclude. I discussed the logic of this kind of case more fully in connection with the dream of self-judgment in Chapter 9.

One consequence of this continuity of defenses with what they defend against is that the result and therefore the appropriate aim of getting past or working through defenses is not straightforwardly the freeing of what is defended against—for example, the freeing of what we might contrast (in important ways wrongly, I am suggesting) with the defenses as the true person or her true feelings. Instead, it is the emergence of an integration of what was until then separated into defense and something defended against, and now is not simply either. That is, what the true person or her true feelings turn out to be includes something of the feelings and attitudes in which the defenses consisted. We can also see this in that defenses are expressions of the person or are of the person's substance, just as what they defend against is. Consequently the substance of the defenses needs to be included in a true emergence of the undefended person.

This is not to say that we cannot become or be truly undefended. Instead, what the undefended feeling or characteristic truly is in its own nature (that is, in light of the shifting meanings in this self-canceling kind of structure, what its own nature sometimes always truly is) includes something of the character of the defense against it, and it is understood only in a distorted way as long as it is understood in separation from the defense. Just as what the defense defends against is internal to the defense, something of the character of the defense is internal to the feeling or characteristic itself that is defended against. So, for example, if someone is defended against her own vulnerability or capacity fully to feel and be appropriately affected by the important events in her life, then that vulnerability itself consists partly in, say, the resilient strength in which the defense consists. Without that resilience, it cannot sustain itself, and so it is not vulnerability but something more like fragility. Like the self I discussed in Chapter 9, the defense and the defended against are essentially one thing in conflict with itself, and the true nature of both (sometimes always) emerges only after the resolution.

It is still true, however, that defenses are also barriers against and so are separate from what they defend against. Consequently, as in other cases of these kinds of coordination of mutually exclusive attitudes and modes of sense, it is also sometimes or in some respects true that what is defended against is simply separable from the defenses against it. This is self-cancelingly the case or part of the case during the transition to the undefended state, when the continuous and discontinuous aspects of this self-contradictory structure are working themselves out against each other and so are both present in opposition to each other. It may perhaps also be the case, for example, before the transition to the undefended state, in limited contexts where only the barrier-like character of the defenses is relevant. Or it may sometimes or in some respects be the case after the transition, when, for example, the undefended character of the person has been established and consequently is identifiable as who the person simply is (and perhaps, in this new context of meanings, as who she always has been), so that who she truly is is clearly separate from the previous or other defenses.

The same kinds of coordination apply to the relation of ourselves as individuals to our social, political, and natural environments. It is true that we are what we are in virtue of these environments. What we are is constituted, for example, by the cultural sense frameworks into which we are born and socialized, as well as by the concrete relations that we are in with others and with social institutions. We could not describe as a human individual a creature that was in no way constituted by any social order, that was not, for example, fundamentally shaped or structured by social institutions like language or norms of thought and feeling. One of the ways our social being is expressed is that we are arguably responsible for what the society we participate in does to its members and to other societies, even if we have done none of those things ourselves. But this "sometimes always" framework allows us to understand how it can also be true that we are essentially individuals, independent of that social and political environment. We are, for example, arguably wholly responsible for our own personal actions; and there are many forms of suffering and joy that can only appropriately be regarded as simply our own. When someone is in agony because he has broken a leg, it surely misses the reality of the situation to refuse to indulge in sympathy for him because he is structurally and without being able to help it complicit in his society's misdoings, or to require him to set his pain aside because he is currently structurally and without being able to help it involved in much more serious social suffering. To be clear, it is not that the social issue really is more serious even in this context but is temporarily treated as secondary only for the pragmatic reason that the person is incapacitated from attending to it or is blinded to its greater seriousness by his distorting immediate experience of pain. The expression I used above is appropriate: to lecture the person on their social responsibility in this situation misses the reality of what is happening. Similarly, when someone is grateful for a kindness from another person, broader social issues are irrelevant in that immediate context. They are not part of the meaning of the reality of the situation.

In these kinds of context, among a wide variety of others, large and small, complicity with the broader doings of society is not part of the meaning of relevant reality and specifically of the reality of ourselves, and we are innocent of those doings.[17]

Similarly, we can legitimately feel wholly relaxed joy, despite the reality of the great, often unredeemable sorrows of our lives and the world, without deluding ourselves about that other side of reality that also legitimately entirely excludes joy. The reality of *each*, the good and bad of life,

---

[17] Chapter 6, on the exclusive legitimacy of our own moral givens while also allowing for the exclusive legitimacy of moral givens that are not ours, is relevant here.

is absolute and to be respected for its own unqualified truth, as well as sometimes or in some respects to be balanced and weighed against the other. I would say it this way: the badness of life is overwhelming, in a way that cannot legitimately be denied; but so is the goodness of life.

These mutually exclusive ways of our being are sometimes meaningfully simultaneously true. We have, for example, a personal responsibility as individuals that no other can take over for us for our complicity in the ills of our society, in which we have nonetheless also played no personal part in our lives as individuals. As in the cases of our relations with others and with ourselves, we are, as it were, wholly of the substance of our social environment or wholly continuous with it, but also wholly independent of it so that its processes are irrelevant to us, and sometimes we are both of these at the same time and in the same respect.

As I discussed in the case of intimacy, in these kinds of contexts a thing is sometimes always (and this self-cancelingly) not the same as itself. This also applies both to ourselves and to our social and political environments respectively. As I noted above, what it means to be a separate human individual, for example, *is* partly to be in essential—consubstantial—relationships with a social order. Conversely, what it means to be a social environment *is* to be the environment for individuals with at the least the potential for their own idiosyncratic meanings and perspectives. In other words, as I argue in these essays with respect to all relevant meanings in situations where mutually exclusive sense structures simultaneously apply, our independent selves and our social and political environments are sometimes each themselves what they are partly by making room for the other which their own sense excludes.

It is already built into the nature of social orders, then, that individuals are both essentially continuous with them and so complicit with them in their structural doings, and also essentially independent of them and so free of that complicity. And it is already built into the nature of individuality that our doings are both essentially our own and also essentially an act of society at large. One way this is expressed is that we as individuals are true to shared principles we sustain and in that way represent something that goes far beyond ourselves (and in fact, because it is principles that we are true to, what we represent also goes far beyond what the social order includes). Other people can then, for example, be heartened by our conduct because of what it says about the world in general that living by principles is possible, and because of the endorsement of their own lives that fidelity to those particular principles might signify.

Similar considerations are true of other kinds of relations we have with our social environment. Because we are (sometimes always) both essentially of our environment and essentially independent of it, we can make sense of ways in which what we respond to in the world can be both of our own substance and an external influence on our independently existing selves. So, for example, it is true that our social norms of sense and conduct (and, for that matter, our sense framework in general) are applied to us externally: they preexist us, we are socialized into them, and we can take up a critical attitude toward them. But it is also true that these norms *are* us: there is no meaningful "us," or at least not the particular one (black, male, middle class, adult, Ghanan, and so on) that we are, until we have already entered into our social norms. And to have a critical attitude toward those norms is already to rely on and express them or norms that are ultimately derived from them, since they are at least in large part the standards we have by which to judge and criticize.

The same kinds of considerations also apply to our relation to our natural environment. For example, we can understand in this light how it can be simultaneously true that we *are* our relation to the environment, and yet also externally affected by it, so that we can say that one environmental influence is bad for what we are independently of it while another is good. And vice versa: we can be good or bad for the environment, over against us, that we nonetheless also are. We can also understand in this light how we might be able legitimately to understand the things in the environment both as wholly and exclusively brute, meaningless things but also as wholly and exclusively embodiments of meaning toward which attitudes like respect and fairness are appropriate, and, as Latour points out, how *we* can truly be both of these too.[18]

Similarly, again, we can understand how mind and body might be essentially and exclusively aspects of one and the same thing (or simply one thing) and yet also essentially and exclusively separate entities, and also how they might be both simultaneously. Among other things, this would allow us to conceive of interactions between them while recognizing that

---

[18] On Latour, see Chapter 6, section 2.

they belong to mutually exclusive conceptual orders for which interaction is inconceivable.

This would in part be a case of the "resolvedly unresolved" aspect of the resolution that self-cancellation brings here, a recognition of the simple legitimacy of incoherence or confusion that I mentioned above in connection with our relationships with others. Our grasp of it would then in part or at times involve our partly not understanding it and not pursuing further understanding that I discussed there too. And perhaps in part or at times it would involve an analogue of what I discussed there as our sense of the shared rootedness of both conceptual orders in their self-cancelingly nonself-identical or self-divergent being.

In general, this case exemplifies that in situations where mutually exclusive conceptual orders are simultaneously relevant, internal or essential relations of continuity between elements of the situation function at a (self-canceling) point or moment through discontinuity, or by being themselves external relations, without deeper grounding of connection; and vice versa.

I have discussed personal identity and our relations as individuals to our political environment. One pressing concern for contemporary political thought that combines the concerns of both is that of political identity: we can be simultaneously women, black, gay, working class, and so on. Each of these has priorities that do not exist for the others and that conflict with the others' priorities. As the various accounts I have given in these essays suggest, there is no solution to this problem that does not recognize their inescapably contradictory complete mutual exclusivity.[19] I suggest that the kind of self-canceling "sometimes always" framework I propose allows us

---

[19] Georgia Warnke, for example, argues that we can resolve issues of this kind by recognizing that the meaning of a concern is given by its context, so that if we place each conflicting concern in its own separate context, the conflicts turn out to be only apparent; Georgia Warnke, *After Identity: Rethinking Race, Sex, and Gender* (New York: Cambridge University Press, 2007), e.g., 245. This view clearly has similarities with the separate "grammars" or "contexts of inquiry" lines of thought I discussed at the start of the Coda. (In fact, it is directly in one of those traditions, as Warnke's work is largely informed by Gadamer's.) But while Warnke recognizes the need to coordinate these contexts, I think that she does not recognize the wholly mutually exclusive character that they can give the meanings of the relevant concerns, and the consequences that this mutual exclusivity has for coordinating them.

to work constructively with this kind of situation.[20] As in the other cases I have discussed, this involves the disciplines of living with deep perplexity, being at a loss, and giving ourselves over to the truth of ourselves and to the self-canceling working of sense.

Let me end with a context that is immediate to that of this book, the context of the practices of scholarship. One of the principles of the logic for which I argue here is illustrated in the usual practices of scholarship, including in the relation of the essays in this book to one another. When we go about demonstrating a general thesis, we typically do so by discussing different relevant lines of thought or examples of an issue. In each case we explore the line of thought or the example largely in terms of its own unique details and their relations, without more than tangential reference to the detailed working of any of the others. We do this necessarily, because in each context the principle or thesis we are exploring functions in ways that can only be accurately expressed in terms that are largely unique to that context. The general thesis or principle therefore in a sense means something different in each instance, a difference in meaning significant enough to require this extended independent work with each set of different terms. These different demonstrations or illustrations of the thesis, then, are incomparable as expressions of a single meaning. And yet it is these incomparable instances that we rely on to demonstrate a general principle or thesis whose meaning consists in expressing what they commonly illustrate or show.

As I have argued, however, this kind of coordination of incompatible sense structures can be conceivable and legitimate. What it would mean in this case is that the successful grasp of the thesis *is* partly the grasp of its instantiations in various incomparable contexts, with the moments of incoherence and confusion that are self-cancelingly (and so not always or in every respect) built into that awareness. It is not that we always or even often need to grasp a principle or thesis differently from the way we are accustomed to doing, but that we often need to understand differently what we are doing when we grasp it as we ordinarily do. There are sometimes less ordinary implications that then follow about the status and scope

---

[20] Chapter 6, on the exclusive legitimacy of our own moral givens while also allowing for the exclusive legitimacy of moral givens that are not ours, is relevant here again.

of the truth we grasp, and about how it relates to other truths. But the grasp of the thesis itself is also (sometimes always) simply a grasp of the thesis.

It follows from the discussions in these essays that this same sometimes always simplicity of a grasp of the unity of incompatible contents, and the sometimes always simplicity of the unity itself that is grasped, is also true of the grasp and unity of being, of essence, of truth, and of personal and political identity.

Where simultaneous incommensurable sense structures or the vantage from outside the sense structure at issue are not relevant, the whole account I have given in this book has no relevance and in fact no meaning. In much of life, there is no reason to have "stepped outside" our structures of sense in the first place, and the issues I have discussed never arise. The questions we try to answer are often given their own meaning wholly within our framework of sense, so that any answers that would meaningfully respond to them can also only be given wholly within that framework. Further, even when issues involving stepping outside our sense structures have arisen, they are self-canceling, and their self-cancellation in turn establishes their meaninglessness. This then also establishes, in these contexts, the meaninglessness of the account I have given here.

If, then, as I have argued, all of these overviews are sometimes always true, they are also sometimes never true.

References

Agamben, Giorgio. *Potentialities: Collected Essays in Philosophy.* Edited and translated by Daniel Heller-Roazen. Stanford, CA: Stanford University Press, 1999.

———. *State of Exception.* Translated by Kevin Attell. Chicago: University of Chicago Press, 2005.

Alcoff, Linda, and Elizabeth Potter, eds. *Feminist Epistemologies.* New York: Routledge, 1993.

Alderman, Harold. "The Dreamer and the World." In *On Dreaming: An Encounter with Medard Boss,* edited by Charles E. Scott. Chico, CA: Scholars Press, 1977.

Allen, Barry. *Truth in Philosophy.* Cambridge, MA: Harvard University Press, 1993.

Almeder, Robert. "On Naturalizing Epistemology." In *Foundations of Philosophy of Science,* edited by James H. Fetzer. New York: Paragon House, 1993.

Arac, Jonathan, ed. *After Foucault: Humanistic Knowledge, Postmodern Challenges.* New Brunswick, NJ: Rutgers University Press, 1988.

Aristotle. *On the Art of Poetry.* In *Classical Literary Criticism: Aristotle Horace Longinus,* translated by T. S. Dorsch. Harmondsworth: Penguin Books, 1965.

———. *Aristotle's Posterior Analytics.* Translated by Hippocrates G. Apostle. Grinnell, IA: Peripatetic Press, 1981.

Austin, John L. *How to Do Things with Words.* Cambridge, MA: Harvard University Press, 1962.

Badiou, Alain. *Manifesto for Philosophy.* Edited and translated by Norman Madarasz. Albany: State University of New York Press, 1999.

Barris, Jeremy. "The Convergent Conceptions of Being in Mainstream Analytic and Postmodern Continental Philosophy." *Metaphilosophy* 43, no. 5 (2012): 592–618.

———. *The Crane's Walk: Plato, Pluralism, and the Inconstancy of Truth.* New York: Fordham University Press, 2009.

———. "The Foundation in Truth of Rhetoric and Formal Logic." *Philosophy and Rhetoric* 29, no. 4 (1996): 314–28.

———. *Paradox and the Possibility of Knowledge: The Example of Psychoanalysis.* Selinsgrove, PA: Susquehanna University Press, 2003.

Barris, Jeremy, and Jeffrey C. C. Ruff. "Thoughts on Wisdom and Its Relation to Critical Thinking, Multiculturalism, and Global Awareness." *Analytic Teaching and Philosophical Praxis* 31, no. 1 (2011): 5–20.

Barthes, Roland. *Mythologies.* Translated by Annette Lavers. London: Granada, 1972.

Bersani, Leo. *Homos.* Cambridge, MA: Harvard University Press, 1995.

Binswanger, Ludwig. "Dream and Existence." In *Being-in-the-World: Selected Papers of Ludwig Binswanger.* Translated by Jacob Needleman. Riverdale, NY: Baen Books, 1963.

Blackburn, Simon, and Keith Simmons, eds. *Truth.* New York: Oxford University Press, 1999.

Blanchot, Maurice. *The Unavowable Community.* Translated by Pierre Joris. Barrytown, NY: Station Hill Press, 1988.

Blasius, Mark. *Gay and Lesbian Politics: Sexuality and the Emergence of a New Ethic.* Philadelphia, PA: Temple University Press, 1994.

Bloch, Ernst. *The Utopian Function of Art and Literature: Selected Essays.* Translated by Jack Zipes and Frank Mecklenburg. Cambridge, MA: MIT Press, 1988.

Boss, Medard. *The Analysis of Dreams.* Translated by Arnold J. Pomerans. London: Rider, 1957.

Bradley, F. H. "On Truth and Copying." In *Truth,* edited by Simon Blackburn and Keith Simmons. New York: Oxford University Press, 1999.

Bredbeck, Gregory W. *Sodomy and Interpretation: Marlowe to Milton.* Ithaca, NY: Cornell University Press, 1991.

Bremer, Manuel. *An Introduction to Paraconsistent Logics.* Frankfurt am Main: Peter Lang, 2005.

Butler, Judith. "Competing Universalities." In *Contingency, Hegemony, Universality: Contemporary Dialogues on the Left,* edited by Judith Butler, Ernesto Laclau, and Slavoj Žižek. London: Verso, 2000.

———. *Gender Trouble: Feminism and the Subversion of Identity.* New York: Routledge, 1990.

———. "Imitation and Gender Insubordination." In *Inside/Out: Lesbian Theories, Gay Theories,* edited by Diana Fuss. New York: Routledge, 1991.

Cavallero, Corrado and David Foulkes, eds. *Dreaming as Cognition.* London: Harvester Wheatsheaf, 1993.

Champagne, John. *The Ethics of Marginality: A New Approach to Gay Studies.* Minneapolis: University of Minnesota Press, 1995.

Collingwood, Robin George. *An Autobiography.* Oxford: Clarendon Press of Oxford University Press, 1978.

———. *An Essay on Metaphysics.* Oxford: Clarendon Press of Oxford University Press, 1940.
Connolly, William. *Pluralism.* Durham, NC: Duke University Press, 2005.
Corlett, William. *Community without Unity: A Politics of Derridian Extravagance.* Durham, NC: Duke University Press, 1989.
Coward, Rosalind, and John Ellis. *Language and Materialism: Developments in Semiology and the Theory of the Subject.* London: Routledge & Kegan Paul, 1977.
Cvetkovich, Ann. *An Archive of Feelings: Trauma, Sexuality, and Lesbian Public Cultures.* Durham, NC: Duke University Press, 2003.
Davidson, Arnold. "Archaeology, Genealogy, Ethics." In *Foucault: A Critical Reader,* edited by David Couzens Hoy. Cambridge, MA: Basil Blackwell, 1986.
Davidson, Donald. "A Coherence Theory of Truth and Knowledge." In *Truth and Interpretation: Perspectives on the Philosophy of Donald Davidson,* edited by Ernest LePore. Cambridge, MA: Basil Blackwell, 1986.
———. "Empirical Content." In *Truth and Interpretation: Perspectives on the Philosophy of Donald Davidson,* edited by Ernest LePore. Cambridge, MA: Blackwell, 1986.
———. *Inquiries into Truth and Interpretation.* Oxford: Oxford University Press, 1984.
———. "A Nice Derangement of Epitaphs." In *Truth and Interpretation: Perspectives on the Philosophy of Donald Davidson,* edited by Ernest LePore. Cambridge, MA: Blackwell, 1986.
———. "On the Very Idea of a Conceptual Scheme." In *Inquiries into Truth and Interpretation.* Oxford: Oxford University Press, 1984.
———. "Paradoxes of Irrationality," In *Philosophical Essays on Freud,* edited by Richard Wollheim and James Hopkins. New York: Cambridge University Press, 1982.
de Lauretis, Teresa. *Technologies of Gender: Essays on Theory, Film, and Fiction.* Bloomington: Indiana University Press, 1987.
Deleuze, Gille. *Foucault.* Minneapolis: University of Minnesota Press, 1988.
Derrida, Jacques. "Différance." In *Margins of Philosophy.* Translated by Alan Bass. Chicago: University of Chicago Press, 1982.
———. *Positions.* Translated by Alan Bass. Chicago: University of Chicago Press, 1981.
Dewey, John. *Logic: The Theory of Inquiry.* New York: Henry Holt, 1938.
Dreyfus, Hubert L., and Paul Rabinow. *Michel Foucault: Beyond Structuralism and Hermeneutics.* 2nd ed. Chicago: University of Chicago Press, 1983.
Dunlop, Charles E. M., ed. *Philosophical Essays on Dreaming.* Ithaca, NY: Cornell University Press, 1977.
Emerson, Ralph Waldo. "Self-Reliance." In *The Best of Ralph Waldo Emerson: Essays, Poems, Addresses,* edited by Gordon S. Haight. New York: Walter J. Black, 1941.

Engel, Pascal. *The Norm of Truth: An Introduction to the Philosophy of Logic*. Translated by Pascal Engel and Miriam Kochan. Toronto: University of Toronto Press, 1991.

Eribon, Didier. *Michel Foucault et ses contemporains*. Paris: Fayard, 1994.

Feyerabend, Paul. *Against Method*. 3rd ed. London: Verso, 1993.

Fornet-Betancourt, Raul, et al. "The Ethic of Care for the Self as a Practice of Freedom: An Interview with Michel Foucault on January 20, 1984." *Philosophy and Social Criticism* 12, nos. 2–3 (1987): 112–31.

Foucault, Michel. "Afterword." In Hubert L. Dreyfus and Paul Rabinow, *Michel Foucault: Beyond Structuralism and Hermeneutics*. 2nd ed. Chicago: University of Chicago Press, 1983.

———. *The Archaeology of Knowledge*. Translated by A. M. Sheridan Smith. New York: Pantheon, 1972.

———. *Foucault Live (Interviews, 1966–1984)*. New York: Semiotext(e), 1989.

———. *The History of Sexuality*. Harmondsworth: Penguin Books, 1978.

———. *Power/Knowledge: Selected Interviews and Other Writings 1972–1977*. New York: Pantheon, 1980.

———. "The Subject and Power." In Hubert L. Dreyfus and Paul Rabinow, *Michel Foucault: Beyond Structuralism and Hermeneutics*. 2nd ed. Chicago: University of Chicago Press, 1983.

———. *The Use of Pleasure*. New York: Pantheon, 1985.

Freud, Sigmund. *The Interpretation of Dreams*. Translated by James Strachey. Harmondsworth: Penguin, 1953.

Fromm, Erich. *The Forgotten Language: An Introduction to the Understanding of Dreams, Fairy Tales, and Myths*. New York: Grove Press, 1951.

Fuss, Diana. *Essentially Speaking: Feminism, Nature and Difference*. New York: Routledge, 1989.

———, ed. *Inside/Out: Lesbian Theories, Gay Theories*. New York: Routledge, 1991.

Gadamer, Hans-Georg. *Hegel's Dialectic: Five Hermeneutical Studies*. Translated by P. Christopher Smith. New Haven, CT: Yale University Press, 1976.

———. *Truth and Method*. 2nd ed. Translated by Joel Weinsheimer and Donald G. Marshall. New York: Continuum, 1995.

Gaita, Raimond. *Good and Evil: An Absolute Conception*. 2nd ed. New York: Routledge, 2004.

Gasché, Rodolphe. "Introduction." In Andrzej Warminski, *Readings in Interpretation: Hölderlin, Hegel, Heidegger*. Minneapolis: University of Minnesota Press, 1987.

Gendlin, Eugene T. *Let Your Body Interpret Your Dreams*. Wilmette, IL: Chiron Publications, 1986.

Goodman, Nelson. "Notes on the Well-Made World." *Partisan Review* 51 (1984): 276–88.

Griggers. Cathy. "Lesbian Bodies in the Age of (Post)mechanical Reproduction." In *Fear of a Queer Planet: Queer Politics and Social Theory,* edited by Michael Warner. Minneapolis: University of Minnesota Press, 1993.

Haack, Susan. *Philosophy of Logics.* Cambridge: Cambridge University Press, 1978.

Hacking, Ian. "Self-Improvement." In *Foucault: A Critical Reader,* edited by David Couzens Hoy. Cambridge, MA: Basil Blackwell, 1986.

Halberstam, Judith. *The Queer Art of Failure.* Durham, NC: Duke University Press, 2011.

Hall, Calvin S. *The Meaning of Dreams.* New York: McGraw-Hill, 1966.

Hall, Everett W. *Philosophical Systems: A Categorial Analysis.* Chicago: University of Chicago Press, 1960.

Halperin, David. *Saint Foucault: Towards a Gay Hagiography.* New York: Oxford University Press, 1995.

Haraway, Donna J. "Situated Knowledges: The Science Question in Feminism and the Privilege of Partial Perspective." In *Simians, Cyborgs, and Women: The Reinvention of Nature.* New York: Routledge, 1991.

Harding, Sandra. "Is There a Feminist Method?" In *Feminism and Science,* edited by Nancy Tuana. Bloomington: Indiana University Press, 1989.

———. "Rethinking Standpoint Epistemology: What Is 'Strong Objectivity?'" In *Feminist Epistemologies,* edited by Linda Alcoff and Elizabeth Potter. New York: Routledge, 1993.

Heidegger, Martin. *Basic Writings.* Edited by David F. Krell. New York: Harper & Row, 1977.

———. *Kant and the Problem of Metaphysics.* Translated by James S. Churchill. Bloomington: Indiana University Press, 1962.

———. "The Nature of Language." In *On the Way to Language.* Translated by Peter D. Hertz. New York: Harper & Row, 1971.

———. "On the Essence of Truth." Translated by John Sallis. In *Basic Writings.* Edited by David F. Krell. New York: Harper & Row, 1977.

———. "The Onto-Theo-Logical Constitution of Metaphysics." In *Identity and Difference.* Translated by Joan Stambaugh. New York: Harper & Row, 1969.

———. "The Origin of the Work of Art." Translated by Albert Hofstadter. In *Basic Writings.* Edited by David F. Krell. New York: Harper & Row, 1977.

———. "Plato's Doctrine of Truth." Translated by Thomas Sheehan. In *Pathmarks,* edited by William McNeill. Cambridge: Cambridge University Press, 1998.

———. *Schelling's Treatise on the Essence of Human Freedom.* Translated by Joan Stambaugh. Athens: Ohio University Press, 1985.

———. "The Word of Nietzsche: 'God Is Dead.'" In *The Question Concerning Technology and Other Essays.* Translated by William Lovitt. New York: Harper & Row, 1977.

———. *Zollikon Seminars: Protocols—Conversations—Letters*. Edited by Medard Boss. Translated by Franz Mayr and Richard Askay. Evanston, IL: Northwestern University Press, 2001.

Hillman, James. "Silver and the White Earth, Part Two." *Spring* (1981): 21–63.

Horton, John. "Three (Apparent) Paradoxes of Toleration." *Synthesis Philosophica* 17 (1994): 7–20.

Horwich, Paul. "The Minimalist Conception of Truth." In *Truth*, edited by Simon Blackburn and Keith Simmons. New York: Oxford University Press, 1999.

Hoy, David Couzens, ed. *Foucault: A Critical Reader*. Cambridge: Basil Blackwell, 1986.

Irigaray, Luce. *This Sex Which Is Not One*. Translated by Catherine Porter with Carolyn Burke. Ithaca, NY: Cornell University Press, 1985.

Jaspers, Karl. *Reason and Existenz: Five Lectures*. Translated by William Earle. Milwaukee, WI: Marquette University Press, 1997.

Johnstone, Henry W., Jr. *Validity and Rhetoric in Philosophical Argument: An Outlook in Transition*. University Park, PA: Dialogue Press of Man and World, 1978.

Jung, Carl G. *Dreams*. Translated by R. F. C. Hull. Princeton, NJ: Princeton University Press, 1974.

———. *Two Essays on Analytical Psychology*. 2nd ed. Translated by R. F. C. Hull. London: Routledge & Kegan Paul, 1953.

Kant, Immanuel. *Critique of Pure Reason*. Translated by Norman Kemp Smith. New York: St. Martin's Press, 1929.

Kapferer, Bruce, ed. *Beyond Rationalism: Rethinking Magic, Witchcraft and Sorcery*. New York: Berghahn Books, 2003.

Kingwell, Mark. *A Civil Tongue: Justice, Dialogue, and the Politics of Pluralism*. University Park: Pennsylvania State University Press, 1995.

Kuhn, Thomas S. *The Road Since Structure: Philosophical Essays, 1970–1993, with an Autobiographical Interview*. Edited by James Conant and John Haugeland. Chicago: University of Chicago Press, 2000.

———. *The Structure of Scientific Revolutions*. 2nd ed. Chicago: University of Chicago Press, 1970.

Laclau, Ernesto, and Chantal Mouffe. *Hegemony and Socialist Strategy: Towards a Radical Democratic Politics*. Translated by Winston Moore and Paul Cammack. London: Verso, 1985.

Larmore, Charles E. *Patterns of Moral Complexity*. New York: Cambridge University Press, 1987.

Latour, Bruno. *Politics of Nature: How to Bring the Sciences into Democracy*. Translated by Catherine Porter. Cambridge, MA: Harvard University Press, 2004.

———. *Reassembling the Social: An Introduction to Actor-Network-Theory*. New York: Oxford University Press, 2005.

———. *We Have Never Been Modern*. Translated by Catherine Porter. Cambridge, MA: Harvard University Press, 1993.

Latour, Bruno, and Steve Woolgar. *Laboratory Life: The Social Construction of Scientific Facts*. London: Sage, 1979.

LePore, Ernest, ed. *Truth and Interpretation: Perspectives on the Philosophy of Donald Davidson*. Cambridge: Blackwell, 1986.

Livingston, Paul M. *The Politics of Logic: Badiou, Wittgenstein, and the Consequences of Formalism*. New York: Routledge, 2012.

Love, Heather. *Feeling Backward: Loss and the Politics of Queer History*. Cambridge, MA: Harvard University Press, 2007.

Lyotard, Jean-François. *The Differend: Phrases in Dispute*. Translated by Georges Van Den Abbeele. Minneapolis: University of Minnesota Press, 1988.

MacIntyre, Alasdaire C. "Relativism, Power, and Philosophy." In *Relativism: Interpretation and Confrontation,* edited by Michael Krausz. Notre Dame, IN: University of Notre Dame Press, 1989.

———. *Whose Justice? Which Rationality?* Notre Dame, IN: University of Notre Dame Press, 1988.

Malcolm, Norman. *Dreaming*. London: Routledge & Kegan Paul, 1959.

Marlan, Stanton. *The Black Sun: The Alchemy and Art of Darkness*. College Station: Texas A&M University Press, 2005.

Martin, Biddy. *Femininity Played Straight: The Significance of Being Lesbian*. New York: Routledge, 1996.

McLaren, Peter. *Critical Pedagogy and Predatory Culture: Oppositional Politics in a Postmodern Era*. New York: Routledge, 1995.

Micklem, Niel. "I Am Not Myself: A Paradox." In *Jung's Concept of the Self: Its Relevance Today,* edited by Niel Micklem. London: BAP Monographs, 1990.

Mouffe, Chantal. *The Democratic Paradox*. New York: Verso, 2000.

Mumon. *The Gateless Gate*. Translated by Nyogen Senzaki and Paul Reps. In *Zen Flesh, Zen Bones*, edited by Paul Reps. Harmondsworth: Penguin Books, 1957.

Muñoz, José Esteban. *Cruising Utopia: The Then and There of Queer Futurity*. New York: New York University Press, 2009.

Nagel, Thomas. "The Absurd." In *Mortal Questions*. Cambridge: Cambridge University Press, 1979.

Nancy, Jean-Luc. *Being Singular Plural*. Translated by Robert D. Richardson and Anne E. O'Byrne. Stanford, CA: Stanford University Press, 2000.

———. *The Inoperative Community*. Translated by Peter Connor, Lisa Garbus, Michael Holland, and Simona Sawhney. Minneapolis: University of Minnesota Press, 1991.

Nye, Andrea. *Words of Power: A Feminist Reading of the History of Logic*. New York: Routledge, 1990.

Ortega y Gasset, José. *What Is Knowledge?* Edited and translated by Jorge García-Gómez. Albany: State University of New York Press, 2002.

Perelman, Chaim, and L. Olbrechts-Tyteca, *The New Rhetoric: A Treatise on Argumentation.* Translated by John Wilkinson and Purcell Weaver. Notre Dame, IN: University of Notre Dame Press, 1969.

Plato. *Theaetetus.* Translated by Robin H. Waterfield. Harmondsworth: Penguin Books, 1987.

Priest, Graham. *Beyond the Limits of Thought.* Oxford: Oxford University Press, 2002.

———. *An Introduction to Non-Classical Logic.* Cambridge: Cambridge University Press, 2001.

Priest, Graham, J. C. Beall, and Bradley Armour-Garb, eds. *The Law of Non-Contradiction: New Philosophical Essays.* Oxford: Oxford University Press, 2004.

Putnam, Hilary, *Realism with a Human Face.* Edited by James Conant. Cambridge, MA: Harvard University Press, 1990.

———. *Words and Life.* Edited by James Conant. Cambridge, MA: Harvard University Press, 1994.

Quine, Willard Van Orman. "Ontological Relativity." In *Ontological Relativity and Other Essays.* New York: Columbia University Press, 1969.

———. "Speaking of Objects." In *Ontological Relativity and Other Essays.* New York: Columbia University Press, 1969.

———. "Two Dogmas of Empiricism." In *From a Logical Point of View: Nine Logico-Philosophical Essays.* Cambridge, MA: Harvard University Press, 1961.

Rajchman, John. *Truth and Eros: Foucault, Lacan, and the Question of Ethics.* New York: Routledge, 1991.

Rawls, John. *Political Liberalism.* New York: Columbia University Press, 1993.

———. *A Theory of Justice.* Cambridge, MA: Belknap Press of Harvard University Press, 1999.

Reps, Paul, ed. *Zen Flesh, Zen Bones.* Harmondsworth: Penguin Books, 1957.

Riley, Denise. *"Am I That Name?" Feminism and the Category of "Women" in History.* Minneapolis: University of Minnesota Press, 1988.

Roditi, Edouard. *Oscar Wilde.* New York: New Directions, 1986.

Rorty, Richard. *Contingency, Irony, and Solidarity.* New York: Cambridge University Press, 1989.

———. *Objectivity, Relativism, and Truth: Philosophical Papers, Volume 1.* New York: Cambridge University Press, 1991.

———. "Pragmatism, Davidson, and Truth." In *Objectivity, Relativism, and Truth: Philosophical Papers, Volume 1.* New York: Cambridge University Press, 1991.

———. "Transcendental Arguments, Self-Reference, and Pragmatism." In *Transcendental Arguments and Science: Essays in Epistemology.* Edited by P. Bieri, R.-P. Horstmann, and L. Krüger. Dordrecht: D. Reidel, 1979.

———. *Truth and Progress: Philosophical Papers Volume 3*. New York: Cambridge University Press, 1998.

Russell, Bertrand. "The Philosophy of Logical Atomism." In *Logic and Knowledge: Essays 1901–1950*. Edited by Robert Charles Marsh. London: George Allen & Unwin, 1956.

———. "The Study of Mathematics." In *Mysticism and Logic and Other Essays*. London: Unwin Books, 1963.

Sainsbury, R. M. *Paradoxes*. 2nd ed. Cambridge: Cambridge University Press, 1995.

Sallis, John. *Being and Logos: The Way of Platonic Dialogue*. Atlantic Highlands, NJ: Humanities Press, 1986.

Schiller, F. C. S. *Formal Logic: A Scientific and Social Problem*. London: Macmillan, 1912.

Sedgwick, Eve Kosofsky. *The Epistemology of the Closet*. Berkeley: University of California Press, 1990.

———. *Tendencies*. Durham, NC: Duke University Press, 1993.

———. *Touching Feeling: Affect, Pedagogy, Performativity*. Durham, NC: Duke University Press, 2003.

Seidman, Steven. *Difference Troubles: Queering Social Theory and Sexual Politics*. New York: Cambridge University Press, 1997.

Shakespeare, William. *Antony and Cleopatra,* edited by Maynard Mack. Harmondsworth: Penguin Books, 1970.

Simpson, David. *The Academic Postmodern and the Rule of Literature: A Report on Half-Knowledge*. Chicago: University of Chicago Press, 1995.

Smith, Barbara Herrnstein. *Belief and Resistance: Dynamics of Contemporary Intellectual Controversy*. Cambridge, MA: Harvard University Press, 1997.

Sōhō, Takuan. *The Unfettered Mind: Writings of the Zen Master to the Sword Master*. Translated by William Scott Wilson. New York: Kodansha International, 1986.

States, Bert O. *Dreaming and Storytelling*. Ithaca, NY: Cornell University Press, 1993.

———. *The Rhetoric of Dreams*. Ithaca, NY: Cornell University Press, 1988.

Stone, Alison. "Essentialism and Anti-Essentialism in Feminist Philosophy." *Journal of Moral Philosophy* 1, no. 2 (2004): 135–53.

Suzuki, Shunryu. *Not Always So: Practicing the True Spirit of Zen*. Edited by Edward Espe Brown. New York: Harper, 2002.

Taylor, Charles. *Philosophical Papers, Volume 2: Philosophy and the Human Sciences*. Cambridge: Cambridge University Press, 1985.

Thomson, Iain D. *Heidegger, Art, and Postmodernity*. New York: Cambridge University Press, 2011.

Tuana, Nancy, ed. *Feminism and Science*. Bloomington: Indiana University Press, 1989.

Tully, James. *Strange Multiplicity: Constitutionalism in an Age of Diversity.* Cambridge: Cambridge University Press, 1995.
Valberg, J. J. *Dream, Death, and the Self.* Princeton, NJ: Princeton University Press, 2007.
Walzer, Michael. "The Politics of Michel Foucault." In *Foucault: A Critical Reader,* edited by David Couzens Hoy. Cambridge, MA: Basil Blackwell, 1986.
———. *Spheres of Justice.* New York: Basic Books, 1983.
Warminski, Andrzej. *Readings in Interpretation: Hölderlin, Hegel, Heidegger.* Minneapolis: University of Minnesota Press, 1987.
Warner, Michael, ed. *Fear of a Queer Planet: Queer Politics and Social Theory.* Minneapolis: University of Minnesota Press, 1993.
Warnke, Georgia. *After Identity: Rethinking Race, Sex, and Gender.* New York: Cambridge University Press, 2007.
———. *Justice and Interpretation.* Cambridge, MA: MIT Press, 1992.
Weimer, Walter B. *Notes on the Methodology of Scientific Research.* Hillsdale, NJ: Lawrence Erlbaum Associates, 1979.
———. "Science as a Rhetorical Transaction: Toward a Nonjustificational Conception of Rhetoric." *Philosophy and Rhetoric* 10, no. 1 (1977): 1–29.
Wilde, Oscar. *Complete Works of Oscar Wilde.* Edited by Vyvyan Holland. London: Collins, 1966.
———. "The Critic as Artist." In *Complete Works of Oscar Wilde,* edited by Vyvyan Holland. London: Collins, 1966.
———. *The Importance of Being Earnest.* In *Complete Works of Oscar Wilde.* Edited by Vyvyan Holland. London: Collins, 1966.
———. "Lord Arthur Savile's Crime: A Study of Duty." In *Complete Works of Oscar Wilde.* Edited by Vyvyan Holland. London: Collins, 1966.
———. "Phrases and Philosophies for the Use of the Young." In *Complete Works of Oscar Wilde.* Edited by Vyvyan Holland. London: Collins, 1966.
———. *The Soul of Man under Socialism.* In *Complete Works of Oscar Wilde.* Edited by Vyvyan Holland. London: Collins, 1966.
———. "The Sphinx Without a Secret." In *Complete Works of Oscar Wilde.* Edited by Vyvyan Holland. London: Collins, 1966.
Williams, Bernard. *Ethics and the Limits of Philosophy.* Cambridge, MA: Harvard University Press, 1985.
Williams, Michael. *Unnatural Doubts: Epistemological Realism and the Basis of Scepticism.* Princeton, NJ: Princeton University Press, 1996.
Winch, Peter. "Understanding a Primitive Society." *American Philosophical Quarterly* 1, no. 4 (1964): 307–24.
Wittgenstein, Ludwig. *Culture and Value.* Edited by G. H. von Wright and Heikki Nyman. Translated by Peter Winch. Chicago: University of Chicago Press, 1980.

———. *Philosophical Investigations.* 2nd ed. Translated by G. E. M. Anscombe. Oxford: Blackwell, 1958.

———. *Remarks on Frazer's* Golden Bough. Translated by A. C. Miles. Atlantic Highlands, NJ: Humanities Press, 1979.

———. *Tractatus Logico-Philosophicus.* Translated by D. F. Pears and B. F. McGuinness. London: Routledge & Kegan Paul, 1961.

Wolin, Sheldon S. "On the Theory and Practice of Power." In *After Foucault: Humanistic Knowledge, Postmodern Challenges,* edited by Jonathan Arac. New Brunswick, NJ: Rutgers University Press, 1988.

Wollheim, Richard, and James Hopkins, eds. *Philosophical Essays on Freud.* New York: Cambridge University Press, 1982.

Index

absolute truth(s): circular justifications of incompatible absolute truths, 47–51; Donald Davidson's arguments for, 35–38; metaphysics and, 206–7; queer theory and the recognition of, 168–69
Agamben, Giorgio, 11–12n17, 177–78, 180
Agrippa's trilemma, 54n1
Alcoff, Linda, 79, 84, 87
Alderman, Harold, 250–51
Almeder, Robert, 55, 65
antiepistemology: debates with epistemology, 81–82; overview, 88–90; Michael Williams's approach to, 92n30
antirelativism, 34–39
arbitrariness, 52
Aristotle, 55n3, 229–30
art: Oscar Wilde's idea of, 124–28
artificial: Aristotle on, 229–30
Austin, J. L., 204n5
authentic existence: Heidegger's notion of, 177–78

Badiou, Alain, 5
Barthes, Roland, 155, 159
Bersani, Leo, 157–58
biases: in epistemology and the problems of self-reference, 84–88
big question philosophy: deep pluralism and, 10–12, 15, 181; the problem of self-contradiction, 11–15
binary opposition, 9–10
Binswanger, Ludwig, 257–58

Blasius, Mark, 157
Bloch, Ernst, 112n26
Boss, Medard, 245, 256–57
Bradley, F. H., 207n9
Bredbeck, Gregory, 158, 160
Butler, Judith, 4, 156–57, 159, 161, 162, 163–64

Cavallero, Corrado, 235
Champagne, John, 157
charity, principle of, 36
circular justification(s): of conflicting absolutes, 47–51; epistemology and, 82, 83, 97; knowledge and the problem of, 55–57. *See also* foundational circularity
coherency of the subject, 156–57
Collingwood, R. G., 196, 260–61
communitarianism, 105–6
conceptual analysis, 204n5
conduct: meaning and value of, 16–18
conflicting frameworks: absolute justification of relativism and of the unintelligibility of relativism, 45–51; the explicit self-cancellation of Rorty's and Davidson's standpoints on the meaninglessness of comparing, 39–42; the problem of foundational circularity and, 60–61, 64; Rorty's and Davidson's standpoints on the meaninglessness of comparing, 34–39, 59–60, 67n29; self-cancellation of Rorty's and Davidson's self-cancellation, 42–45;

293

conflicting frameworks (cont.)
    the truth of singular standpoints,
    52–53; the truth of the knower, and
    negotiation between truths, 51–52.
    See also mutually exclusive sense
    frameworks
Connolly, William, 109–10
constitutive change: Oscar Wilde's
    concern with, 110–15
construction/constructionism:
    heterosexual normativity and the
    logical character of construction,
    154–58; incompatibility but
    necessity of essence and
    construction, 158–66; pluralist
    comparisons and the nature of
    truth, 33–34
continuous consistency, 177, 180, 181
contradiction(s): and the concepts of
    "nature" and "essence" in sexuality
    and gender theory, 152, 153–54;
    and the contemporary problem
    of pluralism, 2–9; dreams and,
    231–33; of foundational circularity
    (see foundational circularity); as
    having a given, self-same sense,
    161; Karl Jaspers on, 206n6; the
    Jungian notion of total personality
    and, 252; law of, 72–73 (see also
    noncontradiction: exclusive
    principle of); the logical structure
    of dreams and, 244–49; logic and,
    72, 95n32, 243; metaphysics and
    the contradiction of absolute truths,
    206–7; pluralist comparisons and
    the nature of truth, 33; the possibility
    of legitimate logical contradiction,
    20–23; theories of Jungian dream
    interpretation and, 253–56; in
    understandings of reality as a
    whole, 237–44; unnatural logic
    and, 166–78 (see also unnatural
    logic); usefully contradictory
    connection of logic and rhetoric,
    57–64. See also self-cancellation;
    self-contradiction
contradictory multiplicity, 161
Corlett, William, 109

Coward, Rosalind, 155, 156
Cratylus (Plato), 189
creationists, 240–41
"Critic as Artist, The" (Wilde), 113,
    115, 126
Critique of Pure Reason (Kant), 198
Cvetkovich, Ann, 5, 152, 169, 175n50

Davidson, Arnold, 143
Davidson, Donald: antiepistemology and,
    81, 89–90; on common-grounds
    situations and epistemological
    doubt, 97; explicit self-cancellation
    of the standpoint on the
    meaninglessness of comparing
    conflicting frameworks, 39–42; on
    the idea of meanings, 38–39; on
    the incommensurability of contrasting
    understandings of reality as a
    whole, 97, 99, 242–43; logical focus
    of, 62; on the meaninglessness of
    comparing conflicting frameworks,
    6, 35–38, 45–50, 59–60, 67n29;
    on pluralist comparisons and the
    nature of truth, 32; on the problem
    of foundational circularity, 65; the
    problem of self-cancellation and,
    14–15; self-cancellation of the
    self-cancellation of the standpoint
    on the meaninglessness of
    comparing conflicting frameworks,
    42–45; on the underlying paradox
    of irrationality, 13n18
deep pluralism. *See* pluralism
Deleuze, Gilles, 146, 180
democracy: plural, 106–8
Derrida, Jacques, 10, 74–75, 233
Dewey, John, 176–77n51, 261
dialetheias, 22
difference: Oscar Wilde's concern with,
    110–15
Differend, The (Lyotard), 195–96
dream interpretation, 236, 251–58
dreams (dream narratives): contradiction
    and, 231–33; as simultaneously
    expression and transformation,
    249–51. *See also* logical structure
    of dreams

Ellis, John, 155, 156
Emerson, Ralph Waldo, 178
environmental thought: Bruno Latour's reconciliation of essence and construction, 164–66; notions of "nature" and, 152–53
episodic thought: problem of foundational circularity, 65
epistemology: contemporary problems, 78–79; debates between different types of epistemologies, 79–80; debates with antiepistemologists, 81–82; problems of infinite regress and ultimate circularity, 82–83; rejections of, 88–90. *See also* feminist epistemology
errancy, 184–85
error, 184–85
essence: heterosexual normativity and the logical character of essence, 154–58; heterosexual normativity and the problem of the concept of "essence," 150–54; incompatibility but necessity of essence and construction, 158–66; nature and, 159; pure essences, 160, 167–68
essentialism: incompatibility but necessity of essence and construction, 158–66; pluralist comparisons and the nature of truth, 33–34
essential relations. *See* internal relations
ethnocentrism: the nature of truth and, 34–39
evolutionists, 240–41
exception. *See* state of exception
existence: discussion of the experience of, 16–18; Heidegger's notion of authentic existence, 177–78
existential dream analysis, 257–58
existential practice: dreams as, 249–51
external relations, 54–55, 197–201, 270n15, 277

Fechner, Gustav, 245
Feminism and Science (Tuana), 79–80
Feminist Epistemologies (Alcoff & Potter), 79
feminist epistemology: biases in epistemology and the problems of self-reference, 84–88; debates between different types of epistemologies, 79–80; debates with antiepistemologists, 81–82; problems arising in the historical examination of sexism, 90–93; problems of infinite regress and ultimate circularity, 82–83; a solution to the problem of truth incompatibility, 93–101
feminist theory: frameworks and logics of contradiction, 153–54
Foucault, Michel: criticism of the emphasis on power, 91; on the multiple self-disparities of rationality, 149; notion of disciplinary and normative strategies of power, 135–36; the problem of self-cancellation and, 15
Foucault's pluralism: challenge to the concept of truth and resulting problems, 134–40; conflicting truth frameworks and the meaninglessness of ideology critique, 129–30; deep contextualization of truth, 141–49; metaframeworks concept, 131–34
Foulkes, David, 235
foundational circularity: correspondence with the world and, 71; problem of, 60–61, 64–66; the problem of conflicting frameworks and, 60–61, 64; the problem of the undecidability of meanings, 74–75; relevance to the experience and conduct of everyday life, 75–77; rhetorical dimension of, 66–71; and the usefully contradictory connection of logic and rhetoric, 61–64; viability and aptness of the contradiction, 71–74
freedom: Foucault distinguishes from power effects, 139–40
Freud, Sigmund, 245, 251–52
Fromm, Erich, 235n13
Fuss, Diana, 91, 159, 161, 162, 163

Gadamer, Hans-Georg, 195, 261
Gaita, Raimon, 260, 264

gender identity: and the logical character of nature, essence, and construction, 156–58
gender theory. *See* sexuality and gender theory
Gendlin, Eugene, 234
genuine open-mindedness, 76–77
German Idealism, 194
Goodman, Nelson, 7
Griggers, Cathy, 158

Hacking, Ian, 138
Halberstam, Judith, 175n50
Hall, Everett, 59
happenstance. *See* external relations
Haraway, Donna, 81
Harding, Sandra, 84, 88
Hegel, Georg Wilhelm Friedrich, 66, 194, 195
Heidegger, Martin: criticism of Ludwig Binswanger's existential analysis, 257n44; notions of authentic existence, 177–78; the problem of self-cancellation and, 14–15
Heideggerian interpretation of metaphysics: Heidegger versus John Sallis on Plato, 188–93; problem of simply continuously consistent logic, 194–201; problem of the decisiveness of, 179–83; truth and the violence of interpretation, 182–88 (*see also* truth(s): as concealing-revealing and also as correctness; truth(s): as an essential or inner strife)
heterosexual normativity (heteronormativity): character and value of unnatural logic, 166–72; incompatibility but necessity of essence and construction, 158–66; the logical characters of nature, essence, and construction, 154–58; overview, 151; problem of the concepts of "nature" and "essence," 150–54; sense and practical dimensions of unnatural logic, 172–78
Hillman, James, 256

History of Sexuality, The (Foucault), 144
homosexuality: unnaturalness of, 151, 159
Horton, John, 2n1
Horwich, Paul, 204n5

identity: and the logical character of nature, essence, and construction, 156–58; Butler on the historical construction of, 163–64
ideology: Foucault's challenge to the concept of, 134–36
ideology critique: Foucault on, 129–30, 138–39, 148
Importance of Being Earnest, The (Wilde), 122, 205, 210–29
incommensurability: Donald Davidson on the incommensurability of contrasting understandings of reality as a whole, 97, 99, 242–43; feminist epistemology and a solution to the problem of, 93–101; Thomas Kuhn on rational decision between incommensurable scientific frameworks, 102–3n11; Kuhn's notion of incommensurability, 86; Bruno Latour's reconciliation of nature and social construction, 165–66; the presence of contradiction in understandings of reality as a whole, 237–44; Richard Rorty on, 95
infinite regress: epistemology and, 82–83, 97; knowledge and the problem of, 55–56
infra-language, 133n8
internal (or essential) relations, 54–55, 180, 188, 194–98, 200–1, 270n15, 277
intimate relationships: and the coordination of mutually exclusive sense frameworks, 269–71
Irigaray, Luce, 81, 161
irrationality: rationality and, 62–63; underlying paradox of, 13n18

Jaspers, Karl, 8, 202–3, 206n6
Johnstone, Henry W., Jr., 21, 57–58, 59, 62, 268n14
Jung, Carl G., 252–55

Jungian dream interpretation, 252–56
justification: absolute justification of relativism and of the unintelligibility of relativism, 45–51; knowledge and the problem of, 55–57; the rhetorical dimension of foundational circularity and, 66–71; Richard Rorty on truth and justification, 68n30; unnatural logic and, 171; Walter Weimer on, 62. *See also* circular justification(s)

Kant, Immanuel, 182, 194–95, 198, 200
Kant and the Problem of Metaphysics (Heidegger), 184
Kapferer, Bruce, 4–5
knowledge: the attitude of genuine open-mindedness and, 76–77; Foucault's use of, 141–42; foundational circularity and (*see* foundational circularity); a legitimate foundation for, 54; the problem of justification, 55–57; skepticism and Agrippa's trilemma, 54n1; as ultimately paradoxical, 76; and the usefully contradictory connection of logic and rhetoric, 61–64
Kristeva, Julia, 161
Kuhn, Thomas S., 7–8, 35, 59, 86, 102–3n1, 239

Laclau, Ernesto, 106–8
language: mediating function of meaningless language, 133n8; metaphysics and, 202–3, 204–5n5
Larmore, Charles, 109
Latour, Bruno, 133n8, 164–66
Lauretis, Teresa de, 154n7
legitimate logical contradiction, 20–23
Levinas, Emmanuel, 270n15
liar's paradox, 42–43
Livingston, Paul, 20–21
logic: contradiction and, 20–23, 72, 95n32, 237–44; of dreams (*see* logical structure of dreams); foundational circularity and, 57–64, 71–74; internal and external relations, 54–55; meaning of, 18–19; the undecided nature of logical connection and Heidegger's reading of metaphysics, 194–201. *See also* simply continuously consistent logic; unnatural logic
logical structure of dreams: discussion of, 244–49; dreams as simultaneously expression and transformation, 249–51; the inactivity of sleep and, 235n13; logically valid violations of sense and, 231–33; the logic of waking life and, 235–36, 237–44; partial and indirect support in theories of dream interpretation, 251–58; sense of reality as a whole and, 233–35, 236
"Lord Arthur Savile's Crime" (Wilde), 119–22, 126
Love, Heather, 175n50
Lyotard, Jean-François, 195–96

MacIntyre, Alasdair, 46, 105–6
Marlan, Stanton, 255–56
Martin, Biddy, 5, 152, 169
McLaren, Peter, 109
meaning(s): Davidson and Rorty on the idea of, 38–39; formal structure of metaphysics and, 202–10; foundational circularity and the problem of the undecidability of, 74–75; *The Importance of Being Earnest* and, 205, 210–29; misunderstanding and, 212–29
meaningless language: mediating function of, 133n8
metaframeworks: in Foucault's pluralism, 131–34, 143–49; self-cancellation of, 133–34
metalanguage, 41
metaphor, 72n33
metaphysics: the contradiction of absolute truths and, 206–7; Heideggerian interpretation of (*see* Heideggerian interpretation of metaphysics); *The Importance of Being Earnest* and, 205, 210–29; logic and, 18–19; preliminary

298   Index

metaphysics (cont.)
    sketch of the formal structure of, 202–10; self-cancelling moment of thought and, 207–10; sexuality theory and, 151
Micklem, Niel, 255–56
misunderstanding: meaning and, 212–29
moods, 237–40
Mouffe, Chantal, 105, 106–8
multiplicity: contradictory, 161
Mumon, 14n19
Muñoz, José Esteban, 175n50
mutually exclusive sense frameworks: big question philosophy and, 10–15; contemporary pluralist problem, 2–10; and the personal experience of existence and value, 16–18; possibility of legitimate logical contradiction, 20–23; self-cancellation, 262–63; simultaneous relevance of, 261–62; viewed by contemporary philosophy, 259–61
    coordination of: in clashes between other people and cultures, 263–68; in intimate relationships, 269–71; in relation to one's personal identity, 271–73; in relation to the natural environment, 276–77; in relation to the political environment, 277–78; in relation to the practices of scholarship, 278–79; in relation to the social environment, 273–76. *See also* conflicting frameworks

Nagel, Thomas, 233
Nancy, Jean-Luc, 109, 180, 270n15
natural environment: and the coordination of mutually exclusive sense frameworks, 276–77
nature: environment thought and, 152–53; essence and, 159; heterosexual normativity and the logical character of nature, 154–58; heterosexual normativity and the problem of the concept of "nature," 150–54; Bruno Latour's reconciliation of nature and social construction, 164–66; unnatural logic and, 166–78 (*see also* unnatural logic)
Nietzsche, Friedrich, 182, 201
noncontradiction: exclusive principle of, 72, 95n32, 243. *See also* contradiction(s): law of
Nye, Andrea, 81

Olbrechts-Tyteca, L., 58
"On the Very Idea of a Conceptual Scheme" (Davidson), 89–90
"Onto-Theo-Logical Constitution of Metaphysics, The" (Heidegger), 184
open-mindedness, 76–77
Order of Things, The (Foucault), 144

Perelman, Chaim, 58
personal identity: and the coordination of mutually exclusive sense frameworks, 271–73
phenomenological dream analysis, 256–57
philosophical argumentation: as necessarily contradictory, 57–58; rhetorical dimension of, 58–59
"Phrases and Philosophies for the Use of the Young" (Wilde), 128
Picture of Dorian Gray, The (Wilde), 113, 114, 116–19, 124, 127–28
Plato, 55n3, 188–93, 196
plural democracy, 106–8
pluralism: connection to big question philosophy, 10–12, 15, 181; the contemporary problem, 2–9; internal and external relations, 54–55. *See also* Foucault's pluralism
pluralist comparisons: absolute justification of relativism and of the unintelligibility of relativism, 45–51; the explicit self-cancellation of Rorty's and Davidson's standpoints on the meaninglessness of comparing conflicting frameworks, 39–42; the nature of truth and, 32–34; Rorty's and Davidson's standpoints on the meaninglessness of comparing conflicting frameworks, 34–39; self-cancellation of Rorty's and

Davidson's self-cancellation, 42–45; the truth of singular standpoints, 52–53; the truth of the knower, and negotiation between truths, 51–52
Poetics (Aristotle), 229–30
poetry, 229
political environment: and the coordination of mutually exclusive sense frameworks, 277–78
political epistemology: contemporary problems, 78–79. *See also* feminist epistemology
political force: rhetorical context and, 93–94
political liberalism, 104–5
political pluralism: current approaches to, 102–3, 104–10; Oscar Wilde's achieved position of pluralism, 115–24; Wilde's artificiality of wit and style and, 102, 103–4; Wilde's idea of art and the logic of pluralism, 124–28
postcritical dogmatism, 115n29
postmodernism: the problem of binary opposition, 9–10
Potter, Elizabeth, 79, 84, 87
power: Foucault on truth and power, 142–43; Foucault's notion of disciplinary and normative strategies of, 135–36; Foucault's use of power as a trope, 144
power effects, 139–40
Priest, Graham, 20
primitive truth, 36–37
psychoanalysis, 146–47
pure essences, 160, 167–68
Putnam, Hilary, 42, 50n15, 262

queer theory: the contemporary problem of pluralism, 5; frameworks and logics of contradiction, 153–54; notion of heterosexual normativity, 151; on the origins of transformative insight, 175n50; recognition of more than one absolute truth, 168–69
Quine, W. V. O., 35, 59, 64–65, 83, 261

Rajchman, John, 147
rationality: Foucault on the multiple self-disparities of, 149; irrationality and, 62–63; Thomas Kuhn on rational decision between incommensurable scientific frameworks, 102–3n1
Rawls, John, 104, 105
reading: Heidegger versus John Sallis on Plato, 189–93
reality: dreams as simultaneously expression and transformation of, 249–51; logic and, 18–19; the presence of contradiction in understandings of reality as a whole, 237–44; reality as a whole and the logical structure of dreams, 233–35, 236, 244–49
reason: (self-) critique of, 115n29
regimes of truth, 129–30, 136
relativism: absolute justification of relativism and of the unintelligibility of relativism, 45–51; Donald Davidson's arguments against, 35–38; the explicit self-cancellation of Rorty's and Davidson's standpoints on the meaninglessness of comparing conflicting frameworks, 39–42; Rorty's and Davidson's standpoints on ethnocentrism and antirelativism in comparing different frameworks, 34–39; Barbara Herrnstein Smith on, 87
repressive discourses, 146–47
Republic (Plato), 189
rhetoric: appeal to an audience's preexisting commitments, 58–59; foundational circularity and the usefully contradictory connection of logic and rhetoric, 57–64; internal and external relations, 54–55, 197–98, 201; rhetorical dimension of foundational circularity, 66–71
rhetorical context: political force and, 93–94; truth and, 92–93, 94, 100–101

Riley, Denise, 85, 157
Roditi, Edouard, 114–15
Rorty, Richard: antiepistemology and, 81, 88–90; on arbitrariness, 52; on circularity, 50; on common-grounds situations and epistemological doubt, 96–97; concept of the "unnatural" and, 172–73; explicit self-cancellation of the standpoint on the meaninglessness of comparing conflicting frameworks, 39–42; on the idea of meanings, 38–39; on incommensurability, 95; logical focus of, 62; on the meaninglessness of comparing conflicting frameworks, 6, 34–35, 36, 38–39, 60, 67n29; on pluralist comparisons and the nature of truth, 32–33; the problem of self-cancellation and, 14–15; self-cancellation of the self-cancellation of the standpoint on the meaninglessness of comparing conflicting frameworks, 42–45; truth and justification, 68n30; on untranslatability, 46, 95–96
Russell, Bertrand, 18n22, 214–15n15

Sallis, John, 188–93, 196
Schelling's Treatise on the Essence of Human Freedom (Heidegger), 184
scholarship, 278–79
scientific frameworks, 102–3n1
Sedgwick, Eve Kosofsky, 151–52, 153–54n7, 157, 169, 175n50
Seidman, Steven, 157, 162
self: dreams as simultaneously expression and transformation of, 249–51; personal identity and the coordination of mutually exclusive sense frameworks, 271–73; relationship to itself as a whole and the logical structure of dreams, 246–49
self-cancellation: of Foucault's metaframeworks, 133–34; of foundationally justified theories, 71; metaphysics and, 207–10, 211–29; of mutually exclusive sense frameworks, 262–63; the problem in big question philosophy, 11–15; Rorty's and Davidson's explicit self-cancellation of the standpoints on meaninglessness of comparing conflicting frameworks, 39–42; self-cancellation of Rorty's and Davidson's self-cancellation, 42–45; Oscar Wilde's notion of constitutive change and, 111–12; Wittgenstein on, 207n8, 207n9
self-consuming theory, 145–46n42
self-contradiction: concept of the "unnatural" and, 167; the contemporary problem of pluralism, 2–9; the problem in big question philosophy, 11–15
self-inclusion: our sense of reality as a whole and, 234–35
self-reference: biases in epistemology and the problems of self-reference, 84–88; paradoxes of, 20–21
"Self-Reliance" (Emerson), 178
self-variance of truth, 182–83
sense frameworks: big question philosophy and, 10–15; contemporary pluralist problem, 2–10; foundational circularity and, 64–71 (*see also* foundational circularity); internal connection between logic and rhetoric between frameworks, 54–57; and the personal experience of existence and value, 16–18; possibility of legitimate logical contradiction, 20–23. *See also* conflicting frameworks; mutually exclusive sense frameworks
sensemaking: unnatural logic and, 172–78
sexism: epistemological problems arising in the historical examination of, 90–93; sexist biases in epistemology and the problems of self-reference, 84–88
sexuality and gender theory: character and value of unnatural logic, 166–72;

incompatibility but necessity of essence and construction, 158–66; logical characters of nature, essence, and construction, 154–58; metaphysics and, 151; problem of the concepts of "nature" and "essence," 150–54
simply continuously consistent logic: defined, 15; Heideggerian interpretation of metaphysics and, 180, 181–82, 194–201
Simpson, David, 5
singular standpoints: truth of, 52–53
skepticism, 54n1
Smith, Barbara Herrnstein, 60, 87, 92
social construction/constructionism, 91, 159, 161, 164–66
social environment: and the coordination of mutually exclusive sense frameworks, 273–76; problem of complicity in, 17–18
social epistemology, 88
sometimes always continuous consistency, 177, 180
sometimes always paradox, 13
sometimes always simplicity of unity, 279
sometimes always true: complicity in one's social environment and, 17–18; the contemporary problem of binary opposition and, 9–10; defined, 9; Heideggerian interpretation of metaphysics and, 183; the individual in relation to the political environment, 277–78; the individual in relation to the social environment, 274, 275, 276; legitimacy of inconsistency and, 22–23; nonself-identity and, 270; personal identity and, 273; Oscar Wilde and, 15
sometimes always true logic: and the relationship between reflective and nonreflective people, 265–67; Oscar Wilde and, 15. *See also* unnatural logic
Soul of Man under Socialism, The (Wilde), 110–11, 124, 125

"Sphinx Without a Secret" (Wilde), 123–24
standpoints: the contemporary problem of pluralism, 2–9; pluralist comparisons and the nature of truth, 32–34; the presence of contradiction in understandings of reality as a whole, 237–44; the truth of singular standpoints, 52–53. *See also* conflicting frameworks; sense frameworks
state of exception, 11–12n17
States, Bert, 233–34, 235
Stone, Alison, 162
storytelling, 23
strategy: Foucault's use of, 144–45
subjectivity, 156–58
Suzuki, Shunryu, 14n19

Taoism, 13–14n19
Taylor, Charles, 105
Theaetetus (Plato), 55n3
theory: correspondence with the world, 71; problem of foundational circularity, 64–66 (*see also* foundational circularity); self-consuming, 145–46n42
Thomson, Iain, 180
toleration, 2n1
Tractatus Logico-Philosphicus (Wittgenstein), 69n31
truth(s): as concealing-revealing and also as correctness, 183; as an essential or inner strife, 185–87, 195, 197–99; Aristotle on the artificial and essential truth, 229–30; contemporary problem with sense frameworks, 3–4; ethnocentrism, antirelativism, and the nature of truth, 34–39; Foucault's challenge to the concept of truth and resulting problems, 134–40; Foucault's deep contextualization of, 141–49; negotiations between, 51–52; pluralist comparisons and the nature of truth, 32–34; as primitive, 36–37; rhetorical context and, 92–93, 94, 100–101; Richard

truth(s) (cont.)
    Rorty on truth and justification, 68n30; self-variance of, 182–83; of singular standpoints, 52–53; and the violence of Heideggerian interpretation, 182–88; Oscar Wilde on telling the truth, 229. *See also* absolute truth(s); meaning(s)
truth frameworks: Foucault's deep contextualization of truth and, 141–49; in Foucault's pluralism, 129–30. *See also* metaframeworks
truth incompatibility: feminist epistemology and a solution to the problem of, 93–101
Tully, James, 109

unintelligibility of relativism: absolute justification of, 45–51
unnatural: concept of, 167; homosexuality as, 151, 159; as the opposite of what is natural, 157
unnatural logic: character and value of, 166–72; overview, 150–51, 154; sense and practical dimensions of, 172–78
untranslatability, 95–96

Valberg, J. J., 234
value: experience of, 16–18

violence: truth and the violence of Heideggerian interpretation, 182–88

Walzer, Michael, 91n29, 105, 137, 139
Warminski, Andrzej, 190, 193
Warner, Michael, 156
Warnke, Georgia, 277n19
Weimer, Walter, 61–62, 63
Wilde, Oscar: achieved position of pluralism, 115–24; concern with constitutive change and difference, 110–15; genuine political pluralism and Wilde's artificiality of wit and style, 102, 103–4; idea of art and the logic of pluralism, 124–28; *The Importance of Being Earnest* and the formal structure of metaphysics, 205, 210–29; sometimes always logic and, 15; on telling the truth, 229
Williams, Bernard, 38
Williams, Michael, 54n1, 92n30
Winch, Peter, 50n15
Wittgenstein, Ludwig, 69n31, 203n2, 204n5, 207n8, 207n9, 229, 237, 262–63
Wolin, Sheldon, 145–46n42

"Young King, The" (Wilde), 126

Zen Buddhism, 13–14n19